Language, Politics and Writing

Language, Politics and Writing

Stolentelling in Western Europe

Patrick McCarthy

palgrave
macmillan

LANGUAGE, POLITICS, AND WRITING
Copyright © Patrick McCarthy, 2002.
All rights reserved. No part of this book may be used or reproduced in any manner whatsoever without written permission except in the case of brief quotations embodied in critical articles or reviews.

First published 2002 by
PALGRAVE MACMILLAN™
175 Fifth Avenue, New York, N.Y. 10010 and
Houndmills, Basingstoke, Hampshire, England RG21 6XS.
Companies and representatives throughout the world.

PALGRAVE MACMILLAN is the global academic imprint of the Palgrave Macmillan division of St. Martin's Press, LLC and of Palgrave Macmillan Ltd. Macmillan® is a registered trademark in the United States, United Kingdom and other countries. Palgrave is a registered trademark in the European Union and other countries.

ISBN 1–40396–024–0

Library of Congress Cataloging-in-Publication Data
McCarthy, Patrick, 1941-
Language, politics, and writing : stolentelling in Western Europe / Patrick McCarthy.
   p. cm.
Includes bibliographical references and index.
ISBN 1–40396–024–0
   1. European fiction—20th century—History and criticism. 2. Politics and
literature—Europe—History—20th century. I. Title.

PN3503.M36   2002
809'.93358—dc21

2002025822

A catalogue record for this book is available from the British Library.

Design by Letra Libre, Inc.

First edition: December 2002
10 9 8 7 6 5 4 3 2 1

Printed in the United States of America

TO ALL THE EX–BOLOGNA CENTER STUDENTS WHO STUDIED POLITICS AND CULTURE WITH ME.

Contents

Introduction ix

Chapter One	A word about words	1
Chapter Two	Left-wing commitment 1940–1960	25
Chapter Three	Depicting the working-class	75
Chapter Four	Italian political language and writers who criticize	105
Chapter Five	Breaking the silence of violence: Seamus Heaney as a Northern Irish poet	117
Chapter Six	Three right-wing novels	135
Chapter Seven	Stories of hell: from the Auschwitz of Primo Levi to the fairy-tales of Céline	157
Chapter Eight	A tale of two Margarets	171
Chapter Nine	The selling of *Ulysses*	183
Chapter Ten	Struggling on the left	195
Chapter Eleven	The empire strikes back	213
Chapter Twelve	The long, unfinished march toward women's rights	239
Conclusion		257

Endnotes and suggestions for further reading 263
Index 281

Introduction

The topic of politics and writing has interested me for a long time: I wrote my first two books on French writers, and the aspects that I studied most were Céline's role in the Occupation and Camus's ties to Algeria. As I began lecturing more on politics and contemporary history, my old interest returned in a new form and I began thinking about the language of Italian and British politics.

It seems obvious to state that the bits and pieces of a period—the political trends, the leading works of literature and painting, and the manifestations of popular culture—all fit together. There is, of course, no reason why they should. Poetry is a specialized form of language that has its own rules and, increasingly, its own readers. People who read short stories and essays do not read modern poetry.[1] Language itself is the first and greatest problem: closely linked with culture, a word that requires precise definition, it underlies the other "bits and pieces." There are various kinds of language, each competing with the others as well as overlapping with them.

The notion of period is also far from simple: can we say that our period began when the Beatles changed style and made the album *Sergeant Pepper's Lonely Hearts Club Band*, or when the young Mohammed Ali, then called Cassius Marcellus Clay, took the world heavyweight championship from Sonny Liston with much "stolentelling" of rhymes and doggerel poetry? Anyway, periods, whether political or cultural, do not have nice tidy endings and beginnings: when did the "period of de Gaulle" or the "age of Sartre" start and finish? More important, why should a novel like *Wuthering Heights,* written on the remote Yorkshire moors, have anything in common with the parliamentary debates taking place in an 1840s London interested mostly in itself?

Then, too, if a period has an orthodoxy, it is very likely that it will spawn a group of heretics. Jean Paulhan defended non-political, avant-garde writing after the Second World War when left-wing commitment was the dominant view.

Answers to these questions and explanations of these contradictions exist, even if most of us no longer believe in one grand Hegelian answer.

History is the storm we blunder around in, incapable of turning our lives into destinies, as Sartre advised us to.

The questions that most interest me—the link between a novel and a political trend or between the language of literature and the language of politics—can be broken down into different relationships that dominate at certain times and for specific reasons. One category is committed writing, where politics reigns almost supreme and producers of literature are—for a while—content to let their work serve a political goal. Commitment usually takes place in times of political crises when the social group one favors is fighting to stay alive. The Depression of the 1930s was such a phenomenon. The unemployment in Northeast England helped produce the Jarrow marches on London as well as a change in the literary avant-garde: the politicized poets, Auden and Spender, replaced Bloomsbury.

Very different is the category that might be called *anti-politique*, where politics starts off as an impulse to reform but is unable to bring about change and leaves literature to depict society in all its varied antagonisms. The working-class is not marching confidently toward hegemony, but it occasionally shows that strain of anarchy that Ken Loach catches so well in his films, but that Tony Blair does not appear to relish.

The first chapter of this book provides an overview of language that has our own concrete, familiar experience as a starting-point and then gets into some not too arduous theory. All the problems discussed come back in later chapters, hopefully not to haunt us: graffiti, names and the unsaid are treated again later. Chapter two deals with commitment, more on the left but also on the right. Chapter three looks back to the France of the early 1900s and to the almost Edwardian England of Harold MacMillan in the 1950s. We rediscovered a working-class that denies Hegel, Gramsci and politics itself, but not class.

There are other kinds of language discussed in the book. In chapter seven the ostentatiously literary language of *Féerie pour une autre fois* almost severs the link with reality as it defends the artist Céline, denounced by Sartre as a "collabo." By contrast chapter six depicts three discourses that seem unpolitical but that spin off a right-wing worldview.

Running through several chapters is the theme of feminism, which is in search of its own language that it will then impose on literature and politics alike. Boldly it carves out space for itself next to what is no longer a universal but a male discourse. Feminism is also lived as a painful absence in the period before the women's movement breaks through in the 1960s. Orwell and Sartre are capable of creating strong female characters but not of maintaining and developing them throughout a work. For that we must await Crista Wolf in chapter twelve.

Certain works of literature may help create an identity, which is usually but not always national. Such was the case in Ireland, where Yeats's interpretation of the 1916 rebellion was at least as important as the rebellion itself. Drifting through some of the authors I discuss—James Joyce and Valery Larbaud—is an elusive European identity that was too weak to challenge communist and fascist identities in the inter-war period and may today be too weak to overcome the national identities. This does not protect the Europeans or the European Union from the sin of arrogance. The EU's reaction to the Irish referendum of June 2001 was appalling in its dismissal of the Irish voter, who must simply be set aside while the EU moves on to Enlargement. Language frequently works against the European identity, which, conversely, attaches more importance to translation. In chapter nine I provide one early example from the 1920s. Political power plays a major role in shaping many kinds of language, but there is nothing necessary or inevitable about its uses, at least in Western Europe. The Soviet Communist Party wanted to block the publication in the West of Boris Pasternak's novel *Dr. Zhivago* and it appealed to the PCI to bring pressure on the publisher Giangiacomo Feltrinelli. The PCI (Italian Communist Party) succeeded in delaying publication but Feltrinelli went ahead despite the party's opposition.

The economic study of a period should be accompanied by study of its culture. A history of painting may throw light on the education, the taste and the worldview of the dominant economic group. Caravaggio was not "merely" a great painter!

The aims of this book are firstly to show how our knowledge of the twentieth century may be enhanced by looking at political and literary history together. There is a narrative thread in the work that runs roughly from the Dreyfus case to the present, although it concentrates on the period from the Second World War to the Maastricht Treaty and the Gulf War. It is interrupted by flashbacks to the turn-of-the-century and to the Paris of the 1920s.

This is also a narrative that crosses national barriers. The comparative dimension involved fresh difficulties because traditions of political and literary language vary from country to country. The superiority that the Germans accorded to the French—Friedrich of Prussia invited Voltaire to his court and kept him there as long as he could—produced a reaction, of which the most famous example is the remark attributed to Heidegger—"Nur auf deutsch kann man denken" ("One can only think in German."). It also seems arbitrary to omit Spain and much more so Eastern Europe. How can one leave out the Polish writers who supported the Solidarity movement? The shameful answer is that I have limited myself to languages in which I can read texts in the original, and I know no Polish except the word for "beer." A slightly more respectable answer is that I agree with Tony Judt that Eastern and Western Europe are very different and the East (whose inhabitants hate the word) requires a book of its own.[2]

Most—but not all—translations are my own. Italy seems to me to give less space than it merits in books on modern Europe and here I have tried to redress the balance. As for the choice of authors, no attempt has been made to include all of the best. Salmon Rushdie has been omitted because to read him well seems to me to demand a knowledge of India, which I do not possess.

The second aim of the book—pursued in chapter four—is to see how language helps shape politics and how a politician, a party and a political system construct a language—or languages—of politics. The task of writers is to criticize that language, to show that there are many other kinds of discourse and to reveal what is special about the literary language.

There are various ways of analyzing political language, but the one that suits this book is storytelling or stolentelling. The politician and his/her party guide the voter/reader along a road where there are already signposts. Political language is concerned less with itself than with the outside world. It wishes to guide the listener from point A to point B and it tries not to let him stray to point C, which is the headquarters of another party. The existing signposts are the tradition of the party. Special words explain to the voter the party's ideology. But if these are too numerous the listener feels trapped and s/he may turn to another party. Good stories often foretell the future utopia that the party will construct. Great political language, such as Gramsci's *Quaderni del carcere*, succeeds in injecting into its content a freedom that belongs usually to the literary language. An example of bad political writing, where there is too much ideology, is "My son the six-year-old trotsky-ite." This is absurd but the Stalinist listener knows that a trotsky-ite is not a follower of Trotsky or a believer in the primacy of world revolution over socialism in one state. To Stalinists, Trotskyism is a generalized form of evil. It is thus perfectly natural to talk about a six-year-old Trotsky-ite. Knowingly or not the speaker has absorbed Trotskyism.

The role of the writer is to act as the watchdog and guardian of the political language. He can do this not because s/he is a literary genius but because s/he knows language well. Leonardo Sciascia goes further when he claims that the literary language is truth and will allow him to lay bare the mysteries of the Moro kidnapping. But *L'affaire Moro* is not convincing.

Heinrich Böll does a better job, but the most arduous task is left to Seamus Heaney. In Northern Ireland political language has broken down into two solipsistic monologues, so Heaney tries, not to lay bare the truth of the "Irish Question," but more humbly to sketch out forms of dialogue (chapter five).

Chapter nine is our example of the rare European identity: it is an account of the marketing of *Ulysses*. Chapter ten is a continuation of the politico-cultural history of the Left, taking up where the early chapters stopped and introducing the very good Italian novelist Nanni Balestrini.

Culture—hopefully defined more precisely—gets a long chapter of its own because it is probably the greatest problem that young Europeans will have to face. European culture is becoming one of many and has to confront "others." In particular it must confront "the other," namely, Islam. Europe's record is not encouraging (nor is Islam's), but we have the resources in our culture to create a dialogue rather than a war. Whatever President Bush may say, September 11 was not just an act of terrorism; it was the fruit of a breakdown of communications that has deep historical roots. Catching Osama Bin Laden may be an excellent undertaking, but the real goal is to learn to live with and talk to, not about, Islam.

Chapter twelve concentrates on the long march of women. They have still some way to travel but the impact they have already made is great. They have succeeded in penetrating much of this book, including chapter eight, which depicts the clash between a woman-novelist and a woman-politician famous for her direct language. In chapter twelve Crista Wolf shows the values of women rising phoenix-like from a moribund Marxism.

A short conclusion tries to pull these themes together. Scattered through the book are pessimistic comments on our society because I believe that Europe has paid a high price for monetary union. A class of "exclus" has been created, composed of immigrants, the young unemployed, women living on their own and other groups.

If I were asked to sum up the book's theme in a sentence, I would refer to Primo Levi's statement that a man who gives up trying to be understood by those around him is headed only for the gas chamber. (And what of Auschwitz? Is it not good that the last half-century has not produced another set of death camps in Western Europe? Yes of course, even if that is a low target to set oneself. Moreover the ex-Yugoslavia has witnessed forms of cruelty almost equal to the crimes of the Nazis.) When he arrives at the center of Auschwitz, beyond the "salvati" and among the "sommersi," those who are certain to die, Levi finds a silence. Language too is being destroyed, which means that our task is to keep language alive, hence the subtitle of this book, which is taken from James Joyce.

He is playing with the world "storytelling" and he wishes to indicate not merely that Shaun the Post has been plagiarized by his twin, Shem the Penman, but that all language is spawned by other language and is thus second-hand or stolen. Shem is "the last world of stolentelling"[3] so he is using language that has been used-stolen many times over. If this be a crime, then life itself is a crime. But these repeated words are our substitute for the authentic language of which Anna Livia Pluribelle's monologue is a hint, but that we can never know.

Such at least is the starting-point of my interpretation of a book, *Finnegans Wake*, which I have never read from beginning to end but have "dipped into" many times. The notion of a language game is the closest I can come to stating my own opinion on these problems. But is it not conceited to fill valuable space talking about my own political or cultural stance? On the other hand it would be absurd for me to lay claim to a Flaubertian kind of objectivity and to hide, like God behind his creation. So let me try to explain where I stand as author.

Despite all my interest in commitment, I do not believe in history sufficiently to allow it the hegemonic role it plays in much post–Second World War writing. History is an object of study as well as something we live through but it is not a force of redemption. Anyway it is much easier for me to believe in original sin than in redemption whether via history in the shape of revolution or via divine grace. André Gide and the whole body of pre-1914 writing are closer to me than Sartre because they are less extreme and doctrinaire but more playful. Gide's *Paludes* is an example of what I mean.

Where does the author stand politically? I drifted in or near the Labour Party (how could I do anything else after growing up in Aberavon, South Wales?) but I went over to de Gaulle because it seemed to me that only he could end the Algerian War, in which French friends of mine were being killed. It took me rather longer to appreciate that young Algerians were being tortured and killed in far greater numbers. After de Gaulle left office I drifted back to the British Labour Party and the French Socialists. In Italy, however, I supported the Communist Party as long as it was led by Enrico Berlinguer. I did not expect great changes in my own life from my political stands, at most a tiny improvement in society.

But it would be foolish to admit solely to a pragmatism that makes little or no difference in my own existence. To return to Joyce it seems to me that *Finnegans Wake* is a work of great freedom that liberates the word from its role as sign. The reader is invited to join in this "stolentelling," which enables him too to liberate himself from the everyday speech that shapes his banal existence. One might draw a semi-serious parallel with the Thai language, where there are accents that are put "near" the letter that they modify. They have no precise place but can be put wherever the writer wishes. One cannot imagine the circumflex or the umlaut enjoying such freedom. But Joyce's pleasure is much greater. If he tried in this novel to continue the attempt at the "summa," which is present in *Ulysses*, his object here is to draw everyone into a huge game.

The reader plays with or against Joyce but always as an individual. I believe that, barring famines, nuclear wars or ecological disasters, the individual will remain at the center of our culture. Solidarity will continue to be a "keeping-guard" word and a reaction to crises like September 11. The daily struggle against the mass media and governments that intervene too much or too little but always badly will be fought by the individual. S/he will need the qualities of courage, silence and irony. Like Leonardo Sciascia, s/he will have as watchword "I do not believe, therefore I am." The Europe in which she lives will be plagued by wars on its boundaries and by terrorism from within. The terrorists will come from the excluded, many of whom will be immigrants. Yet the world will be, if not good, then beautiful. There will be excellent writing, dancing and painting.

This brief—but perhaps excessively long—statement of the author's worldview will now give way to the worldviews of more interesting people. But first we must say a word about the necessary figure of the reader. The material discussed in this book is too important to be left to the jargon of political science or of literary criticism. The writing has been kept as simple as possible. Moreover no special knowledge is required of the reader. An interest in politics and writing will suffice.

As the book begins, a convention of writing intervenes and demands to take precedence. Fortunately it is a pleasant task: the acknowledgments.

I wish to thank Robert Evans, the director of the Bologna Center (BC), for his unfailing support as well as for giving me an extra semester of sabbatical leave to write this book. The Parachini family, who provided funds for faculty research, has been more than generous in my case. To my colleagues goes my gratitude for their willingness to discuss with me the themes of the book. The same applies to David Calleo and others at SAIS (School of Advanced International Studies), Washington. Roya Ghafele Bashi and Jennifer Brant were talented, industrious research assistants. Libraries are important places to a researcher and I was lucky with the tireless, knowledgeable staff of the BC library. It would also be wrong not to mention the staff of the Istituto Gramsci and all my Italian colleagues and friends, especially Fernanda Minuz and the Hanna Arendt society. I have incurred a debt of gratitude toward Monash University in Melbourne, which awarded me a Fellowship for the Summer 1999 to start writing. I am also indebted to Barbara Wiza who, in the midst of the myriad tasks she performs, found time to prepare an excellent manuscript.

Last but by no means least, I wish to thank my wife Veronica and my daughter, Kate.

Patrick McCarthy
Bologna, October 15, 2001

Permissions

Some of the themes and ideas in this book were first explored in *Il Silenzio e le fiabe* (L'Harmattan, 1997). Permission granted by Edizioni L'Harmattan Italia s.r.l., Via Bava n. 37—10124 TORINO

Portions of this book appeared in "Pasolini e Il Setaccio alle ricerche di Parole Politiche," in *Pasolini e Bologna* (Pendragon Press, 1998). Permission © Pendragon, Italy

Portions of this book appeared in "Italy: a new language for a new politics?" in the *Journal of Modern Italian Studies,* 1997, 2:3, pp. 358–377. Permission granted by the Journal of Modern Italian Studies (Taylor and Francis, www.tandf.co.uk).

Chapter One

A Word about Words

The words that concern us most are political and literary words. But, while one cannot conduct politics without language, not all language is, in our opinion, political. In Italy the post-1992 reformers—an almost extinct breed—have tried to reduce the space conquered by politics and to allot some of it to civil society. This is an appeal for other kinds of discourse: for a Sardinia that is indeed the home of Antonio Gramsci and Enrico Berlinguer but also of the nuraghi, of sheep-herding communities, of the novelist Salvatore Satta and of the singer, Maria Carta, all of whom may speak in the island's name and who are tainted but not taken over by politics.

As for the language of literature, it is marked by its freedom. Its aim is not to represent anything outside itself but rather to exhaust the possibilities of language. Supreme examples of the freedom of literature might be James Joyce's *Ulysses* and Louis-Ferdinand Céline's *Féerie pour une autre fois*. Not only do they bring new words into English and French but they add fresh meanings, change the order of words and undermine the unity of the sentence—Céline uses three dots, which launch his narrative headlong forward without the relaxing pause of the full stop. Such writing seems light years distant from the language of politics. The latter makes up a story about the world and tries to convince people that it is true. If it succeeds, then a party or a regime may be formed around the worldview present in the story. Political language deals with what it is not, with what is in the world and outside of itself. It is a means to an end.

Precisely because of this contrast, however, the two seek each other out, each recognizing the power of the other. Political language perceives that the freedom of literary language gives it an ability to convince that the politician must envy. Literary language sees how political language is at ease among people and things. On closer inspection the two share certain traits: both perceive the world as incomplete and people as subject to change. Both tell stories designed to change them. Political language is more jealous than literary language: it knows precisely where it wishes to lead people and it tries not to let them stray. One word leads to the next and key words contain a special meaning, which one might call ideology and which guide the reader to the next signpost. But political language cannot avoid being language and become information instead. In turn literary language cannot avoid telling us something about the world in which language exists. Pietro Ingrao, the communist leader, recounts that John Steinbeck's novel *The Grapes of Wrath* did more to win him over to socialism than any political writing.[1]

The language of literature may have monopolized, as Roland Barthes claims, the French language for nearly three hundred years.[2] But today it is a specialized form of writing, that presents itself as literature by a series of signs that begin on the cover and continue throughout the text, such as the use of the past historic tense in French novels. Clearly these signs place limits on its freedom. Literature may reflect the problems of society as a whole, but it has to defend its linguistic space against popular culture, against the flood of images from TV and cinema and against the e-instruments such as fax, internet, and so on.

These raise the problems of the too many words, of anonymous words and of other people's words, which may well, I shall claim in the conclusion, become the leading politico-linguistic battle of the new century if not of the new millennium. First, however, we must glance at a theme that is virtually inseparable from language, silence.

Silence and privacy

Silence can be a defiance as well as a defeat. It is a defeat when it is imposed, not chosen. Usually this involves refusing to allow a group of people to speak freely. The ultimate form of silence was the gas chambers at Auschwitz. But many dictators sought to maintain their power by robbing a people of its language. Mussolini banned the teaching of German in the province of Alto-Adige-Sud-Tirol, which Italy took from Austria in 1918. To confuse the German-speaking population's sense of place, he renamed the villages in Italian. The imposition of a new calendar, in which 1926 was Year Four of the Fascist Era, was designed to disrupt the population's sense of time. The German-speakers fought back by teaching German in the aptly named "Katakombenschulen." Their children resisted by siding with Italy's enemies in their history classes. They were taught that the Ethiopian king, Menelik, won the battle of Adwa, because of treachery against a gallant Italy, but they applauded him as a superior warrior.[3]

In this way the Sud Tirolesi found words to resist the various forms of silence that Italian Fascism tried to impose on them. But silence becomes a weapon of resistance when a prisoner refuses to speak under torture. A model of silence as stubborn resistance was the Secretary of the Italian Communist Party (PCI), Enrico Berlinguer. He was famous for the unflinching silence with which he opposed the bullying and insults of the Soviets.

The value of silence depends on the value of the words to which it is opposed. At the other extreme from Berlinguer's resistance is the traditional Mafia practice of "omertà." A rejection of justice and reason in favor of force, it holds that reality means the domination of the many by the few. Words are superfluous and even the powerful do not speak. Things live on as they have supposedly always done and the term "society" has no meaning.

By contrast, the Trappist monastery is a fortress of active, positive silence. The non-speech of the monks drives back the words of the world and creates space for the upsurge of prayer, which, in the eyes of a believer, is the most revolutionary of discourses. Here silence is allied with one form of language—the Word of God—against another. Cardinal Martini explains what kind of silence and what kind of words: "Every genuine communication is born of silence. In fact all human speech involves saying something to someone: something which must be born inside one. This presupposes a sense of one's own identity, a self-understanding, a gathering of one's own inner richness. Every true communication demands silence and reflection."[4] Rilke understood this and stated at the outset of the *Sonette an Orpheus* that when Orpheus sang, every living thing was silent but in this silence "a new beginning was present."[5]

In general silence cannot be analyzed in its own right. A philosopher, attacking the complicity between his discipline and theology, argues that there is a contradiction between an all-knowing God and a caring, accessible God. An omniscient, omnipotent God who permits the evil of Auschwitz must be beyond human comprehension. The insights of mystics and of poets deal with human emotion and can offer no special dialogue with this God, who remains profoundly unhuman. Logically religion must view such a God in silence, while philosophy can have no reason for believing in His existence.[6] This is a very different silence from Martini's and Rilke's and it inevitably evokes Wittgenstein's famous comment: "Whereof one cannot speak, thereof must one be silent."

Literature, however, which is haunted by not-writing—by Mallarmé's tenaciously white sheet of paper—occasionally adopts another view of silence, different from both religious forms and from the poet's insights. Silence becomes a source of words or else a reward for words written. To Louis-Ferdinand Céline the night was a great fountain of silence from which an army of sounds emerged, more authentic than the sounds of the day, which were now stilled, and almost always hostile to humans. They included the thunder of bombing as the Allied airforce arrives to destroy Montmartre in *Féerie pour une autre fois*. To travel through the sounds of the night, of which words are only one form, means listening to prisoners crying out in their cells or to soldiers, wounded and shell-shocked in the trenches. One's reward is silence: the "let's say no more about it," which terminates *Voyage au bout de la nuit*. The imperative verb follows the barman's appeal that Ferdinand should tell him everything. This is an ironic reference to the novel, which sets out to provide a "summa" of human misery. When it is written and read, then one may be silent. Such silence is liberation but Céline quickly becomes discontented and attempts fresh "summas" in *Mort à crédit* and *Féerie*. This kind of silence may be an image rather than a "real" absence of words. But then "omertà" is not just an absence of "real" words.

In Céline's novels words are only one form of communication. There are many others such as the "brrts" of the cat Bébert, the companion to the dancer, Lili, who communicates via the beauty of her movements.[7] Some observers think that people cannot avoid communicating and that all things communicate. On the first assertion Primo Levi holds that loss of the ability or desire to communicate is the mark of a man who has given up and is resigned to the gas chamber. The second assertion implies a universe full of messages, which is a happy view. Yet the same observer maintains that a common culture (Kultur) is needed before the message can be understood and communication can take place.[8] We shall return to the theme of culture in a later chapter as well as to the theme of the historical moment. In the present perspective political and literary language would be no more than two of the many forms of communication and gesture or body language would be just as important. An example of a "thing" wishing to communicate in several different ways would be the later works of Paul Klee.[9]

The nature of the communication would vary in accordance with the means deployed. Non-verbal methods are more likely to convey implicit knowledge than precise information. Ballet must surely be one of the most expressive forms of communication. The French critic Charles du Bos quotes from another admirer of dance, Paul Valéry, a phrase about dancers: "their hands speak and their feet seem to write." But Du Bos recounts that Isadora Duncan's movements were a "liberation without a monologue."[10] Dance does not need words and, although it is usually accompanied by music, contemporary groups like Merce Cunningham's have experimented with not using music. Here silence is allied with a non-verbal form of communication.

In the context of the new technology silence is a form of resistance and it is linked with privacy. Both are threatened, privacy more gravely. Strict rules have been advocated by a magazine devoid of luddite sympathies: use cash where possible, keep your phone number unlisted, check your medical records regularly. The list goes on: assume your e-mail and voice-mail are monitored, remember that your every internet entry is recorded somewhere by somebody. When one comes to the suggestion that one should try to use a computer that belongs to a friend, one wonders what sort of world lies in wait for unwary contemporaries.[11] Even with such elaborate defenses, the *Economist* thinks the battle is lost. Privacy will have been a short-lived virtue, peaking among the rich classes of the pre-1914 era and centered in the London clubs. It cannot be maintained in an age of mass high technology. Yet one cannot quite agree that the outcome is so pre-determined.

Spoken, written and recorded words

Political language hides a great historic divide, between the written and the spoken language. The literary language is almost always written although such writers as Céline and Pasolini talk much about introducing into it the slang of the socially excluded groups. The slang is changed when it is put between the covers of a book and it is no longer the same slang as when it is used by a tramp. This is also true of dialect. Pasolini's early poems are written in the Friulan dialect but he innovated within what he regarded as the organic boundaries of Friulan. His poetry is not the same language as was spoken in his home village of Casarsa.

A distinguished example of written political language is de Gaulle's three-volume *Mémoires de Guerre*. De Gaulle begins with an "I" but, as his historic mission to continue the struggle against Nazism unfolds, he emulates the Caesar of *De bello gallico* and invents a protagonist called de Gaulle. This hero engages in constant dialogue with "la France," which is a living entity, separate from "les Français" and incarnated in historical figures like Joan of Arc. The language of the *Mémoires* is old-fashioned and literary. Indeed without the conventions and structure of literature de Gaulle could not have told the tale of the Free French.[12] By contrast Gerhard Schröder's message to the SPD faithful was delivered as a speech at their assembly or "Parteitag" 1999. Schröder uses the spoken language to give structure to his report: as he spots a minister in the crowd, so he talks about that department and its achievements. He interrupts himself frequently to involve the audience by addressing them directly as "Genossinnen und Genossen" (Comrades, ladies and gentlemen) and he calls on them to go out and repeat what he is telling them. He thus triggers more political language, spinning off from his text. This speech could not have been written, for it uses the conventions of spoken German.

In general the written word weighs more heavily than the spoken. Peasant societies often view literacy as a weapon of oppression. In the years after Italian Unification, Southern bandits, with strong popular support, fought the government troops in the South. Whenever they seized control of a village of any importance, they entered the public offices and burned the land deeds. The written language is associated with the state. The French Third Republic established its power via the figure of the elementary schoolteacher who fought several kinds of battles. One of them was to substitute French for the local patois. To speak French linked the individual with a wider group but it was not enough. By teaching him the rudiments of written French the "instituteur" instilled in him respect for the difficult, non-phonetic spelling—"the sacred, correct writing of the language of the lay and obligatory state."[13] In turn the schoolgirl/boy was guided to the great French writers with whom s/he was, however remotely, connected. Their authority arose with the centralized monarchy of the seventeenth century and it survived the Revolution intact. With certain mild changes of interpretation—moral values were ascribed to Molière and La Fontaine—and with certain new names added—Victor Hugo but not Charles Baudelaire—they were brought out again after 1870 to launch the lay Republic. They were frequently read in the form of "selected extracts," which made them both more accessible and more remote, hence worthy of respect.

So the link between language and nation varies according to the historical and geographical factors. Language helps unite people; the nation is a set of shared memories, which could not be revived and renewed without language. The spoken language is not altogether reliable as a nation-builder. Still it is valuable. Making Italians was a slower process than it would have been, had more than approximately 2 percent of the population spoken Italian. Had teaching Italian been a better-funded and more prestigious activity, this too might have made more Italians more rapidly. Moreover ascribing a special place to one dialect—in the Italian case the Tuscan—to certain grammatical rules or to a particular accent can serve to unite people even if they speak other dialects or have other accents.

These differences can also have the opposite effect of creating resentment among the non-favored segments of the population. Or they may do both simultaneously, as the so-called Oxford accent did in Britain at least until recently. It was/is not a regional but a social accent, which summoned up memories of medieval universities, nineteenth-century country houses, amateur cricketers and simple snobbery. It led Margaret Thatcher to work hard on her vowels to acquire something close to it and Neil Kinnock into consciously maintaining against it the working-class accent with which he had grown up.

In Britain the next step was not taken: people may rally around a subordinate form of the spoken language and demand that it be legitimized as a symbol of their struggle for emancipation. Often these languages are rich in emotion, full of slang (because, according to Céline, slang was the language of hatred), devoid of grammatical complexity and hence well-suited to protest, ritual and celebration. Such is the language of *When We Were Kings* (1997), the film about the Muhammed Ali–George Foreman world title fight.[14] Ali, who adds to the black American tongue his own flair for doggerel-poetry and one word of Swahili—"boma ye" or "to beat" as in the chant of "Ali Boma Ye" (Kill him Ali)—uses the spoken black-American language as a weapon in his psychological war against Foreman, cast in the role of a white man. Ali also satirizes the dictator of Zaire, General Mobutu, who is holding the fight to demonstrate to the world the modernity of Zaire. Mobutu did not welcome Ali's cries of "Let's rumble in the jungle."

Ali, whose verbal messages are reinforced by the body language of a boxer–ballet dancer, seeks above all expressivity, which the speech of black Americans possesses in abundance. Ali launched his new career as an opponent of the Vietnam War with the line "Man I ain't got no quarrel with them Vietcong." Tossed into an interview where Ali showed little knowledge of the complex Vietnam phenomenon, this sentence struck home by its simplicity, reinforced by grammatical shortcomings.[15] Spoken languages tend to be weaker in the areas of analytical experience, and the demand that they be used in the school or the courtroom can backfire on the minority community. In 1997 the city of Oakland, California, decreed that Ebonics, a language or dialect of the black population, could be used in the schools but the experiment ran into opposition and was abandoned.[16]

One wonders whether the spoken language can retain its expressivity and the written language its authority in a world increasingly dominated by the internet. Here words are not said in different ways. They are not re-shaped by and they do not re-shape their context. They do transmit information but in atomic isolation. The creative process by which spoken language renews itself depends on the interplay of many participants in many different ways. Meanwhile the authority of the written word is undermined by the ease with which electronic words are transmitted and reproduced. The language of internet is both too meager and too fluent.

This view may be unduly pessimistic, however, because the communication structure of an internet entry is open, designed to allow the largest possible number of people to discover it. Similarly the reader who surfs the internet is free to move in any direction. One can imagine a new discourse, flexible and innovative in grammatical structures and order of words (breaking away from the all too frequent subject-verb-object). It will not be a jargon designed for specialists and it is unlikely to be the instrument of power of an international technocratic class, since only the embryo of such a class exists. There will probably be different languages, at least one of them satirical. These languages will transcend the nation-state and reflect-shape newer political forms, which are as yet unclear. They will not, however, be neutral, mere mules that carry information.

Moreover there will be a great deal of such discourse. The mass media are experts in packaging and (re)-distributing words. They reach greater numbers of people than a governmental decree or a papal encyclical. Computers store words more easily and transmit them more quickly. Printed out, this amorphous mass, masquerading as information, may well swamp the area of the written word, which has been losing prestige already as literacy has increased. Neither spoken nor written but recorded language will be the dominant form. It was symbolic that the Red Brigades used e-mail to send one of their latest messages, demonstrating that they were not a relic of the 1970s. The computer they used was located in a bowling alley, which may be read as an attempt to prove that the BR are a working-class organization. The police retraced the message to its source in two days, by which time the sender was far away. E-mail does not bring impunity but it does bring time.[17]

The adventure of the sirens will cease to be dangerous and their song will cease to lure people. Ulysses cannot allow the sailors to hear the sirens sing and he himself would run the risk of death, if he had not taken the precaution of binding himself to the mast. Today he would plug his own ears as well as the sailors' and record the music on his disks. Later he and the sailors—a triumph for democracy!—could settle around a fire far from the haunted island and listen to the songs. But would they be as enchanting? If Ulysses thought not, he could always sell his tape to Virgin Records and consider himself a competent capitalist.

POWER, AUTHORITY AND PROTEST

Language is associated with power. Orwell's tramps use slang to form a community that is weaker than the larger community that excludes them but stronger than they are as individuals. In a truly democratic society there should be no such languages. Everyone would join in discussions about how the polis should be run and everyone would be able to understand everyone else. Orwell's plain English presupposes such a society. In reality, as Orwell, Barthes, Foucault and a host of other modern thinkers have shown, language is a kind of power. More correctly it is various kinds of power: linked, according to Foucault, with various kinds of knowledge.

Foucault is far enough removed from us—he died in 1984—to allow us to make comments on his work that he would have instantly rejected. One of these is that Foucault had a utopian vision of humans in harmony with the world,[18] which he keeps hidden but that enables him to see by contrast the many kinds of alienation in which humans are forced and force themselves to live. Language is no exception: it is subordinated to power and the various kinds of knowledge it discovers or creates are used to enhance that power. What causes the will to power? Power and protest seem to Foucault the fundamental traits of humankind.

In his most famous example he shows how the sane exploit the right to decide who is mad and who is not. The definition changes as society alters its goals and its work methods. So the discourse of the sane is an act to promote the existing social order. Within that framework the doctor takes his place: the medical discourse ensures it is a privileged place. His judgments are not necessarily wrong but they are guided by his own and society's will to power. Taking up what we have called the silence of submission, Foucault notes that there are no books on the sane written by the mad. So language contains these concessions to power, which might find expression in silences and absences but are more often revealed in the fluency of the storyteller who has on his side reason, plausibility and the support of the majority. Against this storyteller, frequently backed by famous publishing houses and distinguished universities, Foucault pits a discourse that is based on sources considered inferior or invalid and that adopts a structure that includes discontinuity and that distrusts logic, causality and coherence.

Discontinuity is essential to any attempt to use language without turning it into a mere instrument of power. Because there is no dominating, Cartesian subject, language displays a radical otherness. It problematizes the communications, refusing to become an "unsaid." In literature its exponents might be Bataille or Artaud.

In general the language of authority is or rather was surrounded by pomp and circumstance. It consisted of a grand design, was given by a charismatic leader and was welcomed by an enthusiastic crowd. War provides the best context for this language, which is exemplified by Churchill's rhetoric about fighting on the beaches and about never surrendering. Time and place give way to an eternal universe where the main protagonist is an entity called Britain that has never been defeated and therefore will not be defeated now. Hitler and Goebbels invented a protagonist called "das tausendjährige Reich," which made even greater demands on its population, represented by similar enthusiastic crowds. They were forced to welcome something called "der totale Krieg" before they could emerge victorious.

An interesting variant on this theme was offered in 1961 by Charles de Gaulle, who was confronted with the Generals' Revolt during the Algerian War. Faced with military leaders who wished to continue the war and keep Algeria French, de Gaulle denounced them as a "quarteron de généraux," appealed to the nation as a whole but in particular spoke over the heads of the generals to the conscripts who listened to him on their transistor radios. His message was that they should obey him rather than their officers. They were convinced and they went over to de Gaulle's view that the war must be ended. The authority of the nation was divided but de Gaulle's version won out. He was aided by what was at the time a new form of information technology.

De Gaulle's action shows us that the line between authority and protest is unclear. At the core of his language is the entity called "la France," which is more than the sum of the French, of whom de Gaulle did not think highly. Indeed it has nothing to do with numbers since in 1940 de Gaulle decided that he incarnated this "France," although he had a mere handful of followers while the Vichy government had a majority of the population. This makes "la France" into a protest against the established order. In other respects it is an orthodox part of the discourse of authority: it presupposes a Nietzschean rather than a Hegelian view of history and in the present it calls for the French to make sacrifices for "la France."

The discourse of authority has waned along with the decline of charismatic leaders, wars and dictators. In France, where the presidential system favors authority, Giscard d'Estaing won the 1974 election by using the language of economic competence. Instead of stressing military power he projected the image of a professor of economics who could cope with the crisis caused by the Arab-Israeli clash and the rise in oil prices. This brought him a narrow victory. But at the next election in 1981 the electorate rejected him for Mitterrand, who could lay no claim to superior economic competence nor to charisma.

The language of authority likes symbolic settings like the Westminster parliament with the Thames flowing by or the Champs-Elysées, where the July 14 parade takes place. By contrast the language of protest, although it favors great assemblies, such as the Jarrow marches of the Depression or the PCI's rituals on the crowded Piazza San Giovanni, often prefers to be anonymous and indirect.

Graffiti represent a language of discontent, which traditionally uses anonymity and pseudonyms as a defense against police action. Rapid and seemingly spontaneous, graffiti invade so-called public places that are in practice open only to certain public groups. Graffiti are a simple kind of resistance to the dominant languages and to their ability to monopolize the mass media. Writing on walls can be erased quickly and replaced as quickly. The ease with which it can be erased projects the vision of a world where all written or recorded words, such as the signature on a contract, could be made to vanish with equal facility. This vision has no use for private property, financial investment or libraries full of books. It stresses the values of mobility, imagination and indifference to money. It reminds those in power that the "excluded" exist.

Graffiti flourish when protest movements are strong and linger when they are weak. One individual can make an impact: when Piazza Carducci in Bologna was turned into a concrete desert, an anonymous protestor began drawing a large, slight bird along with a slogan invoking Carducci against so-called urban renewal. This established a brief alliance between popular protest and high culture, while the drawing of the bird indicated both possible flight and the resistance of nature. The introduction of the visual links graffiti with posters and murals and underlines its status as street work, which does not share the prestige of the (traditional) written word.

Graffiti are a way of saying things that cannot be said in "ordinary" language. These things are not necessarily pleasant. Near Piazza Carducci, in huge writing, was the judgment "Turchi siete merda" (Turks! You are shit). Strictly anonymous, it represented a strand of anti-immigrant feeling that could not be expressed in mainstream debate. It provoked fear in some parts of the neighborhood, fear of the instigators but also of immigrants' taking revenge. Until a few years ago the graffiti in the New York subway was entertaining but also horrifying for several reasons, of which one was its totalitarian occupation of every single inch of space.

Paris in the summer of 2000 abounded in more fanciful graffiti. The yellow French postboxes were transformed with smiles, quite unbecoming to the solemn, dignified French state they represented. The artist, the Smiler, told curious journalists that he was undertaking "a poetic act." He was stressing the human element in the written word—in demands for income tax as in letters to friends. A fellow-graphologist flooded Paris with small flying-saucers. He described his graffiti as a game but added they were a way of undermining the dominant language of publicity (which is not so easily undermined)! A third artist drew the shadows of trees, statues and metro stations. He too sees his work as restoring a poetic dimension to urban objects deprived of it. All three remained anonymous because their work is illegal: the French postal service is particularly irate. Their influence is, however, spreading and smiling postboxes have been sighted in London and Amsterdam.[19]

Graffiti have already made the not so long leap from street to museum via the painting of Jean-Michel Basquiat. In a work like *Zydeco* (1984) words and objects are mixed up in various ways: names are listed in the same or different color and are then sometimes struck out. The accordion player and the zydeco music (the popular music of créole, black French-speaking people from Louisiana, influenced by the Arcadian French community that made its way down from Canada under pressure from Britain) represent a celebration of popular culture, and a modest film is being made of them. A reference to Westinghouse satirizes both the big media companies and Basquiat's artisanal effort. An African mask provides another cultural support for the zydeco (also spelt "zodoco"). In general words are an alienated or at least remote form of culture. There is a corrected spelling mistake—"film" is first written as "tilm," which introduces a rhyme and is yet another case of the links between words and music. The word "subject" is written on the unfinished outline of a drawing and thus has no meaning or identity, beyond its visual presence.

Is Basquiat's work a pure protest? Not if set in its context. Success came quickly to him and he found buyers in the New York and international bourgeoisie. They were in no sense the puritanical, thrifty class described by Weber. They consumed food, art and elegance, while Basquiat consumed food, alcohol and drugs. Words, whether or not accompanied by visual communication, are rarely pure. Basquiat died of an overdose but one cannot conclude that society drove him to it.[20]

Literature contains a good dose of dissent: Pasolini's *Ragazzi di vita* and *Una vita violenta* are attacks on the post-war economic development in Italy that created, as a by-product, a subproletariat without money or hope. But, although literature criticizes, it is also a part of that broader skein of culture that provides the backing for a society's initiatives as a whole. The two kinds of action may be reconciled, if one remembers that our culture is strongly empirical and that empiricism is only possible with constant criticism. But that is too facile an explanation. Literature may also hide from itself problems to which it can see no solution: colonial writers run this risk. The murder of the Arab in Camus's *L'Etranger* is an example. Certain truths about the colonized may remain "unsaid." Culture in its links to society may merely justify the practice of that society, as Greek or medieval philosophy justified slavery. Here again, graffiti is welcomed by the advertising industry, which relishes its rapid, violent impact, however much the Smiler and his friends may dislike such a welcome.

As *Zydeco* reveals, the link between words and painting is broader than graffiti: the Paris graphologists rarely use words, possibly because elsewhere in Paris they are too abundant. The alliance between paintbrush and pen is a motif of modern art, especially of conceptual art. One reason is the sheer beauty of certain kinds of script: Japanese or Turkish characters, for instance. European poets are occasionally sensitive to the visual impact of their work: Paul Claudel liked the letter "i" to be printed in red, capped a "U" with a circumflex accent and watched over the color and texture of the paper his publisher used. Erik Satie went further: he was interested in the visual impact of his partitions and he then turned the visual shape into words for his titles, such as *Morceaux en forme de poire* (Pear-shaped Pieces). Western script presents the advantage that the observer can grasp its meaning, or more likely can enjoy the hints of meaning that may soon vanish. But there is more: the systematic use of words becomes a theme in itself that is interwoven with the purely visual themes. Painting often uses only one or two words that are renewed by being isolated from their usual context and hence meaning. They also become verbal objects to be looked at as well as read.

Paul Klee's later work contains intricate drawings that are in search of meaning both as shapes and as representing objects. The title was important to Klee, who referred to the naming of a work as the baptism of a child. The title would give a third kind of meaning and Klee played with this by calling one painting "Without a title," but inserting letters to hint at such a meaning. Klee's later work is a refusal of silence and a juxtaposition of many kinds of significance.

The Bologna artist Maurizio Osti has done a series of works based on the word "IO" ("I" in Italian), which is also the number ten and is the visual representation of the male and female genders. By rubbing out some parts of IO, Osti creates an array of different relations between male and female as well as within the self. Osti's erasions show the multiple possibilities of 10 as a visual object, which in turn trigger differences in the kind of "I" we are using or, simultaneously, with our view of gender. As if to highlight the ambiguous relationship between high culture and publicity, Renault has been advertising its Clio model by a simple Cl(io), in order to emphasize that identity is determined by one's choice of car.

A protest, which involved newish technology and revived hope that, like the transistor radio, it would not reinforce authority, took place in 1994 with the revolt of the Italian fax-people. It was not the first time the fax had brought together protestors, for the students who took over their universities in the 1991 Pantera movement had used the fax machines to coordinate their activities. But it was the first time the fax was successfully deployed on a particular issue.

Prime Minister Silvio Berlusconi (of 1994 vintage) sought an end to the Clean Hands investigation. He persuaded his Minister of Justice,

Alfredo Biondi, to issue a decree, letting out of prison virtually all the politicians who had been arrested and placing restrictions on the operations of the magistrates. That same evening Italy defeated Bulgaria in the semi-final of the World Cup, so perhaps Berlusconi thought the electorate would not notice. Instead there was an outburst of protest that revolved around two poles. Antonio Di Pietro went on TV, where he had displayed no special expertise, and expressed all his anger. The second was that the politicians, newspapers and most political actors were bombarded with faxes. Whether the fax-people could have won without Di Pietro or the reverse will never be known, but Berlusconi announced he was going to be tough and then gave in. The fax had demonstrated that, like the TV videocassette, it could serve the grassroots against the central authority.

In a democratic society most political language stresses neither authority nor protest, but aims at consent. The politician moves from an "I," which engages only him, to a "We," which is broad enough to legitimize his action. In so doing he tells a story—about Europe and austerity (Romano Prodi) or about the creation of a new Germany (Konrad Adenauer). Even after he has attained a wide base of support, language continues to be an important part of his action. Tony Blair uses the vocabulary of old Labor and of Thatcherism to create a higher synthesis, which is the Third Way.[21]

By appropriating language Blair is heading down a dangerous road in the eyes of Norberto Bobbio. An intransigent democrat, Bobbio refuses all systematic thought that subordinates reality to abstract creeds. Bobbio rejects the primacy awarded by Croce to such notions as culture or liberalism. He does not believe in absolute truth nor in any brand of silence. Bobbio starts with the political conflict in which the role of language is to guarantee freedom of speech. But language in itself is of very secondary importance. Bobbio's thought does not allow for the complex view of language held by Foucault. Not only are some kinds of language more legitimate and hence more powerful than others, but discontinuity undermines the confident rationality of the debate. Once more, freedom of speech is no simple matter.[22]

So far we have said little about the "small" languages that are dying by an at least apparent consent. Half of the world's 6,800 languages will be lost in two generations' time.[23] In fact behind this apparent consent lies a pattern: the small language is menaced by large neighboring languages, which are better suited to work, a scientific culture and a global economy. One cannot make globalization the villain of this tale because the decline of small languages predated it. The French nation-state turned Breton into a marginal language by using French as a weapon in its own struggle to unite the territory of France. The fate of the Celtic languages, especially Irish, will be discussed in chapter five.

Does it matter if the language of the Navajo Indians dies out? If one thinks a language is just a set of signs, then probably not. If one thinks that a language is just the expression of one particular culture, then possibly not. If one thinks that both language and culture are capable of changing and of producing new words and things that are different from English words and things, then yes. The "apparent consent" is a form of authority—oppression and the defense of small languages is a form of protest. *New Scientist* mentions the great success story of Hebrew, which was revived as a spoken language after centuries during which it existed only as a written language associated with religion and study. The suffering involved in the historical events that contributed toward the revival of Hebrew is, however, not encouraging. Yet Hebrew is interesting because it usually places the verb not the subject at the head of the sentence and because it has no exact equivalent of the verb "to have." So the concept of possession is different from the English concept.[24]

At present language's links with the nation seem looser than in the past. Then an attack on a language would be seen as an attack on the nation. A perceived attack might have the same effect. Yet the most recent examples of European nationalism—in ex-Yugoslavia—do not reveal language to be as significant a theme as it was in Sud-Tirol. Serbs, Croats and Bosnians have other reasons for their nationalism than Sud Tirol–Alto Adige did. How long will this last and to what extent is it a phenomenon of the Balkans?

Meanwhile French is in its turn threatened by "Bretonization" as English moves remorselessly forward to become the language of globalization. French still presents itself as the language of high culture, but English is driving it out of the workplace. Yet English too has its enemies who are most enthusiastic supporters. The price English pays for these new adherents is the simplification of its grammar and syntax. The subjunctive has all but disappeared. Indeed English runs the risk of becoming a new global patois that one uses to buy croissants and orange juice at those non-places, airports.

NAMES

Basquiat's habit of putting the name next to the object but then hinting that there is a vast difference between the two, opens up a whole category of words specialized in one of the functions of language. The *Encyclopedia Zanichelli* defines the name as the "distinctive sign" of a person. It bestows an identity on her/him and on places and things. Once they take on this identity people can be catalogued and, metaphorically, stored in a computer. At a quite different level of modernization, primitive tribes often believe that, if one holds power over a rival's name, one has power over her/him. Religious societies would sometimes not allow their divinity to be named lest He should lose His strength. Once more Rilke understood that humankind lived in a universe where the stars were "namenlos."[25] Perhaps following the example of primitive peoples, Umberto Bossi, the secretary of the Lega Nord, used to refer to Berlusconi as Berluskaiser or Berlusca, thus indicating that he had a sorceror's power over his supposed ally.

In Western Europe one takes a surname or family name from one's father. This is a rule made by the state and it could be argued that babies are named at birth so that the state may keep track of them from the outset. The rise of the woman's movement explains why often—as in Italy—the mother has the right to give her family name to the child. The first name is a choice made by parents with input, if relevant, from the Catholic Church, which encourages them to choose a saint's name. We would like to offer three examples that indicate the importance of the process of naming and exceptions to it.

The first is Jean Genet's speech to the students who occupied the Sorbonne in 1968. Genet claimed that names imposed restrictions on people and hence that they should all be abolished. The students were taken aback: there is nothing about the tyranny of names in Marx or Mao. Yet Genet was right in maintaining that the name, whatever it may be, imposes an identity, whatever that may be. It is usually a psychological unity and it may be held responsible, morally and legally, for that person's actions. Changing one's name can change one's personality: Eric Blair perceived his life as a string of failures; as George Orwell he turned these failures into important books. The Reggio Emilian writer Silvio D'Arzo was haunted by his lack of a surname. He had been born out of wedlock and suffered from the absence of a father. True to his artist's vocation, he sought a father and a principle of stability via words, in this case surnames. His view was the opposite of Genet's. He was best pleased by the name D'Arzo because it is based on "arzàn" the dialect name for Reggio. The presence of place atoned for the lack of family and father.

Secondly, after Italian Unification there was a period when the masses were excluded from politics by a limited franchise. They demonstrated their desire for a role by giving their children "ideological names," such as "Libera."[26] Under Mussolini the red peasantry of the Romagna found space to resist by calling their offspring Lenin and Trotski. After 1945 Hollywood made its presence felt and created little Kims (Novak) and Marilyns (Monroe). So there is a link between names and general history, and family choices are influenced by the historical moment.

Changing one's name may have more effect on others than on oneself. When Cassius Marcellus Clay became Muhammed Ali after winning the world title, he alienated those whites who saw in the Black Muslims a refusal to integrate into the traditional American melting pot. For himself Ali was merely giving up a name derived from the practice of slavery.

Northern Irish names have lost their ability to designate objects and have been drawn into the tribal struggle between Catholics and Protestants. Thus when one names the second city in the North, one is primarily declaring one's religious allegiance: Catholics say Derry and Protestants Londonderry. One's life and death in the North are linked to membership in one or the other tribe, so words are limited, too.

The last example is taken from *Pinocchio,* an Italian children's classic but also a book about the Italian state that emerged from the Unification struggle. The debate revolves around the Catholic doctrine that the moment the child receives a name from her/his parent is also the moment when s/he is freed from original sin and becomes a human. According to Catholic analysts,[27] Geppetto gives Pinocchio his name, becomes his father and from that moment on the novel is primarily the tale of a family that splits up and reunites at the end. One obvious argument against this interpretation is that Geppetto makes this vital act into a joke by explaining that he has chosen the name Pinocchio because he knew a family with that name, the richest member of which was a beggar.

A stronger argument is that Pinocchio has already assumed an identity, not by acquiring a name but by defending himself against Maestro Ciliegio, who wishes to turn him into an object—a table leg. The methods Pinocchio uses are verbal—once again language as protest. He demands not to be carved into a table leg and then he causes a quarrel between Maestro Ciliegio and Geppetto by using the former's nickname. This may be seen as a deliberately false, heretical version of baptism that draws attention to the fact that Pinocchio is not baptized—the Italian state was lay. More important, Pinocchio discovers his identity and does not receive it from anyone. It emerges from a struggle with outside authority, which does not augur well for the new Italian state. Alternatively one might argue that Pinocchio's identity comes from Collodi's writing. In this case it remains true that the text disrupts the naming process, which is secondary to Pinocchio's words and acts of rebellion. Collodi's novel is not an example of how the state uses the written language to legitimize itself. Indeed Pinocchio learns to write using instruments drawn from nature—a twig and the juice of wild fruit. He is not taught by an elementary school teacher but rather teaches himself. The implications for the Italian state are far-reaching.

A general conclusion might be that the family's assumed right to bestow a first name can be blocked or re-directed by social disorder. Another conclusion is that an unusual or an obviously ethnic first name may impose a direction on the child's character. S/he may then inwardize this pressure: a Rhiannon may take it on herself to learn Welsh. Or else, like Pinocchio, she may display an identity of her own making. So, according to our interpretation, nicknames are important because they are imposed by the peer group or the local community and the individual may find it hard to resist them. One may add a third conclusion that names are to words what the machine-tool industry is to manufacturing.

Language and violence

The example of (London) Derry is merely a hint of what may happen when language breaks down. Where there is no political language, there is no politics and a void is created that may well be filled by violence. Northern Ireland is the best-known case and it may be less unusual than we would like to think. Here words have lost their power to name things and to provide dialogue. They have not lost all meaning, for they unfailingly evoke two tribes, each of which finds an identity in hostility to the other. A first name tells the listener not who the individual is but to which tribe he belongs: Seamus means he is a Catholic and Norman that he is a Protestant. The reason for this is not just linguistic but rather lies in the listener's frame of reference, itself shaped by culture. Even in post-war Italy, torn between communism and Catholicism, there was a common text, the Constitution, which could serve as the basis of a political community. Northern Ireland had—at least until the Good Friday agreement—no such document.

I shall argue in chapter 5 that this void may be explained by Irish-British history. It will suffice here to note that until recently the IRA (Irish Republican Army) did not recognize the Dublin, Belfast or London government's right to exercise authority in Ireland. It thus adopted toward them a strategy of silence. Since it did not admit the right of their law courts to pass judgment on its "soldiers," these did not speak in their own defense when they were put on trial. Northern Irish violence has "nothing personal" about it (to borrow the title of a Thaddeus O'Sullivan film). It represents a choice consciously made—at least on the Catholic side—because language is seen to have failed in its task of creating political solutions.

Terrorist groups have usually given up their belief in politics and hence in language. The Red Brigades started by combining examples of violence with left-wing political militancy. Then they discovered that Western European governments of the 1970s were not willing to conduct dialogue with groups that also used violence (the same discovery was made a few years later by a second group, Prima Linea). So they resorted to more extreme forms of violence, which required stricter clandestinity and cut them off from the language of left-wing politics. Living in a closed environment, their own language became a jargon that was vaguely reminiscent of the Third International, itself banned in many countries. They wrote in clichés about non-existent entities like "the heart of the state" and "the combating Communist Party." At the same time their need for words increased and one of their most frequent demands was that their statements be read on TV and published in newspapers. They were either convinced by the many observers who argue that power lies in the media or else seduced by Andy Warhol's promise that everyone can be a celebrity for fifteen minutes. Probably both. The Red Brigades also wished to be talked to: they sought legitimacy from the Italian government and excoriated it all the more because it would not grant them recognition.

Beyond these extreme attempts to speak lies the silence of death. It takes the form of collective suicide in the case of the Rote Armee Fraktion (the Stammheim deaths, which are sometimes not considered suicides) and the IRA's hunger strikes. At least the latter represent an attempt to speak via death: Bobby Sands stood for parliament and his writings were widely divulged as he starved himself.

Primo Levi discussed the kind of language that is caught up with death. In Auschwitz there was a "Lagerdeutsch," a crude version of German that was designed to communicate only the few things the prisoner needed to know. It was helped in this task by arbitrary acts of violence. It did not and was not designed to communicate feelings—aside from the contempt of the SS for prisoners—or anything personal or extraneous to the camp. Indeed it contained a number of expressions that were incomprehensible to the prisoners, whose weakness was thus reinforced.

At an earlier stage, on entering the camp, the prisoners had encountered the language of bureaucracy. An ironic comment on the link between bureaucracy and violence is made by Harold Pinter in *Mountain Language*. Here an oppressive regime bans the use of a language that allows people to talk about love and community. The soldiers use a bureaucratic jargon that does not seek dialogue, backed up by violence. Pinter satirizes this non-language when he has a soldier say of the guard-dogs: "Before they bite, they say their names. It's a formal procedure. They say their name and then they bite."[28] The juxtaposition of "say" and "bite," the mockery of naming and the repetition of the statement with a different temporal sequence emphasize the willful inadequacy of the language of bureaucracy.

The Unsaid

The summa is a literary dream. Even James Joyce did not say everything in *Finnegans Wake*, although he did say enough to inspire in Samuel Beckett, who was transcribing it, a distrust of language that drove him to write brief plays and novels with a restricted vocabulary, slight plots and much repetition. What is left out is the "non-detto" or unsaid. This is not left out for lack of space or because too many things have already been said. It is left out because it is dangerous: it is a more extreme version of Foucault's "discontinu." It is what honest citizens do not wish to know.

Foucault lists cases of the unsaid. The narrative of the mad is unsaid or, if told, it is filtered through the narrative of the doctor who removes the direct experience of the mad. Society would find this uninteresting because the mad by definition do not know anything about their madness. The will to truth causes the omission of all kinds of things derived from forms of knowledge considered unreliable or that do not fit into the coherent pattern of the narrative. Not that the unsaid is necessarily right or wise, but it deserves a hearing.

Literature is aware of the unsaid and strives to include it. But it constantly fails and its successes lead to fresh failures. In the example of colonial writing, Conrad or Forster undermines the fictions that the European community in a colony invents to justify its presence and power. Such novelists can depict "good" colonizers who see the exploitation carried out by their community. They cannot, however, describe the colony as the colonized see it. At best the colonized is present in all her/his otherness, which the good colonizer lives as a painful riddle.

Political language is plagued by the unsaid. Since it is, in a democratic society, a discourse of consent, it is reluctant to offend its listeners. But, if we define a party's knowledge of itself and the world in which it operates as its political culture, then the gaps or contradictions in that culture constitute the unsaid of its discourse. The French Communists knew (the past tense is somewhat harsh!) that they had, in order to flourish, to be a French rather than a Soviet party. In their post-war account of their wartime history they, therefore, stressed their role in the Resistance and their support for de Gaulle. The unsaid is that this is true only after Hitler invaded the USSR. From 1939 to 1941 the Communists supported or did nothing to oppose the Nazis who occupied France, but were allied with Stalin.

Political language, while it tries to be objective when it takes the form of good journalism, mostly wishes to convince. Its goal is to usher the listener/reader from point A to point B and it tries to prevent her/him from straying off toward point C. This creates a tendency to leave out what could serve as a distraction. Gaullists joined the Communists in spreading the tale of the Resistance and they too exaggerated the numbers of members but, unlike the Communists, they stressed de Gaulle's speech of June 18, 1940, which in reality attracted few listeners and fewer still recruits.

Leaving sections of history unsaid is dangerous because the unsaid often re-emerges and threatens the established order. To continue with the French case, the official attitude was that anti-Semitic measures were the work of the Nazis and that only a few French people were involved, therefore the Republic bore no guilt. This was blatantly incorrect. In the fifty years since the war ended sundry Maurice Papons—high French officials who played a role in organizing the deportation of Jews—have turned up to confound the official view and hence call into question the post-war regime. Mitterrand's image as a Socialist and as a president was damaged when he refused to recognize that the Republic bore any responsibility for the roundup of Jews in the Vél d'Hiv incident. He left out the facts that the Third Republic tolerated much anti-Semitism and also that it had voted Pétain into power. In 2000 the French government finally acknowledged the role of the French state in anti-Semitism. Historians had long underlined this role but in our society an "unsaid" in one milieu can be openly stated in another. The truth had not been told in order not to threaten the unity of the post-war political order. That it can now be said shows that the political order is stronger and that, fifty years later, the Second World War is not, except in certain cases, an issue.[29]

In Italy the problem is more complex. A whole series of so-called state massacres was left unsolved—the killing of 16 people in Piazza Fontana (1969) is only one example—or else only minor figures were sent to prison. The real perpetrators were probably right-wing terrorists with the help/connivance of the Italian secret service, of politicians who may have been in the government and of foreign secret services like the CIA. The expressions of doubt are important. Was the goal of the real perpetrators, whoever they were, a right-wing coup d'état? More likely they wished to hold over the heads of the ruling DC (Democrazia cristiana) and of the PCI the threat of a coup. Or perhaps not even that but an ill-defined menace and precisely a doubt. The only way for the state to defend itself was to bring these crimes out of the area of the "non-detto."

But the state could not reveal who the culprits were. Probable reasons are that its incompetent services could not find them or that it was itself involved and divided or that it feared the power of the perpetrators. So Italy acquired a whole zone of what Giovanni Pellegrino calls "indicibilità." Its effect on Italian opinion was to increase the distrust of governments and of the political system. Such distrust makes political and all other reforms more difficult. It also takes the form of "dietrologia": of the belief that reality is not what one sees but is shaped by mysterious forces over which one has no control.

The sense of being unable to control one's destiny leads to the view that everything is manipulated by unnamed "Grand old men" or that every leaf that falls from a tree is pushed by the CIA. So political language is useless because the zone of what cannot be said is so great. This allows political debate to become a game that is played not only on TV talkshows but in local cafés up and down Italy where people gather to drink their cappuccino. We have come full circle: the unsaid creates a discourse of its own: theatrical, ironic and convinced of its inadequacy.

Since Foucault or even earlier, there has been a tendency to believe that the unsaid (and what Foucault calls the *discontinu*) are the most valuable parts of political discourse. This attitude is a luxury that the observer can permit her/himself, but the electorate cannot. It must base its judgment on the story that the party is telling her about itself and the world. This is not just a story about policies, for the language may constitute or create policy itself. Tony Blair's Third Way is only one example.

One is right to be wary of political narrative because it deals with topics that cannot be vetted by science and declared true or false. But it seems unduly pessimistic of Hannah Arendt to write that "It may be in the nature of the political realm to be at war with truth in all its forms."[30] Arendt argues that truth has a despotic character that makes it a rival for dictators and unwanted by democratic societies that rule by consent, hence according to majority opinion. Arendt sees the truthteller as a solitary figure, perhaps like Orwell's Winston who tries, unsuccessfully, to maintain that two and two make four. In a democratic society a government running for reelection might well be tempted to give the GNP a boost by declaring that two and two make five. It will probably hold back, however, because few people will believe it. The unsaid is not the same as Arendt's big lie.

Literary and Political Language

Is the difference important? Both Foucault and Pierre Bourdieu (who died just after this book was completed) would probably argue that it is not. To Bourdieu all language is political because to speak well gives one a symbolic power that is accepted as real in the class struggle. But in Claude Chabrol's film *La Cérémonie,* culture makes the key difference between the bourgeois family and the two "exclues," one of whom is illiterate while the other reads only Céline. Culture has various languages, such as those of music and opera, but all confer power and none (except Céline's?) is qualitatively different from the others. The illiterate servant is excluded because she knows none of these languages.

In 1960—the date is significant—Roland Barthes distinguished sharply between "écrivain" and "écrivant." Barthes describes what is special about the language of literature: the "écrivain" considers language an end in itself. The various "whys" that the universe poses are resolved into a "how" these can be written about. "Ecrivant" means to write about something, about some of the whys posed by the universe. In practice the two kinds of writing can co-exist in one text—George Orwell's *1984* is an example. But the difference remains, even if it is not total. The "écrivain" is deliberately unreal and his world is devoid of cause and effect. It is a matter of form and vision. The second has to do with things, one of which is politics.[31]

Che fare? What is to be done? This is one of the great dilemmas of the post-war when the left—especially in Italy—was awaiting the arrival of the Red Army with ever increasing impatience. One suspects, however, that Barthes, who had been subjected to various brands of populism and had read more "proletarian" novels than he cared to remember, enjoyed this wait and was in no hurry to see the Cossacks return to Montmartre. As early as 1953 and even before,[32] he had worked out a solution that combined avant-garde writing with an edge of political criticism that was present in the writing itself. Although his thought at this period was influenced by Marx, Barthes preferred questions to certainties. Here he maintains that the work of literature contains a silence or a hollowness that is the mark of alienation: "writing is inseparable from silence."[33]

This silence is not trappist, but Rilke would have understood it. It leads the poet or the novelist to combat the bourgeois elements that are inherent in literature because of the bourgeois hegemony in society. One of these is the use of the past historic tense in the novel—"il donna"—which endows the past with a disguised causality. Good writers will shun this as an illusion-instrument of bourgeois power. An example is Camus's *L'Etranger*, which uses the perfect tense—"J'ai donné"—throughout. This is a moral rather than a political matter, Barthes decides; it produces a neutral writing or *écriture blanche*.

This distinction, in which literature perceives itself only as language whereas political language perceives itself as politics, is useful when used pragmatically. We see that the role the literary language can play in politics springs precisely from its refusal to make judgments that lie outside language. As for the language of politics, a politician like Michel Rocard can, by "telling the truth"—"parler vrai"—remove from political language the temptation to say, decide and promise too much.

We shall tackle these difficulties in chapter 4 and next we shall look at the phenomena of commitment and anti-politics, which are two very different ways for the literary language to deal with the political.

Chapter Two

Left-wing commitment 1940–1960

The dates in this chapter's title are as arbitrary as the dates I criticize elsewhere in this book. Left-wing commitment began long before 1940 but lack of space prevents us from tracking it down, via a full discussion of Malraux's *La condition humaine* and *L'Espoir* or of the 1931 collapse of the KreditAnstalt, to the Bolshevik revolution and beyond. Commitment does not mean writing about politics. To reverse the statement of chapter one, a text, even a song by Maria Carta, can barely avoid being tinged with politics, although it shows that politics is not all things.

Commitment presupposes that politics is almost everything, even if that "almost" is rich in diverse meanings. Therefore the intellectual sets his writing at the service of a particular kind of politics, in this case socialism. The initial step leads on to others: there are various brands of socialism, at the very least a communist and a social democratic version, and how is one to choose? Are there particular tenets of socialism that attract intellectuals? Is anti-communism or anti-fascism a form of commitment? Certainly there is much right-wing committed writing. How far does the "almost" reach? Is the work judged solely by its value to the cause it professes to serve? Or is there life outside agit-prop and urging the reader to reach the targets laid down by the Five Year Plan? Are there still autonomous canons of aesthetic judgment?

To these questions may be added the corresponding organizational questions. What is the correct relationship between a revolutionary writer and the leadership of the revolutionary party? More precisely, does Palmiro Togliatti have the right to prevent Elio Vittorini from publishing translations of Ernest Hemingway in *Il Politecnico?* It has been said that the PCI exercised great power over post-war publishing houses and newspapers. In so far as this is true, it is the result of certain traits of the historical moment. But it is also the fruit of a careful strategy undertaken by Togliatti. In any case neither the PCI nor its leader could have won much power unless writers and intellectuals were ready to grant it to them. Why were they so disposed?

Brief historical sketch of commitment

Many observers date the appearance of the politically committed intellectual from the Dreyfus case.[1] But of course the Enlightenment was committed to spreading the values of empirical thought and individual reason. From that point on its exponents divided: Voltaire, for example, liked to dally with supposedly enlightened despots. Closer to our period are the novels of Anthony Trollope like *Phineas Finn* that offer superb political analysis; yet Trollope certainly did not consider himself committed. In the twentieth century there were more writers and intellectuals—the two are not the same and there are subgroups of both. The Dreyfus case has been seen as the victory of provincial schoolteachers, imbued with the ethic of republicanism and subscribers to Charles Péguy's *Cahiers de la quinzaine,* over Parisian writers who have the Academy as their fortress.[2] A recent author puts it succinctly: "From now on intellectual power falls into the hands of the teachers."[3] Some political leaders went about signing up intellectuals in a more systematic way than Friedrich of Prussia had done. Yet the mighty PCI was unable to prevent Giangiacomo Feltrinelli from publishing *Doctor Zhivago,* although it was under pressure from its Soviet comrades to do so.

Certainly the presence of a strong left-wing party fosters commitment. But at the Liberation young Italians, like Italo Calvino or Pier Paolo Pasolini, embraced the Communist Party because they believed that Italian intellectuals had failed the nation by not opposing fascism. To the young, it was a matter of social justice, as well as the attraction of the fraternity that supposedly held sway in the Party. Gramsci provided the reasoning for this choice, arguing that Italian intellectuals had neglected their historic task of writing for and about the Italian working-people. Instead they had become "cosmopolitan": they looked to the Church for patronage and later to France for appreciation and readers.[4] Yet the neo-Hegelian current, which ran from De Sanctis to Croce, had provided the vision of a society that could change. It had helped guide many young men, including Gramsci, to socialism. An important part of Togliatti's cultural policy lay in presenting the PCI as the heir to this tradition. Croce was praised for having opened the way to Gramsci and then he was buried.

Commitment requires a choice by an individual writer, and a strong party is helpful, as is a tradition of intellectuals who get involved in politics. Italy had the first but supposedly not the second. Guilt for past betrayals or for one's own social advantages increases the influence of the party. This is the "il-ne-faut-pas-désespérer-Billancourt" principle. It holds that a middle-class intellectual must not weaken the workers' faith in their party by irresponsible skepticism.[5]

If one looks at the historical moment, one discovers that writers enter politics at the same time as the masses. The right to vote, the need for literate citizens and workers, the formation of mass parties and of trade unions are features of the late nineteenth century. It became harder than before to remain outside politics. George Bernard Shaw and the Fabians were just one example of intellectuals who decided they must get involved. Since the historical moment contains various and contradictory impulses, this was also the period when art for art's sake flourished—Mallarmé and the symbolist poets epitomized it, as did the painter Gustave Moreau, whose canvasses of Salomé bearing the head of John the Baptist have little to do with trade unions.

Right-wing commitment in France, where it was especially strong, is best seen as a protest firstly against the modernization that accompanied democracy and secondly against democracy itself. Then too it was an attempt to strengthen the nation-state, which had been humiliated by Bismarck in 1870. An early example is Maurice Barrès, who first wrote three slight, rather precious books about the moods and movements of his inner self. The so-called *culte du moi* novels were published between 1889 and 1891: *Sous l'oeil des barbares, Un homme libre* and *Le jardin de Bérénice*. They were successful but Barrès was not satisfied. The self, he felt, must be strengthened by being rooted in the soil of France. Modernity entails mobility, but this for Barrès was *déracinement* or being uprooted. The step forward to nationalism is a short one and Barrès finds his first cause in Boulangism. In the late 1880s General Boulanger looked good on a horse, he attracted crowds, Germans disliked him and he was quite willing to be generous in social policy especially when industrialists had to pay. But he was not the man to lead an army and to overthrow the despised Third Republic. Boulangism soon collapsed. In many ways it was a trial run for the Dreyfus case, which began in 1894, three years after Boulanger's death.

Here anti-Semitism was the cement of the French nation, while the Jew, cosmopolitan and nomadic, was the necessary other. Each side had its battery of intellectuals—Péguy and Zola crossed swords with Barrès and Maurras. Proust and Gide also joined in. In right-wing commitment one sees the twin traits of gaining strength and then deploying it against an invented enemy, the Jew, and—perhaps—against a real enemy, Germany. Or perhaps not: one remembers the "better Hitler than Blum" slogan of the late 1930s. By contrast the left sees itself as crusading on behalf of a victim and as defending democracy: the guilt or innocence of Dreyfus was the more important issue, not the honor of the French army. The right of a Jew to be treated like all other French citizens was a complementary cause and it recurs today in the shape of Arab immigrants and the attempt to "exclude" them. Left-wing commitment gave shape or integrity to one's own life—turning it into a destiny, is how Brunet, Sartre's communist, defines it.

Since commitment contains the modernist trait of totality, it is fostered by—although it may clash with—a political interlocutor that believes it can change humankind in its entirety. Communism and fascism were ideal except that they did not permit freedom of speech. But that was not an insurmountable problem. Behind the safe frontiers of drearily democratic France one could be communist or anti-communist, fascist or anti-fascist.

The Dreyfus case was emblematic of a more democratic society in that it posed the question of citizens' rights versus raison d'état. Anti-Semitism might be the cement of a certain kind of nation but the supporters of Dreyfus discarded it to defend democracy. Ireland's Parnell affair, which posed the question of whether one could be Irish without being Catholic, is also still important.

Crises drive writers into politics: the Depression and Hitler helped create the second wave of left-wing commitment. Lucien Goldmann states that communism's failure to dominate Western Europe means there could be—at least according to traditional Marxist theory—no widespread communist culture.[6] But certainly there was some.

Such a culture differs both from the *Nouvelle Revue Française* (NRF) cult of the problematic individual and from the psychological analysis so prevalent in France from the seventeenth century onward. The hero of the new committed novel is simple (although less docile than his socialist realist comrades). He wishes at all costs to act. Self-analysis gives way to the collective judgments of the infallible communist party. Disappointment with commitment often created a new commitment. *1984* reveals the inferno of communism: the main traits of the party as future utopia are reversed. The shabby, whining Winston is a parody of Bolshevik man; the flood of people, perpetually in search of soap or razor blades, is a mockery of the party. Yet *1984* was written by a man who considered himself an active left-winger.

Death is a great theme in this wave of committed writing—as Paul Nizan's work will show—because the individual is dying. But s/he will be replaced by the revolutionary group—Kyo, Katow, May and the others in *La condition humaine* (1933). Heaven has returned in the form of socialism but it has also been realized on earth: the pilgrimage to the USSR is made by the faithful.

The left has no monopoly on commitment. In Italy the possibility of a Catholic revival was also present at the Liberation and there were interesting Catholic intellectuals like Carlo Bo, who admired Jacques Rivière, an unorthodox French Catholic and from 1919 to 1925 editor of the *NRF*. But the Vatican did not want lots of meddlesome thinkers who would be hard to control. Pius XII liked to have men about him who were obedient, such as Luigi Gedda, who claimed the credit for the 1948 election victory but did not claim intellectual originality. Innovative thought came from France in the shape of Jacques Maritain's *Humanisme intégral*, which was read and commented on especially by the Dossetti wing of the DC (Christian Democrats). From France too came the worker-priest movement, which seemed dangerously left-wing to Pius XII, who banned it.

Fascism had used censorship and force against its opponents but it had also penetrated Italian culture. Initially it influenced less than it was influenced by Italian writers and painters. The Futurists and D'Annunzio are only two examples. But the young people who were around twenty-one years of age when Mussolini was overthrown had known nothing except fascism. They had, as one of them said, absorbed it into their bodies.[7] This second generation was offered magazines that were (almost) under its control, a brand of fascism that excoriated the party apparatus, the promise of a return to the left-wing origins of the movement and the very intelligent Giuseppe Bottai in his second incarnation as minister of education. As we shall try to demonstrate in the case of Pasolini, the many-sidedness—the "poliedricità"—of fascism made it difficult to arrive at an anti-fascist position. It has been argued that the populism that dominated at the Liberation was itself born of fascism.[8]

France was superficially much further to the left. The Nazi occupation and the weakness of the Vichy government after September 1942 sent people into the Resistance. This had leaders of all political hues: from de Gaulle, who was a Catholic and a nationalist, to the communists, who now called themselves the "Parti des Fusillés" (The Party of the Executed). But the Resistance was generically left-wing: France's élites had let her down and the working-class had borne the brunt of the Occupation. Anyway Vichy, the fairly small bands of fervent collaborators who supported such would-be Führers as Jacques Doriot and Marcel Déat, and the Action Française members who had supported Vichy, forced the old anti-Dreyfusard right virtually into silence. Slowly it re-emerged and took the political forms of the "Algérie française" movement and then of Le Pen's Front National. But in the 1950s it was too discredited to be an intellectual force. When Céline published one of his greatest novels, *Féerie pour une autre fois* (Part 1 in 1952 and Part 2 in 1954), it received no attention. The same was true of Lucien Rebatet's *Les deux étendards*. By contrast Simone de Beauvoir describes Camus working at the *Combat* office during the Liberation: he was radiant, for his hour had come.[9]

Combat was the clandestine newspaper of the Resistance movement of the same name. It was edited by Pascal Pia, Camus's old boss at *Alger-Républicain*, and Camus was its number two. Sartre was considered the other great writer of the moment. He set out the creed of left-wing commitment in *Situations II*, a chunk of which appeared as a bugle-blast at the head of the first number of *Les Temps modernes*. The initial sentence is sweeping and belligerent: "All writers of bourgeois background have been tempted by irresponsibility." From here on the term "bourgeois" is used as a synonym for evil. The writer cannot, however, escape so easily: "whatever he does, he is caught up in things." Thus Flaubert is held responsible for the repression of the Commune because he wrote nothing to avert it. There is to be no more idealistic talk about posterity or immortality: "we write for our contemporaries."[10] Sartre's sentences are dense with emotion and it was clear that outside of *Les Temps modernes* there was to be no salvation. Inside there would be excommunications and a constant search for heretics. The term "situation" was too broad to be limited to politics, but (wo)man could act to change her/his situation only via politics. There could not, therefore, be autonomous aesthetic canons. Sartre's aggressive language came partly from his temperament and partly from this Manichean period. Clearly Sartre considered that the language of literature could be made to serve political goals.

In reality things were neither so new nor so simple. The Dreyfus case was in the background. Emile Zola, who wrote the letter *J'accuse*, had sought in his long series of novels about the Second Empire, the Rougon-Macquart saga, to take the objective position of an empirical scientist—in this case the medical researcher, Claude Bernard. From objectivity or from the desire to be objective, Zola moved to denouncing leaders and institutions of the Third Republic. Charles Péguy was also an early defender of Dreyfus, although by 1914 he was an ardent nationalist. Perhaps one key to the political stands taken by French writers is that they were impassioned and flamboyant. Writers rarely supported the "stalemate" Third Republic. Alain is the exception who proves the rule. There were two entities that were more legitimate than the Third Republic: the ideal republic born of the Revolution, which should be socialist and should add to the "equality-before-the-law" principle of the Revolution an "equality-before-money"; and the real country as opposed to the legal country. France had existed from the depth of the ages and could not be identified with capitalism, the reign of money, or with parliamentary democracy, the reign of corruption and selfish ambition. On the side of the real France stood Maurice Barrès and the future Action Française, led by Charles Maurras.

The role of André Gide

Philosophical arguments about principles are better suited to writers than the specialized debates about economics that are the raw material of today's political language. But writers grew worried in the aftermath of the Dreyfus case about the invasion of politics on their territory. André Gide may be taken as an example: his writing from *Nourritures terrestres* (1897) to *L'Immoraliste* (1902) and *La porte étroite* (1909) marks the attempt by the individual to free him/herself—more often himself—from the influence of a conformist society. It is true that in *L'Immoraliste* this struggle involves a stay in North Africa, where young, unprotected boys are drawn, by their poverty, into the narrator's quest for liberation. But the way they live is not a major theme. Political writing contains a critical force directed against certain socio-political targets but it is not, on that account, critical of the entire cultural framework of which it is itself a part. Pre-1914 Gide took French colonial rule in North Africa largely for granted.[11]

As 1914 drew closer, the Agadir incident, Kaiser Wilhelm's rantings and the patriotic rhetoric of Maurras turned Gide back to politics in the shape of resistance to Germany. His was not the stand of a Rupert Brooke and he did not discover corners of foreign fields that would forever France be. But when war broke out he went to work as a volunteer at the Foyer Franco-Belge. The *Nouvelle Revue Française,* the magazine of which Gide was the leader but not the director, tended to follow his example.[12]

So Gide went from a Dreyfusard stand, via a non-political period, to a tempered nationalism. His changes of position were characteristic of this subtle writer, determined to live out each of his many selves. Polyphony requires prudence: one cannot allow oneself to be monopolized by any adventure, however fascinating it may be. This was not atypical of writers at this period. They took political stands but did not believe that politics brought salvation. If anything brought salvation—which was unlikely—it was writing itself: "the revolutionary claims for man the right not to be sold into slavery, but the poet demands for man the right to be a man."[13]

The themes of freedom or cowardice were framed as individual choices. Converting them into language was the principal task of the writer.

Commitment to Europe began at this time but its earliest form was the writer who left behind the constraints of his native land and discovered freedom in travel to other countries. An example is another *NRF* writer, Valery Larbaud, who like Gide was fleeing an authoritarian mother, in his poem *L'Europe*. Since the supposed author is A. O. Barnabooth, a South American, Europe is a break with his past.[14] Via diversity, Larbaud moves to the awareness of European unity, albeit in an ironic and non-political form and influenced by Walt Whitman's vast, varied but united America. This too is complex, for earlier Whitman had offered to Yeats and the Irish literary revival the model of the national poet.

The trenches would give new urgency to "Europe," but to return to Gide there was one political issue especially dear to him: homosexual rights. Having hinted at his own pederasty, Gide went no further. Then, disapproving of a translation of the ubiquitous Whitman that did not do justice to his pederasty, Gide decided the *NRF* would publish a new translation.[15] But the more overtly pederastic poems were translated not by Gide but by Louis Fabulet, whose own sexual preference led him to them. Meanwhile Gide translated the heterosexual Children of Adam poems so Claudel need not have withdrawn from the project as he did.[16] The introduction to the new translation was written by Larbaud, who chose to emphasize the religious aspect. So the leading motive for the *NRF* project was not obvious in the final version.

Part of Gide's discretion stemmed from the terrible example of Oscar Wilde, with whom he had gone hunting for boys and who was the model for Ménalque in *L'Immoraliste*. Pasolini, who had of course no direct dealings with Wilde, also reflected on his fate and thought Wilde an exemplary, sacrificial figure. Gide, however, had no desire to finish up like Wilde. When he made his tardy decision to publicize his sexual choice, he published *Corydon* (1924), in which pederasty was disguised with lots of talk about its role in education around the time of Plato as well as a harangue, sprinkled with anti-Semitic comments, against Léon Blum, who had advocated premarital sex among heterosexuals. So the political stand for which Gide is remembered was well dosed with prudence. Gide did not think that one text was going to decide the fate of French pederasts much less provide the material for a judgment of his writing.

One might conclude that, despite his later critique of colonialism in the Congo, his embracing of communism without ever joining the party and his trip to the USSR in 1936 that produced, instead of the usual panegyrics, the critical *Retour de l'URSS*, Gide never believed that politics could transform the human condition, his own or anyone else's. His sense of the writer was of an individual filling up a white sheet of paper in order to communicate with another individual, the reader. Gide's greatest work is his *Journal*, precisely the kind of writing that Orwell's Winston finds the most important and the most difficult. The age that Winston harks back to, when people valued objects because they found their shape aesthetically pleasing and when privacy was taken for granted, was the age of Gide.

COMMITMENT ON THE RIGHT

Gide's world began to break down with the Soviet victory, which provoked a dispute within the *NRF* about the new collectivism. But the communist tide seemed to have peaked and the fledgling communist parties in Western Europe did not attract great numbers of intellectuals. The Western European economies grew well in the mid-1920s. Yet the temptation of commitment was already present. On the right it had taken organized form in the Action Française (AF), which had a clear, dogmatic view of literature to accompany its monarchism.

To Maurras and his followers the great period of French writing was the seventeenth century, which was the age of classicism. The modern French writer should seek inspiration in the plays of Racine or the maxims of La Rochefoucauld. Romanticism was associated with the Revolution and should be ignored. If the modern writer looked outside France, he should look back to classical Rome. German or English literature could be of no help to him, since literature expressed the national genius.

Overlapping with the entry into politics was a surge of interest in Catholicism. Should religious commitment be considered in the same way as political? Many French Catholics were organically linked with the Action Française, and Pope Pius XI's condemnation of AF in 1926 caused them much heart searching. One might also argue that political commitment substitutes politics for religion. The communist party offers the militant eternal life, the human condition will be transformed by the arrival of socialism as by the second coming of Christ and the militant's task is to give up all his possessions and follow the Party. The differences are also great for, if the Catholic Church can be as demanding and as jealous as a communist party, God is more remote than a party secretary.

Historically the great cultural upsurge of French Catholicism is triggered by Third Republic anti-clericalism and it is as strong as the interest in politics in the years before 1914. The Church's defeats over Dreyfus and schools sent it into an opposition that was fruitful for its writers. By the 1950s the energy that had produced Claudel, Péguy and Bernanos was running dry, although French theologians like Henri de Lubak exerted great influence on the Second Vatican Council. Meanwhile François Mauriac's weekly *Bloc-Notes,* acerbic and critical of "the world," bore witness to a great tradition.

Nor must we forget the right. Mussolini's authoritarian government, which did away with parliamentary democracy and indulged in a cult of ancient Rome, appealed to many in the AF. Younger men did not find AF itself so appealing: monarchism and classicism were hardly exciting to a generation growing up in what it believed was its "pre-war."[17] Fascism appealed to a small but significant number of writers: the magazine *Je suis partout,* staffed by Brasillach and Rebatet among others, was virulent in its language, strongly anti-Semitic and professed to believe in a France regenerated by fascism. Rebatet also wrote about the cinema and about music. Indeed it has recently been suggested that his ability to penetrate the world of contemporary music was linked with his belief in fascism.[18] Certainly both he and Brasillach were talented writers. Drieu la Rochelle was a fascist who believed in Europe rather than France. His long novel, *Gilles,* which describes the evolution of his hero to fascism, depicts a Frenchman, an Irishman and a Pole fighting on Franco's side in the Spanish Civil War. Gilles sums up: "From 1918 on he believed in Europe. What was it? Several forces had to come together, none of them weakened by the others. Geneva had been a dirty, little abstraction which humiliated all the powerful, diverse lives. The nations of Europe must meet."[19]

For such writers the anti-parliamentary riots of February 1934 were a first step toward a fascist coup. If Hitler's arrival in power revived the old anti-German feeling of the Action Française, the prospect of an alliance with the Soviet Union, advocated by the opportunistic Laval, and of the Popular Front, led by a Jewish prime minister, caused others to swallow the bitter pill of Hitler. When the defeat came in 1940 it was, in Maurras's eyes, a divine surprise.

The road to collaboration was easy. Drieu became editor of the *NRF,* although he was not without his doubts, while *Je suis partout* hid any trace of doubt at least until the Allies landed in North Africa. The collaborators were very critical of Vichy, which they considered lukewarm, corrupt and self-serving. Rebatet spent a couple of months there before he returned to Paris and pressed for a fascist government. Both he and Brasillach were admirers of Mussolini. Hitler's attack on the Soviet Union delighted Rebatet, who was disappointed only that there was no French contingent in the first Nazi onslaught. In 1942 Rebatet published a long pamphlet, *Les Décombres,* in which he excoriates French élites for the 1940 defeat, although this is also caused by communist and Jewish intriguers, who are also responsible for the confusion of the Popular Front. All this, recounted in a language full of obscenity and blasphemy, virulent even by pamphleteer standards, albeit dedicated to his mother, found an eager audience among French people, shocked by the collapse of their world. *Les Décombres,* published by Céline's publisher Denoel, sold out its first edition of 20,000 in a few days.[20]

Céline even managed to get one of his books, the pamphlet *Les beaux draps* (1941), banned by Vichy, a distinction he never tired of mentioning at the Liberation. As the war swung against Germany, the *collabos* grew worried. For Brasillach the fall of Mussolini was decisive. Rebatet was one of the contingent that fled from Paris on August 17, 1944, just before the Allies arrived. The French collaborators and Vichy supporters followed Pétain and Laval into what they hoped would be temporary exile at Sigmaringen in South Germany. Their hopes soared when Von Runstedt launched his Ardennes offensive, but then Patton stopped him and despair settled on Sigmaringen. Céline managed to get a visa, which allowed him to travel through a devastated Germany and find refuge in Denmark. Rebatet went on working at his long novel, *Les deux étendards,* which has nothing to do with the war or fascism but is a mixture of eroticism and mysticism. He was taken prisoner and returned to France, where he was tried and condemned to death in 1946. Drieu remained in Paris and committed suicide, while Brasillach was tried and executed. In 1947 Rebatet's sentence was commuted and he was released from prison in 1952. *Les deux étendards* was published in the same year. Meanwhile Charles Maurras had been sent to prison shouting that this was Dreyfus's revenge. Maurras was forgotten in the post-war years except by right-wing philosophers like Pierre Boutang.[21] Céline was imprisoned in Denmark but he was allowed to return to France in 1951 and in 1957 his *D'un château l'autre,* a much inferior novel to *Féerie,* was a popular success, probably because it satirizes Sigmaringen.

The collaborators who survived regrouped around a magazine called *Rivarol* but the revelations of Auschwitz discredited them. Young, new writers like Roger Nimier claimed to be right-wing but they were mostly critical of the left's dominance. Nimier brought into literature "style, impertinence, the air of a French cavalryman."[22] He had no patience with the left's longwinded debates about the class struggle. Gaston Gallimard found a use for Nimier: he sent him out to Meudon to deal with Céline.

A third group, which also belonged to the historic moment, resisted the trend to commitment in the name of sophisticated writing. Jean Paulhan, who had played an important if unpublicized role in the Resistance, turned against it after the Liberation: "There are too many so-called Resistants for whom the Resistance is no more than a means of making their way in the world." Paulhan considered Camus's writing too simple and he was willing to publish Céline. But he and those who thought like him were in the minority.[23]

In Italy Mussolini had found support among intellectuals who just wanted order. With a few, however, there was an organic link: with D'Annunzio, who went off and occupied Fiume (now Rjeka) and who rivaled Mussolini in his taste for theatrical rhetoric; and with the philosopher Giovanni Gentile, who believed in the pure act unsullied by thought. At an infinitely higher level this provided a seeming justification for beating up one's opponents. Gentile was responsible for an educational reform that survived the regime and is still discussed today. He was named head of the prestigious Scuola Normale at Pisa, where he showed an interest in many kinds of neo-hegelianism, not merely in fascism. Gentile's interests occasionally led him to tolerance toward Mussolini's enemies but he was an ardent fascist who supported the Salò republic. This did not, naturally, save him from execution by the partisans.[24] Croce voted in favor of Mussolini but then opposed him; he was protected (rather inadequately, since his house was looted) by his European fame. He broke with Gentile and survived fascism. If he did not himself take action to oppose it, many of his young followers ended up in the partisans. Some affirm that Croce's sense of the independence of culture provided them with insights into fascism's totalitarian vocation.[25]

Anti-fascism threw up the most famous Italian novel of the period—Ignazio Silone's *Pane e Vino* (1938). Silone joined the PCI when it was founded in 1921 and left in opposition to Stalin in 1930. Accusations that he spied for Mussolini's secret police have gained rather than lost strength in recent years and they can no longer be dismissed as the usual communist tactic of labeling anyone who opposes them as an informer or a fascist.[26] *Pane e Vino*, republished after the war as *Vino e Pane*, is an anti-fascist novel that satirizes both the regime's claim to have transformed the South and its war in Ethiopia. There are at least two versions of the book and the earlier one is very Catholic—communion is taken with bread made in the village. Although Silone's work cannot be considered popular Catholicism, it draws on that rich vein. It also suggests that Marxism will achieve less in the South than Christianity. Silone may be seen, if his more curious side be left aside, as a committed anti-communist. Certainly this was the role he played in the post-war years.

Antonio Gramsci

The finest example of commitment was provided by Antonio Gramsci, the PCI secretary who was arrested in 1926, suffered from poor health and died after approximately ten years in prison. That Gramsci was able to continue thinking and writing throughout this time is amazing. That he endured long periods of ostracism by his fellow communists in prison makes it even more amazing. He was also at the mercy of the prison director and one vindictive man allowed Gramsci to have paper and pen for only one hour a day. No matter, Gramsci spent the day either reading or walking up and down his prison cell thinking. When the pen and paper arrived, he threw himself on them and wrote intensely for an hour. (Interview with Gustavo Trombetti, Gramsci's cellmate, now deceased.) His prison notebooks were smuggled out of the jail and sent to Russia in the diplomatic bag, where they were read by Togliatti and—until 1945—by almost no one else. Gramsci deepened his analysis of fascism, which he saw not just as an exacerbated form of capitalism but as a separate phenomenon with its own class-base. He outlined a Western road to socialism different from the Bolshevik seizure of the state and emphasizing the role of culture. He defended freedom of discussion within the party.

This is committed writing at its best because Gramsci, instead of allowing himself to be imprisoned by Marxist ideology, uses it to lay bare the workings of capitalist and fascist societies. Having disagreed with Stalin over a range of issues that run from the treatment meted out to Trotsky to Stalin's 1928 decision that revolution was imminent, Gramsci made up his own mind and paid scant heed to the Third International. His is an "open" book and he is an "écrivain" in the Barthean sense, although he is also "écrivant." He does not believe in economic structures alone but rather in the interplay of such structures with the awareness of social groups and the parties that represent them. He rebukes Paul Nizan for taking a particularly obstinate stand on the grounds that one cannot know the correct relationship between structure and superstructure until long after the events in question have taken place. Until then tolerance is better than dogmatism.[27]

Gramsci is a case—perhaps the best case—in which commitment was a vast choice that conferred meaning on all one's life. Certainly this was true of the prison years. But commitment did not interfere with intellectual freedom. The thinking it produced was influenced by the party but independent of it. Had Gramsci not been out of his reach in the late 1920s, Stalin might have found work for him in a Soviet labor camp. As it was, Gramsci did not deal much with the utopian future but rather with the need to establish hegemony before attempting an assault on the Winter Palace. Still the future existed already in the Soviet Union and, of the many writers who made the pilgrimage to the USSR, one was Sartre's friend, Paul Nizan. He came back delighted with everything but surprised that ordinary Russians were still afraid of death.

Nizan was one of the first young intellectuals to join the PCF (Parti communiste français): he became a member in 1928 after a long stay in Aden, then a British colony. In *Aden Arabie* Nizan does not go deeply into colonialism, although the parade of bankers and businessmen making profits out of Aden and Djibouti may have confirmed in him the rejection of existing French society. From 1928 to 1939 Nizan was, at least in the eyes of the world, a model militant who preserved what Sartre calls "his violent purity."[28] Sartre's dealings with Nizan during the 1930s were complex: he was fascinated by this sophisticated friend who talked about international politics with the air of a man who knew a lot more than he was allowed to say. At the same time the Party came between them, since the pre-1939 Sartre was in his own eyes resolutely unpolitical. Nizan disagrees and argues that the metaphysical alienation of *La Nausée* will lead its creator to resolve it by political action. Nizan would become a weapon in that action since in his 1960 essay, partly written in Cuba, Sartre tries to present his former friend as the model rebel for a young generation that was disappointed with commitment.

It has been Nizan's posthumous misfortune to be much discussed but usually only as Sartre's friend.[29] But Nizan is well worth reading in his own right and as an independent example of commitment. One theme he exemplifies is that committed language must attach itself to some other more traditional form of literary discourse, if it is to gain a hearing. So *Aden-Arabie* and *Les chiens de garde* (1932) were recognizable to the French reader as political pamphlets. They did not contain enough economics to suit the PCF but then Drumont and Béraud did not care much about economics either. They and Nizan relied on a particularly virulent kind of language, which the reader considered typical of the pamphlet genre. *Les chiens de garde* does not refute the idealist philosophers whom Nizan thinks dominate the education system. Instead it buries them beneath a mountain of invective. Nizan writes an open-ended novel, *Le cheval de Troie* (1935), where a group of communists try to invent a revolution with no Stalin to guide them. *La Conspiration* (1938) provoked from Sartre the view that there could no more be a communist than a Catholic novel because both narrators had pretensions of infallibility. In fact the standpoint of mature Marxism allows Nizan to satirize the naive group of young communists and briefly reveals a whole new genre: communist satire of a dying capitalist order. There is another theme of the communist party at war with the bourgeois family and Nizan suggests that the bourgeois family, weird and horrible as it might be, might well win. In short Nizan combines traditional French traits with new communist but only indirectly Stalinist traits.

His experience was not untypical of a writer-communist. He sacrificed himself to the party, followed its switches of policy and rose within it. Its worldview gave structure to his instinctive anger with French society. It offered him a language that reversed the official French discourse of bravery in the trenches, noble sentiments and the technocratic brilliance of the *grandes écoles*.

Like so many other committed writers, his relationship with the party ended in crisis: Nizan could not accept the Nazi-Soviet pact and left the party, which automatically expelled him. He was killed in 1940 and the PCF both denounced him as a traitor and tortured him with silence.

André Malraux never joined the party but remained a fellow-traveler, to use a word that communists dislike. Malraux cast a glow of myth over left-wing commitment: he had supposedly been on the Long March with Mao and had taken part in the Shanghai uprising. He fought in Spain at the head of a tattered air force, with pilots, planes and spare parts collected across Europe.

La condition humaine exalts the value of fraternity. The Shanghai uprising fails and the communist group is to be executed by being thrown into an oven. Katow has cyanide so he can die in relative comfort. But, seeing that two younger communists are terrified, he gives them the cyanide and goes to his death in the oven. Nor is this sacrifice vain, for one of the group escapes and goes to work as a doctor in the Soviet Union.

In *l'Espoir* (1937) Malraux shows the tragedy of commitment. The party asks the militant to sacrifice his integrity—which had led him to commit himself—in order to further its cause. In Spain the end—defeating Franco—justifies the means. The solution most commonly found by Koestler, Silone and many other ex-communists is to refuse the party's request, pleading some "Western" moral conscience. Malraux, however, admires the communists because they want to "do" something, whereas the anarchists want to "be" someone. This view of the act will be taken up again by Sartre. Here Malraux opts for efficiency at the expense of personal integrity.

Having entered the Resistance when he judged it had a chance of winning (until that time he refused all invitations to join with a "Soyons sérieux" or "Let's be serious" that intimidated his young interlocutors, already over-impressed by myths of the Long March), Malraux abandoned the left at the Liberation and went over to de Gaulle, who had furnished convincing proofs of his ability to act. When de Gaulle returned to power in 1958, Malraux became Minister of Culture for eleven years. During this time he transformed Paris by cleaning its buildings.

True to his ethic of sacrificing oneself to a cause, Malraux supported the repression of the May riots and fired Jean-Louis Barrault as head of the Odéon theater on the grounds that he had sided with the students. Malraux contributed to the myth of de Gaulle (and of himself) with *Les chenes qu'on abbât*,[30] a long conversation with de Gaulle where it is hard to separate the general's contribution from the author's. In this switch from the communists to the Gaullists Malraux remained faithful to the logic that explains alternating commitments as always anti-centrist.

To seek parallels across Europe in the difficult dialogue between politics and literature is one of the main aims of this book. It must not lead one to forget that language varies doubly: in the ordinary sense that most nations have their own and in the differing concepts of politics and literature as well as in the differing linguistic traditions that most languages bring with them. To take only one example, a much used term in contemporary Italian politics is "indicibilità," whereas the nearest French equivalent is "illégibilité." Behind this distinction lie two very different education systems. We shall return frequently to the comparative dimension but let us here limit ourselves to rounding out the introduction to commitment.

Britain and Germany saw less commitment for opposing reasons. In Britain, where a certain tradition of alliance between intellectuals and the Labour Party existed from the Fabians onward, the interwar period brought much economic hardship, especially in the old industrial areas. The marches on London organized from Jarrow in the North East made it impossible to ignore unemployment, which Orwell treats in *The Road to Wigan Pier*. Yet political institutions held. The General Strike of 1926 was defensive: a protest against the government's decision to go back on the gold standard, rather than a Sorelian bid to take power. The split in the McDonald government in 1931 left the Labour Party in disarray but the National government took over without a general crisis. Donald Maclean's father was in the new Macdonald government, and its inability to confront the Depression may have guided his son toward communism and spying. But even Chamberlain's policy of appeasement toward Nazi Germany, retrospectively so disastrous, did not at the time arouse widespread opposition.

This did not prevent the emergence of a committed left, which gathered around *The New Statesman* and the Gollancz publishing house. The latter published Orwell's *Down and Out in London and Paris* after Faber and Faber, the avant-garde publishers of the 1920s, had refused it. Institutional stability did, however, limit the extremism and virulence of disputes. Orwell, although thoroughly English in his views, was a "continental" in the importance he ascribed to politics. Arthur Koestler felt, by contrast, that the British Communist Party was like a garden tea-party compared with other communist parties he had known. There was a Catholic revival among British writers, too: the generation of Chesterton and Belloc was giving way to that of Greene and Waugh. At this time neither of the last two writers could be considered politically committed, although Greene was attracted by the left, while Waugh, who would go deeper into religion in the Guy Crouchback trilogy, represented a "squire toryism" that provided him with the distance he needed to satirize his contemporaries.

The swing to the left among intellectuals was marked in 1932 by John Strachey. Within Britain the Progressives were on guard against a gradual, slow drift to fascism. Abroad Strachey's *The Coming Struggle for Power* laid down the law. A "progressive" intellectual—to use a word then much in vogue—Strachey saw the world divided into two blocs. One was the fascist bloc, which was a mask for capitalism, and the other was a democratic bloc led by the USSR, which was pursuing its own highly eccentric road to democracy. Meanwhile in Britain the progressives were the heirs to a tradition of dissent (which would re-emerge in the 1950s in the form of CND, the campaign for unilateral nuclear disarmament). In 1936 the Progressives' belief in the Soviet Union soared because Stalin came up with a new constitution, which in fact was never more than a sheet of paper, (undefended by Mallarmé's whiteness). But in 1937 *Tribune* was founded as the voice of the Labour Party Left led by Aneurin Bevan.[31]

Germany could boast of a thriving literary life under the Weimar Republic, but the Nazis wanted writers who were not only committed but docile. In philosophy the Frankfurt school was broken up and Herbert Marcuse went off to the United States, where we shall rediscover him in the 1960s. By contrast Heidegger retained his post and prospered under Hitler in a way that has disconcerted his admirers. Bertolt Brecht, who was a communist, had to emigrate and found his way, via Denmark where he wrote *Leben des Galilei,* to Hollywood, where he attracted the attention of the House Committee on un-American activities. Thomas Mann weighed the decision carefully before he left: he was, after all, an "unpolitical" man. Eventually he decided to speak out against the Nazis and leave. The Nazis pumped money into the cinema, which was thriving when they came to power. They found scant enthusiasm for films extolling Nazi values and lost their best-known directors and actors—many of whom departed before Hitler came to power—from Fritz Lang to Marlene Dietrich. Hitler did not lose his liking for architecture and he and Albrecht Speer drew up plans for a new, colossal Berlin that fortunately was never realized. It was to have a hall that would hold 180,000 people and a Führer's palace that could be defended like a fortress. Nothing came of this Berlin, which seems to have had nowhere for ordinary people to live. The Nazis did build a new stadium for the 1936 Olympics but their theories of racial superiority took a blow when the black American athlete, Jessie Owens, won four gold medals. The gold for soccer went to the Italian team that also won the World Cups of 1934 and 1938. Even this did not turn Mussolini into a soccer fan; he preferred fast cars and planes. But the team's star forward had the Milan stadium named for him—Meazza Stadium.

The dictators took up artists who thus became retrospectively committed. Hitler relished Wagner, whose anti-modernism and sense of fate appealed to him. On Hitler's forty-fourth birthday German radio played Siegfried's *Schmiedelied*.[32]

Meanwhile Ireland was living in its own time, which took some but not very much account of European time. In 1922 Michael Collins, whose military skills had put the price up too high for the British occupiers, was killed. In 1932 de Valera was given the opportunity to create his Celtic, Catholic, Irish-speaking Ireland, but the Free State remained obstinately English-speaking. There seemed no link between nationalism and language. The bond with European time was asserted when an ex-IRA group, led by Frank Ryan, went off to fight against Franco. Ryan was captured but in July 1940 he was rescued from Franco's jails by Hitler, who sent him back to Ireland to organize an uprising against the English. Nothing came of the uprising and Ryan returned to Germany. He had not changed his left-wing views and Hitler's defeat in the USSR delighted him. He submitted to the massive Allied bombing and died in a clinic in Leibzig in 1944.[33] In July 1940 he had been taken to lunch at the Tour d'Argent where he met Olier Mordrel, head of the collaborating wing of Breton separatism. Mordrel fled at the end of the war and some of his friends—but not he—found refuge in Ireland, the only Celtic state.

Meanwhile writers abandoned Dublin for Paris where Joyce, acclaimed as the great European writer but rather overshadowed by fascist and communist commitment, toiled at *Finnegans Wake* with the help of Samuel Beckett. Yeats, who had helped turn the 1916 uprising into a myth, had now to face the reality of the Free State that had emerged from the 1921 negotiations and the civil war that followed them. Yeats defended the rights of the Anglo-Irish minority, "the children of Burke and Grafton"; he denounced the narrow-minded audiences at the Abbey Theatre who were shocked by the plays of Sean O'Casey; he wondered whether he had not contributed to violence by his own writings—"Did that book of mine send out certain men the English shot?" Yeats's last poems are full of shabby country-houses, neglected gardens and lonely if "arrogantly pure" swans that could be murdered by writing.[34] Literary words are dangerous and committed words still more dangerous. Moreover a text can move quickly from being an instrument of protest to incarnating authority.

To go more deeply into committed writing I have chosen four examples: the attempt of the young Pasolini to find a political language to express his anti-fascism or, more precisely, Pasolini as the study of an awareness in search of itself; the examination of *1984* seen as a triumph of political writing but also as a more contradictory work than is sometimes imagined; a look at Bertolt Brecht's *Der kaukasische Kreidekreis*, which represents the best use of Marxist thought in the theater; and the inevitable retrospective portrait of Sartre after whom this period is often called.

PASOLINI, OR THE QUEST
FOR POLITICAL WORDS

Pasolini's articles, written in 1942 and 1943 for two official but also mildly heretical fascist magazines, reveal the cultural struggle between fascism in its death throes and a would-be antagonist. Pasolini was born the year Mussolini seized power and he had known no other regime. He too had absorbed fascism with his body. His situation was all the more difficult because his father was an army officer and a great admirer of Il Duce, while his mother, who seemed ill-used by her husband but tended to make the decisions for the family, came of Friulan farming stock and had no love for fascism. Pasolini sided with his mother on personal as well as political issues. Anyway by 1942 his father had been taken prisoner by the British and it was growing obvious that Mussolini would lose the war.

Pasolini had gone to the Liceo Galvani in Bologna and he continued his studies at the University of Bologna. He was extremely interested in Italian literature, although Roberto Longhi was teaching at Bologna and Pasolini thought about doing his thesis or "tesi di laurea" on Carrà, De Pisis and Morandi (the omission of Giorgio de Chirico was deliberate— Longhi disliked him). Pasolini attended the activities of the Giovani Universitari Fascisti (GUF) where one observer remembers that he kept very much to himself.[35] He told no one of his homosexuality and may not have been aware of its implications. Finally these were good years for soccer at Bologna—the city's team won the Italian championship four times—and Pasolini played regularly for his faculty's team.[36]

His articles may be read as an unsuccessful attempt to discover an anti-fascism to which he could commit himself. He teaches us an important truth of commitment: the need for a great political cause but also for a mighty force that provides the army in which writers can enroll, discuss issues and find readers. In Italy the regime had destroyed all such forces. The PCI maintained a skeleton organization with great difficulty and Pasolini knew one communist—Antonio Meluschi, whose companion, Renata Viganò, later wrote an excellent novel about the partisans, *L'Agnese va a morire*. Then there was the Church whose leaders cordially despised the fascists but that had been neutralized—consciously and willingly—by the Concordat. Pasolini devises for himself a position of cultural opposition but he cannot take the next step into politics. Part of the reason was Mussolini's censorship and his willingness to use force, but another was fascism's "poliedricità." It allowed young people some freedom in order to keep them active inside the fascist movement and prevent them from straying. Pasolini understood this and he was critical of second-generation fascism. But he could not get outside it and find the words of anti-fascism. To borrow Foucault's concept, Pasolini has become his own jailer. Fascism has reduced him to that silence, which is an amputation. Later, after Mussolini's overthrow, his brother's death, the partisans' struggle and the discovery of Gramsci, Pasolini will speak political words. But we are studying a frustrated awareness that is seeking in vain to become political.

There seemed no alternative to Mussolini's rhetoric and to his regime's many-sidedness. Pasolini and his young friends would have preferred to have their own magazine, but fascism allotted paper and money only to its own publications: to *Architrave,* which was the Bologna organ of the GUF, and to *Il Setaccio,* published by the Gioventù italiana del Littorio (GIL), also of Bologna.

Pasolini had another weapon in his cultural struggle against fascism: the Friulan language. Every summer he retreated to his mythical Casarsa, a large village in lower Friuli, within cycling distance from the Tagliamento River. Pasolini's first poems, although published, in a very small edition, in Bologna, were written in Friulan. *Poesie a Casarsa* appeared in July 1942. Fascism had conducted its own battle, entitled "strapaese" versus "stracittà"—countryside against town—and, although the towns won out in the name of modernity, elements within fascism were favorable to the countryside. Still fascism disliked the dialects, which militated against centralization, so Pasolini's poems could be seen as anti-fascist and certainly they constituted what has been called "the search for the other,"[37] for a dream world of innocence that is tangled up with a nascent populism and from which fascism is conspicuously absent.

Similarly Pasolini's drawings of the human figure were considered by his friends an implicit rebuke to fascist grandiloquence. The term "implicit" is important because Pasolini's articles in the journals of second-generation fascism appear as a discourse on culture, principally on poetry. One of its contributors stated that *Il Setaccio* was an "élitist magazine, private or personal, the work of young people who were thus able to express their cultural preoccupations."[38] Certainly Pasolini's starting-point was cultural and his preoccupations were different from those of second-generation fascism.

His great theme seems, however, similar at least in origin. He maintains that culture should not be separate from society. When he argues that Ungaretti's poetry should be read not as an exquisite exercise of language but as a broad ethical lesson,[39] he is both denying fascist claims to control and define culture and he is seeking societal space for his brand of culture.

Architrave has been described as mainstream "giovani" protest.[40] That means that it was allowed some freedom and the illusion of more; that it accepted the tutelage of Giuseppe Bottai; that it was allowed to attack the local fascist organization and to appeal over its head to Mussolini and that it talked of a return to fascism's left-wing origins. *Architrave's* notion of culture was founded on two rejections: of art for art's sake and of art as propaganda. In taking such a stand, these provincial young Italians were at the center of the Western European debate about art and the revolution. Their answer was no more lucid than anyone else's. "Far be from us to claim the pre-eminence of culture over the many other forms of life," proclaims one contributor.[41] There was great discussion of "neoumanesimo";[42] it castigates the old humanism, which was Hegelian and emphasized thought over work. This led to the "domination of one class—the cultured and educated class over the others." Such humanism must be replaced by a new humanism that upgrades the value of work.

The names, Ungaretti and Montale, figure prominently in *Architrave*. If Carlo Calcaterra, who belonged to the traditional academic world, exalted them as men of literature, a younger contributor felt the need to point out—rather as Pasolini did—that in Ungaretti intellectual saturation leads, miraculously, to a renewed simplicity.[43] Suspicion of academic judgments, a hint of primitiveness and a liking for strong emotions, such are some of the many moods of *Architrave*.

The debate was carried over into the realm of painting. Although praised by Maccari in *Selvaggio*, Giorgio Morandi was admired in Bologna as the model of a culture that existed outside of politics. Both Roberto Longhi and Francesco Arcangeli, who became the leading Bologna critic, ranked Morandi's bottles way above the canvasses of rural families so dear to Farinacci. *Architrave's* appreciation of high culture opened up another of the tensions that ran through the GUF magazines. *Architrave* was able in this case to resolve it: it supported Renato Guttuso, "who may serve as an example of the need felt by the young to escape from the sterile constraints of academic formalism."[44] Guttuso's nuanced view of the Paris school, his emotional outbursts and his polemics made him the ideal cultural spokesman for the second generation. *Crucifixion* and *Flight from Etna* were influential works, even if Archangeli thought there was something brutal about Guttuso.

As long as Roberto Mazzetti was editor, advanced aesthetic taste was masked by left-wing political language: "For us, the young who have grown up under fascism, culture is politics."[45] There might be room to debate the value of individual artists but culture was at the service of the new/old fascism: "instead of being a dead superstructure it must be with the people, by the people and for the people."[46] Small wonder that Renzo Renzi, whose articles on the cinema exalted Julien Duvivier and Marcel Carné, could later write, with conscious provocation, that the passage from the (fascist) Cinéguf to the (communist) Circoli di cinema was short and easy.[47]

Mazzetti was too critical for the delicate, supervised freedom that the GUF were allowed and in 1941 the entire editorial team was sacked after *Architrave* had advocated the right of unions to operate on the shop floor. But Mazzetti considered himself a fascist. Indeed the editorial team was committed to fascism and believed that the young would revive the enthusiasm of the "squadristi." The war gave them the opportunity to show their commitment: Renzi was one of many who volunteered in 1941 before he was drafted. Here already lie significant differences between Pasolini's *Setaccio* and the *Architrave* of 1940-41. Pasolini had no enthusiasm for the war and no belief in fascism. He had scant interest in power, except perhaps an unspoken desire for the counter-power of the artist.

He wrote his first piece for *Architrave* after Mazzetti had departed and he attempts to shift debate toward high culture. Luigi Bartolini, whose engravings were then on display in Bologna, was admired as the artist not just of his home province in the Marché but of all the Italian provinces. Defended by Maccari in the "strapaese" dispute, he was also famous for his anarchistic outbursts. Moreover all Pasolini's circle had read Bartolini's first novel, *Passeggiata con la ragazza*.

Architrave's reviewer applauded the exhibit and wrote banally about Bartolini's "affection for natural truth and for the myriad creatures of nature."[48] But it was left to Pasolini to assert that Bartolini had become a sophisticated artist. He noted the transition to *L'Orso ed altri capitoli amorosi*: "this is a male confession, which comes modestly and morosely from Bartolini's pen." Bartolini has left behind the facile exercises of polemic and rhetoric and he has undertaken the task of transforming his raw material into art.[49]

Art is difficult and it is the opposite of nature. In this debate it hardly matters whether Pasolini is correct about Bartolini. Pasolini's view of writing is the real issue. He is turning Bartolini into an example of high culture and he adds that the obstacles that art places in the path of confession add both a moral dimension and a note of "human lament" to the emotion expressed. There is nothing very new about this concept of art but it is important in 1942 to distinguish between the difficult phase of reshaping the confession and the movement of reaching out toward the reader. There remains the act of engaging the reader in his historical awareness. This will be the dilemma of the Weimar essay.

By the time it was published in August 1942, *Architrave* had changed. Although the second editorial group had been orthodox, a new note had been struck when an old friend of Pasolini, Luciano Serra, published *Un esame di conscienza*,[50] a meditation by a young man who is leaving for war. Gone are the exaltation of 1940 and the dream of a fascist Europe. Serra stresses that the war is worldwide and will be long. Anticipating Pasolini, Serra withdraws into himself and undergoes a new "mal du siècle": "What we lack, Faith, we will build in ourselves. Through doubt and suffering."

The political dimension of this view becomes clear when the editorial group changes again in June. By now the fronde had tuned into genuine anti-fascism. Three of the four numbers were confiscated by the authorities. The September number calls for freedom to criticize and discuss and for a tilt in power from the state to the individual. In general *Architrave* does not go as far as this and it would be wrong to suggest that the GUF magazines offer any alternative to Mussolini. *Architrave* does, however, flaunt its disillusionment with fascism. Many pages are devoted to revelations of corruption (as if prefiguring the Clean Hands operation!). The difference between 1942 and 1940 is that two years before, the criticisms were made from within fascism by zealous believers, whereas they are now made by disenchanted observers who do not wish to identify with fascism. Moreover as the tributes to fallen GUF members take up increasing space, there is a sense that *Architrave* is waiting for the final curtain to fall.

Cultura italiana was written after Pasolini's return from one of the many propagandistic conferences foisted onto Goethe's city. Pasolini declaims against art as propaganda. He singles out Nazi Germany as the most guilty party and suggests that in a fascist Europe Italy might have to defend itself. His tone changes when he sketches the relationship between Italian culture and fascism.

> The adhesion of our Italian and we might almost say European culture to our new conception of the State and of society does not take place according to a formal likeness of color, of intention and perhaps, as yet, not of spirit, but it is a parallel and complementary force that acts at the same time in another camp, under another sky, with a faith and an enthusiasm that, although separate from political or social enthusiasms, act with the same force and for the same ideals of civilization until finally they identify themselves with and join with those political and social enthusiasms.[51]

This extraordinary passage, as turgid as the attacks on propaganda are concise, shows how tortuously Pasolini has to search for societal space, partly but not entirely because of the censor. Again and again he divorces his cultural discourse from the politics of fascism—"formal likeness, spirit, another camp" and "separate"—only at the end to admit some link. The reason is that he is trapped in an ambiguity imposed on him by the regime. He is not content to make a purely private or literary discourse, but fascism will allow no intrusion into its political realm. Finally in the last sentence he has to admit defeat and state that his brand of culture might be "politically" useful to Mussolini's Italy.

After the September number of *Architrave* was confiscated, the editorial team was once more sacked and Arcangeli also withdrew. This was the end of second-generation protest and of left-wing fascism. During a fourth and last period *Architrave* was conventionally triumphalist, but this was less than convincing because the list of GUF dead grew ever longer.

Pasolini had now moved on to *Il Setaccio*. The GIL organizers wanted a publication that was a little fuller than their bulletins and that would give young people a chance to write. Its circulation was small, at most 1,000 copies. It was supposed to be politically safer (that is, tamer) than *Architrave*. Control was entrusted to Italo Cinti, a painter associated with futurism and a journalist at the *Corriere Padano*. Further respectability was provided by the director, Giuseppe Falzone, who contributed to each number a front-page article full of rhetorical platitudes. The magazine was also littered with the obligatory quotations from Mussolini.

Pasolini's presence gave *Il Setaccio* an interest it would otherwise have lacked. He filled the magazine with drawings and paintings and one number had a Morandi-ish still life on the cover, which was considered very daring. So *Il Setaccio's* six numbers from November '42 to May '43 had a coherence that came from the period: fascism was dying but it still retained enough power to withstand its pen-wielding opponents.

Pasolini's articles may be divided into three groups: the assertion of the "mal du siècle" and the bid to turn it into a public philosophy suited to a lost war; an impossible escape into the Friulan myth, which has overtones of religion; an analysis of Italian writing that leads to the plea for a sophisticated and yet lyrical-populist poetry.

Pasolini's first piece, "I giovani, l'attesa",[52] sets the break with the second-generation at the head of *Il Setaccio:* he attacks the "facile pomp of young people who indulged in robust and burgeoning arrogance." Does this foreshadow his attitude in 1968? He makes a point of rejecting "neo-humanism." He follows Arcangeli in his dislike of the brutality of Guttuso's painting. All these are contrasted with the values of the "mal du siècle:" weariness, self-awareness and a lucid irony. Adolescence is not a time for political triumphs but for exile. The word "wait" in the title hints that the exile may be resolved historically.

Italy must go to the end of its disastrous war because "we lack the hero who can, like a beacon, guide us and shape events."⁵³ To write this in a magazine full of quotations from Mussolini was an affront and, in simply dismissing Mussolini from history, Pasolini has gone as far as he goes—before the overthrow of the Duce—in attacking the government. Of the positive content of anti-fascism there is no trace and the limits of civic suffering as a political statement need no elaboration.

Pasolini turns to another option: Friuli. This is the mother's territory and in a poem Pasolini describes her as "the silence within the cry"—here the silence is not an amputation but is akin to Rilke's active silence. This Friuli offers no escape from the disasters that have befallen the nation. It does allow Pasolini to develop the themes of suffering and sacrifice: the son, Pasolini-Christ, suffers on behalf of the nation. Innocence is a sterile virtue, which raises for the first time the theme of Pasolini as the necessary bringer of scandal. This theme is destined for a great future once Pasolini goes public with his homosexuality, but by then it will have separated itself from Friuli. Here the notion of departure is never absent. It reminds us that Friuli is invented by Pasolini, who does not hesitate to introduce new vocabulary and grammatical constructions into his poems. Yet Friulan cannot engender a political language that might combat Mussolini's. At most it offers Pasolini some privacy.

More space is devoted to contemporary writing. As a critic, Pasolini continues to argue that art is difficult and sophisticated. Yet his great target is cerebralism and he demands above all lyricism and ethical teaching. A piece on Ungaretti examines his avant-garde language but concludes that Ungaretti's greatness lies in his ability to distil from it moral proverbs.⁵⁴ A distrust of style colors Pasolini's attitude to prose writers. From the Voce to Vittorini they have constructed castles of language and "arrogantly forgotten or transcended human reality."⁵⁵ This is the *trahison des clercs*, and the task of Pasolini's generation is to prune literary Italian. Bilenchi is praised for fixing the idea without transcending it. Turning back to poetry, Pasolini criticizes Mario Luzi and the "ermetici" for intellectual game-playing, while lavishing praise on Sandro Penna, whose poetry is "dense and pregnant with incorporated human suffering."⁵⁶

Pasolini's appreciation of Penna, who would later show him around the haunts in the Rome suburbs where boys could be picked up, reveals his good literary judgment. But Penna, aside from a strong sense of class acquired during "the hunt," was the least committed of writers. This underlines Pasolini's failure to find political words that would lead on from the literary words where he was so self-assured. After Mussolini's overthrow, Pasolini wrote, "I feel something new rising and growing with unexpected importance in me: the political man that fascism had deceitfully suffocated without my realizing it."[57]

I chose to begin this chapter with Pasolini and fascism because it emphasizes a theme improperly neglected: the difficulty a writer encounters in committing her/himself, the arduous task of finding political words.

THE REIGN OF JEAN-PAUL SARTRE

A *Le Monde* article in April 2000 was headed: "We haven't finished with Sartre."[58] Nowadays the media block the fluctuations in a writer's posthumous reputation. A piece on why people are no longer reading Malraux causes people to read at least one thousand words about him. Several of these readers will discuss the neglected author with their friends, while a few may go as far as to read him. There are, however, other methods of evaluating a writer: the reactions of young people—although the young read much less than they did—and whether contemporary writers are interested in her/him. If s/he was widely read in his/her own period, that provides a different reason for reading her/him. In the case of Sartre he dominated his époque so that to understand the mid-twentieth-century one has no choice but to read him.

Tony Judt argues that French Marxism is the product of a particular historical moment.[59] It is, however, a difficult moment to analyze, full of contradictory elements. In the 1930s, when Marxism was growing stronger, Sartre played no role in politics and, despite the riots of February 1934 and the Popular Front, he did not even vote. He was an anarchistic young writer who enjoyed flaunting his cynicism. He won over the more sheltered Simone de Beauvoir by his diatribes against "les belles âmes" and by taking her to see lowbrow American films instead of the art-films she was used to seeing.[60] Judt claims that in the 1930s there was a need for an ideological framework, which was answered by Hegel. But Sartre, of course, was more interested in Heidegger.

Sartre always maintained this bohemian life—spiced by the groups of young women attracted by his fame and eager to be exploited or to exploit—which entailed a rejection of the visible signs of middle-class culture, such as marriage and thrift. Today the cafés Sartre frequented, like the Deux Magots on Saint-Germain and La Coupole in Montparnasse, still draw crowds of tourists by their associations with him rather than by their food. In the years before 1939, Sartre's life suited his work, for his version of existentialism remains individualistic.

Certainly he must also have been influenced by Nizan, who was doing grown-up things like representing the Communist Party in foreign policy debates. Sartre had no real desire to emulate him but he was impressed. Nizan talked about international affairs like a man who knew things he could not say. Both would have to go to war and Nizan would have to die before Sartre's visceral but inchoate hatred of the middle-classes would take political form.

He emerged from the war as the uncrowned king of Saint-Germain, who imposed the law of committed writing. The road that took him from existentialism to Marxism has never seemed well-signposted to Anglo-Saxons. But once he set out along it Sartre never turned back. He declared existentialism an enclave in Marxism and he barely looked around to see how many were following him. In the late 1940s one may talk of "Sartre's party," electorally insignificant but intellectually the most influential group in Western Europe.

In 1960 *La critique de la raison dialectique* aroused less interest than *L'être et le néant* (1943), which was the bible of existentialism, or the bitter quarrel with Camus had done. *La critique* was an attempt to outline a libertarian brand of Marxism with greater emphasis on the militant's awareness and a less dogmatic party leadership. But, although the Algerian War posed the issue of commitment in an acute form and led left-wingers like Francis Jeanson to form networks of support for the FLN (Front de Libération nationale), the integration of the French working-class into the population as a whole went ahead, spurred by the first EC boom. Marxism seemed less plausible than in 1945 and consumerism more important than the class struggle. May '68 seemed Sartre's revenge on a country that was ignoring his call for socialism. Sartre went to the Sorbonne, where he was acclaimed by the students. Later he sold the Maoist newspaper, *La cause du peuple*, at the Censier-Daubenton metro stop. He was challenging the government to arrest him but it would not. Sartre's revenge was short-lived as the political thrust of May '68 soon wore itself out.

Sartre went blind, learned to hide the whisky bottles from Simone de Beauvoir and was surrounded by young girls and dubious people promoting dubious causes. He consciously refused to live out his last years as "a great writer" and although the stands he took were often confused, he remained faithful to his brand of committed writing as the "nouveau roman" waxed and waned around him and as Foucault disagreed publicly with his notion of commitment. Sartre continued to frequent la Coupole, which had become expensive and crowded. He would sit, a frail figure, watched over by the faithful Simone de Beauvoir and by the delighted management. At his death in 1980 he was given a huge funeral. The mourners might never have read him but they knew something important had vanished with Sartre.

This is, however, too simple a demonstration of Judt's notion of the historical moment. Why did Sartre opt for socialism in 1944? I have said that the Resistance was generically left-wing and the PCF's share of the vote rose to approximately 25 percent at the Liberation. But when one looks back on the period from the early twenty-first century, one sees it through Jean Monnet's eyes as the start of high economic growth and of European unity. This ignores, however, the revolutionary words that came from the PCF even as it marginalized leaders like André Marty and Charles Tillon, who wanted to move from words to action. Sartre's relations with the PCF were much less good than is sometimes thought. He never joined the party and he was its rival in the struggle for what Gramsci called cultural hegemony. Unable to control him, the PCF attacked him. Yet Sartre's revolutionary position helped the party leadership: the communist party and "Sartre's Party" were allies against what they considered reformist or modernizing forces that ranged from the Socialist Party (SFIO) to the "dirigistes" who surrounded Monnet. So Sartre had an army, even if he could not control it. He also had a tradition: the segment of the left that believed in the ideal republic and drove the church out of the school system and those who supported the PCF in the 1930s. One could argue that elements of Gaullism belonged in this tradition, but Gaullists were unlikely to go public with their admiration for Sartre.

How many of Sartre's readers believed in his brand of libertarian socialism? Few, one suspects. But there were many who agreed with the notions of a strong Jacobin-Bonapartist state and of the citizens' very limited talent for trust, face-to-face relationships with the civil service and general dealings with one another. Sociologists like Michel Crozier and historians like Michel Winock have seen in this cluster of attitudes an important force that has worked to block the spread of change in France. It has survived until today, although prosperity has increased trust in the authorities and in one's fellow citizens, while the Jacobin-Bonapartist state is in crisis because it has lost power to the EU and to the forces of globalization.

In 1944, however, what we are calling the revolutionary words fitted into the "Crozier syndrome" as well as into the Resistance struggle. Moreover Sartre's Marxism represented the triumph of the individual through the collective struggle of socialism. In his pre-war books Sartre had portrayed existentialist man as thoroughly miserable: in *La Nausée* there is no omniscient narrator and no lyrical-reflective view from within. Roquentin's awareness does not allow him to make contact with the subject of the biography he is writing, so he gives up the book. His failure is foreshadowed by his inability to pick up the piece of white paper from the pavement (back to Mallarmé again!) This loss of the literary language is accompanied by the loss of names—"things freed themselves of their names."⁶¹ But they did not cease to exist. Rather they pressed on Roquentin with all their might. Behind them there was nothing—no Proustian life of their own and behind a table no Cartesian ideal table. Man is lost in a world of things, strange and hostile; his awareness is empty and he becomes the chestnut tree while remaining remote from it. Like Orwell's Winston, Roquentin cannot keep a diary because he has nothing to put in it.

In *Le Mur* (1939) Sartre depicts various attempts to escape. They range from a bid to enter the world of a mad husband to the murderous-suicidal mania of L'Erostrate. The final story, *L'Enfance d'un chef*, depicts the link between the empty awareness and authority. Since such an awareness is lived as a lack, there is an urge to take refuge from it by accepting other people's awareness as real. So Lucien becomes what his parents want him to be, then in a supposed rebellion he joins the Surrealists—for whom Sartre has as little use as Orwell—and finally he discovers the Action Française and anti-Semitism.

The outlines of the existentialist Sartre's view of literature and politics have become clear. The writer has no special status: Roquentin decides at the end of *La Nausée* to write a novel instead of a biography but he does not write one and the reader is left with this diary that flaunts its faults. Sartre is careful to distinguish between his view of language and what one might call the 1920s *NRF* view. To Jean Paulhan and Brice Parrain language was a mystique, whereas to the young Sartre it was merely the way one made contact—or failed to make contact—with other people. The white paper on the pavement was no different from the chestnut tree.

Clearly no committed writing could be constructed around a protagonist like Roquentin. One might accept that his pessimism was merely one part of Sartre's view and that the complementary critique of Nizan and Mauriac in *Situations 1* points the way to a novel with multiple points of view or that the essay on Heidegger describes a "Being-in-the-world" endowed with an authenticity that makes dialogue possible. There is still neither the belief in one cause nor the political content to make commitment plausible.

The Second World War provided the impetus: the Manichean division between occupiers and occupied, the Nazi display of arrogance, the working-class and the Resistance. Such were the ingredients of the historical moment. Sartre may have done little in the Resistance and he had to endure the reproach that at the opening night of *Les Mouches* (1943) the best seats in the house were reserved for officers of the Wehrmacht. Still his plays show how the solution to existentialist anguish lay in political action.

The path is too well known to require much discussion and the numerous Anglo-Saxon skeptics will not be convinced by one more analysis. *Huis clos* (1944) exposes the problem: each of the three characters wants to be assured by one other that he is not a coward or that she is beautiful. Only a free human being can give such an assurance precisely because s/he does not have to. None of the characters is free because they are all dependent on one another, hence they are living in inauthenticity and therefore none can help. Authenticity is seen in *Les Mouches,* where Oreste faces a choice between continuing his comfortable life as a wandering scholar and re-becoming Oreste, who must undertake the task of avenging his father, Agamemnon, by killing his stepfather Aegistus and his mother Clytemnestra. He makes the second choice and his action is presented as a rebellion against the Vichy government. Oreste frees himself of Zeus-Aegistus (Hitler-Pétain) by his act, which lacks, however, one dimension. The citizens of Argos do not follow him.

Sartre is reviving the 1930s debate about the end and the means, about the anarchists (and the existentialists) who want to be something and the communists who want to do something. Having made scorched earth out of traditional individualism—introspection, feelings, the Cartesian conquest of the outside world—Sartre has swung round to the viewpoint that one can only benefit oneself if one's actions have others as their prime target. To put this differently, Sartre chooses the communist notion of efficiency over the Catholic emphasis on intention and he prefers responsibility to remorse. Inevitably he moves on from Oreste, who cannot in this context be said to have liberated himself, to the figure of Bolshevik man.

Les mains sales (1948) depicts two communists: the first, Hugo, is of middle-class background, an intellectual and a journalist whose aim is to break completely with his family and act for the party rather than write for it. Hugo still has the moral sense he imbibed with his upbringing. Hoederer is older and his world is the party for which he is willing to lie and cheat. Yet Hoederer is also a man who likes other people, male and female, who is at home among things and who is willing to talk of his defeats and discouragement. In general communists did not like *Les mains sales,* which tended to reinforce the figure of the ruthless, lying Marxist. But today Sarte's portrait of Hoederer seems all too flattering.

The same is true of Brunet, the communist in Sartre's *L'Age de raison* (1945). Sartre describes him: "he was there, heavy and massive . . . the room was full of his presence, of the smoke from his cigarette, of his slow gestures."[62] The contrast with the emptiness and isolation of Roquentin could not be greater. The Second World War is about to start and Brunet knows the French authorities will put him in the front line. He will be killed "but nothing can rob my life of its meaning. Nothing can prevent it from being a destiny."[63] Mathieu, the principal narrator, explains what Brunet means: "He had committed himself, he had given up his freedom, he was no more than a soldier ... but here he was quite real with a taste of real tobacco in his mouth ... and yet he extended across the whole world, he was suffering and fighting with the proletariat of all countries."[64] The working-class struggle gives meaning to Brunet's life and the revolution to which he devotes himself will transform the entire world.

Yet Mathieu does not follow Brunet into the party. He retains a freedom that would allow him, if he thought it necessary, to criticize the party and adopt positions to which it was opposed. Mathieu is what has survived into the post-war of the critique of Nizan and Mauriac. He is Sartre the fellow-traveler who exists alongside Brunet, the revolutionary Sartre. This critical Sartre, who did write about the Soviet concentration camps, albeit with nuanced language, and who condemned the 1956 invasion of Hungary, made the first Sartre more convincing. The occasional sorties of the critical Sartre reminded Saint-Germain that French intellectuals had been *against* the condemnation of Dreyfus and the presence of the Church in the schools. Sartre never failed to add, however, that his criticism of the USSR was different from vulgar anti-communism, because it came from within the socialist camp.

Sartre imposed his authority by applying his "existential Marxism" to other issues and by wrapping it up in violent language. Simone de Beauvoir spun off from existentialism the theme that women were trapped in inauthentic lives because they allowed themselves to be defined by men: "humanity is male and man defines woman not in herself but as relative to him; she is not regarded as an autonomous being."[65] De Beauvoir has been berated in recent years for her subservience to Sartre and it seems both astonishing and implausible that he was always the intellectual leader and she the plodding follower.[66] But between them they opened the road to what became in the 1960s an extremely influential international women's movement. Much of *le deuxième sexe* has dated: women no longer regard being in the workplace as automatically liberating nor is the spurning of marriage such a bold gesture of liberation as it was in Simone de Beauvoir's France. The flight from biology into history belongs to the age of commitment. But the theme of not allowing themselves to be judged (or empowered) by men remains a basic theme of women thinkers.

The Sartre who is influential here is the early Sartre who also spurred a debate on the body that echoes through post-war thought. The body in all its stubborn materialism is the opposite of bourgeois idealism, which uses its speculations and its abstract thought to exploit the body. But the body fights back, using what to idealism are its defects, its blemishes and ugliness. In *L'age de raison* a bourgeois public is watching a girl dance nude. It is supposedly a piece of art but the girl cannot dance. Her clumsy movements force the audience to recognize that it is engaged in voyeurism.[67] Camus has a strong sense of the body's grace and happiness—Meursault on the Algerian beaches. Sartre, however, experienced the revelation of his own ugliness and makes few concessions to physical beauty. What counts anyway is not who is beautiful but who decides who is beautiful: Pasolini will take up this theme.

One may end this all too brief portrait with a comment on Sartre's quarrel with Camus. This too is best seen as part of the historical moment. In 1952 General Ridgway arrived in Paris to take over the post of Supreme Allied Commander of NATO. The PCF organized demonstrations against him that were widely regarded as unsuccessful. This did not stop the police from overreacting and they arrested Jacques Duclos, the communist number two and widely regarded as "Moscow's eye" within the party. Sartre, angry at the PCF's failure to challenge Ridgway, published in *Les Temps modernes*, *Les Communistes et la paix*, in which he declares that the PCF cannot fail because it alone represents the working-class. Indeed a worker gained his identity when he rebelled against his condition by joining the communist party: "when he is docile, the worker rejects what is human in him; when he rebels he rejects the inhuman."[68]

This is not even consistent with Sartre's writing because it denies to the worker the critical awareness that Mathieu possessed. It also ignores the rampant Stalinism of the PCF. Both these sins of omission are the result of the Cold War, which was growing colder. This was also, not coincidentally, the moment when Camus finished and published *L'Homme révolté*. The war, the Cold War and the Sétif riots had sharpened Camus's fear of violence. Personally he and Sartre were not close. They had briefly been good friends after the Liberation. Sartre admired the working-class elements in Camus—his humor, his Humphrey Bogart mannerisms and his flair for seduction. Sartre had written a very perceptive and favorable article on *L'Etranger*.[69] Camus had never felt a similar liking for Sartre and, much as he admired the author of *La Nausée*, he had grave doubts about Sartre's pro-communist stance. Camus had been a member of the Parti communiste algérien and had left it. He knew more about the daily round of politics than Sartre. He was far more critical of the USSR. He did not share Sartre's view of commitment and did not write for *Les Temps modernes*. Although he viewed his own writing as a protest against the human condition, he did not consider that condition to be shaped solely by politics.

L'Homme révolté anticipates the post-modern view that pursuit of totality is inseparable from gulags and terrorism. The absolute goodness of the end is thought to justify the removal of groups that resist or simply block it. The flaw in Camus's thinking is that the next step should be toward a desacralization of politics, where revolt should take the form of social democracy or reformism or some other pragmatic kind of thought. But Camus will not desacralize because the initial attraction of God seems to him to be intrinsically good and even to constitute the key factor in the human condition. Yet to pursue this end is to risk violence.

It is, therefore, hard to see what the political content of revolt is. This was pointed out first by Francis Jeanson and then with greater violence by Sartre, in whom there was a strain of the pamphleteer. But if one leaves aside his accusations that Camus is both too arrogant and too vulnerable, Sartre has the unanswerable argument that Camus is in effect supporting the status quo. Sartre knew less about politics than Camus, but he understood that the French ruling-class was using the Cold War to re-establish itself in power.

Moreover Sartre was pleased with the period in which he was living. It allowed him to find in commitment a solution to the pessimism of some of his early writing. It offered him a counter-power. It added to the space that writers traditionally occupied in France and French writers in Europe. In the United States Camus was perceived to have won the battle with Sartre and he was hailed as a good man and writer. In France the opposite was true; it was a quarrel of political philosophy. Then too the age of Sartre saw the victory of commitment, and literary words were summoned as a reinforcement by political words. Sartre did not agree with Barthes that the literary language was concerned only with itself, and he thought language could make statements that would help change the world. Indeed, unless it did that, it was not literature.

George Orwell,
or Inferno Replaces Utopia

Unlike Sartre, Orwell did not wield intellectual power. He was acutely aware of power in the shape of authority: his books may be read as angry depictions of various kinds of authority seen from the viewpoint less of the rebel than of the victim. His lasting claim on our attention is his prescience in analyzing a new form of authority—totalitarianism. His vision was fundamentally pessimistic. His biographer demonstrates that the piece he wrote about his childhood at Saint Cyprian's preparatory school, *Such, Such Were the Joys,* was not a piece of Eric Blair's autobiography but one of George Orwell's maps of hell.[70] Like Céline, whom he admired, Orwell blackened his existence, seeking out the guilt and failures that are less important to the man than to the writer, who also dealt with them better.

Such, Such contains penetrating comments on English society. The change of name from Blair brought Orwell increased freedom.

For a committed writer this worldview meant that he would not depict future utopias but that he would expertly point out the shortcomings of the revolutionaries in the present and of their blueprints for the future. The literary language would be used to satirize and to deconstruct. Orwell would be alert to attempts to manipulate political language and would seek to write clearly: plain English, the language of common sense, which was democratic because easily understood. Orwell would defend the innovations of avant-garde literature—Joyce and Céline—but his own long struggle was to eliminate the pretensions and obscurities of both discourses and to fuse them. If Barthes thought that impossible, so much the worse for him. Commitment was above all a literary-political discourse that did not try, like fascism and communism, to deceive readers and voters but rather to defend the weak and protect them against verbal oppression.

From an organizational viewpoint the leaders of the revolutionary movement will not be able to tolerate such a heretic. Harry Pollitt, secretary of the CP (Communist Party) cold-shouldered Orwell, while Victor Golancz published *Down and Out* and *The Road to Wigan Pier*, but he broke with Orwell over the Spanish civil war. The heretical writer may find friends s/he does not want: the right seized on *1984*, which became a weapon in the Cold War. Alternatively this writer may feel betrayed by his former comrades, who are hard on the "exs." Anyone who left the Communist Party was automatically expelled, his former friends who remained in the party were instructed to shun him and his wife was encouraged to divorce him. Orwell was fortunate that in Britain the intellectual left and the Communist Party were weak. The Labour Party, which Orwell considered a trade union and not a socialist party, was more tolerant. Orwell had a happy spell as literary editor of *Tribune* when Aneurin Bevan was running the paper.

Although the biographical reasons for his rebellion are less clear than they seem, the young Orwell was generally distrustful of any and every kind of authority. "I never went into a jail without feeling . . . that my place was on the other side of the bars."[71] But we have noted the close ties between authority and protest and Orwell could be hard and dogmatic—toward himself or his political opponents. He found his own way to his positions, guided more by personal experience than by reading sacred texts or listening to stories told by others.

One suspects, despite Bernard Crick's warnings, that the formative experiences for Orwell were the conflict between a lower-middle-class upbringing and the upper-class world of Eton and then the five years spent in Burma as a member of the police force. He used the paper of the Burma Government to write anti-colonial words and in 1935 he published *Burmese Days,* a critical novel, discussed in chapter 11. Like Camus, Orwell did not limit himself to condemning imperialism but showed an awareness of its complexity. It may be more than coincidence that both writers emerged as leaders during Europe's crisis in the Second World War: they had seen Europe at its worst in the colonies. There remain, however, great differences between them: Orwell could pack up and leave Burma but Camus carried Algeria on his back until his death.

Both Eton and Burma guided Orwell toward the left. He was personally ill at ease with working-class people and much more at ease with other old Etonian writers, however right-wing they might be. But he set out to learn about the poor of Paris and of London. His spell of work in a Paris restaurant and as a tramp in England produced *Down and Out In London and Paris* (1933). Written with a massive concern for detail—especially unpleasant smells—this book skips over the stable, employed working-class and shows a horrified fascination with what our marxless but Foucauldian generation would call the excluded. Orwell went on to write *The Road to Wigan Pier* (1937), which reveals an ambiguous attitude toward the working-class: it was suffering from the Depression and so it must be supported; but it was ugly, inert and passive.

Orwell's trip to Wigan was remembered with resentment in *1984*.[72] But in his lifetime perhaps the most important moment and certainly the most controversial came in 1937. He decided words were not enough and set out to fight against Franco in Spain. He joined a POUM (Partido obero de unificaciòn marxista) unit and with his Burmese experience he was appointed corporal and led his men efficiently at the front. In 1938 he was wounded when a sniper's bullet hit him in the throat and he was invalided back to Britain. From this experience comes *Homage to Catalonia* (1938), the opening pages of which are perhaps the best he ever wrote. They describe democratic and socialist Barcelona, where relationships among people are free of oppression and class conflict. Orwell knows this will not last but he savors it while he can.

The rest of *Homage* is a political analysis in which Orwell is so hard on the communists that the editor of the *New Statesman* and his publisher never really forgave him. Yet Orwell's position is more nuanced than it might be. He does not blame the communists for wishing to postpone the revolution until after the war. Indeed he himself was switching to the International Brigades when he was wounded. But he will not forgive the communists for taking action against their anarchist and Trotsky-ite allies, who were accused of being on Franco's payroll. To use Malraux's terminology, Orwell did not think the anarchists only wanted to "be" something or that the communists wanted to "do" what was necessary to win the war. The anarchists wanted to strengthen the anti-Franco forces by bringing the revolution to the people, while the communists were eager to come to power themselves. The British left refused to listen to such anti-Stalinist propaganda when the communists were doing much of the fighting.[73]

Orwell had his own version of where communist ruthlessness fitted into a more general historical pattern. He was still an anti-fascist; he believed the communists were growing ever more fascist, a view that the Nazi-Soviet Pact would confirm. Meanwhile so-called democracies like Britain and France would have to become more fascist in order to combat Germany and Italy.[74] The three blocs of *1984* are present already. Indeed until war broke out Orwell was preaching for a pacifist policy and planned a guerrilla campaign against the British government, if it should go to war against the Nazis. War, however, made him turn instead to patriotism.

In England—although not solely there—Orwell saw the values of decency, common sense and grown-up-ness. He contrasted them with the hunger for power and the contempt for morality, which were the marks of totalitarianism. They were also the values of democratic socialism and Orwell, showing his prescience, thought they would emerge strengthened from the war. Dickens was a great defender of this tradition, Bertrand Russell a contemporary exponent and on a simpler level decency was at the core of popular English culture. Crick argues that this is Orwell's creed and that *Animal Farm* and *1984* are satires or warnings about what happens when the creed is abandoned. The trouble is that the so-called satires are so much better—and have so much more imaginative power—than *Coming Up For Air* or the essays of *Inside the Whale* (good as these last two books may be) that these attracted fewer readers and do not make the same impact as *1984*, which is written in blood.

By now Orwell had emerged from the crushing poverty and readers' indifference that had marked his early years as a writer. But his very real success at political writing and the simple language that was his trademark still did not prepare the literary public for the success of his next—last but better seen as next two books—*Animal Farm* and *1984*. In the meantime Orwell strayed into the minefield of national character and published *The Lion and the unicorn,* which extols the gentle nature of British popular life. In November 1943 he had his first official contact with the Labour Party when he became literary editor of *Tribune,* the weekly of the Labour left. Orwell liked *Tribune,* which, according to him, managed to combine "a radical Socialist policy" with a "civilized attitude toward literature and the arts."[75]

If there is a hint of conservatism in that remark, it is not out of character. Orwell's commitment to socialism was intermingled with a dislike of various aspects of modernity. In *1984* Winston is aware that there used to be something called privacy. There was also a time when people bought an object not to serve some function but because they liked its shape, which they considered beautiful. It is then particularly treacherous of the Party to have a member of the Thought Police play the role of an antique dealer. Orwell did not altogether relish the concept of commitment and he looks back with nostalgia at the age of George Gissing, when the writer was a man of letters.

Orwell wrote *Animal Farm* in 1943–44. The manuscript was turned down by both Gollancz and by T. S. Eliot at Faber and Faber. It was finally published by Secker and Warburg and Orwell, whose first wife Eileen O'Shaugnessy had just died, went off to farm in Jura, an island off the coast of Scotland. His own TB was getting worse and he toiled to finish *1984*. It was published in 1949 and sold 400,000 thousand copies the first year. Orwell's TB grew worse and he died in January 1950. He had no chance to enjoy his wealth, which went mostly to his widow Sonia Brownell, whom he married just before he died.

To the end Orwell was a non-conformist: he considered himself well to the left of the Labour government; he was searching eagle-eyed for communists who infiltrated the party and he was trying to prevent *1984* from being used as a weapon by the right. He had insights into political developments: he foresaw the Cold War as a balance of terror—"an epoch as horribly stable as the slave empires of antiquity."[76]

THE INFERNO OF 1984

In general Orwell defended plain English, but he saw it decline all around him. The concrete melted into the abstract, unnecessary foreign imports like "Weltanschauung" or Latin words like "ameliorate" grew more common, as did prepositions like "in respect of" and "in relation to," which failed to define that relation. Orwell could see the link between linguistic difficulties and political exclusion. The language of pre-1992 Italian politics would have had no secrets for him.

In *1984*, however, the Party goes much further and develops newspeak, a new language from which many words have been excluded. Newspeak also turns concepts on their head: "war is peace." In reality it is unlikely that one can destroy concepts or emotions just by destroying the single words that represent them. A person who wishes to express her dislike of war will find a way to do it, refusing to be content with the transformed word "peace." What Orwell is offering is a deliberately exaggerated critique of the way the Party tries to control the language to which the people have access. As the young Pasolini discovered, one needs words to rebel. Orwell shows how the word "duckspeak" takes on whatever meaning the Party ascribes to it: it can be a compliment or a condemnation. This variation shows the weakness of language, its willingness to serve all masters and hence the need to care for it. Newspeak even finds its poet in Syme, who enjoys its concision. His reward for studying the language as an autonomous entity is that he vanishes.

So Orwell sees the link between language and power. There are several other languages in *1984:* the proles speak a grammatically incorrect, mid-twentieth-century brand of English that does not enable them to analyze political developments but serves to set them apart from members of the Outer and Inner Party and allows the direct expression of emotion. It is a prole woman who complains about the horrors of the war film. Then there is the song turned out by the Party's Music Department but transformed into popular culture by the woman who sings it while putting out her washing. Then there are genuine, old, popular songs like *Oranges and Lemons,* which have been appropriated by the Party. None of these presents a challenge to the Party, but Julia's speech does.

Limited to the abrupt expression of what she feels, Julia combines speech with body-language. This includes sexuality, which is a radical form of opposition to a Party that treats sex as a grave threat to its own dominance. Desire is the opposite of the fear that the Party wishes to inspire. If Julia has had lots of lovers, that adds to the strength of her rebellion; the Party prefers monogamy and joyless sex. Julia pits mobility against stasis.

Julia's rebellion is put down not by the Party but by Winston. Their first meeting in the countryside is arranged by her, but, as their relationship continues, Winston chooses the places and guides them to the antique shop and to O'Brien. The original trait in the novel of having a woman take the lead in a sexual relation of her choosing gives way to the traditional couple, led by the male.

Julia is just one of the many original female characters created by male authors who are not able to maintain their insight and who revert to male dominance and other stereotypes. Sartre does the same with Electra in *Les Mouches* and with Jessica in *Les mains sales.* It is useless to blame Orwell's lack of awareness of women's condition. As already argued, male writers cannot dispense with the women's movement. As a text, *1984* changes, and the discourse on gender becomes less interesting.

Julia had been called by Winston a rebel from the waist down, but Orwell commented that "the sexual act, successfully performed, was rebellion."⁷⁷ The political struggle against totalitarianism pits the body-language of a woman against a language that does not allow the expression of desire or freedom.

Winston too has tried out heretical languages. He buys a diary and writes in it. At once he faces the problem of the reader: who will read him with any comprehension? Stendhal asked himself the same question, did not have to answer to Sartre and opted to believe in the future. Winston, faced with the spread of newspeak, is thrown into crisis by the lack of readers. Gide's diary is a long reflection on his daily experience; action and awareness move together. Winston, however, is living in a world where his individual existence has been voided of meaning. Meaning supposedly comes from the Party in which Winston participates—its hate sessions and its mythical statistics of ever-rising productivity. Alienated from the Party, Winston tries to find meaning in the written language, but he is unable to construct sentences in the diary and he breaks down into automatic writing. Some surrealists had turned automatic writing into a literary form, but Winston can do no better than a string of "Down with Big Brother." This marks the failure of the literary avant-garde to combat tyranny. Instead Winston invokes Shakespeare's name but links it with Julia's body-language. Shakespeare's work is absent, presumably unread, but his name is valuable as an evocation of the past and of literature. One remembers that under Mussolini names were a form of protest in the red countryside.

The past is ally and puzzle for Winston. He is drawn to the antique shop as the repository of the lost Britain. The objects he sees have all lost their utility, but this does not confound Winston, as it worries Sartre's characters. The objects possess aesthetic quality: the paper-weight stranded in a world without paper or the diary whose beauty outlives its function. The past is also to be investigated. The Party re-shapes the past after purges or perhaps for no reason at all. Winston's attempt to unearth the truth of the past comes to nothing because he uses the language of reason, whereas the prole he interrogates does not. Winston has to be content with shreds of the past—Shakespeare's name or the paper-weight. If he were able to interpret it, he might learn more about the past from the proles' language.

But the only opposition discourse remains Julia's body-language. She is not like Céline's dancers, who are there only to communicate by movement. Julia allows herself to be guided by Winston, who wants to fight the Party with the discourse of historical truth. There is a conflict between Julia's more aesthetic and more sexual discourse and Winston's. The difference between them is illustrated by Goldstein's book.

Bernard Crick advises us to remember that Orwell was gravely ill when he wrote *1984* and that he did not get everything exactly as he wanted it.⁷⁸

This included the treatment of the proles, the explanatory section on Newspeak relegated to an appendix and Goldstein's book. This argument is used by Crick to promote his interpretation of *1984*. It does not depict the certain future but is a warning; the warning is directed not merely at Stalin's USSR but at totalitarianism in general; and the popular value of decency runs through the sections on the proles. Orwell, so Crick maintains, was still a socialist. To take the last assertion first, Orwell certainly thought of himself as a socialist, but this does not mean that his greatest text is in any way socialist. Winston (certainly the name is ironic) cultivates what one might call a Tory liberalism, in that he approves of individualism and sets it in the past. The depiction of the proles is not very different from the portrayal of working-class Wigan. There are indeed traces of other forms of totalitarianism in *1984*, such as the anti-Semitism in the Party's war film, but they are far fewer than the allusions to Communism, which had been Orwell's main target since 1937. On this point one agrees with Crick that *Animal Farm* and *1984* do not reveal a new Orwell. The first question seems to us unanswerable: *1984* is convinced of its own inevitability but that does not mean its author was.

One returns to Goldstein's book. It purports to offer what Winston is looking for: the Party destroyed opposition by its monopoly of language; now Winston will gain a new awareness from this explanation of the Party. In particular the causes of its authoritarianism will be spelled out. Sure enough, Goldstein's book reads like all ex-communist analyses: he explains the evolution of the Party and what went wrong. He is superficially another Trotsky. Yet Goldstein is the worst of Winston's mistakes. His book was written by O'Brien and it is used to make opponents of the regime reveal themselves. Moreover Goldstein's argument repeats the discourse of the Party. It is different in the subjects it chooses to discuss but the same in the unfailingly simple logic that gives form to its discussion. It lays bare the mental gyrations of doublethink but in its list of the various states of mind it is, or professes to be, as exhaustive, as methodical and as objective as the good Party member is taught to be.

Unsurprisingly, Julia is not interested in Goldstein's book: it depicts a world where one cannot dance, wear make-up or make love. Its exploration of the past is interrupted, suitably, by the Thought Police, who have appropriated the chopper of *Oranges and Lemons*. Goldstein's book is the key to *1984*, for it brings back a male view of things based on force and on power.

The torture reserved for Winston is that he must give up the apparently logical view that two and two make four. Yet in Brecht's *Leben des Galilei*, students of the Copernican universe are taught that two and two can just as easily make five. This is unlike *1984*, where two and two make whatever the totalitarian state wants them to make. But it is also unlike Winston's simple rationalism. In this conflict over nothing Julia has no place. Orwell does not describe how she is tortured, for men are now dominating the readers' attention. But one might speculate, based on one's last glimpse of Julia, that her body has been damaged. Of Winston we know that he feels a latently homosexual attraction toward O'Brien and that he comes to love Big Brother, which is not going to save him from the death the Party has allotted to him.

This interpretation, which ascribes much importance to the early presence and late absence of Julia, offers solutions to two other questions. The first is that Winston's journey into the past is also a personal and Freudian quest. With an absent father, he was able to have an incestuous relationship with his mother at the price of behaving selfishly toward his younger sister. He carries the guilt of this past into a joyless first marriage. Now he meets Julia, the woman, who can offer him a guilt-free relationship. Instead he falls into the clutches of very severe father figures in O'Brien and Big Brother. The second question is, What drives the Party? Crick is far from alone in criticizing Orwell for not providing more explanation for the Party's urge to dominate. If it is seen as an aggressively male organization, then O'Brien's statement that the Party wants nothing more than to be a boot smashed into the face of its victims, acquires greater plausibility.

There is no need to deny the traditional reading of *1984* as an "inferno," an analysis of totalitarianism in general and of communism in particular. Once Winston takes the lead from Julia the "inferno" theme dominates. Nor is it surprising that such a condemnation should come from a man who considered himself a left-winger. Koestler and Silone are two other names that come at once to mind. Anyway the evolution of Orwell's brand of commitment leads him with perfect logic to demolish the new utopia of communism.

But the essence of Orwell's onslaught is on the language of communism. Newspeak is a simplified, exaggerated version of Stalinism. Huge ideological leaps are contained in single words: "freedom is slavery" presupposes a whole chunk of reasoning about bourgeois freedom. Against newspeak Orwell pits the discourse of the proles, of twentieth-century innovation and the name of Shakespeare that conjures up a great tradition. He looks for subversion in the writings of the ex-leader Goldstein. But the only real subversion lies in Julia's body-language, which cannot be introduced into the text except as written language, but that confers movement and brevity on the writing that expresses it.

In his switches of language, Orwell reveals his own ability as a writer. At other times he is more concerned to describe the communist system and to explain how it works. This in itself shows that Barthes's concepts of "écrivain" and "écrivant" are not mutually exclusive but may be found side by side in the same text. For a committed writer the discovery of a literary-political language is a necessity, as argued above.

Bertolt Brecht, or the Curious Marxism of Azdak

Brecht wrote *Der kaukasiche Kreidekreis* while he was still in the United States. It dates from 1944–45 and was first performed in 1948 in English. It was not until 1954, after Brecht had returned to Europe and made the choice to live in the German Democratic Republic (DDR)—while having his Western royalties paid in D-marks into a Frankfurt bank—that it was performed in German. Despite its early genesis, one feels that its popularity in Western Europe was linked not merely with its strong lyrical strain but with the fading of hopes for massive social change. Azdak's reign, which ends with the Grusche decision, is short and "almost just," which hints at another more perfect justice that would be socialism.[79] But the Great Prince has been returned to power, socialism is remote and Azdak, who has just created a children's park with the funds from the governor's estate and has called it after himself, sets people dancing and then vanishes.

The name may be seen as an attempt to leave some trace of his being in the public realm and to associate it with children and with spending—rather irregularly—public money on them. The dance is an expression of corporeal freedom and a popular festivity. But once the dance stops, there will be no justice. Azdak does not die but vanishes, which leads all of us who like myths to hope that he will return, like Merlin or Arthur. But there is no hint of this in the text.

Brecht grew up in an affluent bourgeois family in Bavaria. According to his biographer, he always liked and demanded bourgeois comforts, along with the respect and privileges offered to Hitler or Stalin, not forgetting easy sex from a whole group of dominated but talented women. John Fuegi not only depicts a model of egotism, he alleges with very strong evidence that Brecht's works were mostly written by these women.[80] Brecht's first and most popular success, *Three Penny Opera* (1928), was written 80–90 percent by Elizabeth Hauptmann.

In the years of Hitler's rise to power Brecht wrote little to oppose him and, although he was active in Comintern politics, he was not a Communist Party member and he was even more active in selling under his own name work done by his group. This now included Grete Steffin, a superb writer who came from a working-class family and had tuberculosis, which Brecht ignored. After the fire in the Reichstag Brecht began to think of leaving Germany but it was not until 1938 that he established himself in Denmark in considerable comfort and with no lack of money, married to Helene Weigel and with Steffin to do the literary work. It was now that Brecht produced one of his—or the group's—best works, *Leben des Galilei*. While they were writing it they were reading the transcripts of Bukharin's trial.

Brecht likes the movement of history in which he sees the hope of change. In *Leben des Galilei* he depicted the Copernican universe as a threat to the Catholic Church and its allies. They rally and treat Galileo almost as badly as Stalin treated Bukharin. But now the Pope was dislodged from the center of the universe and sent flying around the sun. "The old age is gone and there is a new age," says Galileo.[81] The new age will adopt as its basic values doubt and knowledge; the second follows from the first and is no longer the set of certainties handed down from Aristotle. Knowledge is not depicted, however, as controlled by a particular group. Rather it is dispersed throughout society and the task of the scientist is to place it at the disposal of the people. Certainly new forms of capitalism will emerge as the telescope permits more accurate meteorological predictions and hence safer navigation and trading. But Galileo foresees greater democracy, too: "For the new thinking, we need people who work with their hands."[82] Scientists will write in the vernacular so that they are not read solely by the educated classes who know Latin. Thus there will be no clear distinction between social classes. Here again Galileo's unheroic submission to the Inquisition sets his cause back decades, although the threat from his last, unpublished book remains. Brecht had scant use for heroes, as he would demonstrate before the House un-American Activities Committee (HUAC).

Brecht lingered in Denmark as the Nazi-Soviet pact was announced and belatedly decided that the Nazis would invade and that he would be safe only in America. He and Steffin had just written *Arturo Ui*, a satirical account of Hitler's rise to power. By the time Brecht was ready, the only safe route to the United States was to cross Russia by train and find a boat to California. The band set out and had to leave Steffin in Moscow, where she died of TB.

Once ensconced in Hollywood Brecht worked at *The Caucasian Chalk Circle* and felt aggrieved because he was not recognized as a star. The FBI, however, took an ever stronger interest in him, as did HUAC, which called him to appear before it in 1947. When asked whether he was a member of the Communist Party, Brecht did not invoke the first amendment, which might have brought reprisals. Instead he said "no." This was seen as cowardice by all the other people summoned to testify, but what could one expect from the (part-)author of *Galilei*?

Brecht promptly left for Europe and considered his options. It was the Russians rather than the DDR who offered him the Schiffbautheater in East Berlin. There Brecht had a generous budget and lived a life of luxury while most DDR citizens toiled to get through the winter. The Russians may have thought their money—or rather the DDR's money—was not wasted as propaganda because in 1954 Brecht took the company to an international Paris theater festival. There *Mother Courage* was a great success, all the more disquieting to the audience because of the recent French defeat at Dien Bien Phu. Brecht, who had done almost nothing to help or explain the workers' protest in the DDR in 1953, was acknowledged as a great dramatist and one who was left-wing in his technique and worldview.

Certainly he was seen in Western Europe as a model of the committed writer and his decision to opt for East rather than West Berlin proved there was an anti-capitalist theater of protest. Brecht's writings on the theater were examined to find out what this was. His statement "I don't let my feelings intrude in my dramatic work . . . I aim at an extremely classical, cold, highly intellectual style of performance" placed him on a pedestal way above other playwrights. It does not, however, seem to explain very much about his theater.[83] The key to Brecht's theater seems to us to lie in Fuegi's comment that Brecht was a man accustomed to contradictions who believed that "the certainty of the ego is a myth. A man is an atom that perpetually breaks up and forms anew."[84] The reiteration of another Brechtian term, "Verfremdungseffekt," is also misleading, if it means the spectator is supposed to remain cold and reflective throughout the play.

One might begin this all too brief discussion of Brecht's aesthetic with Artaud's comment that the bourgeois went to the theater as he went to the brothel. The aim of left-wing, committed theater was to shake up this theater-goer, who wanted only to be taken out of himself and amused. A standard feature of such theater was to break the illusion and make the spectator think. In pre-1939 Algiers Camus interrupted a play he was staging and had the audience sing the *International*. In the same play the audience became a mass jury to judge a character-actor.

But this was designed to create a bond among the onlookers. An aloof, intellectual stance was fine for a moment but then the spectator must form a new group. The constant shifts of emotion and perspective are what counts in Brecht. In *The Caucasian Chalk Circle* Grusche is associated with a simple lyricism that wins the viewer's sympathy. By contrast Azdac's discourse is ironic, every word a play on other discourses. The "Volkslied" side of Brecht rarely pervades a work as it does this one and rarely too does he create a character like Azdak.

If the revolution is a long way off, then one must find a way to live in the meantime. This essentially moral question is posed to Grusche early in *The Caucasian Chalk Circle* when the baby is abandoned. Brecht's answer is an ethical one that also becomes political. There are certain values that are associated with the working-class: courage, tenderness, but above all the very capacity for work, which is wasted by the alienation of capitalist society but that the working-class itself prizes. Not that Brecht was a "stahkanovite" or that he depicted the working-class of social realism: transformed by socialism and toiling away happily. But the ethical urge to work becomes the starting-point of a political awareness.

This is the awareness that Grusche is forced to acquire when the upper-class travelers drive her out because she can do housework and has the roughened hands of a servant. Later comes the counterpoint: Azdak tells the Great Prince that he has obviously never known hunger because he does not seize his food and tear it apart with his hands. In both cases the body reveals a truth that the mind is trying to conceal. A theme of much post-war writing, which we noticed in Sartre, is that the dominant scientific-technological culture has arrived at a point when it creates abstractions. But the body retains its realities of pain and well-being, so it is a reliable guide to what is happening.

At all events Grusche is aware of her values from the start. When Simon asks her to marry him, he specifically asks about her health and she replies that she "is strong enough for any work. No-one has ever complained about her." If her reaction to the helpless child can be attributed to instinct or nature, Brecht chooses this moment to intervene with the Singer, who reinterprets the child's cry in rational language. Thus the act of helping is also explained as a form of human solidarity, or what Marx called *Gattungswesen*. The two are separate here but, as Grusche evolves, she will bring the levels of nature and history together. She sums up her feelings toward the baby:

Weil ich dich zu lang geschleppt
Und mit wunden Fussen
Weil die Milch so teuer war
Wurdest du mir lieb.[85]

Here Grusche can express for herself what the child means to her. He has reaffirmed in her those working-class values that the Singer stated at the outset of her journey. A logical consequence is that the child must also become working-class not merely because it has no choice but because it must participate in this ethic. Grusche, whose awareness grows more sophisticated, explains how she has brought up the child: "I told him to show friendship to everyone and from the start I had him work as much as he could, he is only little."[86] Next Grusche receives a crash-course in the disadvantages of poverty from Azdak: she learns quickly and stands up to him, telling him a judge is no better than a criminal hanging on the gallows.[87] Azdak asks her the key question: If she loves the child, why does she not give him up to the rich and let him enjoy a privileged existence? Here again the Singer replies on behalf of Grusche: "let your child be afraid of hunger, let him not be afraid of the hungry."[88] After the treatment she has received in the course of the play, Grusche has learned the ethical superiority of the working-class and the exploitation of the ruling-class, even though Brecht has the Singer state it. This is a good example of Barthes's definition of Brecht's "theatre of nascent awareness."[89]

This use of a chorus, a singer or other interlocutors who stand between the characters and the audience is part of the *Verfremdungseffect*. But if we are right in arguing that the alienation effect was itself part of a greater principle of contradictions, then Brecht's aim was to elicit from the viewer a series of responses: to show where Grusche's awareness might take her, to indicate how far Grusinien is from socialism and to explain the innovations of Azdak. Brecht seeks to draw the viewer into varying emotions of suspense, sympathy or rejection for one or the other character. Despite or because of such multiplicity Brecht's plays are incomplete: the class struggle in Grusinien is still in an early phase.

What will become of the child? Will Simon and Grusche manage to survive after flaunting the rules of class? There are no answers because Brecht's work is tangled up with reality, which is still unfolding. The viewer is not able to leave the theater like Artaud's bourgeois leaving the brothel—convinced of his central role in the universe. Brecht's viewer will go on reflecting on the outcome of the play. This deliberate breaking of the mood of triumph at the end delighted Brecht's Italian admirers, who saw in it an invitation to go out and change the world.[90]

Franco Fortini, whose magazine *Ragionamenti* was financed by the unorthodox left-wing publisher Giangiacomo Feltrinelli, saw the incomplete nature of Brecht's work as a critique of the supposed harmony that idealist thought attributed to art and hence to the world. Fortini republished Barthes's articles in Italian translation and spread the gospel of Brecht. By the mid-1950s neo-realism, having produced a flood of novels about the peasantry and of tapes that recorded their experience in their own words, was moribund. This was the real issue in the debate about Vasco Pratolini's *Metello*, a long novel about the Florentine working-class. Fortini attacked it as not dealing with contemporary capitalism and declared that it was the cultural equivalent of the PCI's soft Gramscian line.[91] Fortini, Pasolini and many others on the Italian left were searching for more modern and sharper left-wing criticism. Brecht was the answer. His "work was in a state of complicity with the world" and it invited the audience to go out and complete its task, which was an ever higher level of awareness and the creation of socialism.[92]

Brecht's use of Marxism, claimed Barthes, was the opposite of the determinism that posed as a scientific, Marxist discourse. Since reality was a mere superstructure it was unpredictable and could take surprising turns in response to unfathomable changes in the economy. It was riddled with ideologies, many of them false. History was plastic in the playwright's hands.

This meant that the peasantry was often confronted with forms of necessity it did not choose or want. They destroyed the continuity of the ego, creating unstable characters. It also meant that the ebb and flow of the class struggle could throw up one of the great characters of modern writing—Azdak.

Azdak's social position must have intrigued Ernst Gellner, who saw the written language as the weapon by which the state imposed itself. Azdak was a public writer, hence the lowest form of state intellectual and the intermediary between the peasants and authority. As such he sees the class struggle at its sharpest. It follows that he is no positive hero and no Bolshevik man such as one finds in Sartre or Malraux. His level of awareness is much higher than Grusch's, but it leads him to grovel before the rich. He does not consider work a value. He has sympathy for the Great Prince, who is an anonymous refugee and whom Azdak does not turn over to the police, just as Grusche feels sympathy for the executed Governor's baby son.

When he discovers the Prince's identity, Azdak goes to the soldiers and (anticipating 1968!) accuses himself. He professes to believe that Grusinien has entered a phase of popular democracy where actions like his are condemned. In reality he demonstrates his ability to live under all regimes and he shows that there is no fixed category of enemies of the people. He becomes judge by his outspoken criticism of the army leadership, which appeals to the soldiers who are running this topsy-turvy interregnum. Here is an example of where a particular moment in the class struggle produces a random legal structure. It has of course its own logic: the people have never believed in the legal system so they appoint someone who denounces the system and the rich who take advantage of it. This is a play within the play, where Azdak wins the job over the Prince's nephew by his ability to tell the truth as the people see it. The very soldiers who have put down the weavers' revolt and will later knock Azdak around, appoint him a judge. Ideology takes various, contradictory forms.

As a judge Azdak demands bribes and exacts sexual favors. He acts as a pedagogue, telling the working-class that justice is like meat and must be paid for. In Marxist terms it is part of the superstructure and depends on economics. He acts, however, like "the poor people's judge" even if Brecht points out to us once again that this is not fair, socialist justice: Azdak is "well-equipped with false scales."[93] Brecht includes as Azdak's ally the well-known figure of Eric Hobsbawm's social bandit, who also flourishes when capitalism is weak but has not collapsed. Then, as Azdak puts it, "the time of confusion and disorder has gone and the time of Greatness has not arrived."[94] Azdak is dethroned and beaten up by the soldiers before a document from the Great Prince reappoints him judge. Contempt is at once transformed into fawning respect and the Grusche case begins.

The didactic introduction about the two Soviet co-operatives vying for a piece of land emphasizes the value of utility over ownership. This is a crude version of the play that stresses, among the values of the working-class, Grusche's inability to tear the child apart. Here caring rather than know-how is at stake. The most important feature of the ethic in *Der Kaukasische Kreidekreis* is, however, the way that it evolves into a political awareness. Just as Galileo begins by not understanding the economic and political forces that are eager to profit from his research but by the end grasps that he has unleashed a struggle between two different kinds of society, so Grusche learns that the class struggle pervades even the most private feelings.

Conclusion

Grusche is aware that she is governed by necessity—"We do not choose the road we take."[95] Yet there are, in the historical crises that so intrigue Brecht, moments when the characters are free and able to impose their own language. Azdak's brand of justice is one example. These temporary victories, which hold out the hope of socialism, reveal Brecht's ability to imagine different societies. Here he is an "écrivain" who sets aside what capitalism calls reality. This makes *Der Kaukasische Kreidekreis* a superb piece of left-wing theater.

To conclude, commitment produced excellent writing when the author realized that he was a writer whose main tasks were to combat authoritarian language and to offer examples of freedom. When he merely tried to refute the stories told by authoritarian regimes, he ended up unable to impose his own language (Pasolini) or imitating the enemy.[96] "Writing" (écrivant) has its merits, but it does not match the moments when Julia smears make-up on her face or when Azdak decides to sit on the book of laws rather than to consult it.

Of what help were these works to the kinds of politics they were ostensibly supporting? *1984* was the most influential, although Orwell may have been displeased by the narrow-minded anti-communism of some of his admirers. Sartre was the most famous but perhaps his early "existentialist" works exerted more influence. Certainly it was they who shaped the atmosphere of Saint-Germain at the Liberation. But then the limits on the support supplied by good writing were narrower than Gramsci believed.

The signs of literature limited its impact. The name of the publishing house sets a tone at the outset: the name "Gallimard" invited the reader to filter Nizan's communism through Gide's irony. A work may itself invite the reader to approach it in a certain manner. The pre-1939 French pamphlet was a genre in which language was exaggerated and opinions were not meant to be taken literally. Few readers of his pamphlet thought that Henri Béraud actually wanted to reduce Britain to slavery and fewer still agreed with such a view. These signs cannot be discarded as easily as Sartre considered. So the overlap with politics may be no more common than the opposite: the reader suspends his belief while he reads Sartre's description of his communist militants before moving on—with a sigh of relief—to the rest of the novel.

The substitution of the language of literature for the language of politics was difficult and brought some, but not many, changes. When successful it introduces into politics the freedom of the literary language. We must next look at the opposite of commitment, anti-politics.

CHAPTER THREE

DEPICTING THE WORKING-CLASS

Literature has never been at ease with its place in high culture. It is perpetually in search of new characters, new material and new readers. It cannot cease being literature because it cannot do without the signs we have discussed. Still literature often becomes aware that there is a vast working-class that should be brought within the limits of its aristocratic and then bourgeois domain. How can this be done? Must there be working-class authors? Is it possible not merely to write about the working-class, as Balzac and Zola did, but to reconstruct the world as the working-class sees and lives it? This is not the same as being committed to a particular political goal, although Gramsci linked the two things in his notion of cultural hegemony. Most of the writers we shall consider hold exactly the opposite view and defend an anti-political point of view. They refuse to dissolve the working-class into either a socialist utopia or a long process of reform. They are the antithesis of commitment.

To gain insight into these and other issues we have selected three topics from different periods: Charles-Louis Philippe and the myth of the French education system; the Angry (formerly) Young Men from the English 1950s, especially Alan Sillitoe; and the contemporary film director Ken Loach, with particular emphasis on *Riff-Raff*.

CHARLES-LOUIS PHILIPPE, OR ANTI-POLITICS

One might begin with the observation that Philippe (1874–1909) seeks to "allow this other,"[1] which is the working-class, to speak. Philippe's characters are convincing as people, which might lead one to interpret his novels as "psychological," but their complexity comes from the class struggle. In *Le Père Perdrix* (1902) Pierre Bousset represents the reliable worker who is integrated into the established order. Superficially he is a social type. Then the reader realizes what a complex figure Pierre is: devoted to his family, he is an authoritarian father. The reader's second discovery is that Pierre's complexity is linked not to individual psychology but to the contradictions of the class struggle. Pierre hates the bourgeoisie but he is determined to make his son a bourgeois. He is an authoritarian father because he knows that the poor can only survive if they are hard-working and prudent. There is no simple determinism in Philippe's writing. Alienation blinds Pierre, driving his contradictions to extremes and breaking through his self-control. He does not understand why he acts as he does. But the reader understands.

Philippe's task is to lay bare the existence of the most important social law: the iron law of class. In his early work, *La Mère et l'enfant,* he describes the initiation of a working-class child into the Third Republic. Philippe's task is primarily negative: he wants to undermine the myth of equality that sustains the Third Republic. Here again the historical moment is important: from the time when it emerged from the 1870 defeat at the hands of Bismarck, the Third Republic represented an alliance between the middle-classes and the peasantry. Measures taken to help the peasantry included the construction of railway branch-lines leading to previously remote villages and protectionist measures to keep out cheap food from the United States and Argentina. The peasantry's position did improve and along with it the artisans', such as Philippe's father, who made clogs at Cérilly in central France. But it was still a very hard life. Emile Guillaumin, who came from Ygrande, a village close to Cérilly, chronicled it in *La Vie d'un simple* (1904). He depicts a "métayer" or sharecropper and shows the pressures on him as well as the strength of character he needs to survive and the gloominess of his worldview.

Despite this work of stern reality the peasantry acquired a romantic haze. In *Le Grand Meaulnes* the hero leaves behind the school but he has to spend a night on a farm before he discovers the magic realm of the Domaine Inconnu. One remembers that Alain-Fournier's parents were elementary-school teachers, so that he lived geographically among the peasantry but socially he was quite separate from them. His position was different from that of another writer: Marguerite Audoux was raised in an orphanage in Bourges, once more in central France. Encouraged by Philippe and his circle of friends, known as the Carnetin group after a house they rented near Paris for weekends, she published the hugely successful *Marie-Claire* (1910), which depicts her life in the orphanage and then as a shepherdess. Written simply and with lyrical passages, the book transmits the child's experience directly to the reader. *Marie-Claire* was introduced to the British reading public by Arnold Bennett; it was translated into many other languages and was acclaimed across Europe as the tale of a peasant girl. The peasantry had reached the point where it was perceived as different by town-dwellers, but that difference could be the mark of a more imaginative as well as a harsher society. Guillaumin continued to underline how hard life was among the peasantry. *Baptiste et sa Femme* (1910) depicts a peasant who abandons the land and goes to the town but fails to overcome its new, strange obstacles. Guillaumin believed, however, in education, and his advice to his neighbors who asked what they could do to help their children was an abrupt "Send them to school."[2]

The question of the education system was at the heart of Third Republic culture. Talleyrand had foreseen schools for all children and had drawn up a plan in 1791. It was an Enlightenment project, for, in disseminating knowledge, the school was supposed to spread freedom and truth. Jules Ferry's law of 1880 continued this process.[3] The curriculum has been criticized as non-technical; it contained little that would make the children of the peasantry better farmers. That was not, however, the point.[4] The aim of the education system was to create Frenchmen by ousting the patois, teaching peasant children to speak French and making them aware of the state by teaching them correct written French. The removal of priests in the aftermath of the Dreyfus case dispatched a rival ideal. The elementary-school teacher exemplified and spread the values of French citizenship.

Another aim was to provide a very limited social mobility. Although secondary education was not free and only the middle-classes had enough money to send their children to "lycée," there were scholarships for the talented sons and—more rarely—daughters of the peasantry. Then, if they passed the exacting entrance examination, they could continue their studies in the "grandes écoles," which led to at least middle-class and at times important jobs. The "boursier" or "scholarship boy" was an admired, significant figure in the Third Republic, the rival of the "héritier," the boy born into a wealthy family.

La Mère et l'enfant is the tale of a boursier who fails to pass his examinations and go on to a brilliant career. Philippe distinguishes between the elementary school "where we acquired a simple, useful knowledge from teachers who were the sons of men who worked the fields" and the lycée, where knowledge was "cold" and was imparted by a teacher "with a big black beard of the kind you don't see in our villages."[5] *La Mère et l'enfant* is not an autobiography. In reality Philippe failed his examinations at the end of the lycée years because he had spent too much time reading contemporary poetry. He was drawn as if by a magnet to the most esoteric kinds of 1890s poetry and neglected his mundane school work. This mishap is then transformed into a choice (Sartre might say that Philippe chose to fail) on which all Philippe's writing is based. He refuses the society that emerged from the French Revolution, which flaunts its empty slogans—liberty, equality and fraternity—to hide its division into rich and poor. This is Philippe's anti-politics: the hope of a socialist revolution is turned into an illusion born of the failures of the past. In *Croquignole* (1906) the character of Félicien, the hero's friend, is associated with the revolution of 1848. But this association is made by others: "Lots of people, on seeing him, thought of 1848 and of the Revolution."[6] It has no relation to political reality and it is at best a vague, moral nostalgia and certainly not a correct piece of class-awareness. Nor does Philippe believe in gradualism. Rather he asserts that there was a period, which he does not name, when "the Republic was serious." Presumably it is not serious now and history is in decline. Philippe does not, however, indulge in any kind of "Untergang des Abendlandes."[7] When the boursier hero of *La Mère et l'enfant* returns after failing his examinations, he affirms his adherence to the working-class: "I too am a man of the people and I am going to work like the others."[8] But jobs are hard to find. It is here that Philippe sets his satire of the bourgeoisie: a local notable, a left-winger, is invoked to help the hero get a job, but he does nothing. The rural middle-classes were supposed to act as intermediaries between their own class and the working-class/peasantry. Their failure to play this role destroys the mystique of republican solidarity.

Philippe's circle of friends contained militant left-wingers like Francis Jourdain, who would go on to become a fervent communist. Nevertheless, Jourdain insisted on the anti-political trait before going on to say that Philippe was unsure of his political views. He could be right- or left-wing but, once again, he was always opposed to the Third Republic.[9] The figure of the mother is also complex. To be sure, she incarnates the love and warmth that the Third Republic lacks, but she is not merely the incarnation of such values, as is the mother in Alain-Fournier's *Le Miracle de la Fermière*. This mother goes to get her unhappy child, a boarder at school, and brings him home to a happy ending. Philippe's mother is associated with work: she helps her son look for a job, which he does not get. The values of the family cannot hold out against the corrosion of society.

Philippe returns to the themes of the boursier and of work in *Le Père Perdrix*. The successful scholarship boy, Jean Boussin, has become an engineer, but, when the workers in his factory go on strike, he joins them and is fired. His father, who had worked hard so that his children might work less, does not understand much less appreciate Jean's action, and the father-son relationship breaks down. For once an orthodox left-winger,

Philippe sees the refusal to work as a protest against the alienation of work and as the desire to work freely.

But the desire remains unsatisfied and work does not become the starting-point of a new discourse. French industrialization lagged behind English and it would be surprising if Philippe wrote mostly about factories. Nor does he, like Gramsci, have before him a historically advanced proletariat such as the Turin workers. He tends to concentrate on white-collar workers and seamstresses. But he ranges from peasants to the unemployed and includes prostitutes and pimps. Although Philippe's sociology is imprecise, he establishes one essential difference—between those who have money and those who do not: the first exploit the second.

For Berthe, the prostitute in *Bubu de Montparnasse*, love means exploitation by her pimp. As the young Pierre Hardy (the name is significant: Philippe admired the compassion of Thomas Hardy's novels) declares his love for her, Berthe is thinking about work and money: after Pierre, she will have to find another man and she will also have to buy new shoes because hers are worn out. Philippe's materialism, pitted against Third Republic idealism, enables him to create a category of reification: love-shoes. Another variant on the work-as-alienation theme is Angèle, the seamstress in *Croquignole*. She has interiorized the law of work so that she finds it unnatural not to work and sees no link between sewing and the money she receives. Moreover the materialism of Philippe is revealed by the way he describes her: her body "looks like a pair of scissors with a thimble on it."[10]

Berthe's pimp, Bubu, incarnates "not working." This is a two-sided portrait, for Bubu's victory over Pierre Hardy is the triumph of force. Bubu sits idly in a café with a like-minded friend and judges the passers-by who are going to and from work: "It was like the day of Creation, when Adam, the king of the world, sat down near an oak-tree to watch the animals go past, examined them and named them."[11] Once more "naming" people, albeit transformed into animals, is a sign of the pimp's power, but the comparison with Adam is ironic too. Bubu is a false king, soon dethroned by the Republic's justice system and thrown into prison. Not that the Republic's justice is very just: Bubu goes to prison for theft—a crime against property—rather than for exploiting a woman. By his "not working" and his brutality Bubu represents a parody of the reality of the Third Republic. In a world without love, the pimp is king.

Bubu is also a parody of the writer, especially of the working-class writer who gives new names to things. There is a good deal of parody in anti-politics: since it deals with inauthentic forms of revolt, forms that reflect but do not go beyond the alienation of work. When Philippe writes that the bourgeois are important like science, he is anticipating the theme of the link between knowledge and power and he is suggesting there may be another kind of science that is non-bourgeois. But he does not develop this theme and the oppressed fail to create the alternative forms of knowledge, of which Michel Foucault will speak.

Philippe does succeed in creating a different kind of writing. It is unlike Zola and Balzac because the omniscient narrator is undermined by the emphasis on class. Since there is no unified class-awareness, there can be no working-class language. Or more precisely, there will be several. As Pierre Hardy unfolds his monologue, the silent monologue of Berthe swells up to confound it. Philippe's novels are on the verge of breaking down into individual worldviews. This disintegration is checked not by class solidarity but only by the struggle between the rich and the poor, which unites the characters around self-interest and hatred. But the point of view changes rapidly: Philippe uses "nous" and "vous," which are traditional indicators of a certain universalism, at least of common ground between writer and reader or among readers. But in *Bubu de Montparnasse* the "nous" changes and becomes the group of prostitutes from which pimps and all males are excluded.

These narrative shifts jolt the reader, who is suddenly obliged to become a member of the group of prostitutes. Yet this is far from being a new development. The group of writers associated with Gide and the *NRF* were experimenting, during the same pre-1914 years, with novels that contained new forms of awareness. These reinforced the *NRF*'s individualistic worldview, whereas in Philippe's work they indicate the presence of different social groups. The parallel development remains a sign of "contamination:" the anti-political cannot develop its own aesthetic and it is contaminated by the dominant literature.

It does not follow a logical much less a Hegelian order. *Bubu* (1901) draws the conclusion from *Le Père Perdrix* (1902). The novel no longer wishes to be accepted as reality but rather to suggest that there are several kinds of reality. Language is not authoritarian and it is not fixed. Philippe does not always use slang for Bubu because that would attribute to class warfare a coherence it does not possess. Such mobility masks the repetition and parody that stem from the anti-political worldview. This kind of writing is not simple, even if Philippe cultivates simplicity—short sentences and few subordinate clauses.

The blend of sophistication and simplicity is often jarring to the modern reader, but the pre-1914 reader was more tolerant of the attempt to allow the people to speak. Philippe returns to his familiar themes of work, non-work, consumption and language in his best novel, *Croquignole*. The reader sees the various stages in the discourse of consumption: consumption as transgression, the superiority of the feasts of the poor over the feasts of the rich, the link with non-work, the role of the prostitute and the temptation for the class that was born to work. Consumption is an inauthentic form of revolt or of evasion, but the gamble of this novel is that it can—for a while—present itself as authentic because it is endowed with its own values: the body, eroticism, the spoken word and humor.

Why does one work? To earn money so that one may live. It follows that the aim of the alienated worker is to sever the link between work and spending and then between spending in order to live and spending on what is unnecessary. Similarly money must not be saved because the cycle of saving-investing creates still more work. To break this cycle, which is at the heart of capitalism, money must be spent, and it is better that it be inherited and not earned and that it be wasted. The notion that luxury goods and expensive restaurants provide jobs for the poor is absent from the novel, although Philippe affirms that human relations are based on power in fine restaurants as in offices.

The first paragraph of the novel describes the contrast between the office, which resembles a prison, and the street, full of apparently free bodies. Next the narrator moves to Croquignole's feast in the country, where eating is merged with nature as the sun shines into the restaurant and as Croquignole and Félicien go for a boat ride, which is an immersion in the feminine nature of the Marne. This seems a real revolt even if Paulat has refused to come, if the servility of the waiter reminds one that this is a bourgeois world and if Claude has brought his double—once more the novel is threatened by disintegration—the peasant, Jean Morentin, who has only once in his life eaten as much bread as he wanted. By creating Jean Morentin, Claude has set Croquignole a challenge.

Croquignole responds by moving to new ground. If consumption is so heretical, then the consumption of women will be important and it will be symbolized by the reign of the prostitute. Convinced that beauty can be bought and sold, Madame Fernande buys creams, clothes and hats. She transforms herself into the kind of woman men like. She then sells her body, advises Angèle to do the same and stays with Croquignole until his money runs out. She does not work and by giving up control over her body, she gains control over her mind. One trait of Madame Fernand deserves a mention: she too believes in anti-politics: there are the rich and the poor as there have always been; she is the most lucid character.

In this context Angèle's suicide does not come about simply because she has been unfaithful to Claude or because Croquignole has seduced her. She is tired of Claude's often repeated thesis that she and he have much in common because they are workers. Tempted by the couple Madame Fernande-Croquignole, Angèle should, logically, go ahead and become a prostitute. But she does not because of her traditional sense of morality. She and Madame Fernande join our list of interesting female characters created by male authors who are unable to follow them beyond a certain point.

By contrast the erotic motif is developed in *Croquignole* and it is primarily oral. The man smells, licks and devours the woman. Croquignole wants a woman's body that is all round and warm like a brioche. Even now the hunger of the past is not forgotten.

The theme that enables us best to appreciate the triumphs and limits of Croquignole's revolt is the theme of language. These men are white-collar workers who earn a living with their pens. Their written pages are, however, work-writing; often they copy out documents so what they write is not really theirs; they are neither écrivains nor écrivant. Paulat symbolizes their plight: he adds to his copies a personal writing that consists solely in naming common objects whose name is already well known: on a pen box he writes "Pen box (in use)."[12] Paulat has no language of his own, only the language of the office. Naturally he cannot maintain it and, after copying a few pages, he gives up. The others understand his plight: he is like "l'administration." To the silence of the authorities, he answers with a silence of his own. Master and slave meet in the alienating work of governance and copying.

Croquignole's task is to break this silence and he succeeds by his conversation, which is rich in verbal fantasy. To him talking is like eating or spending money. His words animate the novel, but it transcribes his spoken words. When his money runs out he loses his ability to talk and he starts to write. But all he can write is a suicide note. In Félicien's view Croquignole was a better orator than writer. As if to emphasize Croquignole's linguistic defeat, Philippe briefly notes his suicide, using his correct name, never before mentioned, and the anonymous language of the newspaper: "a certain Aristide Buffières had killed himself with a bullet to his head."[13] The pluperfect tense makes the act more definitive.

One remembers Gellner's view of the written language as the basis of the state. The anti-politics of Phillipe cannot create a different social order. The humor, energy and verbal skills of Croquignole are not enough, neither are the ability, loyalty and moral sense of Jean Boussac. Another way of interpreting Félicien's judgment is to say that Philippe succeeds where Croquignole fails. Philippe, who worked for the city government of Paris, often uses its official paper, headed Ville de Paris, to write his novels. This marks the imposition of his language on the language of governance.

Philippe succeeds not in creating a new literature but in producing a series of contaminated novels on the fringes of the *NRF.* One might argue this implies that class differences are not fundamental in our societies.

Philippe's achievement is reformist or social democratic and the hard core of class in which he believed is unreal. He might have accomplished something more and different if he had not died in 1909 at the early age of 35. Later working-class writers—Louis Guilloux is the best example from the inter-war period—tackled similar problems and, while they tried to avoid sentimentality and pseudo-simplicity, they fare no better than Philippe. If he has had less recognition than he merits, the reasons lie in the sentimental note and our hasty judgment on the pre-1914 years that leads to the underestimation of many of its writers—Larbaud, Léon-Paul Fargue, who belonged to the Carnetin group and others.

La Mère et l'enfant, the only book by Philippe that is readily available in a relatively cheap edition, holds our interest as a critique of the Republic and its education system. The myth of the Republican school pervades *Le Grand Meaulnes.* Alain-Fournier, who was a friend and admirer of Marguerite Audoux, at first contrasts the school and the Domaine Inconnu, although the strict discipline and hard work of the elementary school are absent from the novel. Insidiously the school makes its way through the novel: the narrator becomes a schoolteacher, Meaulnes lives in a building that used to house a school and his beloved Yvonne des Galais dreams of becoming a schoolteacher. This last allusion directly links the school with the dream world of beauty and innocence. It consecrates the Republican school just as Philippe derides it.

A brief note on Gramsci

From this we may see how Philippe does not fit the Gramscian category of populism. Although he was in favor of freedom for the writer to set down on paper what he saw, Gramsci believed that the writer's vision was backward because he depicted the worker-peasant as s/he was at the time: blinded by bourgeois ideology. The Party, however, also saw her/him as s/he would be in the future socialist society. This was a more complete vision. Since Philippe did not believe in a future that was radically different, the varied depictions of the working-class that he gave in his novels were all there was. This was another aspect of his anti-political stance.

Gramsci's view had, however, at least two merits: his vision of the working-class was not the simplified vision of socialist realism and he maintained—in a critical observation on Paul Nizan—that, since one could not anticipate the forms the class struggle would take, it was vain to commend certain novelists as more progressive than others. A new literature "must necessarily manifest itself in relatively hybrid and different combinations."[14]

Gramsci demanded something else of the writer: that he not limit himself to depicting peasants in rural smocks dancing around maypoles, but that the reader should see them toiling in the fields. The reader should also see workers at the conveyor belts of factories.

After the Liberation Gramsci's work was gradually and carefully diffused by Togliatti through his "new" PCI and among non-communist intellectuals. It helped produce the neo-realist cinema: the depiction of Italian and not Hollywoodian life, broad social themes and an emphasis on anti-fascism, the resistance and the working-class. An example would be Visconti's *La terra trema*. In the novel neo-realism meant depicting the lives and especially the work of peasants, fishermen and the like.

A good example is Franco Solinas's *Squarcio*, set in the very poor fishing community living on or near the island of La Maddalena, which is just off the coast of Sardinia. The hero, nicknamed Squarcio or "The Ripper," stands in an ambiguous relationship to his community. When he is young, his father dies, his brothers all flee and he alone stays to look after the mother. He fishes with explosives so he is not liked by the net-fishermen or by the police. Yet Squarcio marries happily, has four children and loyal friends. It is not fanciful to see in him the ambiguity of an Italian working-class that is all too accustomed to seeing justice used against the have-nots. There is a touch of the bandit in Squarcio, who fishes where he pleases. There is also a touch of the hero in the way he fights for his family, defying the police and his neighbors. He shows a modern side: he is the only fisherman to install a motor in his boat. At the end he dies, the victim of a simple accident with the explosives, but one that is also the logical conclusion of his way of fishing. Solinas has written a good novel because Squarcio is a man who reacts boldly against the hardships that are imposed on the poor.[15]

Populism lapsed into long, almost plotless accounts of a worker presented as typical of his generation or city. This kind of book reached its climax in Vasco Pratolini's *Metello*. The *Metello* controversy dragged on all through the mid-1950s. Pratolini, who translated Philippe into Italian, wrote the story of a Florence worker whose life has a structure that it receives from his participation in the long march toward socialism. According to Franco Fortini, Pratolini took no account of the post-war dynamism of Italian capitalism, of the defeats suffered by the PCI or of the rise of mass culture.[16] Gramscian populism was associated with Liberation hopes of radical change to be achieved by the whole nation guided by the Resistance and the PCI. This did not take place and the novels that took account of defeat were Pasolini's *Ragazzi di vita* and *Una vita violenta*, which depict the Rome subproletariat left out by modernization. These novels, especially the first, displeased the PCI because they depicted non-workers with no trace of that awareness that Marx attributes to the working-class.

So the political development of Italy was like Britain in that it disappointed many people on the left, even as it integrated the working-class, albeit to a lesser extent than in Britain. The PCI provided writers with a more formidable army than the Labour Party, although Labour came to power whereas the PCI remained illegitimate. It helped produce as early as the 1940s a combative "committed" culture, but there is no real equivalent of Silitoe or Braine in the 1950s. The theme is discussed again and again in the PCI magazine, *Il Contemperaneo*, in Fortini's *Ragionamenti* and in the new series of *Officina*, founded by Pasolini and his Bologna friends. The integration of the proletariat into a modern industrial society is the starting-point of a reflection that produces "ingraismo" and Franco Rodano's "opulent society," as well as Marcuse.

Alan Sillitoe and Harold MacMillan

What remains in Britain of this assortment of concepts from the politico-cultural situation of pre-1914 France and of Gramscian Italy? There is as yet scant knowledge of Gramsci and few parallels to the broad socio-political alliances implicit in populism. Philippe is quite unknown, despite Eliot's preface to the translation of *Bubu*, but his fundamental theme still holds: there is a hard core of workers who cannot be persuaded to take to the barricades but cannot either be bought off with political reforms and consumer goods. This social group exists by what it is not: in this second case it refuses MacMillan's appeal that "you've never had it so good." It follows that the conciliatory forces in society, represented in 1950s Britain by the Conservative Party centrists and the Labour right, are doomed not to realize their vision of a fluid, mobile society. The value of work, which is one of the keys to an advanced economy, is undermined. Again, aside from orgies of consumerism, which resemble *potlach* but may also be seen as a parody of Keynesian economics, this working-class offers no new set of values or political vision. In Alan Sillitoe's *Saturday Night and Sunday Morning* it is just there. In the *Loneliness of the Long Distance Runner* it speaks—or rather writes—that it is still there.

There are parallels too in the historical situation. The Second World War had pushed Britain to the left, as it had France and Italy. The working-class may have welcomed Churchill as a wartime leader but the real object of their admiration was Ernest Bevin and in peacetime they wanted to be ruled by the Labour Party. The thought of Keynes and Beveridge became orthodoxy during the war and the creation of the Welfare State had broad support. Like the French peasantry under the Third Republic, the working-class received privileged treatment. But like the Third Republic, the post-war Labour government was cautious in its social policy and mildly reformist, but certainly not revolutionary. This led to the protest of Labour's left-wing and to a sense of frustration with what Sillitoe describes in his autobiography as a miasma of falsity. Just as Philippe's characters say the Republic is not serious, so some young people, often first generation university graduates, often intellectuals, expressed their bewilderment that society was not moving as they had hoped. How many people came into this category is impossible to tell but they represented a "zone"[17] of the reading public and they extended a warm welcome to Jimmy Porter, their spokesman (not spokesperson, for no women need apply) in Osborne's *Look Back in Anger*.

The reader who bought the paperback edition of *Saturday Night and Sunday Morning* (1960, first edition 1958) was told on the cover that it was a novel about the working-class. This meant it would be raw and uninhibited, devoid of the cultural subtleties that novels about other social classes displayed. But the reader was also told he was buying a literary novel that would expand on the innovations of John Braine's *Room at the Top*. This meant that it would depict the working-classes as if they were the main social protagonist and that the world would be reconstructed as they saw it or as some of them saw it. There would be neither deference for the upper-classes nor attempts to hide class conflict. This was a literature, like *Bubu de Montparnasse,* that made such conflicts more important and that demythologized notions of reformism or gradualism. It was not, however, confident of change as the Liberation mood had been in Italy.

The understanding that the working-class possessed was limited. It knew that relations between foreman and workers were based on hostility even if both sides often pretended they were not. The working-class's knowledge was directly linked with its own experience, which was rich in social clashes but vague on their economic causes. Arthur, the hero of *Saturday,* knows that, in the period since the Second World War ended, the bicycle industry in Nottingham has flourished and has provided his generation of workers with jobs, wages that Arthur considers high, and the freedom that comes from the absence of want. Arthur knows that before the war the bicycle industry did much less well but he has no idea why. He is untouched by Marxist analyses of a new phase of capitalism, where the state is drawn into the productive process, as well as by orthodox views on the folly of returning to the gold standard and by Keynesian beliefs in counter-cyclical investment.

Arthur is a piece-worker with a rate that is comfortably low. Yet, although piece-rates were decided by collective bargaining, Arthur has no use for trade unions. He describes one: "the big-headed bastard that gets my goat when he asks me to go to union meetings."[18] Arthur has equally little use for the social workers who run the welfare state. (In this he anticipates Ken Loach.) Indeed he is opposed to the collectivism that inspired the 1945 Labour Party. The closest Arthur comes to politics is when Sillitoe cites him as a member of "anarchistic Labour."[19] But this is at best anachronistic, for by 1958 Labour was settling into a rather unhappy center-left stance. It forgot, under Hugh Gaitskill and a compromising Aneurin Bevan, its promises of radical change. But Arthur does not want radical change; he wants to be a rebel under the existing system.

This was also the period when the Conservatives flaunted their claim to working-class votes because of their success in modernizing the economy. MacMillan's famous slogan "you've never had it so good" runs implicitly through *Saturday,* as Arthur reflects on his good fortune. When they returned to power in 1951 the Conservatives felt they had to yield ground to the powerful working-class and to its strong trade unions. In the eyes of future prime minister Margaret Thatcher, the Conservative governments from 1951 to 1964 wasted resources on consumption and neglected productive investment. But the Conservatives were traumatized by their defeat in 1945. They knew that the country blamed them for the Depression and they considered that unemployment was the worst of evils, while inflation was to be preferred, although it caused a run on sterling and displeased the City of London. The state intervened whenever unemployment approached 3 percent, but, having reflated the economy, it was obliged reluctantly to intervene again and raise interest rates to bring down inflation. This stop-go strategy helped create a business community that had no trust in long-term investment. Growth in the Britain of the 1950s ran much lower than in Germany or Italy.

MacMillan, who came to power after the Suez fiasco (1956), which Sillitoe supported, restored the confidence of the bewildered and despairing Conservative Party. In reality MacMillan was shy, hated emotional scenes and the rough side of politics—muckraking journalists and colleagues who had to be fired. But he disguised these traits behind an Edwardian style that was flamboyant and ironic and behind an ability to dominate cabinet and parliament. He had a theatrical strain that may have inspired John Osborne's character Archie Rice in *The Entertainer*. He was born into a middle-class publishing family but married (unhappily) into the Devonshires, a grand aristocratic family allied with the Cecils.

In 1956 he gave priority to re-establishing the special relationship with the United States and then tried to solve the growth problem by entering the European Community, which Britain had snubbed when it was first proposed. MacMillan was a profoundly ambiguous figure. Before the war he had been a Keynesian and, as the member of parliament for Stockton in the industrial north, he favored state intervention in the economy. After the war he was a curious blend of old and new. New in understanding that Britain no longer had the strength to play a world role, old in that he was determined to play such a role via the special relationship with the United States. Old in his lack of enthusiasm for Europe, new in his understanding that Britain could no longer stay aloof from Europe. He did not possess de Gaulle's vision of a revived country strong enough to defend itself and shape its own future.

The early years of his premiership were successful: he won the 1959 elections with his slogan that was, like everything else about him, both true and false. Then things started to go wrong: in 1962–63 his government was dragged through the Profumo affair, which involved very minor breaches of security but photogenic call girls like Christine Keeler and a moral carelessness that the fastidious, puritanical MacMillan hated. In January 1963 de Gaulle vetoed Britain's application to join the EC. Suddenly MacMillan seemed old, his Edwardianism anachronistic and his verbal skills useless. In late 1963 he was hospitalized and resigned.[20]

MacMillan's historical importance is that he understood Britain's postwar situation and tried to find a solution that would keep his England intact. He is the exact opponent and counterpart for Sillitoe's heroes. He presided over the prosperity they enjoy but that does not appease them. His social and economic policies were paternalistic, like those of the Borstal director in *Loneliness*. Despite Arthur's contempt for trade unions one could argue that his sexual mores and aggressive temperament were typical of the forces MacMillan had to face. Conversely MacMillan's theatricality hid a void, which the narrator of *Loneliness* sees behind the banalities of the prison director. MacMillan's mixture of modernity and Edwardianism is akin to Sillitoe's heroes, who are simultaneously living in the boom of the 1950s and in the inter-war Depression. MacMillan's literary taste did not lead him to Sillitoe or Braine. He preferred Trollope and Jane Austen. His language is the antithesis of Arthur's—polished, rhetorical, with a flair for the happy phrase—"little local difficulties" were how he described the resignation of his three top ministers in the key area of finance.

The Entertainer, first performed in 1957, bears the marks of Suez. Mick, Archie's son, has been captured by a group of people who are known only as the "wogs." They also look forward to the "wind of change," another happy phrase invented to indicate the decolonization MacMillan would undertake. Mick's death is a proof that British greatness cannot, as the Conservatives hoped, be maintained. Archie Rice's brand of theater, based on the music hall, is also dying out. In one of his turns

Archie makes fun of the exploitation of the Second World War victory. Flanked by a large nude Britannia, he sings a song that parodies Churchill's most quoted speech: "For this was their greatest shower." Osborne, however, writes an introductory note to express his regret for the death of music hall: "Some of the heart of England has gone; something that once belonged to everyone, for this was truly a folk art."[21] The nostalgia for a working-class past turns up everywhere in this writing—in John Braine's sense of a lost innocence—and it offers a parallel with Philippe's sense of a time when the Republic was serious.

As a character Archie drinks and laments—"We're drunks, maniacs, we're crazy, we're bonkers, we're characters out of something that nobody believes in."[22] He cannot keep his theater going, but he will not give up. Aside from the parallels with MacMillan, this play remains full of life today.

The same cannot be said for *Look Back in Anger*. Its title emphasizes the peculiar nature of the 1950s: that it was a period when the working-class advanced but was also aware that it had been more radical in the past. Jimmy Porter is constantly harking back: to his father, who fought in the Spanish Civil War; according to Helena "he thinks he is still in the middle of the French Revolution"; and, according to Allison, he thinks he is an "Eminent Victorian."[23] The only person who can sympathize with him is Allison's father, who was a soldier in India from 1914 to 1947. It is hardly necessary to dwell on MacMillan's Edwardianism. Jimmy Porter is turned toward the past in his personal life, too: he runs a sweet-shop and his marriage to Allison contains a good dose of infantilism.

Politics, either of the revolutionary or reformist brand, means little to Jimmy, as is evident from the way he reads the Sunday newspapers. If this is a sign of "anti-politics," it is also accompanied by a strong sense of class. Jimmy is loyal to Cliff as well as to Hugh's mother because both are uncomplicatedly proletarian and he is hostile to Allison's middle-class family and friends. This enmity is Jimmy's dominant trait and it inspires some of his song-and-dance acts—such as "We'll send our kids to public school/And live off bread and marge."[24]

But his sense of being working-class is inseparable from a sense of being a victim. Identification with a class that has no sense of moving toward hegemony involves suffering. In the absence of political action, Jimmy seeks relief from suffering by bullying his own victims—Allison and Helena. The anti-political theme thus becomes a sadomasochistic game that quickly turns serious. The contemporary theatergoer has also been shaped by the women's movement and s/he is more likely to see Jimmy as a tyrant than as either a rebel or a victim. Osborne invites such an interpretation by having both Allison and Helena wear one of Jimmy's shirts while they do the ironing and Jimmy reads the Sunday papers and abuses them. This theatergoer is not likely to be mollified by Jimmy's evident fear of middle-class women or by his ability to attract them through his vulnerability. It is fitting that his child should die during Allison's pregnancy and that he should re-launch their marriage with an appeal to their old infantilism.

As in Philippe, there is not much development in the play where the Helena period is a variant on the initial Allison period. *Look Back in Anger* is a contaminated version of the traditional family drama in which the usual hates, grievances and alliances are explained by class instead of by individual psychology. Moreover the audience of the 1950s was prepared to see the justice of Jimmy's grievances and the novelty of such a character. Arthur Sillitoe, a severe judge, writes that "to me it was a revelation to see people like Jimmy Porter shown on the stage at last."[25]

In *Room at the Top* (1957), class is not a complex matter. The ruling elite in the North of England town of Warley makes no attempt to deny that it is nouveau-riche. As in *Croquignole*, a man's importance is measured by what he can afford to buy. This is the North of England, where the textile industry continues to create wealth, and the subtle way that the pre-capitalist ruling class absorbed the new industrialists in the mid-Victorian period is something that happened a long way away in Southern England.

The working-class is emerging from poverty. The hero, Joe Lampton, comes from a town that had an unemployment rate of 75 percent during the Depression. Wages are still low compared with Sillitoe's Nottingham. But there is a new generation of young men rising from the working-class and acquiring white-collar jobs. Joe Lampton used the three years he spent in a German prisoner of war camp to qualify as an accountant. Clearly he did not share the Churchillian view of the Second World War. For the struggle among nation-states and for anti-fascism he substitutes the class struggle: "The rich were my enemies, I felt they were watching me for the first false move."[26]

Class is a matter of possessing objects. Braine describes lots of things and pays great attention to their value. He gives the price of a pint of beer in a pub and the price of a double-whisky. When he first moves to Warley, Joe is delighted to be living in a district littered with expensive cars. Braine describes wallpaper, house-paint and various kinds of dressing gowns.

Seeing all these things is a mere prerequisite to possessing them. The way to the top does not lie via work, better qualifications and changing jobs but rather via a rich marriage. Women are depicted as toys that, once wound up, seduce and are seduced. Male sexuality is a form of ambition: Joe seduces a rich man's daughter, makes her pregnant and is accepted as a son-in-law. Indeed the key conversation is between Joe and Susan's father, who form an uneasy alliance because women have no place in business decisions and because Mr. Brown is able to recognize Joe as a man of talent. Mr. Brown demands and obtains the sacrifice of another woman, Joe's mistress, who conveniently kills herself in despair when Joe tells her—as Mr. Brown insists—that he is leaving her.

The interesting trait of this novel is what is left out. Or rather what is mentioned and quickly dismissed: nature, friendships, hobbies, free time, foreign countries, English traditions, women's tenderness and intelligence. Joe sacrifices them all to his overwhelming ambition, which is the product of the British class struggle but represents no collective solution. Joe will deal with Mr. Brown's workers as Mr. Brown does. In the process of acquiring Susan Brown, Joe consciously loses his innocence, but there was not much innocence and the pain of loss was not great.

Class is a more complex issue in Kingsley Amis's *Lucky Jim* (1954). The hero, Jim Dixon, went to grammar-school rather than to public, that is, private school; he spent the war as a corporal, before becoming a university teacher of history, a job he detests all the more because he is burdened with the medieval period. He is blunt in his dislike of the cultural circle of the provincial northern city, which claims to enjoy classical music, modern painting and lots of other things about which it is pretentious and Dixon is scathing. At first sight this seems the clash between an ambitious working-class intellectual and a sterile brand of middle-class culture. But complexity is introduced by Gore-Urquhart and his niece, Christine, who represent genuine culture and wealth.

If one reads the novel as a competition for Gore-Urquhart's goodwill, then Dixon wins out. Fired by his useless professor Welch, he is offered a job as Gore-Urquhart's secretary-collaborator. Similarly he takes Christine away from Welch's son. This vision of society based on a rich upper-class that can be trusted to act honestly and to recognize working-class merit and the critique of petty-bourgeois cultural and social pretensions is a model of conservative thought. It hesitates between an establishment and individual initiative, between the two poles of Tory-Conservativism and Liberal-Conservatism. Private philanthropy from an enlightened upper-class also replaces massive state intervention.

So there are various readings of *Lucky Jim*. A third and the most popular is to see it as the satire of the red-brick university. Dixon comments on the title of an article he has written for a learned journal. "It was a perfect title in that it crystallized the article's niggling mindlessness, its funereal parade of yawn-enforcing facts, the pseudo-light it threw upon non-problems. Dixon had read, or begun to read, dozens like it, but his own seemed worse than most in its air of being convinced of its own uselessness."[27] This humor would have been enough to ensure the book's success but it also contains a scattered but coherent moral discussion where the virtues of independent thinking, of making up one's own mind and not allowing one's life to be run by so-called superiors or by would-be moral blackmailers, all are stressed. Dixon is helped to free himself of Margaret, and he helps Christine to assert her independence of Bertrand. The Welch family, however, is depicted as a single clan devoted to seizing what it can. Dixon's resistance goes as far as knocking Bertrand down, but he usually uses facial expression—grimaces that exaggerate Welch's, speech that parodies the professor's and a special "Welch song." This use of body-language enlivens the book but it is also part of individual resistance.

Even Dixon's lecture on "Merrie England" is an incoherent protest against mass culture—TV and cinema. *Lucky Jim* does not, like *Room at the Top*, portray a hero who is obviously shaped by his class background before our eyes or whose main character trait is ambition or revenge. By letting Dixon take shape before us, Amis allows him to reveal his lively sense of humor, his battle to overcome his shyness and his preference for pubs over concert halls. The fact of class is presented more lightly. Amis's son, Martin, has declared that the main value in his father's writing is decency.

Nor is it exaggerated to cast Dixon as a latent right-winger. Evelyn Waugh saw this clearly. The upwardly mobile grammar-school élite was bound to have right-wing leanings and, although Dixon defends the postwar Labour government against Bertrand, he and his creator belong on the right.

The depiction of women stresses their dependence on men, although it is hard to see where dependence stops and preying starts. Christine is admirable because she is beautiful, because she needs protection and because she is unpretentious. Running through these books is the theme of woman as prize: Susan Brown, Christine, Allison and Helena are all middle-class women who become the prizes as well as the hostages of the working-class warrior. Working-class women fare rather better—Doreen may also be considered a prize but Brenda is her own woman. There is an organic link between this kind of writing and an unfavorable view of women: traditional working-class life, even where it is matriarchal, gives much prestige to man as the bread-winner and hence to male rituals and male bonding. Since the working-class is seen at its toughest, there is less place for the conflicting woman's values of fostering and tenderness. It would take the woman's movement twenty years of toil before Pat Barker could write the story of working-class women. A recent performance of *Look*, directed by Judi Dench, brought cries of fury from the women who saw it.

Driven by ambition, Joe Lampton uses the war and the army. Sillitoe, whose view of national defense is very similar in his novels if not in his life, reacts by instinct, not calculation: his characters desert. When Arthur does his military service, the army puts him into the Military Police because of his height, which does nothing to change his view that life is a matter of "every man for himself."[28]

His model for his dealings with the army are his cousins, Ada's children, with whom he spends more time as the book goes on. They deserted from the army, came back home, were captured and escaped again. Arthur rejects the Cold War with a casual certainty: "'The men at the top' must know that nobody would fight."[29] Arthur never changes in his view of authority and his brand of consumerism; far from integrating him into a modernizing society as MacMillan hoped, take the form of drinking and lead to primitive protest.

Arthur especially dislikes the great 1950s innovation of TV, which he sees as a toy given to the working-classes to turn them away from thinking and acting. Significantly, it is women who want TV. Arthur has reflected on this and his awareness includes a distinction between working-class males who collaborate by accepting the rules imposed by employers and government officials, and those who fight and drink as he does. Women, who marry the former and have affairs with the latter, count as rebels.

Arthur modifies the gender aspect of his awareness to seek out a desirable young woman from the first category, Doreen, to be his wife. Once more the limits placed on female characters by male narrators are considerable. Yet these characters are not spineless: Brenda chooses Arthur as a lover, wearies of him and goes through an abortion voluntarily while he looks on in helpless agreement. (Brenda is brilliantly played in the film by Rachel Roberts.) Her sister, Winnie, fights back vigorously when her husband hits her. Arthur's aunt, Ada, rules like a matriarch over her family.

Nor is the narrator absent from the arena. Phrases like Saturday as a holiday in the "slow-turning Big Wheel of the year" reveal a sophisticated storyteller who adds to ordinary linear time that moves forward a circular time that reinforces Arthur's defiance of the past. Similarly there is a "literary" note about the phrase, that Arthur and Brenda possess "their minuscular coracle of untouchable hope and bliss."[30] The reader will not fail to remember that the coracle was used by Celts who have long since been defeated and have withdrawn from England.

There is a nostalgia for various pasts. On Sunday Arthur persuades a suspicious Doreen to go for a walk in the country. He harks back to rural England because his grandfather had been a blacksmith, who had his own well, his own eggs from chickens he kept and his own potatoes from his garden (all described in Sillitoe's autobiography). This is anarchism of a different kind: born of the sturdy independence of the self-employed craftsman.

Arthur sees no future, however, except working in the factory. This functions along Fordist lines. The workers clock-in, which Marx considered a great innovation because it marked the selling of human time for money. The motors are connected to a central one and Arthur's lathe provides one link in the chain. The various noises echoing through the plant give it a spurious life, so it is not the dehumanized, rational factory of orthodox Fordism. Moreover, although Arthur's work is an integral part of the conveyor belt, the reader sees him mostly alone. His battle is, therefore, less the class struggle of a modern proletariat than a man fighting a living but inhuman enemy.

The Loneliness of the Long Distance Runner, published one year after *Saturday,* shares many of its themes. Here again are the strong feeling of belonging to the working-class and the contradictory sense of loneliness; the MacMillan attitude of benevolent authority and the tempting offer of consumerism. The last is treated differently from the way Philippe handles it in *Croquignole*. There the world contains poverty and luxury but there is no mass consumerism and hence no worry lest spending be a trap. This sense haunts the runner, who notes that the 500 pounds that constitutes his family's windfall is compensation for his father's death. Since the runner's refusal to win the cross-country race is later presented as an act of fidelity to a father who dies of cancer after working all his life in a factory, the 500 pounds are well and truly tainted.

The money is stamped "MacMillan benevolence" by the foreign language with which it is bestowed—"for your bereavement, they said, or words like that."[31] Linguistically alien, the money is transformed into consumer goods. The most important, a large TV, can be enjoyed only once it has been carried across the class barrier. First the advertisements are mocked, then the films have their endings changed so that the cops do not catch the robbers. (The runner dreams of smashing the screen to save the robbers, but in 2000 a TV advertisement in Italy depicts a character in a futuristic crime program who appeals for help to a young spectator. He responds and helps her dispose of a gang of villains. Virtual reality overlaps with ordinary reality but morality is still the triumph of simple good.) The runner learns nothing from TV, whereas he knows what a pterodactyl is because he has heard about it on the radio.

The final act of subverting the TV comes when the runner turns off the sound during a party political broadcast for the Conservatives. Here MacMillan's attempt to integrate a more prosperous working-class is directly ridiculed and linked to the offers of protection made by the Borstal governor.

He personifies the "them" against whom the runner's "us" is waging an eternal war. Sillitoe understands the way the "post-war" is dragged out in

Britain so that the war can be used to project an image of British greatness that has survived into the present. This too is subverted by the runner, who depicts the class war as the only real war and compares the detective with Hitler. As in *Saturday,* his cousins have all deserted from the army. Here too class is a fixed entity and *Loneliness* specifically rejects reformism. Winning the race would be a sign that the narrator accepted it, but he knows, by instinct and experience rather than by reason, that class warfare is "how it will always stand."[32]

In his autobiography Sillitoe denies explicitly and at some length that he was aware of class and also that he should be lumped together with other "Angry Young Men." Sillitoe, whose autobiography depicts a childhood of real hardship, lived his life as an individual and as a writer. Most of *Saturday* was written in Majorca, where the young Sillitoe was living cheaply while serving his apprenticeship as a writer. Yet in a sharp criticism of Britain he also writes that "the complacent upper few percent" impose their values on the people. Included in this élite are "socialists and left-wingers."[33] The real country is still to be revealed.

The runner would agree. Here again his father's example is important. The father was a communist who fought at the end of his life against doctors. They work for the established state, whereas he trusts only a herbster who lives within the working-class community. Yet the father is seen dying on his own and the theme of individualism is strong in the book. The narrator's "mates" play a very secondary role: Mike does not go to Borstal for the robbery, we know little about the other boys held there and the hero enjoys running because it leaves him free to think for himself.

Unlike Arthur, the runner has no sense of a modern, conveyor-belt factory or of working as one of a team. Like Arthur, he has a feeling for the countryside, "for the good, dry soil that at least would never do you a bad turn."[34] This time the negative traits of women are accentuated: his mother is openly unfaithful to his father and, while the runner praises the working-class skill with which she copes with the police, she inspires in him a contempt for her gender. The words "whore" and "tart" are scattered liberally through the text.

The runner's revolt is deeper and more problematic than Arthur's because he is less able to exploit the system by earning high wages and because he affronts it directly by theft. The way the tale is told is also more complex. The runner writes it as a kind of journal or diary. The problem of using this form with a narrator-character who would not have kept a journal is faced by Camus in *L'Etranger* (Sillitoe was an admirer of Camus) and it is an obvious trap for populist writing. Sillitoe sometimes gives up and lapses into conventional literary jargon; he presents the text as an increase in the runner's awareness and he sees it as the sign of new writing.

In the early pages there are colloquialisms and grammatical mistakes to mark the unconventional storyteller: "them fields" and "kick the bucket" are only two examples. Meanwhile Sillitoe casts the reader among the ranks of the collaborators: "blokes like you or them,"[35] which further sharpens the class conflict. Other sentences simply show how hard it is to avoid the conventions of literature (Barthes would not have sympathized): "that first flying leap out into the frosty grass of an early morning."[36] Sillitoe, however, depicts a hero who is changed by his running and this enables him to use a sophisticated vocabulary or to play with words like "honesty." It enables him too to claim that he is not a realistic writer and thus cannot describe his surroundings.

Clearly there is a problem of whether the runner is more articulate than he could convincingly be. Arthur too developed his own homespun vision of the world. The runner does the same but takes the different step of presenting it with written words. This enables him to criticize the writing of the Governor of the Borstal. Since the Governor has written nothing, this can be only a symbolic act. Still the runner mocks the right-wing *Daily Telegraph,* which the Governor is reading in his office, and also the Governor's use of the language of sport. This is interesting because the Governor takes the view of athletics that in nineteenth-century England and especially in *Tom Brown's Schooldays* is attributed to cricket,[37] namely, that it is part of the British heritage and, far from being a mere game, is an institution where God-fearing people are taught moral values. Already the narrator laughs at such a view.

He is convinced the Governor's language is not worth "what I'm scribbling down."[38] That he represents the excluded is proved by the fact that he is using a stub of pencil rather than a laptop computer. How does his text get published? Is it via a mate who acts because the narrator has been sent to prison? Or has the mate or another person proved to be unreliable? This second possibility would—like the first—mark a defeat for a youth who has already brooded on suicide. It would also strengthen the theme of loneliness.

Either way the runner's role as storyteller is reinforced. Here again literature lies in wait and when the runner claims that his story is superior because he has "more fun and fire"[39] in his life than the Governor does, he is indulging in bad literature and ignoring that a good book is made with words. But in proposing the runner's tale as a critique of an archetypal MacMillan story of a working-class that makes steady progress under the guidance of a wise ruling-class in a great nation, Sillitoe is, in a simple manner, doing precisely what the language of literature is supposed to do. He is criticizing the language of authority.

If time permitted and our knowledge were greater, we could find many parallels to Sillitoe and Osborne in popular culture. Tony Hancock is only one name to come to mind. In his radio and TV programs Hancock plays the part of the small man who has an exalted view of himself, who talks much about the war, who appears never to doubt British greatness but constantly belies it, and who is faced with the resolutely proletarian Sid James. The Beatles' early songs also belong to this period. They are set in the context of a working-class Liverpool, the Beatles retain their accents and there is an element of emancipation in the treatment of love and sex. There is also less male superiority than in the Rolling Stones, who made a cult of seduction.

Much of the writing discussed above has not lasted. One might also claim that these are not the great writers of the 1950s but that Graham Greene, Evelyn Waugh and Lawrence Durrell are better and different. But Sillitoe and the others are created by and in turn fix a certain moment in working-class history. Not that they are historians, anymore than Philippe was. But they chronicle the malaise, anger and ambition of a working-class that is changing but is suspicious of change.

In 1960 Harold Pinter's *The Room* was put on at the Hampstead Theatre Club. Here the language was subtle and change was, superficially, much smaller. Pinter, a lover of cricket, demonstrated how deeply language is present in people's lives. Rose, who may have moved up from the basement, has, because of the room, a fragile grasp on a social and personal identity. As if to convince herself, she affirms, "I mean you know where you are," where the switch of personal pronouns between her mental activity and the content of that activity reinforces the fragility. Her doubts about herself as subject are indicated by three, uncertain impersonal phrases: "It's quiet. Be coming on for dark. There's no-one about."[40] The room has a strong existence for Rose—it becomes the subject in "this room's allright" and "the room keeps warm."

So the slightest threat to the room troubles Rose. From the dogmatic "this room is occupied" to the arrival from the basement of the blind Riley, her language grows more vulgar: "You're a blind man . . . Can't see a dickeybird" and "Spit it out." Rose has also to weather an attack on her name: firstly her name is bandied about, so she believes by the other characters; then Riley calls her "Sal" when he appeals to her to "come home." This completes Rose's disintegration and, when her hitherto silent truck-driver husband, tells macho tales about his driving and continues them by beating up and killing Riley, Rose goes blind in his place.

The Room, like most of Pinter's plays, can be interpreted on many levels. The trait that concerns us here—the fact of Riley's being black will be discussed later—is the way a character is defined by her/his words and the way that subtle shifts of language change that definition. The identities are social as well as personal: Rose is a good representative of the lower-middle-classes. So language shapes and is shaped by social groups and the "écrivain's" job is to unravel the skein of words, making the viewer brood on an occasional subjunctive or a personal pronoun that reveal hidden traits. This kind of writing was better suited to the Britain of post–Harold MacMillan, where politics was changing shape.

A Chat about *Riff-Raff*

Ken Loach has been making films about the working-class for a long time. He did *Poor Cow* (1967), which recounts the story of a young working-class woman and her men who keep ending up in jail. It is delightful entertainment, but the heroine, played by the late Carole White, is too pretty and too pleased with the power she exercises over men to suffer hardship convincingly. Had she been able to express how badly her admirers actually treat her, *Poor Cow* might have been the first widely seen feminist film.

In 1969 Loach made *Kes*, a tougher and better film. It depicts a working-class boy who catches, trains and cares passionately about a kestrel. The kestrel is the only creature of grace and beauty in Billy's life. His father has left home, his mother has little time for him and his elder brother bullies him. The brother is a coalminer and Billy, who is about to leave school, has no illusions about what awaits him in the world of work. He is, however, determined not to go down a coalmine. Since the film was made one year after the May Events and in the same year as Italy's hot Autumn, one might expect a touch of political radicalism. But Loach, while he holds leftwing views, is determined not to let them get in the way of his attempt to depict the working-class from his disenchanted viewpoint. So Billy lives on a housing estate that is viewed badly by the rest of Barnsley.

Like the writers discussed in this chapter, Loach knocks down the notions of gradualism and reformism and emphasizes the alienation of poverty. The Labour Party returned to power in 1964, but people's hopes were briefly raised and then "very quickly shattered."[41] Once again the mixture of change and of failure to change helps create this vision of a stubborn working-class. Loach's father was a skilled worker, an electrician, and Loach went to Oxford, where he studied very little law and acted a great deal. He also read John Osborne and Bert Brecht.

Meanwhile Billy undergoes more bullying in school; soccer is debunked via a gym teacher who uses the pupils' soccer games to live out his fantasy of playing for Manchester United. The headmaster tells them that the generation of the 1930s went through worse hardships and had more courage and life, whereas "yours is the generation that never listens" and is "mere fodder for the mass media."

In 1969 this would have been quite a fashionable insult, but the only role the media plays in Billy's life is his paper round. To the man from the employment office, Billy listens with impatient indifference and notes only that when he gets a job, "I'll be paid for not liking it," whereas he attends school for nothing. When asked to talk about his ambitions, he cannot tell a story about himself. This is one of Loach's many unfavorable depictions of the people who run the welfare state. But Billy's inability to recount himself shows a silence born of alienation that is broken only when he uses language as a defensive tactic to avert bullying or as an instrument to obtain something he wants.

His only venture into language-as-creating-an-identity comes when he has Kes on his arm and is talking to the one sympathetic schoolteacher. He describes vividly Kes's flights and we have already seen him run around the field while the bird soars and dips. This is the only time he is not running to school or his paper round or else running away from bullies. In this conversation he explains what he admires most in the bird: its autonomy—it thinks it is doing him a favor by letting him admire its flight.

These few words tell us much of the story that Billy could or would not tell the employment official. The strong desire for liberty and affection come through by this circuitous route. Naturally Billy's brother kills the kestrel. At the end of the film we see Billy take the corpse from the dustbin and dig a grave for it in a scene that remains moving however often one sees it. Loach has a deep sense of the wasted richness of working-class people.

He went on making films while the working-class disintegrated around him. In 1992 he made *Riff-Raff* about a group of construction workers trying to survive in Thatcher's London. This won him a wider audience and launched him on a series of films, one supporting the Nicaraguan revolution, another about the Spanish Civil War seen from the anarchists' viewpoint, another castigating the bureaucracy that runs the welfare state. The 1990s had been a good decade for Loach, whose works were banned or shown as little as possible in the 1980s, the great decade of Thatcher and of "her catastrophic project of revitalizing the economy... by attacking the working-class."[42]

The talented Loach of the 1990s cannot very easily be set in the historical framework used in this chapter. When left-wingers in Europe were energetically defending the Welfare State against the neo-liberal assault, Loach revived an old quarrel between the well-meaning but power-seeking social workers and their clients, the supposedly shiftless, irresponsible working-class. Similarly Loach's success with *Riff-Raff* came some ten years after the working-class was defeated in a series of strikes in the early

1980s—the British coalminers in 1984, the Fiat workers in 1980, a cluster of French unions in 1983–84. Loach's film on the coalminers' strike, *Which Side Are You On?*, which left no doubt, unlike Phillipe's and Sillitoe's, which side he was on, was boycotted, like his other works. He was living in an age that had lost the impetus to change when the very concept of change meant something unfamiliar and disruptive.

Loach seems to have been able to find the money and the support for the expensive operation of making even low-budget films—*Riff-Raff* cost £750,000 and took up a mere 5 weeks—because of a (residual?) belief held in institutions, like the British television networks, that culture should be a critical force. The success of Loach's films comes from their depiction of a working-class that is on the defensive and expends all its energy and talent on survival: this is, so I shall argue, the main theme of *Riff-Raff*.

Visually the film is dominated by the scaffolding that the gang of construction workers has erected in order to transform a hospital into a block of luxury flats. The boom in the London property market was not what Thatcher and Lawson had intended, although arguably it was the result of their arrogance. The generous budget of 1988 triggered not inflation-free growth, but high inflation and property speculation. The banks lent a lot of money to home-buyers and got into trouble.

Construction companies, never the most gentle of employers, scoured London for labor, non-unionized and willing to work without the protection of the safety code. The free movement of labor had been a great Thatcher theme, but it could not be realized, because property values in the provinces, where there was unemployment, were low and a worker could not afford to move to London. So London Transport had busses in its garages that were not in use because it could find no one to drive them. Meanwhile the construction companies widened their search to all of Britain. They found unemployed, unmarried men willing to live in "squats" and work in dangerous situations, like Steve (Robert Carlyle), who came from Glasgow and more recently from prison.

Here already is the starting point of Loach's anti-Thatcher discourse. On the building site, one is first struck by the obscenity, which is part of male bonding. It acquires self-awareness when one of the management team refers to "fucking, foul language." If this unites the workers, they are divided by accent. At the risk of making it hard even for the British viewer to understand, Loach has the workers speak in a variety of geographical accents: Glaswegian and Liverpuddlian, centers of working-class culture, but also Bristol, London, Jamaica and Africa. Thatcher had silenced the working-class by defeating it in strikes, by legislating against trade unions and by letting unemployment rise. Now the working-class talks back in all its irreverent diversity: the Liverpuddlian like a trade unionist, the

Glaswegian like an anarchist. The workers also have graffiti on their side: when the management uses in its official notices "urinate," the graffiti prefer the term "piss."

One's next discovery is how well the workers use language. Someone, tackling a crossword puzzle, asks for a nine-letter word meaning "innocent"; back comes the answer: "ingenuous." The Liverpuddlian, well acted by Ricky Tomlinson, uses statistics and reminds the others that Thatcher won only 41 percent of the vote, which means she had a majority of 59 percent against her. He is calm and logical, but when he presents to management a list of the safety violations on the site, he is fired. He leaves, having figured in one of the film's most comical scenes: he is taking a bath in the show-apartment when a group of veiled Arab women arrive to view the apartment. Their surprise and shock are the revenge of the British working-class on the oil-rich foreigners who have, in alliance with the British upper-classes, taken over some of the most elegant parts of the capital.

It was the Liverpuddlian too who organized support for Susan, the very bad female singer who has an Irish accent and goes to live in a squat, also arranged by Ricky Tomlinson, with Steve. Here we must move from seeing the film as a feast of spoken language—where the mobile phone is a symbol of power that the workers briefly manage to seize and then destroy—to the bleak side of a working-class struggling to survive.

Despite the initial help and her own rendering of a Beatles' song with its comforting refrain "I get by with a little help from my friends," the Irish girl, played by Emer McCourt, is fragile and, when Robert Carlyle has to go back to Glasgow, she has recourse to drugs and is condemned by him on his return as a "junkie." Their relationship breaks up, but one finds it hard to see the responsibility as entirely Susan's. Steve goes back for his mother's funeral but, since he has not kept in touch with her, his family has to send out a radio appeal for him. The cremation ceremony is grotesque as the smoke and grime from the ashes cover the mourners, who are wearing their best clothes.

His mother dead, Steve would appear to need Susan more than ever. Instead he gets rid of this second woman and is implacable when she comes to the building site and wants to speak. This is male territory. Since Susan is the only woman we meet, we cannot help thinking that defending oneself means jettisoning all baggage, especially female.[43]

The long-expected accident duly takes place on the building site, and the victim, a Jamaican who has been planning, despite the mockery of the Africans, to go to Africa in search of his roots, is rushed to the hospital. The bureaucracy at the hospital, suspicious because the Jamaican has more than one name, demands to know Steve's name. The theme of the interfering welfare bureaucracy runs together with the theme that names provide authority with a method of social control.

Steve has the last "word": he sets fire to the building. This simple anarchistic protest is all, so Loach believes, that the working-class can hope for in its weakened state. Steve fades out and the final shot is of the anonymous building in flames. Violence against objects is the correct response to capitalism's casual violence against people. The ending presents it as the response of the working-class rather than of one anarchistic Glaswegian.

In the film the working-class is represented by the gang we have mentioned. Loach uses professional actors, but they had worked on building sites when they were between parts. They therefore know how to handle machinery. This is important to Loach, who divides film directors into those who are concerned with what goes on inside the projector and those more interested in what is happening outside.[44] By this he means the "cinema d'arte," as opposed to his own films, which depict a chunk of society. In Italy Loach prefers the neo-realism of Visconti to the director-centered films of Antonioni.

In pursuit of accuracy Loach allows great freedom to the actors, who are encouraged to invent nicknames and bits of dialogue and to define their own space without paths marked out on the floor for them. Physical freedom is a sign that Loach's characters are not "complete and resolved" but are striving for some understanding of their situation and for the development of a "class-consciousness."[45]

Raining Stones (1993) is a less sophisticated film than *Riff-Raff* but it concentrates entirely on accurate depiction of the working-class and it has one great surprise reserved for the end. It takes place on a shabby housing estate monitored by police helicopters, with unemployment rampant, drug-dealing evident and casual crime endemic. Bruce Jones, who plays Bob Williams, the hero, scrounges a living by adding odd jobs to his dole but, when his van is stolen, he is in trouble. At precisely this moment his daughter is making her first communion. Her dress, veil and first communion breakfast will cost about £150.

Bob is determined she shall have everything, so he borrows money. He falls into the hands of the loan shark–drug dealer and kills him by accident. Now for the surprise: like a good Catholic, Bob heads for the priest, Father Barry, who tells him to steer well clear of the police, that the housing estate is better off without the dead man and that he, Bob, has done no wrong. Father Barry hears Bob's confession and a few days later Bob receives communion along with his daughter. Both sacraments are depicted with the correct ritual and one wonders whether Loach is implying that a popular Catholicism would be a force for working-class protest in Britain or whether Father Barry is an individual radicalized by the housing estate.

Carla's Song (1996) is an attempt to use a non-European revolution, that of the Sandinistas, in order to galvanize the flagging European left. This was common in the 1960s when Sartre, Giangiacomo Feltrinelli and many others used Castro's successful guerrilla war in Cuba. In the 1990s the European situation was far less promising and Loach is too good at depicting the working-class not to know that. The result is that there is little contact between the Glasgow and Nicaraguan segments of the film.

Carla, traumatized by the brutality of the Nicaraguan war, turns up in Glasgow, where she meets George (Robert Carlyle). He represents the anarchistic side of the working-class and manages to get himself sacked from his job as a bus driver. He has, however, his great hour when he absconds with a double-decker bus to take Carla to the Scottish countryside. The episode is visually rich because it juxtaposes the big, empty bus and the small country roads.

George has a woman-friend with whom he breaks up, reinforcing the spectator's view that Loach has a male-dominated vision. George then takes Carla back to Nicaragua. The war between the Left and the Contras is bitter and George gradually realizes he does not want to cope with it. Meanwhile Carla returns to Antonio, by whom she has had a child and who is unable to speak after being tortured. Politically Carla's return makes little sense because the Sandinistas are facing defeat. But, as in *Riff-Raff*, Loach shows how the working-class fights oppression with forms of self—and group—expression. Now Carla will sing Antonio's songs, thus enabling him to emerge from the silence to which the Contras have reduced him.

A sign of the freedom Loach allowed his actresses is Carla's inability to sing well. Loach thought he was hiring an actress-singer but the woman turned out to be an actress-dancer. No matter, Carla dances in Glasgow as in Nicaragua; in both cases she is using body language to resist oppression.

In *Ladybird, Ladybird* (1994), which is a stronger film, Loach takes on an old target—the Social Services. Why do these people act as they do? In their upper echelons class plays a part: they think that proletarian life is brutal and disgusting. The lower echelons take their superiors as a guide and they too believe in the two-parent family with a steady income. Hidden away in the back of their minds is Foucault's drive for power.

Against this sanitized Welfare State stands Crissy Rock, who will have had eight children by the time the film ends. She was taken from her own parents, where her father beats up her mother, and she grew up in a foster-home. Her tremendous vitality, her liking for men especially of minority status and—a favorite Loach trait—the emotion-packed songs she sings in the pubs, make Crissy a problem for the welfare bureaucracy. She takes up with an impeccably nice Paraguayan who has been put on a death list by his government for non-violent opposition. He has the patience to bear with Crissy and he is less macho than Britishers.

The boldness of Loach is masked by the fury of Crissy, by the polite behavior of Vladimir Vega and by the seeming good of the social workers. But this is the Loach who seeks out what is most distinctively working-class about contemporary post-Thatcher Britain and who, having found it, will not lightly let go.

Loach has made other, in our opinion, less good films: *My Name is Joe* (1998), *Land and Freedom* (1995), which harks back to Malraux and Orwell in its treatment of the Spanish Civil War, and *Bread and Roses* (2000), set in the United States and depicting a struggle for union recognition. It emphasizes the hardships that Hispanic illegal immigrants must undergo, via one sister who is forced into prostitution, and their ability to fight back, via the resourceful younger sister. The working-class may be shrinking and changing, although much less in the Third World, but it has found its perhaps last observer-artist in Loach, who chronicles its decline but admires its resistance.

Loach does not, however, admire the left-wing parties that have come to power in the major European countries in the last years of the century. He singles out Blair and D'Alema, but his criticism is directed less at personalities than at their strategy and policies.[46] He denounces the way they came to power by using the traditional methods of social democracy—union support or the promise to retain the social services—and then switched to Thatcherite liberalism. He would doubtless make similar criticism of Jospin and Schröder.

Other film directors have joined him using their own language. In *Aprile* Nanni Moretti is watching a TV talk show in which D'Alema is participating. After long moments of exasperation Moretti yells at the screen: "Say something left-wing, D'Alema, say anything." In the aftermath of the 2001 defeat, Moretti blamed the result on Bertinotti's refusal to come to an agreement with Rutelli. Moretti followed up by denouncing the Centre-Left leaders and declared them incapable of defeating Berlusconi. It matters politically whether or not Moretti was right about this but it is culturally interesting that a few artists still act out political roles.

This shows that the "anti-politique" method of depicting the working-class creates a different working-class from the one shown in committed writing. We must next examine the language of politics and what writers say about it.

Chapter Four

Italian political language and writers who criticize

Man sets out to change the world: such is the goal of politics and of the language that is an indispensable part of it. Dictators like Mussolini do away with dialogue and keep language for themselves. Mussolini made endless speeches and yet what he said had so little meaning for his listeners that his regime may be seen as a twenty-year silence. This silence was greater at Auschwitz and greatest of all in the gas chambers. By contrast contemporary democracies are garrulous and noisy. Since they work by consent, a politician, a party or a government has to convince many social groups that what she/he/it is doing is the best possible solution to their dilemmas. Of course the dangers of a new dictator and a new bout of "rhetorical silence" are still present, but the dangers are slight within the EU.

The EU politician works by sending out information along with specialists like her/himself to explain the issues to the people. These have many chances to register their approval or rejection: elections—local, national and European; referenda; and, most insidious of all, public opinion polls. This does not mean that a healthy dialogue exists between ruler and ruled, for the issues are complex and specialized and the politicians soon learn to simplify and to distort them. One need only look at the reaction to the Irish referendum of June 2001 to see how the EU élite greets democratic opposition. Similarly voters use elections for purposes extraneous to them: the European elections have historically been used as a domestic protest vote. Despite its plethora of words, then, a contemporary democracy is not free of silence. In France the strong franc and the link with the mark are surrounded by silence despite the discussion of them, which is mostly contrived.

Our culture is predominantly scientific and technological but, as Umberto Eco has pointed out, problems like foreign policy and health care are unsuited to scientific discourse, so politics falls back on rhetoric.[1] In my opinion the best way to understand political language is to see it as storytelling. The politician begins with an "I," which is part personal and part constructed (like anyone else's "I"). His aim is to turn the "I" into a "We," which will encompass diverse social groups. As the number of people who believe in his story increases, so he becomes more powerful.

S/he, the followers and the story also become more legitimate. Nowadays the state itself gains legitimacy by bargaining with other states. There are areas of policy that the state used to decide on its own that are now decided by the EU. The member states bargain or negotiate over agricultural prices, steel production and many other things. If the politician and the state bargain well, then they will be invited to bargain again. If not, a different political party or coalition will replace them. Meanwhile people rehash the stories they are told and discuss them with their friends. The line between the political and the non-political is important, in that the political must not be allowed to monopolize the social space, but it is unclear and unobserved. Television ignores the distinction and puts politicians on talk shows. They themselves welcome this, although it is a new development. It is hard to imagine de Gaulle in a talk show.

Meanwhile the stories get tangled up with other, often older stories. Religion provides a great stock of stories for politics: in 1916 the Irish nationalists turned Easter into a feast of rebellion; the Blair government replied eighty-two years later by turning Good Friday into a feast of reconciliation. Stendhal, Balzac and Hugo created a Napoleon who was quite different from the "real" Napoleon, that is, the Napoleon of existing political stories.

The political story seeks, however, to be exclusive. It wants to lead the reader-listener from his starting point at A to point B. It does not want her/him lingering around point C, which is the capital of a different political movement, or point D, which is the center of protest and abstention.

One of the themes of political language is to project the ideal, that the politician or party claims to represent, as an ideal community. Hence the Italian Christian Democrats describe the communion of the faithful, while the left's favorite word is solidarity. So the story the PCI tells about itself is also a story about the future socialist society.

Finally the political story has bits missing. These constitute the unsaid and they are made up of things that the politician or party does not know. There are words that she/he/it prefers not to speak but that is a simple cover-up. If one calls culture the knowledge that a party has, its experience in government as in opposition and the groups it represents as well as its intellectuals and the books they have and have not read, then the unsaid is what has escaped the party. Often it constitutes a threat to the party's worldview. These sudden silences or breaks in the story—what Foucault calls "discontinuity"—are the clearest possible guide to the informed reader/listener of what the party is all about. Togliatti's discontinuity in 1956 showed how embarrassed he was at the invasion of Hungary by Soviet troops but also how constrained he was by the myth of the Red Army.

The DC's Communion of the Faithful and the PCI's Historic Avant-garde

During the post-war the language of DC leaders was crystal clear. Prime Minister Alcide de Gasperi showed no trace of ambiguity or vagueness when justifying his party's claim to rule Italy. Since the new Italy was a democracy, various parties would compete, but the DC should always win because it incarnated "the Christian culture that had ... marked Italy more deeply than any other culture."[2] The PCI was excluded, or, in De Gasperi's eyes, excluded itself from Catholic Italy. Included were the great figures of medieval and Renaissance culture. Indeed De Gasperi warned that "if ever Christian idealism were extinguished in Italy, then the Italian people would no longer, I fear, be able to understand its Dante and its Michelangelo."[3]

So Catholic Italy was one of the first myths of the new republic: it was a projection of the DC's view of itself. One problem was that De Gasperi was using a borrowed language. Nor was this the usual habit of drawing on "other" words. The DC deployed only the vocabulary of Catholicism, while admitting it had obtained the permission of the Church, whose version of such language was more authentic. Aldo Moro spoke of the Church's Christian idealism that in politics takes forms that are "inevitably unsatisfactory."[4]

The inability to construct an autonomous discourse reduced the legitimacy not only of the DC but of the state it governed. The DC's first loyalty was not to the political system of the newly founded republic nor to the Risorgimento tradition. Rather it was—if we leave aside the loyalty that the DC, like most organizations, felt toward its own survival—a loyalty to the Vatican.

Giuseppe Dossetti, who led the DC left, offered a variant on this dilemma. In equally clear but more lyrical language, he maintained that the Christian party should be separate from the Church and should conduct its own mission. This was nothing less than the establishment of a new Christian order in Italy: the DC should act "with a totality of aims and initiatives... capable of changing man's entire social being." The words "totality" and "entire" indicate the absolutist nature of Dossetti's project. But Pius XII was not going to allow "his" party such freedom.

Meanwhile Togliatti was presenting the PCI as a model community, appealing to history rather than to Catholicism for inspiration. He gives an example: "Anti-fascism moves outwards from an understanding of the historical fact in all its necessity... to the precise economic and social groups that dominate... and to the growing awareness and maturing wills of the human actors."[5] Thus anti-fascism infuses the working-class with knowledge of its situation.

The parallels with the DC's vision of communion are obvious. They share the defect that the prime focus of their loyalty lies outside Italy. The merit of the two discourses is that they depict communities united by belief. Even in the 1950s, however, ideology was an imperfect method of encouraging people to join in political life. As the 1960s wore on, both discourses lost confidence in themselves. DC spokesmen grew more obscure: they hid themselves behind phrases like "Catholic interclassism" or "the human person." Aldo Moro's language became the language of the DC: difficult and ambiguous. Since the outward movement of Dossetti had failed, the DC would now use its central position to mediate among the other social groups. A language was needed that was obscure, that sent messages to the initiated but left out most people.

Meanwhile the PCI's Gramscian vocabulary was congealing into a set of clichés. Terms like "hegemony, historic bloc" and "civic and intellectual renewal" ceased to be analytical tools. The "leadership role of the working-class" was supposed to be a goal but Giorgio Amendola, the leader of the PCI right, spoke of it as if it already existed.[6]

THE NON-LANGUAGE OF THE HISTORIC COMPROMISE

Still the PCI was not too spent to create new forms of discourse such as *ingraismo* and Berlinguer's language of austerity. Ingrao's language is all movement. Sentences begin with verbs, especially with reflexive verbs like "si rilancia" or "si comincia." Ingrao's language would play a role in the *svolta*, but before that Berlinguer was striving to construct the language of the historic compromise. In general it lacked originality. Sonorous phrases like "the great popular forces" or "the Catholic and Communist masses," superlative adjectives and an abuse of the word "vast" mask the fragility of the alliance with the Catholics. References to the DC's "popular soul" conceal the unsaid of DC corruption.

But when Berlinguer spoke about waste and consumption, his passion enabled him to discover a whole new language.

Convinced that the decision to become a communist was a moral choice that shaped one's entire existence, Berlinguer saw the PCI as a community based on self-sacrifice. The solution to the economic problems of the 1970s lay in the values, which inspired the policy of austerity. He denounced "squandering and waste, the priority given to special interests, unbridled individualism and the folly of consumerism."[7] Opposed to these evils are the values of work, solidarity and austerity. When asked by none other than Gianni Agnelli what he thought about cars, Berlinguer is said to have replied that he disliked them and preferred public transportation.

His language remained fractured: urgent and clear when he warned against the disintegration of Italian society but turgid when he spoke of the alliance with the DC. Intertwined with the economic issues was the problem of the Italian state, which must be defended and reformed.

But the historic compromise never found its discourse. Berlinguer's interlocutor was Aldo Moro, whose thankless task was to guide his party into some sort of alliance with the PCI, while not telling them where they were headed. From 1975 to 1978 Moro made speeches where the initiated could pluck nuggets of clarity from the quicksand of his rhetoric. On July 20, 1975, Moro moved from the vague admission that "our sense of the state and our respect for the public good have been less than rigorous" to the blunt statement that his party must free itself from "the arrogance of power" and that "a third, difficult phase of our experience has begun."[8] The listener must take the last step on her/his own: the DC will share power with the PCI.

After 1976 Moro piled subjunctives on conditionals and mixed up personal pronouns in order not to explain how power-sharing was to work. His non-discourse was interrupted by the Red Brigades, but its obscurity, without the nuggets of clarity, was emulated by DC leaders of the 1980s. The solipsism of this regime discourse, which found a variant in Craxi's implausible imitations of Garibaldi, had already produced two reactions that might have served as warnings: the first was the parody of PCI language undertaken by the 1977 Movimento, discussed in chapter 10, and the second was the criticism of the language of politics by two very good writers, PierPaolo Pasolini and Leonardo Sciascia.

But the language of politics did not change until 1992, when the system crumbled beneath the hammer blows of the Clean Hands investigation, which was aided by the fairly poor performance of the DC and the Partito socialista italiano (PSI) in the election. The 1992 upheaval produced a change in political language, or, more precisely, the political language of the governing coalition was one of the defects that made it vulnerable to its enemies. There were too many things that could not be said.

This process did not take place in other European countries: in Britain because Thatcher's language of conviction averted the crisis of politics and provided a simpler and bolder, if dogmatic, means of communication, elements of which have been taken up by Blair. In other European countries the change was from a party based on an almost religious belief and sense of belonging (called in Italian "un partito-chiesa") to a catch-all party (called by its French name "un parti attrappe-tout"). This appeals to the citizen's self-interest and judgment. In such a party the militants are less important and their role is taken over by TV or other forms of mass communication. A vote is no longer a matter of belief or belonging but is rather a reward for efficiency, which may be withdrawn. The language of such a party has fewer sacred terms and is more pragmatic. In Germany such language is associated with Helmut Schmidt, but in the Wende of 1982 he was replaced by Helmut Kohl, who was slightly more like Adenauer, but not sufficiently so to interrupt the trend. Meanwhile Mitterrand changed the language of the French Socialists, de-ideologizing it. He allowed the PS (Socialist Party) little say and preferred to them his wide circle of friends who were not very left-wing and not very honest.

In Italy the political vacuum, left by the downfall of the DC-PSI coalition in the 1992 election, helped undermine the complexities of Aldo Moro, now replaced by Ciriaco De Mita. It opened the gate to simpler forms of language—to Bossi—virulent in attacking his foes and to Berlusconi, whose vocabulary was supposedly restricted to the 600 words used by an A.C. Milan supporters' club. Meanwhile the ex-PCI (Italian Communist Party) lost itself in a forest of expressions like, "the communist horizon and the buried left," as well as indulging in a poetry challenge, which pitted Tennyson against the inevitable Whitman. Ochetto deliberately used Tennyson, until then shunned by the PCI as the poet of British imperialism, to widen the horizons of the new party. Ingrao invoked Charlie Chaplin's *Modern Times* to keep the new party on the left, while the women debated how best to obtain a party that would fight the forces of capitalism, while allowing its women to fight for justice within the party.

The aftermath of German reunification and the Maastricht Treaty, which was inseparable from it, weakened all governments that accepted austerity as the price of monetary union. High unemployment and especially youth unemployment led to the phenomenon of "the excluded," who were even worse off than the "marginals" of the 1970s. Political language contained more "unsaid," as peoples were herded into the EU and the group of monetary union. Only in Italy did a political crisis break out and even there the reasons were primarily domestic. The difficult language of Moro gave way to the several champions of populism.

In the meantime one must glance at two clashes between the political and literary languages: Leonardo Sciascia's *L'Affaire Moro* and Heinrich Böll's *Die verlorene Ehre der Katarina Bloom*. Before dealing with Sciascia, one must, however, rid oneself of the Pasolini whom Sciascia invokes. Sciascia seeks an alliance with the late Pasolini, who also criticized political language in the name of the literary language. Pasolini was, however, tracing the outlines of his own inferno, where the language of technology reigned supreme. He saw this as the main threat: the substitution of technology for politics and ideology. But this was not the case with the Italian language of politics: technology was shunned almost as much as clarity. Pasolini's other criticism that political discourse was turning into a new Latin, just when the Second Council had strengthened the vernacular, had more substance.

Leonardo Sciascia,
or I Do Not Believe, Therefore I Am

Leonardo Sciasia was born in 1921, one year before Mussolini came to power, at Racalmuto, inland from Agrigento. He became a young schoolteacher, a job he hated because it entailed teaching Dante to underfed, shoeless village children, and he served his apprenticeship as a writer. These were the post-Liberation years, which were an era of hope. Sciascia's early books were successful and he was able to give up teaching. His short, sophisticated novels had little to do with the neo-realism of the age. But books like *Il giorno della civetta*, with its Mafia villain (actually Sciascia was later accused of being much too kind to Don Mariano Arena) and its sense of mystery, which the hero-policeman Bellodi, who comes from Parma, is on the verge of penetrating when he is transferred to another post, found a lay, predominantly left-wing audience. Sciascia had no use for the DC, whom he satirizes in *Todo Modo*.

Sciascia's novels, which often take the form of detective stories in which the policeman fails to get his man, expose the problem of citizenship in Sicily. The Mafia is the non-state that has succeeded in taking power and in imposing silence, or "omertà," on the local community. Sciascia's heroes are aspirant citizens. Then there are a few other roles: the bystander who sees and hears nothing or the informer who recognizes only the law of the Mafia and trembles every minute for his life because a word to the wrong man means his execution. Women characters might form another category, although they do not offer much variety. They attract men by their sexuality and then destroy them. Essentially when the self moves out to meet the world, it encounters deceit and violence as well as a few politicians and policemen who are a front for the hidden power of the Mafia. The self reacts with caution and skepticism. This is no Cartesian self that goes out and conquers the world. Rather the self is grounded in the act of refusal—"I do not believe, therefore I am."

It is not surprising then that free-flowing language is rare in Sciascia's books. Conditioned by the Mafia, neglected by the state, a danger to the rare speaker, language consists of anonymous letters, blocks of failed dialogue and threats. Speaking is dangerous in Scascia's novels. Conversation implies a trust that does not exist.

The 1970s, which brought the rise of the PCI in Sicily as in the rest of Italy, brought also the possibility of change. Sciascia, who had not exempted the PCI from the suspicion with which he viewed all things and had infuriated the Communists with *Il Contesto* (1971), changed his mind slowly and partially. In 1975 he was elected to the Palermo city council on the Communist ticket, although he was unwilling to join the party. Indeed contact with the Communists brought not trust but rather a return to skepticism. Sciascia disliked the historic compromise, which he had foreseen and denounced in *Il Contesto*. He was disappointed that the Palermo PCI ceased to oppose the DC and sought agreement with them at almost any price. Sciascia broke with the PCI and in the 1979 elections he ran with the Radicals who were then a small party of opposition.

In his diary Sciascia asks himself, "What is truth?" and while answering himself in his usual doubting way he gives an unusually specific reply: "One would be tempted to respond that it is literature."[9] Sciascia uses the reflexive form and the conditional tense of the verb, which is indication of a very strong doubt. He does not elaborate on this judgment. Is literature more moral than other kinds of language? Is it better-suited by its game-playing to out-witting the many lies that keep watch over the truth in Sicily?

The identification of literature and truth is at the heart of *L'Affaire Moro*,[10] which Sciascia published after the kidnapping and murder of the DC president and architect of the historic compromise. Sciascia begins by invoking the aid of the later Pasolini, the author of a famous article declaring that the DC leaders should be put on trial because there were no more fireflies in Italy. Pasolini could have said what he meant in banally rational phrases. Instead he chose a great metaphor because he wanted to enter the polemic armed with the signs of literature. Now his name serves the same purpose for Sciascia, who introduces Borges for extra support.

L'Affaire Moro is essentially a critique of political language from the viewpoint of the literary. When he was kidnapped, Moro's fate inspired his party to flights of fancy about what a great statesman he was. But Sciascia tells a different story: "Neither Moro nor his party had ever had the slightest sense of the state."[11] It suited the DC, which could not, for international rather than domestic reasons, negotiate with the Red Brigades, to declare the old Moro a statesman and the Moro of captivity a man under duress whose letters should be ignored. Sciascia, however, claims that Moro had always been a great politician and continued to be one in the "people's prison." Sciascia analyzes Moro's letters and reconstructs his period of captivity via his writings.

Sciascia debunks the DC's language and dismisses the Red Brigades as the descendants of the Third International. The Communists are also castigated for using the Moro kidnapping to strengthen the historic compromise. Among all the protagonists Sciascia prefers the kidnapped Moro who, in order to explain what is happening, uses a language designed not to explain. This Moro, powerless except for his language, appeals to Sciascia. He is honest, whereas the Brigate rosse (BR) talk about such non-existent entities as "the heart of the state" and the "combating Communist Party."

What then of Sciascia? He is rather too dogmatic and some of his insights are wrong. The PCI did not benefit from the Moro kidnapping and gave up the historic compromise less than a year later. Sciascia relies too heavily on his fluent prose. The Moro affair does not become explicable when recounted by Sciascia. "From the sense of writing as a trap I have arrived at writing as truth," he states.[12] But truth is more convincing when it is caught up with deceit as in Sciascia's early novels. He does not consider the issue of outside forces like the CIA, the KGB or the Mossad. This self-consciously literary book leaves as many unanswered questions as the political commentaries. Sciascia thinks of himself as an isolated voice of truth and his faith in literature grows as his trust in all other forms of human activity declines. But literature falls short of his hopes. There is no special breed of human different from all others.

Die verlorene Ehre der Katharina Blum, or Writing Less

Heinrich Böll offers a very different view of terrorism and the political class. In Sciascia the temptation is, once more, not to say enough. Sciascia comes up with the notion that the language of literature can be a solution. In *Die verlorene Ehre* the bourgeoisie and its allies—the police force and the popular press—know everything. The drama lies in whether they can be brought to realize that certain things are not subject to their supposedly rational, scientific methods. So the narrator leaves out much. His story contains silences, things that should remain unsaid out of respect for Katharina, whose identity lies in her privacy. Böll has reversed the usual judgments of a detective story. There as here, the supposed criminal is irrational while the detective is rational, but rationality becomes authoritarianism and irrationality protest.

Böll was accused of arriving at this conclusion too easily. In his novel Katharina and her fiancé are not terrorists, which makes the police seem brutally authoritarian. The Baader-Meinhof group were terrorists who did not hesitate to kill. Does this not justify police telephone tapping, as well as Bildzeitung's rantings? But Böll is showing a society that set out to be a "Rechtstaat" and has now introduced a "Berufsverbot."

The narrator's opening passage sets the tone. He states that the sequence of events is "not inexplicable but almost logical." "Almost" is a key word, for it marks the presence of a permanent doubt in the narration, which opposes it to the police or Bildzeitung. He also declares that he is writing fiction, but there is a hint that this fiction is more real than the statistics bandied about by the police. The narrator retains a skepticism about language and about the "we," who are either narrating or else narrating and listening. He mentions documents that are never heard about again. In such a narrative there can be no question of omniscience; the narrator becomes briefly a surveyor imposing order on a stream, but the stream soon flows once again where it will.[13] (This is a hard book to translate and I have no faith in my ability to do better than Ms. Vennewitz.)

Much of the narrative is between inverted commas, which change the visual aspect of the page and make the reader think about who is speaking, as well as about whom and to whom he is speaking. The book thus presents itself as several different discourses, which co-exist uneasily. The mark of Katharina's discourse is that it is self-conscious and self-correcting. When the police interrogate her, she changes "amorous" to "making advances" and "kind" to "gracious."

In marked contrast is the language of Biltzeitung, which professes to be omniscient, and sets out to tell the reader the whole truth. From the outset it is convinced Katharina is guilty and, to assure itself of this, it interviews her ex-husband—how can one find out the truth about a woman without asking a man? He delivers a wonderfully comical speech: "Our modest happiness was not enough for her. She was ambitious and how is an honest, modest workman ever to come by a Porsche? That's how false ideas about socialism are bound to end. I could hardly have offered you a Porsche, merely such modest happiness as can be offered by an honest workman who doesn't trust the unions."

Bildzeitung flaunts its knowledge of anything and everything. Katharina's boss, who is a lawyer, thinks this does not matter because he knows no one who reads such a paper, but Katharina states that everyone she knows reads Bildzeitung. In the context of authoritarianism, the popular press is used to keep the working-class under control. Its weapons are paternalism, sentimentality and the threat as well as reality of witch-hunts.

The police using high-tech listening devices are the watchdogs of the bourgeoisie and they work with the élite of the CDU. Böll is too intelligent to imagine they have everything under control: the murder of Schönner, the photographer "who makes things more beautiful," is never resolved even if the reader has her/his own suspicions. When the police interrogate Katharina, they are particularly insistent on the considerable amount of time she spends driving alone around the countryside. They have calculated her expenses for petrol and so are able to work out how far she goes but not why.

This "why?" is perhaps the most important theme of the book because it is a sign that the ordinary citizen is or can be watched, as Orwell showed in *1984*. The reader is fairly certain that Katharina is shunning men who make aggressive advances to her. But the police do not consider that explanation and one is left with the other theme, namely, that the police have no right to ask. Similarly there is no obligation on Katharina to tell. Privacy is her right, even if she does not read the *Economist*!

Lingering behind the pages of this novel is a 1950s realist novel. Böll does not stress explanations by class, but they are there. Why? Perhaps to mislead the reader. Perhaps to show that Marxist notions of class are no longer valid but that authoritarianism and protest are. Anyway Katharina was born into a working-class family and her father was a communist. Here again Böll does not tie up the ends neatly, for Katharina's father is no rebel but a weak man worried about his pension. Nor is this a tough proletarian family. Katharina's brother is in jail and her mother is an alcoholic. Nor is Katharina herself a rebel. Rather she is a child of the "Wirtschaftswunder," eager to get ahead by becoming a caterer. Her friend Elsa comes from a communist family and her mother lives in the DDR. But her father was killed by Stalin and her closest friend is an ex-Nazi, Konrad Beuters. Böll deliberately confuses the ideological categories in order to show that the age of the class struggle and the neo-realist novel is over.

There is a red bourgeoisie that emerged from the '68 movement, but Katharina's employers, the Blorna couple who belong to it, are no threat to the state. Moreover they are friends of Straubleder, the CDU politician who pursues Katharina. They suffer for their decision to stand by her: the radical worldview present in the '68 movement is not strong enough to sustain them.

Die verlorene Ehre has no happy ending, for Katharina is awaiting trial and sentencing, as is her lover, Götten. The case has brought confusion to people's lives but the socio-political order is holding. The reader, however, has been turned against this order and hence he still seeks an explanation for the murder. The most plausible is male aggression against women. Katharina offers this as a reason for Straubleder's pursuit of her and also on other occasions. If this is correct, then her murder of Tötges is an act of liberation, a rebellion against a male-dominated society. This explanation would also explain Schonner's murder: he is killed by the woman dressed as an Andalusian and his crime too is interfering in the lives of others, especially of women.

Until now we have encountered no women characters whose strength of will is sustained throughout the book. Is Katharina the first? The trouble is that she is in many ways a traditional female. She is puritanical, seeing sex either as a form of male aggression or else within the context of love and marriage. With Ludwig she is the eternal woman waiting for her ideal man to come and marry her. This traditional side may be explained by Böll's Catholic, Rheinland culture. Another reason is the date: *Die verlorene Ehre* appeared in Germany in 1974, when the women's movement had not long been underway.

A contemporary left-wing critique of the novel argues that the action of the police is depicted as exceptional, whereas it is common and "West Germans internalize the power-structure of their state and become legislators of their own fears."[14] But Zipes agrees that the narration's task is to block the total explanations that justify police violence.

The role of the literary language is not to spin out utopias or infernos but rather to express a critical awareness of political language, whether it is inventing a total, i.e., completely law-abiding, policed society or, as in *L'Affaire Moro,* trying to conceal from the citizen misdeeds that have been committed. Control over information takes many forms: the popular press supported Thatcher. Listening devices and phone-tapping get ever easier and ever more efficient.

It is important to have storytellers who recount their own story, using their own and not other people's words, who distrust statistics and are suspicious of grand epics. They are not ordinary, but so much the better if they think they are.

Chapter Five

Breaking the Silence of Violence

Seamus Heaney as a Northern Irish Poet

> "O words are lightly spoken,"
> Said Pearse to Connolly.
> Maybe a breath of politic words
> Has withered our rose tree.[1]

One returns to Yeats's much-quoted lines in the year 2001, three years after the signing of the Good Friday Agreement. The agreement is now in crisis because David Trimble has threatened to resign as prime minister unless the IRA agrees to disarm—the jargon term is "decommission"—and the IRA has not at the time of writing done anything except make promises. Yet in many spheres the Agreement is working well, albeit slowly and with many breakdowns, as if the participants had to learn a new language, which is precisely the case.

Pearse knew, of course, that words are not lightly spoken. What he meant was almost the opposite: that the parliamentary form taken by Irish nationalism, with its emphasis on mediation and negotiation, was suffocating the very Ireland it was supposed to be creating. There had been a great period when Charles Stuart Parnell had led the Irish parliamentarians and had come tantalizingly close to Home Rule. But Parnell fell in the Kitty O'Shea affair, which was arguably Ireland's Dreyfus case, and he died in 1891. Implicit in Pearse's observation was that these were English words. The mediation was taking place in the English language, which was ousting Irish, without which the new Ireland would have no identity. Pearse planned to interrupt this idle, dangerous chatter with gunfire.

Silence and Guns

Not for nothing had he chosen Easter Sunday for his rebellion. He knew that his little band had no chance of victory and no solid base in Irish society. He was proved right when they were taken out by the British to be shot: the 1916 rebels were booed and insulted by the Dublin crowd. But Pearse intended to offer an example, which would be taken up by the best in the nation. With their own "red blood" they would "make a right rose tree." By sacrificing themselves at future Easters, which were, according to the myth, the same Easter, they would call forth the young men of Ireland who would continue the struggle.

Pearse was inaugurating a new or at least more explicit discourse of sacrifice, quite separate from the discourse of politics, which is based on the need to convince with words. Pearse's thinking is probably linked to the self-sacrificing strand in Irish Catholicism—Pearse discussed theology and said the rosary during the uprising—and inextricably caught up with violence. He was proven right once again in his gamble on rebellion because the British conducted a brutal repression that sent droves of young men into the IRA. The symbolic uprising of Easter produced an anti-colonial, nationalist struggle.

In the South "politic words" re-entered the fray in 1921. Michael Collins, the head of IRA military strategy, had raised the price the British had to pay for their colony and forced them to the conference table. The peace negotiations retriggered the dispute within the Catholic Irish between the advocates of physical force and the party of "politic words." With the victory of the Free Staters in the civil war, words and politics won out, but Collins himself was killed, a thought that must haunt Gerry Adams.

Although de Valera fought on a platform of refusing the British all concessions that Pearse had not made in 1916, he found Jesuitical ways around his refusal to take the oath to the King. He and his supporters entered parliament in 1926 and formed a government in 1932. Domestic politics in the Republic was, at least superficially, much like those of other democratic European countries. Legitimacy came, mostly, from the ballot box. There was, however, an important splinter of the IRA that did not follow de Valera into the Dàil (parliament) and that did not recognize any of the Free State's institutions, including its law courts. For the IRA, legitimacy came from Easter 1916.

Another difference that separated Ireland from Europe's older democracies and that also ran between the two major parties, Fine Gael and Fianna Fàil, had to do with language and culture. For the latter only a Celtic, Irish-speaking state could be fully legitimate. This was in no sense a minor problem. While de Valera was in power it was considered more important than issues of class and economics. This enabled Ireland to become and remain a special and hence neutral country.[2] Of more real importance was the huge role played in the Free State by the Catholic Church. It was expanded in the 1937 constitution, which was voted into law under de Valera.

Yet "Dev" did not succeed in reviving the Irish language. Today it is spoken by 1 percent of the population. Its decline was not a new phenomenon, for by 1650 it had ceased to be the language of intellectual life. In the nineteenth century a national school system was set up in English, which was thus presented as the language of work and of the state. In the chaos of the post-Famine years knowledge of English provided the Irish who were leaving for America with an advantage over the other immigrant groups.[3] Irish was left dominant only in a few, remote areas on the west coast. The wave of cultural nationalism, associated with Lady Gregory, Yeats and Synge, led a certain number of people to re-learn Irish and inspired in a wider group an interest in the language. But English could not be challenged. The effort of the Fianna Fàil state succeeded in making knowledge of Irish a prerequisite for civil service posts, which in turn forced the Dublin middle-classes to send their children to the Gaeltacht in the summers.

It is interesting that control over the machinery of the state proved of so little value. Of the four major Celtic languages only Welsh is spoken by at least 20 percent of the population. Breton fought an unequal battle against the powerful French state. Wales, under English domination since the Middle Ages, somehow concentrated on what could be done. It diverted the resources of nationalism into preserving and reviving the language. This achievement is blemished by the number of people for whom Welsh is a second language and by tedious debates about Welsh identity (satirized by Kingsley Amis in *The Old Devils* [1986]).

What was the effect of the loss of the Irish language? It was argued out by Brian Freel in *Translations* (1980). A group of British surveyors arrives in an Irish-speaking community in Donegal in 1833. Its task is to rename—again the importance of naming is stressed—the places in English. Hugh, the teacher in a hedge-school whose pupils learn Latin and Greek through Irish, appreciates the importance of this action. Not only does it present English as the modern, practical language but the villagers will gradually be led to conduct their whole lives in English. For Hugh this is a triple defeat: he loses his job, his language and the classical culture he is teaching. Fittingly Hugh comes from a baptism at the outset where the child has been christened Eamon—a satirical glance forward in time to Eamon de Valera. Maire, however, is in favor of learning English, which she considers more useful. She also attacks the pessimistic strand in Irish culture—"some of you people aren't happy unless you're miserable and you'll not be right content until you're dead."[4] Friel holds the balance between the view that the loss of the Irish language is a damaging blow to Irish identity and the view, nowadays heard frequently in the prosperous, practical Ireland, that Irish held people back while English gave them an advantage in the new struggle represented by emigration to the United States. The two interpretations are not mutually exclusive. Each could be true for a segment of the population, and even for one and the same person.

The Republican movement, the loose political force that demanded a united Ireland and was prepared to use violence to get it, paid little heed—until very recently—to the Irish language. Its militants and its hard core, the IRA, feared that cultural questions would distract attention from the political goal.

The IRA continued Pearse's distrust of politic words and believed that only the gun could shake the British hold on Ireland. During the long peace process in the North the strength of the IRA's identity as an army was consistently underestimated by the other actors. The offer of a limited cease-fire could be explained by the leaders to the militants as a strategic move; an unlimited cease-fire was more difficult because it left the IRA with no role; a surrender of weapons was most difficult of all because only defeated armies surrendered their weapons, and the IRA was not defeated. Foreign observers found this hard to grasp: an Italian journalist writes of the IRA's "mythical, fetishist attachment to weapons."[5] But in its own eyes the IRA had, in 1998 as in 1921, brought the British to the negotiation table. Violence was the IRA's language; there was "nothing personal" about the bombs it placed and, despite the condemnation of the Catholic Church, nothing wrong or evil about them. Yeats's famous remark that those who die for Ireland have no need of prayer remained true.

Such intransigent silence flourished among a minority of the Northern Catholics. They suffered discrimination in housing, jobs and elsewhere. But more important they saw no chance of being able to redress the balance. Although their higher birthrate seemed to offer them hope of becoming the larger group in the North and of exercising hegemony, this did not come about between 1922 and 1994, possibly because of higher levels of emigration. So the poorer Catholics saw hope only in changing the boundaries, uniting Ireland or taking in a chunk of Donegal. More prosperous or milder Catholics, who voted for the SDLP (Social and Democratic Labour Party), did not accept the use of force but agreed that reunification was the goal. Either way they were reluctant to give their trust to an alien society, which, located geographically in Ireland, considered itself British; one of whose major religious traditions was bitterly and wildly anti-Catholic in a way more suited to the seventeenth than to the twentieth century; and that was endowed with a population that had grave uncertainties of its own.

Convinced that their national identity was British, the Ulster-men and -women were not at all sure of their fellow countrymen. For the most part they themselves were of Scottish origin, whereas the very different English had won the struggle for Britain. This left the North with certain allies—like the Glasgow Rangers football team—but also with vastly greater numbers of supposed compatriots whose lay, post-family view of the world they do not share. Their historical memories are different and more vivid: Cromwell's campaigns and William of Orange's victories over James Stuart are remote events in England, but Northern Ireland lives them as if they had happened yesterday. The siege of Derry was commemorated and repeated, such was the enthusiasm of the marchers, every year. When they took part in a British epic like the Somme, they were fighting not the Germans but the Catholic Belfastians from the Falls Road. A Protestant poet, Michael Longley, compares the death of Ulster soldiers in the trenches with the assassination of a Belfast city employee. The soldiers die with screams of hatred directed not against the Germans but against the Belfast Catholics. The city employee dies wordless, while his teenage assassin mutters "Sorry Missus" to his victim's traumatized wife. At least the poet thinks he said it. The very uncertainty is more authentic than the solipsistic monologues.[6]

It is important to grasp the fears of the Northern Ireland Protestants. A majority in the North, they are a clear minority in the island as a whole, hence their fear of a Home Rule that would turn out to be Rome rule. The Free State did little to change their minds. Strict self-interest in obtaining government funding provides a link with Northern Catholics. All else, especially elusive issues of loyalties, both religious and civil, separate them. So the Protestants turn onto the Catholic minority the silence that emanates from it. Actually a Protestant Northerner has less in common with an Englishman than with a Catholic Northerner who is, like her/him, fearful of discrimination and historically wronged. The Protestants have paramilitary forces that have been formed to fight the IRA and that have their roots in Carson's volunteers.

The anti-Catholic strand in Protestant Ulster's culture had a long tradition on which to draw. The pattern, represented by Ian Paisley, was set in the early nineteenth century as Belfast was becoming an industrial city and leaving Dublin behind. Henry Cooke anticipated Paisley with rhetoric like this passage:

> To the glorious, pious and immortal memory of King William III, who saved us from brass money and wooden shoes: and whoever denies this toast may be slammed, crammed and muzzled into the great gun of Athlone, and the gun fired into the Pope's belly and the Pope into the devil's belly and the devil into hell and the door locked, and the key forever in an Orangeman's pocket.[7]

Catholics and Protestants developed a political language that takes account of the silence. Firstly a speaker addresses himself in reality to his own tribe, although officially he is talking to everyone. Secondly each monologue has a Manichean structure that is the exact opposite of the other monologue. For the Catholics united Ireland, thirty-two counties and British withdrawal are positive values, whereas union with Britain, the Orange Order and the Battle of the Boyne are negative. Thirdly dialogue between the tribes cannot create a political community, which must be in agreement on basic terms like loyalty to the state or equality of all citizens. The North cannot even agree on what it is. Whereas the Catholics believe they are living in an as yet unliberated part of Ireland, the Protestants believe they are living in a province of Britain. Prior to 1998 there was nothing like the Italian Constitution on which Catholics and communists worked together.

Political language may therefore be seen as a more aggressive form of silence. Or else as a set of two monologues that are launched into space, that never manage to meet and fall back on themselves. It has been argued that Protestants and Catholics use the language differently: Protestants are precise, whereas Catholics use old words to spin off new ones. So the words of an agreement are sacrosanct to Protestants but to Catholics they may be the sign of a much broader agreement that has, however, not yet been reached. This interpretation may well be true. Certainly it corresponds to the historical experience of each tribe. Facing foreign rulers who spoke a different language, the Catholics sought margins of freedom by learning English and then by playing with it in ways the English did not know. Britain was a different entity for the Protestants. It was an ally and friend, but it could not be relied on and hence must be tied down to its promises.

The solipsism of these monologues is self-perpetuating. It brings nothing new and it is incapable of spawning change. There are the expected silences: the Protestants have no wish to expand their dealings with the Dublin government; the traditional insults against the "colonizing" Protestant and the "Papist" Catholic; and the distortions of words.

The distortion of words is perhaps the most revealing factor. When words lose their power to name and to communicate that name, then political debate becomes impossible. Without debate there can be no political community, based on agreement in fundamental areas and healthy diversity in other areas. In Northern Ireland to say the name of the second largest city does not inform the listener of what that city is called. One may call it Derry or Londonderry. But if one uses the former name, one informs the listener that one is a Catholic and by using the second, one is announcing that one is a Protestant.

Names are especially sensitive words. In Christian theology, whether Catholic or Protestant, wo(man) is freed from the devil and acquires a social and psychological self at baptism when one is also given a name. Aside from the protection of a saint, which one obtains by the choice of a traditional Christian name, one's entire individual personality is pulled together and becomes visible to others when one receives a name. In Northern Ireland, however, the name does not convey primarily an individual identity but membership in one of the two religious groups or tribes. As Seamus Heaney puts it, "Norman" signals Protestant and "Seamus" Catholic.[8]

Not just the discourse of politics but most of language is monopolized by the tribal conflict. The most extreme form is taken by the IRA, which kept the Pearse myth alive. This needed no ratification from the ballot box; it did not recognize the rights of British courts, whether in the Six Counties or on the mainland, to try its soldiers much less condemn them; and it was virtually unique among European terrorist organizations in its use of the hunger strike. The IRA's political arm, Sinn Féin, was in the uncomfortable position of being allowed to speak for the IRA, subject to having that right withdrawn or to being contradicted by the Army Council, the clandestine body that governs the IRA.

How did the Good Friday Agreement ever come to be signed? How could this non-language produce a political community? It was all the more surprising because the Anglo-Irish Agreement (1985) had demonstrated that the Dublin and London governments could find a common language to talk about the North, whereas the Northerners themselves were trapped by their mythical past. But the thirty years of fighting had worn down many in the IRA and led to the Hume-Adams discussion. Then too there was an injection of a different language from the United States: Clinton's choice of Mitchell as his envoy over the Kennedy clan and the Moynihans was a choice for pragmatism.

Meanwhile Tony Blair, whose party had no historic ties with Northern Ireland, could speak with greater authority than John Major. But the real novelty was Mo' Mowlam, whom Blair appointed Secretary of State for Northern Ireland.

To understand Mo' Mowlam's innovation one must talk for a moment about women in politics. In my opinion they are systematically given either ministries vaguely related to women's traditional values—Livia Turco is the Italian Minister for the Family—or else the most difficult jobs. Edith Cresson's appointment as the first woman to become Prime Minister of France was made when the French economy was headed downward because of German reunification, over which neither she nor Mitterrand had any control. Similarly Mo' Mowlam was given Northern Ireland and doubtless was reminded of the old saying that Ireland is a graveyard for English politicians.

Mowlam's task was to turn gender into a positive factor. She had one advantage that derived from a combination of nationality and gender: Englishwomen were not supposed to know anything about "the Irish Question," so Mowlam took no heed of the Wolf Tone rebellion or the Battle of the Somme. She specifically denied that the Good Friday Agreement was supposed to be a reply to Pearse's Easter rebellion, although one feels that in this instance Mowlam wanted to have her myth and debunk it. By claiming that it was by chance that the Agreement was signed on Good Friday she was meeting Pearse on his home ground and refusing to admit it.

Mowlam exploited her gender when she visited the Maze Prison. She spoke with IRA men and Protestant paramilitaries, both of whom were accustomed to being told that they must remain in prison for twenty years so that Ireland might be reunited or Ulster saved from the Pope. They were used to talking to men and to women whom the organizations kept in order. Mowlam talked to the prisoners about getting jobs, improving schools and anti-drug programs. Where men talked of heroes and resisting pain or the blandishments of the enemy, Mowlam told the prisoners they could be out in six months and that their families needed them.

To her subject matter Mowlam brought a sense of humor that allowed her to mock traditionally male values like secrecy and endurance. In another speech she took her shoes off, saying that her feet were killing her. She peppered her language with colloquialisms, substituting "fag" for "cigarette" and using the terminology of gambling—"I don't give a monkey's." Instead of the male value of martyrdom, she used the woman's values of common sense and ordinary life lived to the full.[9]

This language was not new to Belfast but it was new as a political discourse. It worked, too: obtaining the release of prisoners was a major reason for the IRA's acceptance of the Agreement. The prisoners were powerful voices in favor of giving up the armed struggle. Alas, Mowlam herself became unacceptable to the Protestants, who felt she was leaning too far toward the Catholics, that she was letting convicted murderers loose on the streets and that she was turning a blind eye to IRA breaches of the ceasefire. In my opinion she was sacrificed—willingly—to the cause of peace. She left the Northern Ireland office to Peter Mandelson, a very different kind of person.

Meanwhile the language used by Irish actors has been changing. Change came first in the South, when Sean Lemass replaced Dev as prime minister in 1959. Lemass did not neglect nationalism but he gave it economic content. Landmarks of his role had been the creation of Air Lingus and of the Irish Tourist Board. By stressing the need for prosperity to block emigration and dismantling the apparatus of protectionism, Lemass turned outward toward the EC. Despite the great celebration of the Fiftieth Anniversary of the Easter Rebellion, the blowing up of Nelson's statue and the revamping of the Post Office, Ireland's eyes looked toward Brussels—with some wavering—throughout the thirty years of Troubles in the North. The language of Irish politics has become more "European" and it has not escaped the developments described in this book.

If the Agreement holds in the North, then the discourse of violence will vanish, as will the silence and solipsism. Catholics and Protestants must learn a new, common language.

Sinn Féin's language should initially draw closer to Fianna Fàil's language as it used to be while Dev's party was making the transition from culture to prosperity. It has also been suggested that there is a tendency in Northern Ireland to keep using the old familiar words that win instant, unthinking support from the various groups.[10] This turns into support for the Agreement, but when the various statements are examined, that support collapses. This is obviously dangerous but perhaps inevitable. One cannot overnight create a new political language but one may evolve from the change in practice.

The Many Dilemmas of an Irish Writer

Let us turn then to the language of literature. Even more than most writers, an Irish author cannot "just write." Can s/he avoid being conditioned by the virulence of political language and by its sudden murderous silences? Recently there has been a tendency to perceive Irish writing as part of the anti-colonial struggle, as an attempt to depict what the country will be like once the colonized have gained their rights. This is a special case of the phenomenon we described as the freedom of the literary language. The depiction of a new identity will be caught up with the revival of old, pre-colonial identities and with the destruction of a language. Thus Oscar Wilde becomes both very English and very Irish, as he makes fun of both sides of the colonial relationship.[11]

This presupposes a black-suited Englishman, stable and content with himself. Opposite him is a clownish Paddy who talks about nothing but racehorses. Wilde can make the Englishman ridiculous and the Irishman decisive. It is no coincidence that he is "the first major artist to discard the romantic ideal of sincerity" and to replace it with the more difficult ideal of authenticity. This means being faithful to one's shifting, constantly moving self, rather than to an idealized, heroic self. Kiberd's argument, while it is based on a good understanding of how the colonized behaves in front of the colonizer, ignores certain aspects of the historical situation. The first is that Wilde—this too is very Irish—jumped over England and embraced the French decadence, in particular J-K.Huysmans's *A Rebours*. The notion of authenticity is perhaps the key theme to the next French generation, finding expression in the *NRF*. So France offered Irish writers a haven and even an inspiration. This does not contradict the anti-colonial theme, because France is acting against a historical enemy who defeated it in the eighteenth-century race for colonies, but it makes it more subtle. If one tosses into the equation the proximity of Ireland to Britain, the time-framework in which the various waves of colonization took place—is the Norman conquest to count? If so then Normandy itself should be considered a Danish colony—the absence of differently colored skin, the large number of Irish people settled and living in Britain from the nineteenth-century on and other obvious factors, then one wonders about the relevance of Frantz Fanon to the Irish-English dialogue. Except that one immediately remembers that Fanon came from Martinique, a privileged and relatively untroubled colony.

Still one feels that the Irish were neighbors and associates of the English—working next to them in the coal and steel industries—as much as colonized facing their colonizer. In the United States, the Irish used their knowledge of English to differentiate themselves from other immigrant groups whom they did little to help even when, as with the Italians and Poles, they were Catholics. In Philadelphia, Irish parishes were separate from Italian. The Irish were much quicker to take on the WASPs. There was an Irish president in 1960, whereas there has still not been even a Jewish vice president. In Australia the Irish may have been more numerous than they merited among the convict population—and certainly among the "bushrangers" or bandits—but they were not almost exterminated like the Aborigines. Moreover it is hard to fit the Anglo-Irish into the colonial framework, except perhaps to say they were a ruling class that never ruled over anyone. Certainly they were not as intrusive or as demanding as the pieds-noirs in Algeria.

The loss of the language must have hit writers harder than the mass of people. Kiberd sees the emphasis on style as the result of working with a language that is not one's own. He also sees in Synge's writing Ireland as it might be, depicted via Ireland as it had been. To reinforce the colonial elements in *Playboy of the Western World* one might add that Albert Camus produced the play and played the role of Christy Mahon with much exuberance in the Algiers of the Popular Front.

Doubt and controversy arise when the question of Joyce's relationship to his native land is posed: my own opinion is that Joyce, the man, wanted to have nothing to do with the Free State. That the negotiations between the Irish and the British came to a conclusion at almost exactly the moment when *Ulysses* was presented to an élite public in Paris is coincidence (see chapter nine). Joyce knew perfectly well that the Free State would and did ban *Ulysses* and he thought of himself as renewing the tradition of the Wild Geese, the Irish soldiers who went to serve in foreign armies after the defeats of the seventeenth century.

Kiberd may well be right when he argues that Joyce carried Ireland around with him in the shape of his wife, Nora, although one must add that, without Nora, Joyce could not have survived in Trieste or Paris. Joyce must have suffered from the loss of the Irish language and, at least when he was writing *Ulysses* and *Finnegans Wake,* he saw the solution not in reviving Irish but in plundering English, contaminating it with foreign words and tormenting its grammatical structures. If *Dubliners* is a search for freedom within Ireland and if the last story, "The Dead," is a rejection of the Gaeltacht and the Irish language in favor of exile and Europe, then *Ulysses* may be read as an attempt to recreate Ireland. It is also, to mention a theme that Kiberd virtually ignores, an attempt to write the "summa."

The need to say everything sprang from Joyce's refusal to make arbitrary choices like those of Balzac and Dickens, which turn the novel into an apparent slice of realism. The anti-British strand in Joyce overlapped with the modernist strand: the reader sees what the narrator chooses to tell him, which is not "a slice of life" but life filtered through the narrator(s)'s awareness. In the context of Ireland's complex dealings with Britain, to switch points of view in each chapter risks having the book disintegrate, hence the need for the central myth of Ulysses's homecoming. Hence too the attempt to write the "summa" and to say everything. Kibert's argument remains: Joyce is turning things around as the key Sartrian moment arrives and the colonized looks at the colonizer: Joyce declares that Bloom is universal and the British Empire is about to crumble. But let us not forget that, if the Martello Tower in which the book begins is a remnant of colonialism, the first words spoken in *Ulysses*—"Et introibo ad altare dei"—are the exact first words of the Latin mass. Uttered by the despised Buck Mulligan, they testify that there is an even greater power in Ireland than the British and that it must be combated—the Catholic Church.

No attempt can be made here to offer a full, much less new, interpretation of *Ulysses*. Kiberd's anti-colonial thesis has many merits. Later we shall argue that the "selling" of *Ulysses* was undertaken by presenting it as a "European" work. But perhaps the only thing we have to say about *Ulysses* itself is that, in its refusal to be explained, it offers many explanations that are roughly equal in merit and that it seeks to avoid becoming a sacred text, while simultaneously refusing to be nihilistic. In its own way it also announces Joyce's next summa: the Molly Bloom soliloquy has less in common with the Ithaca chapter that precedes it than with Anna Livia Pluribelle of *Finnegans Wake*.

THE NORTH: POST-COLONIAL WRITING?

The recent Northern Irish writer faces the obstacles posed by a colonialism that, whatever it may have been originally, has turned into something else: the static face-off of two tribes. Indeed it is silly to talk of colonialism in contemporary Northern Ireland when its great industries, shipbuilding and linen, have collapsed. If a referendum had been conducted in Britain at almost any time during the thirty-year Troubles, a majority would have voted to withdraw the troops. British governments, even Thatcher's, have been able to reach agreement with the Republic on the North. It is not clear that a majority in the Republic wants a united Ireland. To take in the Six Counties would endanger the Republic's new and precious prosperity. Perhaps Brussels has made the "Irish Question" obsolete. Pearse was wrong: consumer goods rather than politic words have withered his rose-tree.

But Dublin and London had not, until 1998, been able to persuade Northerners to tolerate one another, much less to share power. The British tax-payer would be better off without the North, which displays, like gaping wounds, the remnants of its smoke-stack industry: the Harlan-Wolfe shipyard and the rows of small houses built for a working-class that now has no work. The writer is estranged from Britain—the Protestant rather less than the Catholic—but neither is an English writer. As Seamus Heaney puts it, "Ulster is British/But has no rights upon the English lyric."[12]

This is an intriguing statement, for Heaney implies that in a more just society Ulster would have such rights and because the word "English" refers to a language but also to the ethnic group that has won out in Britain. The ethnic and linguistic factors in Northern Ireland's relationship with Britain are very different: the Good Friday Agreement recognizes that the Catholics have their own political goals because they belong to a different people. But it very properly makes no mention of the Irish language.

The political task of the literary language is to clarify, enrich or even create the language of politics. It is one of the most obvious examples of our thesis exposed at the end of chapter 1. All good Northern Irish poets must discover a language of their own, which will have political value if it can throw light on the solipsistic monologues of the two tribes. It is vain to expect a poet to reconcile the tribes, but he may lay bare the stale verbiage behind which they hide from each other and themselves. To liberate the language of Northern Ireland would be a great achievement. Derek Mahon broadens his task by setting the victims of the Troubles into the context of other twentieth-century massacres, a subject to which we shall return. The poet must break the silence of oppression: "They are begging us, you see, in their wordless way/To do something, to speak on their behalf."[13]

For a Protestant poet the first step must lie in the recognition that he is born of colonizers. Michel Longley becomes aware of his foreignness when he hears Irish spoken. But today's Protestant community is not made up of foreign exploiters and has its own values and culture. Another Protestant poet, John Hewitt, asserts the existence of the two tribes and goes on to criticize the Catholics: "not these my people, of a vainer faith/and a more violent lineage." Here, for once openly admitted, is that Protestant fear of becoming a minority in a united Ireland. Hewitt explains what it is: "I fear their creed as we have always feared/the lifted hand against unfettered thought." The identification of Catholicism with authority and Protestantism with liberalism is not objective, but Hewitt is drawing on a founding myth not just of Northern Ireland but of Britain. He goes beyond it to admit that Irish Catholics have "a savage history of wrong," which he offers to help repair. With a modesty more complex than it seems, he adds "if voice avail." The subjunctive stands in sharp contrast to the certainty of the two tribes' monologues.

This poem, entitled *The Glens*[14] because it draws on the bond Hewitt feels with the Northern Irish countryside, reveals a rationality that acts as a critique of the screams of hate and the rock-hard certainties of the two monologues. Hewitt's "avail" is the mark of a poetic discourse that doubts itself, of a skepticism that wants to insinuate itself into politics. It seems pessimistic but it plays a positive role by acting as a barrier against facile moral judgments and against the tendency, strong in the aftermath of the Good Friday Agreement, to oversimplify the tenacity of hatred. For

Catholic poets, rationality is even more necessary and perhaps more difficult. They have to confront the great myth of Irish nationalism, that a united, independent Ireland, Celtic and Catholic, can only be brought into being through blood sacrifice. Yeats, who had previously constructed the very different (and more useful) Parnell myth, contributed to this one via Cathleen Ní Houlihan's exhortation to young men. Later Yeats had second thoughts about sending young Irishmen out to be killed by the English but by then there were too many Liam Mellows and they had learned their lesson too well.[15] This myth overlaps perfectly with the silence of the IRA. Both the austere charm of sacrifice and the refusal to negotiate with the British are present in Bobby Sands' hunger strike.

In that part of his poetry, which is written as a Catholic but not specifically Northern poet, Heaney explores the Irish "past." He writes of the Famine as a part of the present for the people: "Stinking potatoes fouled the land, you still smell the running sore."[16] Behind the new and superficial prosperity of the Republic the old fears and loyalties linger: the peasants pay homage to the Famine God. The Famine is an obligatory theme for the Irish poet—as Patrick Kavanagh demonstrated—but Heaney delves deeper into the Irish past. The towns and ports were taken over by the British who left to the Irish only the infertile peat bogs of which Heaney takes jealous possession. Since the peat guards faithfully everything and everybody thrown into the bog, it acts as a repository of Irish history, which cannot be confined to the British occupation.

Heaney uncovers pre-historic fortresses, Celtic bracelets and embalmed Viking warriors. Not only were the Vikings not British but they were not Christians either. The dream of being Irish without being Catholic recurs here. The poet's journey is not merely into time but into geological shapes and forms. The crest of a hill is the spine of a woman whose breasts are the morenas. From the earth the Bog Queen emerges. But it is a betrayal to separate her from the peat: betrayals have occurred in Irish history but they are the work of nobles—a touch of populism is present in Heaney's sense of the Irish people. The poet's exploration is an act of love, endowed with a rich erotic sense. The woman who emerges from the Irish countryside is both mother and "insatiable bride." The land is not unfertile: it creates, destroys and re creates in an unending cycle.[17]

Here we are drawing closer to the heart of Heaney's poetry, considered still as Irish but not specifically Northern Irish. The creative cycle of the earth is also a linguistic process—"This is the vowel of earth/dreaming its root/in flowers and snow."[18] Following Joyce, Heaney exacts his revenge on the English language by re-introducing Irish words like "crannog" (land near a lake) and "kerne" (a poor soldier). The Vikings return too via the word "ret" (to go bad). Heaney's revenge takes the form of a liberation.

There is indeed the goal of compelling the colonizer to scurry for dictionaries and submit to unfamiliar constructions. But the reader can participate in the freedom of linguistic invention. No longer does s/he have to submit to uses of the subjunctive laid down by an absolute monarch. S/he works with the literary language to expand its possibilities. One thinks of Joyce and Beckett weaving the strands of *Finnegans Wake*.

Yet it is at this very moment of liberty that one has doubts about the experience that Heaney offers to us. The union of the poet and the mystical land of Ireland seems all too easy. The various mythical female figures leave us remembering the way that Irish males kneel before idealized women in order to avoid real women. One returns to Cathleen Ní Houlihan. Among the embalmed corpses in the peat-bog, many are the victims of violence: Viking warriors betrayed by their comrades or Viking girls punished for their infidelity.

Heaney sees in them the ancestors of the Belfast girls who are tarred and feathered for going with British soldiers. Unstated but implicit is the explanation of the Northern Irish violence as the most recent chapter of Ireland's tragic history. As such it is a sacred and necessary violence, in harmony with the thought of Pearse, who believed, in Yeats's words, "that in every generation must Ireland's blood be shed."[19]

But Heaney does not take the final step that would make him, however much higher his level, a fellow traveler of the IRA. Instead he displays a rationality that has nothing to do with Hegelian historicism: he brings a critical awareness to bear on the myth. *Strange Fruit* depicts the head severed from the body of a young woman. The head remains obstinately itself, defying the poet to turn it into a legendary offering to the gods of Irish history. The girl remains "nameless," which leaves her outside the poet's imagination, a position reinforced by the title of the poem. Kiberd puts the problem well: "the violence may have been sanitized or even prettified by art." *Strange Fruit* sets aside that temptation.[20]

So far the language of poetry, while it permits a freedom that is the antithesis of the roadblocks and police patrols that litter and divide Belfast, leaves those roadblocks intact. The mythical language of poetry cannot breathe fresh life into the non-language of politics. Indeed it is the accomplice of that language both because it presents a violence akin to the IRA's and because it leaves the monologues intact. Yet Heaney divides his volume *North* into two parts and calls the second part "North." These pages look visually different from the earlier ones because they are full of quotation marks.

Heaney opens by rejecting commitment in the Sartrian sense. This leaves him without an obvious role, so he tries out several. He describes himself as an exile, a clown and a voyeur. Important is not the precise role chosen but rather the multiplicity of possible roles. The structure of these poems is not monological, like the first part of the volume, but rather digressive. As well as the inverted commas, there are lots of commas and full stops. *Whatever you say say nothing* consists of all the clichés one hears and reads about the North—"As the man said when Celtic won, 'The Pope of Rome's a happy man this night.'" The poet's voice comes through—ironic, self-aware and quiet.[21]

Heaney has been criticized for not speaking on the North sooner and more strongly, for being timid and for not creating myths like Yeats.[22] But the comparison with Yeats ignores the very different historical situation both inside and outside Ireland. Yeats was living in a period of European nationalism, within a lifetime of Italian Unification and precisely when the Eastern European nations re-emerged at Versailles. The struggle of one small country against the British Empire was seen as heroic. There is, however, little greatness in the IRA bomb attack on Harrods or in Bloody Sunday at Derry. Ordinariness, self-awareness and caring for others are the values that emerge by their absence from the Northern Irish struggle. Heaney does not allow himself the false luxury of objectivity: he writes about the British Army as invaders who do not belong on his terrain—"I had rights-of-way, fields, cattle in my keeping."[23] Representatives of government inspire fear in him as a child: the constable in his uniform and on his bicycle.

The effort of rationality does not give Heaney any new understanding: "the liberal papist note sounds hollow." Writing about the Northern Catholics, he affirms, in a poem whose title is its own explanation, that their history imposes on them "a sensation of opaque fidelity."[24]

Unsurprisingly Heaney, despite all his success, has been attacked by British Conservatives for not divorcing himself from the men of violence in his community and by the Republicans for not being more forthright in defending that community. Both attitudes seem to me unfair. Heaney gives up much—the incandescent lyricism of *Kinship*—in order to surround the poetic objects of *North*, Part 2 with a critical commentary. He is modest about what a poet can achieve, but he keeps trying. Even when he leaves the North, he views it as an insider, specifically rejecting the Joycean solution of exile. The North remains what it was: "all around us, though/we hadn't named it, the ministry of fear."[25] Since *The Ministry of Fear* is the title of a Graham Greene novel, Heaney may be comparing the lot of an English Catholic writer with his own. Certainly the assertion that the Catholics had no part in shaping the North, in naming things, is an illustration of the poet's alienation, which is a greater version of the ordinary citizen's.

What is the reader who is not from Northern Ireland to make of this poetry? The North is not easily to be categorized: Marxist interpretations are of no use yet clearly people do not massacre one another over the Virgin Mary, even if they define themselves as Catholics and Protestants. But if these self-definitions are viewed as the form taken by an ossified colonialism, now vanished, then they may provide a plausible interpretation. If it be accepted, then Northern Ireland is almost unique in contemporary Europe, unlike Alto Adige- Sud Tirol, Catalonia or Wales.

But if one stresses the economic problems of the North, the sharp contrast with the South and the tribal groupings as a form of nationalism, then Northern Ireland has much in common with the ex-Yugoslavia. Moreover, violence is on the increase in such European countries as France and Italy. As the global economy increases the number of the excluded, so one can imagine mini–Northern Irelands becoming more frequent. Then the European nature of Heaney's poetry will become all too apparent.

Chapter Six

Three right-wing novels

Now that we have looked at literary language in its role as a critic of political discourse in Italy, Germany, and Northern Ireland, we might consider the political ramifications of works that are neither committed nor anti-political nor acting as a watchdog over political language. Such books cannot avoid making statements that have political implications. To describe these, the words "right" and "left" are most commonly used, however imprecise they may be. For the general reader of today the value of the political writing as writing is decisive. It is interesting to examine whether Orwell is primarily satirizing Nazism or Stalinism. But what really matters is whether his insights into totalitarianism are penetrating or not. If he can convince the reader that they are valuable, then he has written a good book. (No book can be good, Sartre reminds us, until it has been read.) There are readers who are still committed and who judge a book by the nature of its political views, and there are writers whose political tale is so aberrant that it makes their work unreadable. This is true of Céline's pamphlets, but not of his novels. His pamphlets should of course be studied because they tell us much about the evil of anti-Semitism. But that is a different kind of reading, in which one is not attracted by the work itself.

Until now we have discussed mostly left-wing writing because more good twentieth-century writing comes from the left or at least presents itself as such. Right-wing writing, however, often presents itself as neutral or outside of politics. Don Sebastiano, "hero" of *The Day of Judgement,* does not vote or take part in politics but in so doing he is limiting the role of history in his and his fellow citizens' lives, which is a right-wing attitude. There is also a tendency for the right to be ashamed of itself—although

Evelyn Waugh was certainly not—because it has been held responsible for Hitler, not to mention Thatcher, the crisis of welfare, the coalminers' defeat and many other welcome or unwelcome developments. But there are many right-wing texts that offer political writing of a high order and here we shall look at three of them.

Giuseppe Tomasi di Lampedusa was born in 1896 in Palermo. His was an aristocratic family and, although its fortunes were in decline, Giuseppe never had to work. He was a shy, undistinguished boy and the dominant influence on him was his mother. He married another strong woman, Alessandra Wolff, a pioneer in the new field of psychoanalysis. The two met in London because the young Lampedusa spent much time traveling. England and France were among his favorite countries and he also read their literature: Proust, Joyce, Stendhal and Shakespeare were among the writers he liked best. In 1943 American planes bombed and badly damaged his family's house in Palermo, which was a trauma for Lampedusa.[1] In the post-war years he spent most days wandering around the Palermo cafés with a big bag full of books and cakes. Some people considered this a wasted, idle life, although it seems rather pleasant to this author. Lampedusa gave private lessons in French and English literature to a small group of chosen students who included Gioacchino Lanza, one of the models for Tancredi. Lampedusa brooded long and hard about writing a novel and then wrote *The Leopard*. He died without establishing a definitive version and after his manuscript had been refused by Elio Vittorini. Lampedusa may have considered *Il Gattopardo (The Leopard)* unpolitical, but the difficulties he and others had in getting it published were proofs that he was wrong. A manuscript of the novel was sent to Elio Vittorini, a fellow-Sicilian, who turned it down on the grounds that it was static: neither the hero nor the historical situation changed. Despite his clash with Togliatti, Vittorini adhered to a view of the novel that the PCI could endorse: the historical situation must be in movement. There was no need for the presence in the novel of the final triumph of socialism, but the Prince's loyalty to the past and a depiction of the Unification of Italy that voided it of meaning were too much for Vittorini to take. Another manuscript found its way to Giorgio Bassani, the author of *The Garden of the Finzi-Contini*, who recommended it to Giangiacomo Feltrinelli. Much to the PCI's irritation, Feltrinelli had just published the Italian translation of *Dr. Zhivago*. This was Feltrinelli's greatest adventure as a publisher. By contrast he was not interested in *The Leopard*, but he trusted Bassani's judgement.[2]

Il Gattopardo appeared in 1958 after Lampedusa's death and around the same time as Pasolini's *A Violent Life*. Pasolini was drawing closer to the PCI and his hero dies a communist martyr. But he depicts the Rome sub-proletariat, and in its own way his novel too marks the end of neo-realism. The Italian working-class was changing and, to catch up, left-wing intellectuals had to flounder their way through the new series of the review *Officina*, through Franco Fortini's *Ragionamenti* and through the criticism heaped on them by the 1963 Group. Meanwhile Fellini's *La Dolce Vita* marked a new age in the cinema of which Visconti's version of *The Leopard* was an important part.

STYLE RATHER THAN HISTORY

There is one sentence in *The Leopard* that has become all too well known: "If we want things to stay as they are, things will have to change."[3]

It is worth remembering that it is spoken by Tancredi, who is not, like the Prince, close to the narrator. Moreover things do change—for the worse. The last chapter depicts the decline of the House of Salina. Tancredi's sentence is used in Italy, however, to define *trasformismo*, the view that Italian history is made up of pseudo-struggles where the new sociopolitical force, instead of defeating the existing order and ruling itself, comes to an agreement with its supposed enemy, which allows them to rule together and leaves the old order intact.

This explains why Tancredi goes over to Garibaldi, an enemy of the Southern aristocracy and of the king of Naples and a great democrat. Tancredi announces his plan in this same conversation: he is not really going over to Garibaldi but to the Piedmont monarchy, which is using Garibaldi to conquer the South. Prudently Tancredi waits until the rebels are on the outskirts of Palermo. His closest friend, when he joins up, is a Milanese aristocrat and both switch as soon as they can into the Piedmontese uniform. Tancredi goes on to a career as a diplomat, after repairing the damage done to his family fortunes by a spendthrift father, via his marriage to Angelica, whose father is a member of the new middle-class that also engages in *trasformismo*.

There is then no expansion of democracy in the process of building the new Italian state. On the contrary the referendum is blatantly faked. Two points about it are revealing, aside from its total triumph. The first is that the peasants come to ask the Prince's opinion: he tells them to vote yes, fearing there will be repercussions on them if they do not. But they think that the Prince is trying to mislead them and that he really wants them to vote no. So they duly vote yes. This lack of trust, only occasionally comic, is endemic in Sicily and to a lesser extent in all Italy. Today it blocks the creation of a flourishing stock market, much less of a new society. The second point is that although the village of Donnafugata was unanimous in its declared support for the referendum—512 votes were cast, 512 said yes—at least one man, the organist Don Ciccio, has voted no. This vote has been conveniently forgotten, although it was a reasoned choice for the feudal order. Don Ciccio had personal ties to the monarchy, which paid for his education. His no vote reflected gratitude and loyalty: emotions for which there is no place in the new Italy.

The Piedmontese élite does not believe that this version of things is correct. A representative of the government manages to find his way across Sicily to the Prince's summer residence. He is horrified by the roads, the poverty and the incessant, exaggerated tales of brigands, but he is confident that Piedmont can bring order to Sicily. He offers the Prince a senate seat, which is hardly democratic (although it cannot be considered unmodern!). The Prince refuses him in an answer where he broods on Sicilian history. He dismisses the Marxist interpretation on the grounds that many countries underwent a difficult period of feudalism. The rejection of this and other rational explanations leaves the Prince—and the narrator—with the notion of Sicily as asleep and resentful of being awakened. This is a religious explanation, based on the belief that God created the world in a certain way and that it cannot be much changed. The chapter ends with the Baudelairian term "irredeemable." It follows a quotation from the poem *Voyage à Cythère* that expresses the unchanging demands of the flesh and the sordid ways they are satisfied. In Baudelaire's poetry there is much sense of sin and very little of redemption. Unsurprisingly, he was one of Lampedusa's favorite poets.

The view of society as fixed and governed by a fallen human nature has political implications. It is opposed to the neo-Hegelianism, which was the closest the new Italian state came to having an official philosophy. It ignores the Marxist belief in a working-class that bears new values and that, in saving itself, will save all society. If it is right-wing, it is certainly not Burkian, since it has no sense of community. It is post-feudal and, except for Don Ciccio and perhaps Father Pirrone, it associates feudalism with injustice. The main criticism made by Lampedusa was also made by Gramsci from an opposing viewpoint: the Unification of Italy was not carried out by a new class full of capitalist zeal and able to establish its own values as hegemonic, but rather by the Don Calogeros, who make money out of grain speculation, buy up church land and marry into the aristocracy. There is nothing corresponding to the French Jacobins, who created a new state, the Republic, and who rallied popular support around it.

Gramsci regrets the absence of the Jacobins whereas Lampedusa does not. But the absence is present in *The Leopard* and it cannot be filled by the existing Sicilian aristocracy or by the supporters of Garibaldi. At a ball for Palermo society held in November 1862 the hero was a Colonel Pallavicino, who had blocked Garibaldi's fresh rebellion at Aspromonte.

Not only was the colonel the idol of Palermo society but he depicted a Garibaldi, who was still great but who was surrounded by thugs and beggars unworthy of him. Thus Garibaldi could become a national hero, even while his attempt to found a democratic Italy was dismissed.

The stifling quality of the old-new Sicily is exemplified by the way women are depicted. In the first chapter the Prince leads his family in the rosary, which is the devotion to Mary. (He omits the first part—the Joyful Mysteries—and recites the other two parts in the wrong order. So he ends with the Crucifixion, which should precede the Resurrection. This is another Baudelairian touch.) Then the whore who receives the Prince's visit is called Mariannina. Woman as ideal and woman as harlot are the two extremes of the male vision. The Prince's wife is submissive, prudish and pious. More interesting is Angelica, who is defined by her beauty. This is a commodity that is paralleled by the size of her dowry. The reification of her beauty is made specific at the Ball when she is the object of covetous glances by men who admit, however, that "Donnafugata was a fief of Don Fabrizio's and if he had found that treasure there, one could no more be envious of that than of his finding a sulphur mine on his land; it was his property, there was nothing to be said."[4]

But Angelica is not passive. The erotic scene where she and Tancredi chase each other through the many rooms of the Prince's palace reveals her active sexuality. If her marriage turns out badly and she is nothing more than a political wire-puller, there is nothing female about this failure. It is part of the general decline.

The most interesting woman character in the novel is the Prince's daughter, Concetta. He admits she has the Salina spirit, which takes the form of a great refusal. When Tancredi does not, as she had hoped, propose to her she refuses the Milan count, just as her father refuses a senate seat. She is proudly Sicilian and rejects the ambitious, crude world of Unification. Not that she looks to Palermo society, for, like her father, she is an outsider in the Sicilian aristocracy. When we encounter her in the last chapter some fifty years later she does not, like her sisters, believe in the relics. She is reliving the events and the period of the novel and the various interpretations of it are an invitation to us to reread it. If the destruction of the relics reveals the falsity of the past, Concetta is finally liberated from the power that her father continued to exercise over her. His stuffed hunting dog joins the relics in the rubbish and Concetta is free.

She has something in common with the woman characters depicted by Sartre and Orwell. Lampedusa does not know what to do with Concetta's freedom. The brief portrayal in the concluding chapter cannot atone for Concetta's virtual absence from the novel after Angelica's entrance. But then Lampedusa clings to the notion that woman's beauty inspires men:

on his deathbed the Prince has a vision of a young, beautiful woman who does not speak and to whom he says nothing. It matters little whether she is Mary, Christ's mother, or a whore; women do not exist in their own right but are invented by men.

To return to our political discussion, such a depiction is no more right- than left-wing. The rightist flavor of *The Leopard* comes from the theme of Unification as a decline and from the way that the Prince lives it. In our opinion there is only a superficial nostalgia for a defeated aristocracy; it is present in the brilliant depiction of the Ball, but it is not dominant. The Prince is a very atypical member of that aristocracy: half North-European and with a strong interest in science. When he is dying he admits that both he and—implicitly—Tancredi had been wrong. "He had said the Salinas would always remain the Salinas. He had been wrong. The last Salina was himself. That fellow Garibaldi had won after all."[5]

Lampedusa's biographer suggests that the book not be read as a historical, much less a political, novel; it is rather a modern novel about an individual in search of values in a disintegrating society.[6] To anyone living in Italy this is a refreshing proposal.

We would, however, argue that precisely this individualism is right-wing. There is scant emphasis on solidarity in the novel and the Prince's decisions are made alone. As society is unable to provide codes of behavior, so the individual falls back on himself. Such skepticism about history is quite unlike the left's ceaseless quest for a historical project. The left is optimistic about the collectivity and, if not pessimistic, then wary of the individual. The right, once again, is the opposite. This, rather than *trasformismo,* is the political theme: the Prince has to find a way to live through a bleak period of Sicilian history. The qualities required are lucidity and courage, in particular the courage to face solitude. Both the Prince, who is not much of a husband or father, and Concetta live alone. Nor can one forget that pessimistic Catholicism that does not guarantee God's grace but demands the courage of which Baudelaire had spoken. Not that the Prince should be taken as a model. From the very start he is content both with the existing social order and with the new Italy, both of which allow him to keep his social position. But, as the shape of the new Italy grows clearer, the Prince's courage asserts itself.

The writing is the other trait that makes this a right-wing novel. In the neo-realist scheme of things, the writer hides behind the world he has created, like God behind his world, as Flaubert put it. Many of the characters are working-class and they must be allowed to speak for themselves. There is nothing absolute about this right-left distinction. Brecht wanted the audience to be aware it was watching a play. Still, in the Italy of the 1950s, the emphasis was on diminishing the ostensible importance of the writer and on increasing the importance of the Italian people who were his subjects. One remembers Pasolini's dislike of Italian prose writers who flaunted the brilliance of their style.

To Lampedusa art was the only worthwhile activity and in demonstrating that he was creating, the writer gave meaning to the world and to his own existence. It follows that the act of writing itself should be avowed and introduced into the work. Thus when Father Pirrone is asked to give his opinion of Tancredi as a future husband, his reply is set between two comments by the narrator: "He took refuge in Prudence, most tractable of the cardinal virtues." "The fund of goodness in our dear Tancredi is great indeed . . . he may become one day an excellent Christian husband." The prophecy, risky but prudently conditional, passed muster. Except for the "may," Fr. Pirrone's reply is banal as well as fictitious. The narrator's ironic comments first place the reply in a theological context and then point out to the reader that it is a conditional statement that he, although not Don Calogero, must interpret as a prophecy of Tancredi's almost certain infidelity.

Lampedusa uses other devices to inform us that this is a piece of fiction and not a slice of life. He does not attempt, for example, to reproduce the Sicilian dialects that his servants and especially the peasants would have used. He breaks out of the linear time-framework to tell us that the Prince's Palermo palace will be destroyed by an American bomb in 1943 and—more important—that Tancredi's marriage will not be happy. Plot poses a problem in this kind of right-wing fiction because it is the sign of a process of change. In *The Leopard* the problem is solved by the substitution of repetition for change. Each chapter offers the same traits—superficial brilliance, then the fight for survival and success. Even Fr. Pirrone's return to his village mirrors, in the family battle over the olive grove, the machinations of Don Calogero, while the young couple are a parody of Angelica and Tancredi. Since the genre of the novel emerged in a period of social change and depicts characters—like Fielding's Tom Jones—who are on the way up, the art that goes into changing this structure must be considerable.

This is the way to read the last chapter, which has puzzled observers, from Mario Alicata on. The great house of Salina's pre-eminence in Palermo is reduced to a collection of relics. A relic is not an image but a part of the true cross or of a saint's belongings. If the collection of relics be taken as what remains of the Salina, then the assertation that most of them are false is a retrospective judgment on the Prince. This is followed by the decision that a supposed painting of the Madonna is in fact of a young woman waiting for her lover. She is not unlike the woman of the dying Prince's vision.

Shortly there will be celebrations to mark the fiftieth anniversary of the March of the Thousand. In this welter of inauthenticity the church does not escape: the Cardinal of Palermo's bureaucrats do not possess the Baudelairian sense of sin that was present fifty years before. The mixture of imitation and banality provides the setting for Concetta's act of liberation.

Visconti's film of *The Leopard* (1962) concentrates on the Prince. It ignores the final chapter and devotes much of its energy to the Ball. Since Visconti was close to the PCI, a major figure of neo-realism, which he had founded with *Ossessione* (1943), and since his most recent film *Rocco and his Brothers* (1960) was a social film about a poor Southern family that resettles in the North, his enthusiasm for *The Leopard* rather disconcerted his admirers. But Visconti's own aristocratic background and his liking for opera drew him to this sumptuous story of decadence in a ruling-class. He would go on to make *Death in Venice* and *Ludwig*.

Visconti's interpretation of Lampedusa, which we do not share, emphasizes the splendor of the Salina. The Prince, played by Burt Lancaster, is the last of his kind, as he realizes when confronted with the beauty of the young Angelica (Claudia Cardinale). He leaves the Ball on his own and kneels before a priest who is taking the last sacraments to a dying man. At the same moment a group of young men who followed Garibaldi to Aspromonte is executed. Tancredi's gamble has paid off and his class will survive Unification. But the Prince sees his own death and knows he is the last of the Salinas.

Mario Alicata took a very different view of the novel. Both he and Pietro Ingrao had collaborated with Visconti on *Ossessione*. They also shared a passion for American writers and Togliatti, showing the cruel subtlety of the Third International, made Alicata into his hatchet man for the battle against Vittorini and Hemingway. Afterward Alicata became an orthodox and talented PCI intellectual. His article on *The Leopard* expresses the left's opposition coherently.[7] Alicata begins by lamenting the lack of realist novels in Italy, which reminds us of the *Metello* controversy. A void has been left that *The Leopard*, decadent rather than realistic, has been able to fill. But Alicata points out that there was peasant protest when the redshirts arrived in Sicily and that Garibaldi put it down. Alicata also affirms that Lampedusa may be mostly correct when he stresses that Unification brought chaos to Sicily, but such chaos was created by historical agents whom Lampedusa ignores. This also makes the book boring because once the author's cosmic pessimism is stated in the first chapter, there is nothing more to be said. Alicata likes the last chapter but considers it completely extraneous to the rest of the book, although its theme is the vanity of all things, which Alicata sees throughout the book.

Alicata's opinion and analysis are logical if one accepts his left-wing starting point. He just does not see that the right can produce culture and that the Prince's pessimism can find expression in such values as lucidity. This is of course only one example of right-wing writing: The Céline of *Féerie*, with his furious diatribes and his embattled narrator, represents a very different kind, while the comedies of Evelyn Waugh are a third. We must next look at another Italian novel that is close in certain ways to *The Leopard*.

The Living Dead of Sardinia

Salvatore Satta too wrote one great novel that was published posthumously. It too is a historical novel that has death as its other main preoccupation. It also seems to us to contain a political tale that could be called right-wing. Here the parallels cease: Satta's book does not have the sumptuous feasts of Lampedusa's, it has aroused little interest in the English-speaking world and its brand of politics is different.

During the Second World War Satta wrote a short book called *De Profundis*. Published in 1948 although written in 1944-45, its worldview anticipates that of Satta's novel. The title indicates a religious perspective that can overlap with a right-wing political vision based on individual rights and—more important—responsibilities. Satta sees the war not as a defeat for fascism because ideology means little to him, but as the collapse of the Italian state and hence as the need for the individual to "become a state unto himself."[8] Fascism was nothing more than the regime of traditional man willing to accept authority in order to defend his privileges. Mussolini's language was a rhetorical device that hid his chronic lack of preparation for war.

But the real weakness was the Italian people. Satta does not like the word "people" ("popolo") and affirms that it is made up of individuals each endowed with a moral conscience. Satta defines freedom: "it cannot be reduced to political or economic terms . . . each person must conquer it and keep it in his heart . . . this is, in a word, Christian liberty based on renunciation and self-sacrifice."[9] This kind of freedom is incompatible with reliance on the state.

Other states are not much better than the Italian: Satta has no great liking for Britain and anti-fascism is as meaningless as fascism—there is no trace of commitment in *De Profundis*. The sign of national decline is the black market, a theme that arouses in Satta conflicting emotions. In general he is opposed to all markets because buying and selling do not constitute work. Satta has inherited the Catholic dislike of usury. With the spread of the black market all the Italian population, even the working-class, is drawn into a moral morass of unearned money and undeclared goods. There was formerly "a mystical sense of property"[10] but that gives way to the omnipotence of money—Don Sebastiano belongs to the earlier world. But *De Profundis's* main theme is not historical but moral. The struggle takes place within each person and it will not be easy because fate is "a mysterious thread woven by the devil."[11]

After this interesting, untimely first book, light years distant from Gramsci and populism, Satta (1902–1975) devoted himself to the study of law. He became Professor at Rome University and the author of many books. A collection of essays written in the 1950s was posthumously published in 1994 under the title *Il Mistero del processo*. It begins with a dreadful scene of massacre during the French Revolution. This is revolutionary justice: the links with the 1940s and 1950s are obvious. To such justice Satta opposes judgment, an act that has no goal but itself. The mystery of the trial is that it is "inhuman and anti-human" and hence it has elements of the divine. Suspecting this, humans have put judgment at the center of their lives. Not punishment nor reward but judgment—a cleansing or an evaluation—is to mark the end of the world.[12]

When Satta died the probably unfinished manuscript of *The Day* was discovered among his papers. It was published by Cedam in 1977, as if it were a treatise on law, and then by Adelphi in 1979. Satta had already tried his hand at novel writing. In the late 1920s he wrote *La Veranda*, which depicts a TB sanatorium. By this if by no other trait, it invites comparison with Thomas Mann's *Zauberberg (The Magic Mountain)*. *La Veranda* was also published posthumously in 1981.

The opening pages of *Il Giorno* re-elaborate *Il mistero* and set the tone. Satta's narrator is more distant from his hero and has greater freedom than Lampedusa's. Most of the language is his and there is little direct speech, although occasional words and phrases from Sardinian are strewn across the pages. Satta begins by presenting Don Sebastiano Sanna Carboni and he himself remains a ghost for the first forty pages. Don Sebastiano is introduced first by his name, which is not exactly what it seems. The reader next encounters him in a setting of exaggerated order and repetition. It is "precisely" nine o'clock in the evening and Don Sebastiano has done what he does every evening: he has read every line of the newspaper. It is his only text since we soon learn that he does not read books, believing there is little to be learned from them and little to be learned in general. Now he folds the paper, tidies his desk and prepares to join his family.

Don Sebastiano belongs to the lesser nobility, created by Charles V of Spain, "if it is true," adds the narrator, introducing a grain of doubt about whether it was Charles V who created the nobility, or whether such a nobility was created or whether the reason was that they were being rewarded for spreading the olive tree across Sardinia. The narrator is certain the minor nobility was authentically Sardinian whereas the grand nobles were from Cagliari and barely Sardinian. Thus a new capital is established: for the duration of this novel Nuoro will be the center of ambitions and passions as well as of doubt. Sassari is important only as a place remote from Nuoro.

Don Sebastiano's double-barreled name is not very true: it is merely his mother's name attached to his father's. This uncertain name is a sign that Don Sebastiano may belong to the ghosts. The next piece of information we glean is that he is a notary. The importance of notaries and their link with the written word and hence with the state has been discussed already. But it must all be reversed here. The narrator informs us that the notary becomes important when the spoken-word agreements, backed only by the protagonists' promise to observe them, began to decline. This is a sign that the narrator does not perceive the process of modernization as necessarily good.

Moreover Don Sebastian does not attempt to represent the modernizing state. He is proud that his name is entwined around the King's name on the official stamp, which he locks away each evening in a drawer of his desk. He does not seek to guide land sales or to spread Italian. He has none of Croce's neo-Hegelianism and the past and future have been and will be much the same as the present. In capitalist Italy he does not charge as much for his services as he could. He accepts as clients mainland Italians who are buying up Sardinia's forests.

Don Sebastiano takes no part in politics. He does not vote or have any sense of society as made up of warring social classes or groups. Rather there is a king, formerly of Piedmont now of Italy, but Unification means little in Sardinia. In any case ruling the country is the task of ministers chosen by the King. They are figures in a pre-political legend rather than real humans. Don Sebastian recounts to his family the good deeds of these ministers, as described in the newspapers. He must have noted that the parliamentary candidates for Nuoro were all lawyers and came from the countryside around the city. They were guided not by duty to the king nor by ideologies but by ambition. They marry into ghostly Nuoro families where the daughters would otherwise remain unmarried. They are the men of the new, post-Unification Italy, members of the political class and aspirant members of the ruling-class. The narrator does not use such terminology and Don Sebastiano barely knows these men whose challenge to the Nuoro élite is rebuffed.

Among the authors Don Sebastiano has not read are Weber, Michels and Pareto. This rural notary is guided by reverence for the monarchy, a certain kind of ambition for his sons and his strong sense of fate. The insult he hurls at his wife in their quarrels is, "You are in this world only because there is room for you."[13] The three threads of his thought run together in a worldview where a kindly, distant king rules but a zealous fate crushes those who do not work hard (and sometimes those who do).

The narrator approves of Don Sebastiano, but his own worldview is broader and simpler. A modern narrator gives statistics so we learn that the population of Nuoro is 7,051, that Don Sebastiano's basic fee is L.3.50 and that the number of times the bell tolls for a funeral is nine for a man and seven for a woman. This goes unchallenged, whereas the rule of slow bells for an important man and faster for a poor man is often violated, although never without creating discord. Isolated amid the fog of uncertainty these statistics lose all value. The dead are forgotten straight after the funeral. The people of Nuoro are too busy leading their own lives, which are a constant struggle against death. Yet they are undermined or undermine themselves by their "instinct of dissolution." (G., p. 15)

Don Sebastiano's family is the most important theme in his life: seven boys to put through school. He is determined that each one shall obtain a "laurea." Yet even as he constructs on their behalf, building his big, uncomfortable house, farming his various plots of land and spending as little money as possible, so his family is disintegrating. The causes are the same: Don Sebastiano's asceticism prevents him from showing affection to his wife and makes his sons resent the sacrifices he is imposing on himself and on his family to pay for their education. So as Don Sebastiano increases his wealth and his standing in Nuoro, his wife, Donna Vincenza, grows ever more alienated from him and his sons set out in their various directions. The conclusion is that life is inseparable from death. Donna Vincenza listens to her children's voices as if they were still in her womb, but they do not inspire her with hope. Since hope places its trust in the future and she sees only perils in the future, motherhood is an anticipation of death.

Far from being an isolated example of an unhappy marriage, this living death, where life does not resist death but collaborates with it, dominates Nuoro. The town too is marked by division. There are three, very different segments: Sèuna, which is home to farm laborers; San Pietro, the fief of sheep herders; and Nuoro proper, where the middle-classes live. They coexist in an uneasy truce with one another and with the outside world. The sheepherder "knows he is always innocent in his own eyes but authority feels differently." (G., p. 33) Relations are conducted via elaborate codes so that no community is formed and there is a violence that erupts when the codes are broken. The Coralles, talented rustlers, are leading law-breakers or rather they impose their own law on their neighbors.

After some forty pages the narrator speaks about himself. "I am writing these pages that no-one will read, because I hope to have enough lucidity to destroy them before I die." (G. p. 42) Why then does he bother writing? The answer is that same contradiction. By writing he is bringing death on his fellow citizens, who must tell the story of their lives, which in religious language means they must confess their sins, before they can rest in peace. We are reminded that "Requiescant in pace" is a subjunctive not an indicative verb. Only after being judged can the characters be freed of the sin of having lived. The last judgment marks the response to the theme of moral conscience discussed in *De Profundis*. The narrator's language is the life that he draws from his characters' deaths. When the judgments are all complete, his life too will be absorbed by death. Judgment is linked with death because it is the opposite of life.

The narrator talks of his house, which he wants to look like an old Sardinian house. But there is a flaw here again, for a real house would be handed down to him from his parents and their parents. Nor does the narrator forget to criticize the language he uses. The flux of human experience cannot be fixed: perhaps music would be better suited to render it? Elsewhere the narrator does his auto critique: his memories are in "an absurd disorder." (G., p. 68) Only the town of Nuoro allows him to write: he goes to the cemetery "to resume the conversation without which these pages could not continue." (G., p. 98)

When he goes to the cemetery the narrator's anti-modern stance emerges: the rituals of death have changed because "our age is characterized by its flair for making everything trivial." (G., p. 100) The cemetery has been re-done and there is less place for the dead. The grave-digger, Milieddu, who was the second identity of everyone in Nuoro, capital of the living dead, is no longer there. There is a difference between ordinary narrators who feel nostalgic for a lost past and this narrator who is searching for the signs of death. Once again his story is made up of words that emerge from the near-silence of death. For these dead are not at peace. As far back as the Etruscans they want their story to be told. The narrator's task is to liberate "the men of my people" by telling how they died. As long as he does this, he must continue writing, continue the life that bears death within it.

The issues at stake become clearer if we look at some of the narrator's stories. The main story of Don Sebastiano has as its theme the motif of construction-disintegration. Early in the book we see Don Sebastiano's pleasure at farming the land in which he has invested the profits of his notary's office. He does not think of shares or even government bonds: the only real wealth is in land. The reader enjoys the description of the various fruits and the wine-making grapes that are ceremoniously brought to the big house to be treated by a team of workers. The richness of nature is heartening and the chapters dealing with wine and bread describe a kind of communion. But the land introduces fresh disputes into the family: Donna Vincenza complains when her husband sells some fields that belonged to her. Don Sebastiano rises early to put in hours of work before he goes to his notary's study; this exacerbates the resentment of his sons.

Later in the book comes Don Riccione's attempt to recover an estate that his father had been obliged to sell twenty years before. He takes the road of politics, seeking to unite the Seùna landless peasants against the landowners. Here one sees Satta's right-wing view, for Don Riccione is acting in the context of the nascent Socialist movement, which Satta reduces to a banal tale of educated ambitious orators manipulating the illiterate peasants for their own purposes. Don Sebastiano is saved by Ziu Poddanzu (as usual this is an affectionate nickname and for the Italian state his name is something quite different and barely known in Nuoro), who vouches for his honesty in Seùna.

His relationship with Ziu Poddanzu is Don Sebastiano's most successful. The two men are separated by wealth and social standing but they are united by their liking for the land and by their agreement on the ethic of work and on fixed social hierarchies. Near the end of the book Ziu Poddanzu saves Don Sebastiano a second time. One concludes that this kind of feudal relationship—generous lord and faithful retainer, which also attracted Lampedusa—fits Satta's worldview.

Don Sebastiano's family ties crumble. One son returns from the First World War to die. Of what, is unclear. Death is so common in Nuoro that one should really ask how anyone manages to stay alive. Ludovico, another son, remains at home, convinced that the world is too demanding and that he will be unable to act successfully. He becomes a lawyer because he can open a studio in his father's house and thus avoid going out completely. Ludovico does well although he has not studied law. He plays on the Nuoresi's liking for long, unresolved lawsuits. Then he sees through the window an eligible and attractive young woman. He becomes engaged to her but, true to himself, he does not marry her and the engagement is broken off twelve years later. Ludovico lives his life in the shadow of death.

Another tale focuses on the religious aspects of this living death. Gonaria is devoted to God, to her brother, who is a priest, to her various relatives and to the children she teaches. Her trust in Providence is great but then her brother, by now a canon, falls ill with one of Satta's unnamed but deadly maladies. Gonaria continues to trust her God but the canon dies. To Gonaria, who had believed firmly that her brother represented God and therefore could not die, this is traumatic. She decides that God must be present somewhere in her brother's bedroom and she closes it up. Years later she is obliged to open it and to confront the reality that if God is not there, he is nowhere and does not exist.

The narrator's sympathy is with Gonaria and he refers to her as "the poor creature abandoned by God." (G., p. 250) But Satta's world is harsh and when she opens the door Gonaria finds much of the furniture devoured by insects, cobwebs everywhere and no trace of God. She flees from the town, across the dark countryside. Satta concludes: "what must happen, happens and God can do nothing about it." (G., p. 264)

Space does not allow us to analyze all the case studies—tales of altered wills, of an unfortunate young man who goes off to Milan to make his fortune and is cheated out of his money and of Don Sebastiano's tenant farmer who commits a murder when a drought arrives and kills off all his crop. The narrator moves unerringly from case to case. His periods are long, he uses subordinate clauses, but often he limits himself to a string of parallel clauses so that his prose moves quickly. Here is an example:

> Baronia was a garden during the winter. If from time to time the river went crazy, overflowed its banks, flooded the fields and isolated the absurd little villages that—who knows how or why—had sprung up in the vast plain, still when it withdrew and turned itself into a gentle stream and here and there lingered in blue pools that looked like patches of sky, it left among the rocks, to make good the damage, a fine, damp soil that was already wheat or barley or above all broad beans or those melons with the bluish flesh that spread the name of Baronia throughout Sardinia. The trouble was that paradise lasted three months in Baronia: then the sun became hostile, was sorry it had brought so much joy to mankind and it too went mad. (G., p. 27)

In the long second sentence four verbs depend on the one "if," while the last sentence ends with three parallel main clauses. Both the river and the sun are personified, which makes the world more alive. Both are dangerous and, like lots of Satta's characters, menaced by madness. Human life is fragile and its origins unknown. Short pithy sentences like the first one sum up the description. The beauty of nature is palpable but it is also arbitrary.

The narrator flaunts his role and since he tells his stories in bits and pieces, he is the principle of unity. Nuoro itself did not exist 300 years ago and no one knows how it came into being, but there may have been a settlement there in pre-Roman times. Space is as uncertain as time: the sheep rustled by the Corrales re-appear out of nowhere.

Politically this is barely a society at all. People do not help one another because they do not trust one another. One cannot imagine a welfare state in this Nuoro. The limits on human ability to resist fate are severe. By Western European standards, *The Day* is a throwback to earlier centuries.

It was published at the moment when the historic compromise broke up and Satta's fellow-Sardinian, Enrico Berlinguer, took the PCI back into opposition. Berlinguer was a man of austerity and it is tempting to see a simple parallel between politics and literature. Tempting but misleading. The cultural setting for Satta's novel is the non-modernity of sectors of Italian society and is not to be confused with mere economic backwardness. It takes the form of showing how little humans can do to change their condition. It depicts an Italy that is still a religious society, since Satta's denial of God does not lead him to embrace pragmatism much less any historical philosophy.

Leadership of the society depicted in *The Day* will fall to those people like Don Sebastiano who are reconciled to the limits of their condition and who will, by definition, not want to lead. Charisma, dictators and democracy are all unlikely to be of any use. Unlike *The Leopard*, this novel depicts no great events and is not nostalgic for great struggles and heroic deeds. Stoicism and silence, more extreme forms of courage and lucidity, are the virtues dear to Satta. Freedom lies only in language: in recognizing that the word brings death—one cannot choose to write love sonnets or drawing-room comedies—but that it also debunks and for a while lives in the shadow of death, which is the only true life.

Ebenezer Resists

G. B. Edward's *The Book of Ebenezer le Page* (1981) was also published after its author's death in 1976 and after being refused by several distinguished publishing houses. It too is about an island, Guernsey, which belongs to a distant, powerful, uncaring nation-state. As in *The Day*, the narrator is all-important and although there is a linear structure, his voice is here again the chief principle of order. But Ebenezer Le Page is very different from Satta's narrator, who flits from topic to topic and hides only to re-appear some pages later. Ebenezer struggles to impose his language on the entire book; he writes mostly of events in which he was involved, for this is the story of his life. He offers great chunks of narrative that are doubly his. He is the main character and he writes in an English that is marked by his Guernsey patois.[14]

The title is biblical: his mother reads the Bible every day. But the title is a hint that Ebenezer will not accept the domination of any other text, however great its authority may be. He establishes himself as the storyteller. His title has an artisanal ring and sure enough Ebenezer tells us about the kind of paper he uses and how much it costs. The title also contains two unsaid statements. Firstly one knows that Ebenezer is not the author and secondly this is not the written but the spoken language. The reader notes on the front cover that "the book of Ebenezer le Page" is also "a novel by G. B. Edwards." Who is this mysterious Edwards? A doubt hangs over the seemingly so clear narrative. The presence of the spoken monologue makes the language ever more a language of protest. This is not the Guernsey that the tourists see nor is it the haven of offshore banking (which is actually centered in Jersey.)

Ebenezer invites us to believe in him as a guide. His cousin Raymond says that he does not believe in anything said or done, nor in God, nor in his own existence. Ebenezer agrees with Raymond on every point except the last one, where he asserts, "I know I am Ebenezer Le Page."[15] His personal identity is closely linked to place—the Channel Island of Guernsey. One of the people I interviewed on Guernsey, in the summer of 2001, described Ebenezer as "a dour, old Guernseyman." He spends much time developing this sense of place, which is more concrete than Sardinia or Sicily in the two novels already discussed. Where Sardinia hovers between life and death, Guernsey is on the side of life. Until 1939 the island is poor but the people survive by growing fruit and vegetables for the British market, by fishing, by quarrying or by something similar.

Ebenezer prefers such occupations to pen work in the government service and to wheeling and dealing as Horace does when he opens his shop. Buying and selling are not work for Ebenezer. Working for oneself is better than having an employer, even if Ebenezer gets along well with the tomato exporter for whom he works. His sister is married to a poor fisherman but they are happy. The patois is the language of such people, whereas the written word is linked with bureaucracy, which quickly turns into government interference in society. Reading is dangerous, as Raymond's theological speculation proves: torn by the question of whether God's love is real, he undermines his existence. He once describes to Ebenezer the new world of Fordism, which seems a hell to his independent cousin.

Contact with the upper-classes offers a different kind of danger: Cousin Mary-Anne's husband is enticed off to England by the Princess whose coachman he is; his wife and family are left to fend for themselves. Only Liza Quéripel can start as a lady's maid and take over the family, and she does not want to stay on but instead returns to Guernsey.

The question of class is secondary to the colonial status imposed on Guernsey by Britain. This is illustrated at the start of the book in an incident barely narrated but that has devastating effects. Ebenezer's father sides with the Boers and the Irish against England. He goes off to fight for the Boers and is killed. Edwards provides no details on this. One suspects that Ebenezer's father is bored with his marriage and some characters draw from the episode the lesson of prudence, which becomes a theme in the book. But it is a powerful influence on the young Ebenezer.

References to England are almost all disparaging. "We are not a lazy lot like they are in England." (E., p. 196) Earlier a wife has gone off to England, while her husband commits suicide in Guernsey. An English company comes to Guernsey with a hare-brained scheme for mining gold; since it is not a local but a London-based firm it is able to obtain finance until the day it gives up and leaves. In general to go to England is to uproot oneself from Guernsey, to waste one's ability and to leave behind chaos on the island. Unsurprisingly, Jim Mahon, Ebenezer's closest friend, looks to the small Celtic countries. He joins a Welsh regiment when he is drafted into the army. "They were more natural: they was more like us." (E., p. 104)

Ebenezer has no sense of any Channel Islands identity. Being from Guernsey implies a rejection of Jersey. Moreover, although Guernsey has a French-speaking community whose spoken French has much in common with the patois of the nearby Cotentin peninsula of Normandy, Ebenezer does not think of himself as belonging to a French-speaking world.

There is an intriguing moment when Jim Mahon visits the site of the Battle of Hastings and comments: "It's a wonder we ever got him at all." (E., p. 85) "Him" is Harold and "we" can only be the Normans. But this is the only time Ebenezer and his friends identify with France and perhaps they are pleased that a king was killed. During the Second World War Guernsey is occupied by the Germans. Ebenezer is firm in his dislike of them, of the restrictions they impose, of the near-starvation of the last year and of the deaths of Raymond and Horace, blown up by a mine. He also makes one German friend as if to show that people count more than the passports they carry. One chapter deals with slave labor but there is nothing on the holocaust. (Note that Edwards was not on Guernsey during the German occupation and the same Guernsey source says that Ebenezer could not have made his long nightly walks because the roads were crawling with German soldiers.)

Ebenezer reserves a special hatred for the increase in bureaucracy that took place under the Germans. "It is a craze have gone on ever since," he adds in his patois English. (E., p. 271) So instead of taking the left-wing view that the greater role of government during the war helped prepare the social reforms of the Welfare State after 1945, Ebenezer takes the right-wing view that there was excessive government intervention, which continued after 1945.

Ebenezer is a right-wing anarchist, a worldview that dominates his private life too. He has male friends but he outlives them and clings to the memory of Jim Mahon. With women he makes a bad start and continues badly. The first time he makes love—"I must say I was disappointed. I thought it was going to be more than that." (E., p. 35)—Ebenezer is caught in a classic male trap: he does not give much but he expects affection and intimacy from the woman who does not, of course, provide them. Ebenezer has no use for women's liberation because he does not consider them unequal.

Logically this champion of male independence meets the most independent of Guernsey women, Liza Quéripel. Each is attracted by the other's strong character, which neither can in practice tolerate. On their first date, they argue repeatedly and at a circus Liza intervenes to interrupt a male hypnotist who is mesmerizing a woman. Shouting "Brutes of men. That poor woman" (E., p. 69), she breaks up the act to Ebenezer's great consternation. This pattern holds: in a squabble about which of the two is the taller, Ebenezer pushes Liza into a rock pond and returns to tell his friends that he has drowned her.

The chase continues: Ebenezer loves Liza but one doubts if he could say to her "j'aime à toi" in Luce Irigaray's sense of the term. Liza's reply when he proposes to her after his mother's death is "I wouldn't be me any longer." (E., p. 205) He worsens his case by telling Liza she would be Mrs Ebenezer le Page, which leads to her refusal to marry him. Names really do matter. In general Liza is the first woman character we meet who can stand up to men. Moreover in the context of the book's values her decisions to remain in Guernsey, to redo her family's house and to shun the new island of tourists and profiteers are admirable. How did Edwards manage to create such a woman character? It is true that by the 1970s the women's movement had begun its long march, but Edwards does not seem the man to pay attention to it. The reason lies rather in his sense of man and woman locked in an eternal battle. In the rural society he describes there is no scope for those exercises of male power that are possible in Margaret Drabble's London. But matriarchism survives and is healthy. Biographically we know that Edwards fought with his mother.[16] This respect for woman's strength is a roundabout way of coming to an understanding of woman in her own right, but Edwards manages it. Counterpoint to Liza is Raymond's wife, Christine, who engages in battle with men and efficiently destroys them. She goes off to England, leaving her husband and lover to be blown up by the mine. (Ironically Raymond reads to her Coventry Patmore's poem about the joys of matrimony, *The Angel in the House*, discussed in chapter nine.)

So the choice is between succumbing to woman and being destroyed by her, or resisting her and living on one's own. Ebenezer makes the second choice and suffers from it: "I have lived without hope." (E., p. 206) This pessimism is present in *The Leopard* and in *The Day of Judgement*, albeit in less personal form. As if to show that class makes no difference, the Prince lives out his loneliness amid his family and Palermo society, while Don Sebastiano too is the center of a prosperous but disintegrating family and the narrator haunts the graveyards.

In all three novels relations between men and women are gravely flawed, but then societal developments are headed in the wrong direction. All three novels deal with the modernization of their islands and in every case modernization is seen as a loss of individual life and of personal feelings that are replaced by the getting and spending of capitalism. All three islands are on the periphery. While modernization goes successfully ahead in Turin and London, the voices from the periphery contain a critical lament.

Yet the Guernsey of his youth to which Ebenezer looks back was a hard, rugged life. He has a cousin, Mary-Ann, who appears miraculously at family tragedies to help out. Ebenezer considers her one of the most intelligent people he knows, but her interventions are not motivated by kindness: "She didn't think of herself as a good woman going around helping people. She said she only went to help people for what she could get." (E., p. 305) This is one of the few occasions when Cousin Mary-Ann speaks: her silence is a form of wisdom since people are unable to distort her views and make enemies for her. As political writing Ebenezer's book goes against the grain. He dislikes what is and sees in it the outline of what will be and the death of what he believed in. Ebenezer dislikes TV because "You can't get your spoke in against it." (E., p. 12) Far from becoming more democratic, society becomes more hierarchical. Mass production takes away beauty and individual vision. Just as the relics in *The Leopard* turn out to be false, in *The Book* Ebenezer finds that his sovereigns have been declared invalid by the English monetary authorities. He does not keep his money in banks, which he does not trust, but in various boxes scattered around his house. He does not draw his old-age pension because he believes a man "ought to be allowed to look after himself." (E., p. 385) The Welfare State here, the coming of socialism in Nuoro and the Garibaldini in Sicily provide the illusion of progress and of a more generous society. They remain, however, illusions.

The Book's ending, much criticized by most readers, reverses the lonely course of Ebenezer's life. He meets Neville, a young man, a painter, a lover of Guernsey and an individualist and his pretty, strong-minded girlfriend. Liking is rapid and mutual. Ebenezer decides to leave all his money and property to the boy. Then he discovers that the boy is a descendent of Liza Quéripel and the girl of Ebenezer himself. A surge of happiness replaces his stoical loneliness: his Guernsey will live on. Improbable as this may be, it allows Ebenezer to use a different kind of language and to end his book on a new note.

In general Ebenezer's language is dense, without many adjectives or adverbs and with short periods. He is aware of Rilke's view that any true communication demands silence and he notes that Jean and his sister "seemed to understand each other with very few words... there was a quietness around them." (E., p. 37) His own prose is, however, aggressive: "I haven't got no children, that I know of, but that don't mean I've been a perfect lover. I haven't led any girl up the garden either. When I took a girl out I soon let her know what it was I wanted. I kept my nose to the ground and, if there was nothing doing, I trotted off" (E., p. 37).

The two double negatives remind us that this is the speech of a man and a social group with little formal education. The analogy with horses increases the sexual and weakens the emotional elements of Ebenezer's relationships. Often Ebenezer sums up his attitude in one short, pithy sentence. At the end of a longish paragraph on Christmas he states that he never sent Christmas cards and adds: "I'm not one for spending my money on such rubbish." (E., p. 87) Similarly after a discussion on games of chance Ebenezer concludes: "I like to know what I am getting for my money." (E., p. 41)

The most striking feature of his language is, however, the ungrammatical use of verb and subject: "he have" for "he has" and "she don't" for "she doesn't." This is so common that it cannot be considered a mistake but rather an integral part of Ebenezer's English, the Guernsey patois that has invaded and occupied the territory of standard English. One returns to the theme of class but also to the theme of periphery triumphing over center. At his happiest, when Neville gives him the picture of his house, he exclaims, "It look nice, my picture." Guernsey has replaced Ireland in the role of teasing and usurping the role of the English language. Ebenezer demands the freedom to use his patois instead of the Queen's English.

When a religious friend offers to pray for him, Ebenezer thinks "the cheek." (E., p. 165) His narration is an onslaught on contemporary governments, churches and élites. John Fowles argues it is part of that tide of suspicion and doubt that is normally suppressed or diverted by the media but that isolates governments. There is no doubt that Edwards is an écrivain. Indeed the growing importance of politics is one of his targets. But the political equivalent of Ebenezer's skepticism is the increasing number of abstentions and spoiled ballots. The voices from Palermo, Nuoro and Guernsey rebuff the contemporary equivalents of the Piedmontese official, Don Riccione and the Guernsey tourists (the EU officials?) in the name of older truths about work, loneliness and death.

Telling such truths is the mark of these novels. The best of them, *The Day of Judgment*, goes further and shows God himself drawn into this harsh world. All three dismiss cherished modern beliefs about the individual's right to happiness and a social group's right to equality. In short: rights as a whole.

Chapter Seven

Stories of Hell

From the Auschwitz of Primo Levi to the Fairy-tales of Céline

Primo Levi (1917–1987) had studied chemistry before joining the Resistance. He was captured by the fascist militia in December 1943 and handed over to the Nazis. As a partisan and a Jew, his fate was sealed. The Nazis sent him to Auschwitz. He survived and took up the challenge that the SS had made to the prisoners. The SS said that they would destroy the camps, falsify the records and offer a mild version of what Auschwitz was like. Against this the prisoners, decimated and suffering enormous psychological as well as physical damage, would have no credibility. No one would believe their terrible tale. Levi's gamble, which he won, was that a few prisoners would manage to survive, to tell their version and to be believed. Levi devoted his life and his writing to this battle for the past that would, he felt, be decisive for the future. That he committed suicide in 1987 has no relevance to his struggle.

Although *Féerie pour une autre fois* was partly written in a Danish prison, Céline succeeded in avoiding the French Resistance and de Gaulle's post-war government. He left Paris on June 17, 1944, when the Battle of Normandy was still undecided. After a stay in a luxury hotel of the spa-town Baden-Baden, he, Lucette (called Arlette and Lili in *Féerie* possibly by an overlap with the film actress Arletty), and their cat, Bébert, destined to become the most famous cat in French literature, joined the main body of collaborators at Sigmaringen, a pretty, South German village on the Danube. Here men schemed and dreamed of impossible German victories, while Céline thought only of reaching Denmark, where he had friends and gold. He managed to get the necessary documents, which most collaborators could not do, and he set off across the collapsing Reich, lit up at night by Allied bombers. Céline reached Copenhagen, although his train often had to wait in tunnels to avoid being bombed. He moved into a pleasant flat in the Danish capital but could not enjoy it because there was a warrant out for his arrest in France. The French popular press got hold of the case, the French government was obliged to ask for extradition and the Danish government was obliged to throw Céline into prison. He remained there from December 1945 to February 1947.[1]

Céline suffered less in prison than the narrator of *Féerie*. But the psychological damage was great, although he worked hard on what would become *Féerie*. He continued the book after his release and hoped that it was good enough to make the French public forgive or forget his wartime role. His hope was unfounded but the French public was growing displeased with the purge and in 1951 Céline obtained an amnesty as a wounded, decorated veteran of the 1914 war. He returned to France, again with Bébert and again working on *Féerie*. In the meantime Jean Paulhan had published a chunk of Céline as part of his battle with "the directors of the Resistance." But *Féerie* was Céline's great hope. It was, however, too far in advance of literary taste and it brought back political memories people wanted to forget.

In my opinion *Féerie* is one of the very best books to emerge from the Second World War. It presents the war as rooted in the hatred that pervades ordinary life. Then in *Féerie II*, published with no greater success in 1954, the power that transforms a city into a mess of ruins is the same power as the artist deploys. In *Féerie I* the artist uses his courage and his linguistic ability to fight off would-be assassins. So the theme of the artist runs through both parts of the novel as an integral part or even as a cause of the war. Céline knew that Hitler had artistic pretensions; that he discussed architecture with Speer and liked Wagner.

The reason for putting Céline in the same chapter as Levi is not an attempt to vindicate Céline, or to suggest parallels between his vision of the war and Levi's. It is simply that the two men have thought much and fruitfully about language and war. The differences between them are enormous: Levi is learning about concentration camps; Céline is sure, beyond his protestations of innocence, of the artist's role in the bombing. Levi is just starting out as a writer; Céline had won fame with *Voyage*.

Telling Stories

Levi speaks of "the need to tell others."[2] He elaborates: "I had a whole stack of vital things to tell the civilized world. They were things personal to me but they concerned everyone, they were drenched in blood, things that, so it seemed to me, ought to shake the foundations of everybody's conscience."[3] This would, so he had thought while he was in the camp, bring him an inner liberation. His unspoken comparisons are with confession to a priest or with recounting one's personal problems to a psychiatrist. But Levi's task is more difficult. He has few points of reference and nothing with which to draw comparisons. This is an important argument that has been made by many observers, notably by Gunther Grass: "Auschwitz has remained inconceivable precisely because it is not comparable, cannot be historically contextualized, is not open to any confession of guilt."[4]

As someone who lays no claim to being a specialist on the holocaust, I cannot help feeling that it is dangerous to put Auschwitz into a category of its own. Surely it could be the worst human crime without being "isolated" from all other crimes.

Although Levi is not guilty, he often feels guilty. He is "guilty of being a man since men had built Auschwitz and Auschwitz had swallowed up millions of humans, among them many of my friends."[5] Survivors' guilt is a well-known psychological phenomenon, which Levi explores in *I sommersi e i salvati* (Turin: Einaudi 1986). But it drives Levi to find a language that can convey what man has endured. Since language was used in the camp to torment the prisoners, it is natural that he should begin his investigation with a discussion of words.

He found in writing "a complex, intense and new pleasure." It is the search for the right word "strong but brief" that can seize the object with "a maximum of rigor and a minimum of interference."[6] Much of the traditional novelist's work is done for Levi by Auschwitz. He does not have to think out a plot or a story and he is presented with a team of characters. Levi is protected against treating words lightly and he will take care not to be seduced by them. He will not indulge in "marbled Italian," so good for inscriptions, to which he prefers the Piedmontese dialect, which is meant to be spoken. In *Il sistema periodico* Levi demonstrates his liking for inventing words, for the way small communities defend themselves with language and for the humor that is present in ambiguity and storytelling. Most of Lévi's writing is deceptively simple: he recounts what happens to him, without juggling authorial voices or introducing myths.

Levi affirms that Nazism has cut the Germans off from one another, thus, as we have argued in chapter 4, weakening people's capacity to criticize the stories they are told by their government. In the death camp this strategy is taken to extremes. Levi writes of "the wall which separates us from the outside world for which we are dead."[7] The entry in the camp is entry to a world that makes no sense: even the word "Zugang," used for new prisoners, means not the "arrival" of new people but a place or a right of "entry." Oppression comes from without but also from within so that there is no "we" to oppose to "them." The "we" of the inmates is an entity riddled with conflicts, as each person fights for his own survival. This atomism is carefully fostered by the SS, who greet each new arrival—or rather arrange for him to be greeted by other inmates—with blows that cannot be understood as a punishment. Some inmates (Kapos, a word with a latin root that has been Germanized) belong to a privileged group that obtains better food or is less exposed to the cold, in return for maintaining discipline and division among the other prisoners.

These privileged "Häftlinge" are the "salvati" because they are able to exploit the system. Only they survive so the Auschwitz of the "sommersi" is a "non-detto," or untold story. Lévi is himself a "salvato" because his knowledge of chemistry is useful to the camp authorities, who are running a chemical plant that requires skilled technicians. As he waits in the morning to be taken over to his comfortable, heated laboratory, he watches other prisoners being marched out in the snow to one kind or another of their useless, exhausting tasks. Although he has maneuvered carefully to get his job, he feels a kind of guilt for his egoism in saving himself. From this springs his feeling after the war that the worst of Auschwitz is not being told, that one story remains neglected and that he is not the man to tell it. In fact this is another piece of survivor's guilt and it may be seen as Auschwitz's posthumous revenge. It may also be the writer's discontent with his work and his permanent resolution to write a new and better book.

The official language of the camp is Lagerdeutsch: a simplified German that horrifies Germans who take pride in the language of Goethe and that is used to abuse the prisoners and give them orders. If they do not understand, then so much the better since it provides an excuse for hitting them, while reinforcing the lesson that German is the language of authority and order. Lagerdeutsch contains slang or familiar words, such as "abhauen" (this was common usage among post-war adolescents) instead of "weggehen" or "fressen," which means "to eat" but that in polite German is reserved for animals, while "essen" is used for humans. Beneath this Lagerdeutsch there is no common tongue but rather Babel, which foments discord among the prisoners. The group of Jews from Salonnica, who speak Greek and Spanish, have left their mark on the camp language: the soup bowl is "caravana" and stealing is "klepsi-klepsi." Even worse: the prisoner is unable to communicate with anyone. The theme, so common in modern culture, of non-communication irritates the post-war Levi, who sees the isolation of the camp as an important step toward death. After Lagerdeutsch, Yiddish is the next language, but the Italian Jews do not know Yiddish. The need for information is so great that new arrivals are eagerly questioned. But Levi discovers that the need for language is different and greater. He learns words in languages he does not know, so eager is he to be able to speak. Here again one reason is practical: soup is distributed in Polish and Levi learns the number of the prisoner ahead of him so that he himself is ready when his number is called.

But Levi learns words for their own sake because language is a fundamental human activity and not to speak is an indifference, which is the harbinger of death. Scraps of poetry float into Levi's mind and he insists on repeating Dante to reluctant fellow countrymen. Conversely he is appalled when a doctor for whom he has worked uses the written word to tell a flattering lie. That the doctor uses school paper with lines on the page makes his crime worse. Levi's task is much greater after the war when, like the Ancient Mariner, he must "my ghastly tale tell."[8]

Another psychological battle had to be fought over the number tattooed on the "Häftling's" arm. The Nazis revealed their primitive side in taking away the prisoner's name and instead allotting him a number. Tattooing the number rather than merely sewing it into the cloth of the prisoner's clothes increased the sense of domination by the SS through the violation of the inmate's body. The prisoners create affectionate nicknames for one another—Levi is Lapé—when their heads are shaven. Here, exceptionally, they are able to use their own language to resist. The tattooing is, however, too much for them. Levi clings to his name but some prisoners adopt the numbers they are given. Thus one man is known only by his last three numbers, which are 018. Since the number was imposed in German he is Null Achtzehn. Levi kept his tattoo after the war, whereas most ex-prisoners had them removed. But for Levi the war was still going on.

Levi underlines the importance of Babel in dividing the prisoners. This should mean that the translator enjoys great standing. But his job is not to permit the prisoners to talk among themselves but rather to translate the Lagerdeutsch to them. So the translator (or Dolmetscher in German) has no prestige.

In *Se questo è un uomo* Levi discovers after the war that no one can understand him: even his sister turns away. This must have been all the more disconcerting because Levi's family seems intensely aware of language, as he describes it in *Il sistema periodico*. Each story in this book is named for a chemical gas but the real unity of the tale lies in the language. Levi's family and the Piedmont Jewish community to which it belonged kept up a patois that contained Hebrew and Yiddish elements. Its role was "to dissimulate and to hide" part of their life from the goy. Although there is no mention of persecution, this is a defensive language that has no word for man or day but does have words for prisoner and night. It also allows the expression of humor, which the Bible does not—or so Levi claims. But this was a language of "frontier and transition" rather than of opposition or segregation, and the elaborate game-playing Levi's family goes through with the non-Jews is carried over from their dealings with one another.

Meanwhile the war comes ever closer and Levi, straying from chemistry into physics, discovers a world of noises: at certain times of the day an intricate set of mysterious messages dominated the air either in Morse code or in human voices deformed and blurred, which pronounced sentences in some incomprehensible language or else in Italian, but then they were absurd phrases in code. It was the electronic Babel of the war, messages of death transmitted by ships or planes, from who knows whom to who knows whom, beyond the mountains and the sea.[9]

This is one of the very few overlaps with Céline, who also depicts the radio messages carried on sound waves and in code as the language of war itself, announcing destruction. But Levi, who grew up with the myth of democratic America, consoles himself by reading Cesare Pavese's translation of *Moby Dick* or Jack London's *The Call of the Wild* (Pasolini read *Billy Budd*), whereas Céline sees the American novelists as commercial rivals and attributes no aesthetic or linguistic value to them.

A "COLLABO" NARRATOR

Féerie pour une autre fois presents itself by its title as a non- or anti-novel. The nineteenth-century novel tells a story that is fiction but that may be offered as a chunk of reality. That the story has to have a storyteller is recognized. That the storyteller needs a language can hardly be ignored. However the title of a Balzac novel usually presents the main character and leads into her/his story—le père Goriot, Eugénie Grandet. Trollope does the same with Phineas Finn and he even adds Phineas's nationality and profession—he is an "Irish member (of parliament)." So the story starts already with the novel's title. Céline, by contrast, chooses a title that is far distant from reality and throws it into doubt: Reality is not here, so where is it? What is it? Here we are offered a fairy-tale, which is not entirely unexpected because the reader remembers the legend of Krogold and the world becoming ballet in *Les beaux draps*. A "féerie" is to Céline not really a fairy-tale, although that is the simplest translation. It is a spectacle that confuses time and place and has the structure of music. By adding the "for another time" Céline stresses the difference between his book and the present or arguably linear time as a whole and he takes another long stride away from the novel.

Trollope describes himself as a fictionalist but his aim is to render reality. Or so he says, for there is much game-playing with most of these writers. In *Phineas Finn,* Trollope declares how difficult it is to describe an event as august as a cabinet meeting. Céline's aim is to attain a different kind of "reality": the fairy-tale does not admit such things as cabinet meetings without transforming them. The emphasis placed on the narrator as a source of truth rather than on the plausibility of the events is one of the traits of modernism. Similarly the characters lack the massive solidity of Balzac and Dickens. The language is more like poetry than prose, for it is rich in images—*Féerie* depicts the roses in Brittany—and in myths—the hero-victim narrator. But Céline's narrator is no ordinary modernist: he clings to his brand of truth about the war and battles his many opponents in order to hold on to it. *Féerie* is his triumph and its commercial success is to justify Céline, the 1914 hero and the writer who tried his hardest to prevent war in 1940. Céline is at the opposite end of modernism from Joyce, who uses several narrators and much irony in *Ulysses.* Yet in his use of free association and in his linguistic invention Céline is a mainstream modernist. He has fused two kinds of writing into a blend of his own: a dogmatic brand of political writing and a freer version of literary discourse.

Next the reader encounters the dedication that he sees as an absence: of Céline's friends and of named individuals. Instead there are three categories: the first is animals, which both suggests the role of the cat, Bébert, and affirms the scarcity of humans. When these appear in the dedication, they are in the shape of two categories—the sick and prisoners. The last category suggests the purge in France and the supposed witch-hunt against Céline. The general impact of the dedication is to create another and different gulf between *Féerie* and reality. This is a book for the excluded. The general mass of people is seen as a lynch mob.

Chabrol understood this, and before him or Céline, Baudelaire ends *Le Cygne* by addressing the poem "aux captifs, aux vaincus, à bien d'autres encore." Yet Céline knows that the sick and the imprisoned do not buy books. Anyway he cannot shake off all the conventions of literary discourse: he is endeavoring, via the Gallimard label, to make contact with the sort of public that reads Sartre and Camus. His relationship with that public will, however, be very different. Céline worked on *Féerie* throughout the purge. He will try to impose on his readers his own sense of place, time and reality, not to mention justice, against which the purge was directed.

According to the terminology I have chosen to use in this book, neither *Se questo* nor *Féerie* is a committed work. Primo Levi presents himself as an individual writer who has as his public as many people as he can reach. He does not wish to teach them a political creed but rather one terrible truth that is not just political. As for Céline, his war is over and lost. He reacts by changing roles and defending himself on the level of high culture.

This explains the word-games in the monologue and the narrator's various stands as caring doctor, wounded veteran of the First World War, and many others. Behind this multiplicity there is a jealous narrator to whom multiplicity is a strategy of defense. His goal is to occupy the entire text. This is a political and indeed totalitarian action but without it the word-game would be shapeless and insipid. His strategy is present in the opening line: "Here is Clémence Arlon. We are the same age, roughly... What an odd visit! At this time... No, it isn't odd."[10] The first phrase introduces a woman who is an old friend and hence could be a main character in a traditional novel. The second phrase is descriptive and it is undermined by the doubt in "roughly." The third phrase is a judgment and it too is undermined by a narrator switching from an ordinary role to a role as teller of fairy-tales. The opening lines of *Féerie* present the story of a traditional novel: one waits to hear the reason for Clémence Arlon's visit, as one waits to know whether Phineas will marry Lady Laura. Instead Céline removes the psychological element with a throw-away but decisive comment that "all beings behave the same way at around the same time," which Lady Laura would have considered an absurd remark. Here is a very different narrator, sure of himself and aggressive but above all determined to impose his language on his visitors.

So the conventional novel present in this new meeting of old friends gives way to a potentially violent confrontation. Céline is "the notorious treacherous villain who will be assassinated tomorrow... the day after tomorrow... next week." The uncertainty has changed shape: it is now inside of a greater certainty: of Céline's execution. But the certainty is short-lived: if Céline can impose his language, then he will not be a treacherous villain, but a persecuted hero.

In order to achieve this Céline needs the reader. He is convinced of the reader's hostility when he returns to France and he is not going to leave the reader a margin of freedom. This is why he intends to occupy the whole text. But first he needs to take away the reader's space and her/his language.

Thus Clémence Arlon's visit is turned into a preparation for the grand assault—by Céline on language and by the visitors on Céline. It is not to be the starting point of a traditional or even a modernist novel. Rather it is to be the model act of persecution Céline must face. Clémence is jealous—another of the many forms of jealousy in the book—of Céline's flat, his furniture. This is the petit-bourgeois side of Céline's vision: people's murderous impulses have no grandeur. Hence the need for allusions to furniture. They gradually fade from the novel as Céline sets the geography of his assassination: it is a plot carried on the airwaves worldwide: from Sydney to Aberdeen and on to Tchad. The radio announcements of the BBC become a universal plot; the disembodied voices are well suited to the fairy-tale. But the occasional, highly specific allusions to the geography of Paris, such as Céline's reference to his school on Louvois Square,[11] add a concrete dimension to the witch-hunt and serve to justify Céline's claim of being authentically French. As the film star Arletty is alleged to have said: How could Céline have betrayed when he was born, like her, in the Paris suburb of Courbevoie? Finally these pieces of concrete geography enable Céline to move to and fro between Louvois Square and the global voices, skipping over the domain of logic and reason.

It is Céline the writer they are pursuing. Céline claims his books were designed to save France, but he receives no thanks for this. From Stalingrad on the nation turned against him. Thus the part of his flat to be sacked first is the library; the first part of him to be attacked is his tongue, which is to be cut out. This would leave only Clémence Arlon's language—they are all Gaullists now that the Nazis have lost the war. But theirs is a poor language: Clémence's son does not speak at all and the narrator speaks for him. For the narrator has no intention of dying in silence.

Thus his language dominates. It has an order of its own that is imposed by the three points. Céline passes to a second piece of supposedly traditional writing. Clémence and her entire family came to take away Céline's furniture when his clinic at Rueil went bankrupt. Here again is the precision of the narrator who describes what they took away: cupboards full of medical equipment; the only thing they do not want are fifty copies of *La Revue des deux mondes*. This time the reader knows that this episode will be seen from the viewpoint of the victim Céline.

And so the first part of *Féerie* proceeds: ordinary "reality" is transformed before our eyes into the fairy-tale. The narrator speaks more directly and about different subjects: he is in Montmartre, he is in a Danish jail. There is the characteristic confusion of time and space. Céline is—sometimes—at his ease traveling. So he cannot resist an allusion to Ulysses.

Then he introduces the various kinds of noise that are included in the fairy-tale: the tam-tam of African drums (heard already in *Le Voyage*), the sounds in his head from his supposed wound in the First World War, the many and varied purrs of Bébert. *Féerie* is, like *Voyage*, an attempt at the summa: all the noises of the world find their way into Céline's cell. Characters appear briefly and only in their relationship to the narrator. Marc Empième, a thin disguise for Marcel Aymé, appears for two pages to symbolize the successful author. The writing changes around here, for the narrator gains the upper hand and arranges his book around his noises, his memories and his hatreds. There is much repetition, but the narrator keeps our attention by his state of fury. Then too he has a set of themes to which he can return since all is suggestion and no subject is exhaustively treated.

One of his themes is his contempt for the new literary establishment of Sartre and Camus. There is a difference between Céline and Camus that is not to be swept aside as Céline's need for hostility. Céline indicates it with a remark about *Le mythe de Sisyphe*, which should be read as a mockery of Camus's judgment that "We must imagine Sisyphus happy."[12] Céline responds: "We are all Sisyphuses and cursed carriers of rocks. With me the rock falls back on top of me."[13] Céline takes a more pessimistic view of things than Camus and does not believe in courage, solidarity or any other "optimistic" values.

This leads into a reflection on Céline's failures: he is compelled to write novels because he cannot write ballet; he has enemies who denigrate him; he introduces medical matters in order to hide the treacherous writer, Céline, behind the goodhearted Dr. Destouches. Weighed down by the burden of hatred and by constant repetition, the narrator's character starts to break up. Only anger remains. But he unifies his enemies into a chorus of abuse and then defends himself or alternatively he imagines a hundred ways to die. In this process he claims proudly, "I am France. I am the colonies." (*Féerie*, p. 31) The sentences are ironic but reminiscent of de Gaulle's claims.

Another Céline habit is to wish illnesses on his enemies: here it is a skin disease, later it will be cancer of the rectum. Another theme is to remind the reader of 1914, when Céline was at the front and France held. Switching back to his Danish prison he calls his fellow prisoners by their numbers (which are sewn but not tattooed on them) but then he mixes these up with other numbers such as dates in the French Revolution—(17)89 and (17)92. The figure of his publisher, Denoel, shot near the Invalides, recurs, alongside the poet André Chénier executed during the Revolution.

Céline indicates his goal of ridding himself of prose—the language of his enemies—by lapsing into a poem-song that depicts him killing one of them and surrounds the act with allusions to music and dance. Then come various war stories: the Russian who kills himself, despite Céline's encouragement, because he is about to be sent back to the USSR. Céline himself is abandoned in his Danish prison. Saint Theresa of Lisieux is mentioned because of the miracles she has worked—and probably because she was much admired by George Bernanos among others—but Céline reminds us that the devil works miracles, too. Céline's books are riddled with allusions to religion that are rarely orthodox but often deal with themes like persecution. Another sarcastic passage depicts the persecuted hero, surrounded by thousands of French admirers on his return to France. Meanwhile Céline is still collecting noises: the mocking laughter of seagulls heading out over the North Sea, the sound that only Céline can hear of the snowflakes descending, the bells from the cemetery, the cry of owls, the scream of a newborn baby and the death-rattle of a dying prisoner.

Céline poses the possibility that he is inventing all these noises only to deny it—"I am not romanticizing." (*Féerie*, p. 43) One's doubts remain. Another familiar theme from his earlier work is lace-making, which is described as "a music without notes, without sounds." Another is the view that no collaborator—here the one discussed is Robert Brasillach—has suffered like Céline.

A typical passage depicting—or rather suggesting—Céline's ideal follows: "the pattern of Time... Time!... the embroidery of Time... blood, music and lace." (*Féerie*, p. 52) This is the fairy-tale world where two and two can—despite Orwell's horror—make three or seven as well as four. Determined to root his utopia, while denying the existence of utopias, Céline sets it in pre-1914 Brittany, contrasted with that contemporary utopia, Siberia. Céline's domain has a casino, built in ten different styles to defy people of "good taste," flowers everywhere, especially roses, the coastline of Jersey visible across the ocean and a band of young English women. Céline adds to this a tale of lice eating up a prince: a classic Célinian piece of deconstructionism!

Although this free monologue seems the reverse of the utilitarian precision of political writing, Céline is engaged in the thoroughly political task of destroying the dominant political discourse of the Resistance. Not merely does he do battle against the intellectuals and the language of the Resistance, but he strives to create a world in which such people and such language become irrelevant. It was perhaps inevitable that Céline, who drew heavily on spoken French in *Voyage au bout de la nuit* and *Mort à crédit*, should use the monologue form. But his language in *Féerie* is not the spoken tongue but rather a mixture of languages that includes, for example, a defense of French "la langue royale" and an attack on English, the growing threat. Passages like the one already quoted on the embroidery of time juggle the relationship between the sign and the signified and create a less- or non-referential language for the fairy-tale, which is a piece of "lace-telling."

The theme of the literary establishment returns when the writers who are Céline's enemies load him onto a wheelbarrow. They include Gide and Mauriac, whose first names are given, while Céline casts himself in the role of Roland, who dies because he will not sound his horn and admit defeat. Céline associates his enemies not merely with wealth but with capitalism: he alludes to De Beers, the Bank of Suez and the firm, Saint-Gobain. Once again the far-right in France shows its anti-capitalism. Both the writers and the companies are linked with the creatures of Céline's private mythology—Toto and Tante extreme—thus the entire scene is still dominated by Céline.

The other writers want to bury him among leeks or carrots—"market-gardening madness" (*Féerie*, p. 91) but also a parody of the Catholic "ashes to ashes, dust to dust." They are now reinforced by "the foetus Sartre, Aragon" and "Claudel"—communists and catholics follow the capitalists. (Paul Claudel told Gaston Gallimard that he would go to hell for publishing Céline.) Fittingly they have been fabricating a false dictionary—"they are massacring my text." Once more Céline's language is depicted as authentic French and as his alone. Sartre's screams of "he is being paid" echo his judgment in the *Portrait d'un anti-sémite*. They urinate on Céline. Aragon's companion Elsa Triolet, who according to Céline translated *Le Voyage* into very bad Russian, is brought in especially to help. But then the spirits of 1914 arrive and hold a trial. In this age of Stalinist show trials and Resistance purges, this is Céline's contribution to the genre. The court of the 1914 spirits proclaims glory to Ferdinand, the decorated veteran of the trenches, and calls on people to buy *Féerie*. Once more *Féerie* as a saleable commodity is a metaphor for *Féerie* as a work of liberation.

There remains only the cancer of the rectum incident, which is a way for Céline to stress the physical weakness of humanity. Then comes the bicycle and Céline goes riding out of his prison and back to Paris. Céline relishes sailing boats and bicycles and dislikes the internal combustion engine, linked with Fordist industry, so his escape by bicycle remains in his world of magic.

On his return to Paris, Céline meets Jules, whom he describes as "my brother, my love, my weakness." (*Féerie*, p. 125) What does Jules represent in a work where imagination is becoming ever freer? Jules is certainly no "ordinary" person like Clémence Arlon. Once he enters, the book's change becomes irrevocable. Ferdinand has escaped from his Danish jailors and his rival writers. Time has changed, moving backward to the bombing of Montmartre in 1944. Jules fits into the fairytale as the opposite of Ferdinand. Ferdinand likes long-legged dancers but Jules has lost the use of his legs in a war wound. If Jules can be seen as a substitute for Ferdinand or a rival in the fairy-tale world, then he represents evil, albeit with the customary dash of humor. Jules is a sculptor; hence we are entering the domain of the *Gesamtkunstwerk*.

Jules is jealous of Ferdinand for all the petit-bourgeois reasons: Ferdinand can walk, he is a successful writer and he has Lucette. But the real reason is that only one of them can re-shape the reality of Paris. This is Montmartre: a mixed brew of artists, artisans and do-nothings; with bitter memories of the Commune and of the Cossacks who were billeted here after the Battle of Waterloo. The clay Jules uses to do his sculpture comes from a secret source identified with divine creation. Jules also has a little mirror in which he keeps looking at himself. His paintings resemble him more and more. But he changes: "I see myself huge! then tiny.... I see myself as a pea... proof that a true artist creates himself!" (*Féerie,* p. 131) Jules goes further toward self-creation when he eats his own paints.

He preys on schoolgirls to strip off and model for him. Even Lili's dance students obey. Then comes Jules' great betrayal: He seduces Lili and calls Ferdinand a boche. Jules is the spirit of evil. This does not prevent him from being a talented artist. Gide had spoken of "the devil's part" in artistic creation but Céline is much more advanced in elaborating on the theme. It is here that one sees the organic link between Jules' art and the destruction of the Second World War. The bombing begins when Jules takes command and it creates new forms of reality. Put the other way around, the work of art involves destruction of self and of place: Céline had opened *Voyage* with trench warfare; now the bombing provides material for his novel about the Second World War. The link with the artist is revealed, for example, in Jules's preference for young women who have tuberculosis, then a deadly illness. Or again, there is Ferdinand's claim that "he tells Jules the truth about things" (*Féerie,* p. 145), but Jules does not pay attention.

The seduction of Arlette accompanies the start of the bombing. Ferdinand could have done more to prevent it than he does, which reminds us of Céline's liking for voyeurism but also of Ferdinand's kinship with Jules. Nothing should be expected from Arlette herself because the dancer lives in her own universe with the cat and does not know how to live in Ferdinand's—or ours. But this is Céline's disguised mea culpa for the Second World War.

He is sick and throws up on the street, which is a sign of his disgust. Yet he also hears music and inserts a few notes into his text. Ferdinand reverts to his monologue and his Danish prison. He ends with a defiance of his enemies—Sartre is honored with another mention—and with a few notes of music.

So Céline has won his battle for he is still alive in his cell, still fighting to impose his monologue. He has dispatched ordinary language and replaced it with free association, sustained metaphors, music and dance: lace-telling. By drawing on all the resources of literary discourse and giving them the force of a "collabo" narrator, he establishes a special place for himself. That he was not successful in 1952 shows us the gulf that lies between *Féerie* and the existentialism that held sway. There can, however, be little doubt which has aged better.

For lack of space our discussion of *Féerie II* must be short. It grows out of the theme that the bombing, which creates new forms as well as destroying the old, springs from the artist's vision. But the artist cannot indefinitely control the forces of destruction that overcome her/him and take over/are taken over by someone else. *Féerie II's* ending, when Ferdinand's manuscript breaks apart and envelopes Montmartre, is the sign of how strong the irrational forces are. In the course of the novel they have been held by Jules, by two dancers and by the actor, Norbert.

The model for Norbert is Robert Le Vigan, a friend of Céline and an actor with a flair for strange, gloomy roles. He was playing the old clothes dealer in *Les enfants du paradis* when he decided Leclerc's tanks were too close to Paris and fled. He and Céline were together at Sigmaringen where they spent the winter quarrelling and making up. Then Céline escaped but Le Vigan did not. According to Céline, Le Vigan was a superb, silent actor whose greatest role was as the Man from Nowhere. Céline's imagination has been at work here, but in *Féerie II* Norbert's dining-room is an oasis of calm, he is dressed in evening clothes and silence reigns. Such calm amid the bombing cannot be maintained for long and as soon as Norbert speaks, his magical power ceases to work and the bombing re-starts.

Féerie II had even less chance than *Féerie I* of attracting a wide audience. It depends even more on deconstructed free-play with words and it has the form of dance. Céline would have to wait three more years for his popular success with *D'un chateau l'autre*. But he had discovered a language that could render the destruction of modern war.

As far as we know, Levi and Céline never read each other. Nor would there have been much value in their meeting and talking. They have nothing in common except a flair for language and their links with the world of concentration camps. They are chroniclers of inferno who tell us the stories of hell.

Chapter Eight

A Tale of Two Margarets

Thatcherism may be viewed in a European as well as a British context. In Europe Thatcher's victory of 1979 was a major step toward discovering a seemingly new but in large part very old method of coping with the two oil price increases of 1973 and 1978–79. In 1973 the oil crisis had come as a shock. It should not have done so, because the major countries were struggling through a period of what economists timidly call "difficult growth." Government-spurred development, Keynesian counter-cyclical investment and American leadership in the form of Marshall Aid, taking over a chunk of European defense costs and providing a strong, convertible dollar had produced thirty years of economic success that had few historical parallels. But now it was running dry: workers could no longer be bought off with annual wage increases nor management failures, the so-called lame ducks, bailed out with public money. In *L'inflation au coeur de la crise* Michel Rocard showed how the various economic forces did not over-produce, as classical Marxists had forecast, but they did show the strain they were under by letting their costs rise and hence their prices. This was at least one reason why the oil-producing nations increased their own prices.

In 1973–74 the European governments dithered. The first to find a solution was Germany, where the Bundesbank raised interest rates when government and unions increased spending. Unable to pass on higher costs by increased prices because of lack of demand, German industrialists were compelled to make tough choices that involved laying off workers. Retrospectively it is obvious that an age of German near-hegemony was beginning in Europe—"near" but not complete because of the Hitler period and the conclusions that most post-war German politicians had drawn from it—and of Bundesbank hegemony within Germany. To remain with the first of these two statements, by the early 1980s most European governments, whether they called themselves left or right, socialist or neo-liberal, were following tougher, more traditionally capitalist policies that left more freedom to market forces.

Thatcher became a model to follow because she was explicit about where she was going. In turn she could speak directly because the British crisis had finally come into the open as a result of the oil price increases. The usual post-war policies had failed. The Labour Party had tried working with the unions and had fallen victim to the Winter of Discontent, while the Conservatives had abandoned MacMillan's policies, which gave priority to fighting unemployment and to conciliating the working-class.

Thatcher represented a very different brand of conservatism and she had found a new kind of language to express and impose it.

THATCHERSPEAK

Language does not merely render in comprehensible form a political project that exists already. Thatcher's language was an integral part of her project. Since it allowed her to defeat the Labour leaders Foot and Kinnock in the House of Commons question time, it was a weapon. In a more subtle way Thatcher's language did not merely express her view of the world but rather embodied it in its own right. It made all other kinds of language seem illegitimate. It contained, of course, its "unsaids," which revealed the weaknesses of Thatcher's view of the world. But it told a story that the British found convincing.

Generally Thatcher's language might be described as "populist." One of many examples might be, "I believe the people of this country understand better the truth of the matter (Soviet Communism) than those who try to mislead them."[1] But that term means not an appeal to all the people living on the islands of Britain and Northern Ireland nor to the very poorest of them but rather to the "ordinary people." Thatcher was deliberately avoiding sociological categories but in reality she was looking for the new working-class, created by post-Fordist industry. These people did not possess the culture of the old working-class—the respect for the skilled craftsman, the sense of the Labour Party, as "our" party and the automatic union membership. That working-class, which Harold MacMillan had faced, was declining. Its decline was reflected in the Labour Party, which could no longer reconcile its reformist and left wings. Thatcher's project was to peel off the reformist wing, not via a political upheaval or a change of constitution, but through the creation of a new voting block. This would run from the self-made Thatcherite élite—men like Tebitt or Parkinson—to the rising working-class who were first-time home owners and would-be members of a broader middle-class. Such groups contain many ancillary workers and between 1964 and 1983 they grew faster than any other social group.

To appeal to them, Thatcher devised a language that was not the way that a nurse or a computer operator spoke but rather incarnated the values that she attributed to such people. Key words were "work, efficiency" and "initiative." By not defining these people as a group, Thatcher emphasized their individuality: one of her goals was to recreate a sense of individual responsibility. The sum of the decisions made by such individuals constituted the market, which is logical, but there exists also a nation that incorporates individual and market. On the level of political thought it is hard to see how the nation could exist or what purpose it might serve. As a practicing politician, however, Thatcher saw the British people in a Reformation context: Bible-reading, intent on salvation and on its modern form, which was wealth creation. Then, in so far as national identity is formed against someone, Thatcher had no trouble discovering or inventing such enemies as General Galtieri, Arthur Scargill, idle aristocrats, Marxist intellectuals, Third World–loving Anglican clergymen and rock-throwing picket lines.

This view of the British nation gave an advantage to the traditional inhabitants and provided a reason not to admit immigrants from countries untouched by the Reformation. Thatcher introduced into her speeches pieces of what Herbert Marcuse called magic. She reinterpreted the parable of the Good Samaritan, stressing that the important thing about him was not that he was generous but that he was rich, without which his generosity would have been futile.[2] Thatcher invents new heroes like the customs official in Germany who succeeded on his own in blocking a terrorist attack by the IRA. It is important that he acted on his own initiative and did not wait for instructions.

The religious sources of Thatcher's worldview emerge from a speech to the Church of Scotland. She draws on Saint Paul and the parable of the talents to show that a Christian should become wealthy. Her interpretation was challenged by Jonathon Raban, a distinguished writer who was at least by culture an Anglican.[3]

Traces of defeated political discourse litter Thatcher's speeches. She makes fun of "theoretical models" and "refined theologians." She professes only to use language as a vehicle for action. The Bruges speech revolves around a clash between "abstract, intellectual concepts of Europe," which dissolve into incomprehensible institutional disputes—Thatcher's opponents, the Federalists—and the use of "practical instruments" to take "efficient measures"—Thatcher's position.[4]

One may also see the logic of Thatcher's language by contrasting it with Neil Kinnock's. Kinnock was not merely working-class, he came from the South Wales coal mines where the "old" working-class culture remained alive. He also saw a future socialist Britain as the epitome of such values, updated in the meantime. So where Thatcher does not hesitate to use words like "arcane," which do not belong to popular speech, Kinnock uses expressions like "flog off," "bunch of twisters" and "quid" and ungrammatical expressions like "an awful funny word" and "a Prime Minister that."[5]

Kinnock's periods are longer than Thatcher's but, to understand her use of sentence structure, one must compare her with Mitterrand. The French president, who was a lawyer by background, loved complex structures and parentheses. He modifies everything he says and introduces other points of view into his discourse. His aim is to create space, to offer a multiplicity of options. Rather than meeting or ordering themselves into neat antitheses, his statements go round in circles, never quite encountering one another. But in the empty spaces one hears the voice of François Mitterrand, who does not command or bully but suggests or proposes the best solution.[6]

As the Bruges speech shows, Thatcher willfully abolishes such complexity. Her "politics of conviction" are Manichean rather than multiple and her sentences allow for no doubt or empty space. She uses few subordinate clauses and her brief periods advance across the page like well-trained infantrymen. Her language is aggressive and she takes no prisoners. Subordinate clauses, which allow for refinement and modification of the statement in the main clause, are not welcome in Thatcher's speeches. The Bruges speech provides examples: "Europe is not the creation of the Treaty of Rome. Nor is the European idea the property of any group or institution." Thatcher also favors the imperative form: "Europe must continue to maintain a sure defense through NATO" and "We must strive to maintain the United States's commitment to Europe's defense."

She has, like most politicians, her favorite words that stem from her childhood and are different from the usual political vocabulary. Thus Thatcher's enemies live in "cloud-cuckoo land," whereas she deals with the "nitty-gritty." She meets and overcomes the opposition of the "moaning minnies." The alliteration and the rhyme provide a rare moment of relief in Thatcher's battle-scarred world. She is not, however, devoid of humor: she asks to be accepted into the working-class because she works so hard. She presents herself as an ordinary housewife, boiling eggs or rushing into the kitchen to peel the potatoes.

More important is the claim Thatcher lays to "common sense." Refuting Keynesianism, which might be described as the common sense of the post-war, she affirms during the '81 recession that common sense dictates that one cannot create jobs by public spending. In British political culture common sense was an important theme. Orwell, having declared in *The Road to Wigan Pier* that the British working-class had no revolutionary awareness, attributes to it a common sense that denies the cult of power and hence is a barrier against totalitarianism. This left-wing definition of common sense plays a role in the Labour victory of 1945. Thatcher takes it back to the right when she affirms that socialism can never be part of popular common sense, whereas Thatcherism, the philosophy of an ordinary woman, is by its very nature common sense.

Thatcher moves directly from common sense to the language of the apocalypse or of a crusader. When she describes the Britain created by the Labour Party, she sounds like an Old Testament prophetess: "Unemployment is a human tragedy" or "Councils must learn to cut costs in the same way as companies do."[7] Problems of political economy are changed into moral problems: inflation is an evil that destroys people's faith in the market and in life itself. The pursuit of equality is inspired by jealousy (Blair has picked up this phrase). To Thatcher economics is just the method, the goal is to save souls.

The faith that inspires this crusade is the Methodism that Thatcher learned from her parents at Grantham. The original role of Methodism was to inspire docility in the working-class of the industrial revolution by its doctrine of submission to the divine will. Once it became the religion of large parts of this class, Methodism was turned into a weapon of protest and strengthened the development of the Labour Party. As with common sense, however, Thatcher took Methodism from Labour's heritage, emphasizing both its individualism and its sense of community, which is linked with civil society rather than with the state.

Thatcher was accused of having no sense of society, but this seems to us unfair. She welcomed such communities as the family, local neighborhood organizations that should run their schools themselves free of interfering (often Labour-dominated) local education authorities, and small businesses in which everyone works together and there is, supposedly, no class conflict.

These communities put together constitute the nation, which is sacred because founded on biblical principles. This leaves no space for multi-culturalism or immigrants who are Moslems or Hindus. Among the unsaids of Thatcher's discourse, there are the excluded: illegal immigrants but also the non-Bible-reading masses of the Third World. Another unsaid is the negative side of the market. To Thatcher the market is the realm of grace, and the choices made by individuals are moral choices, signs of the liberty God has bestowed on humankind.

Thatcher does not believe the market needs regulation. The exchange rate of the pound sterling rises and falls: to try and fix it is an act of hubris. When Lawson introduces his medium term financial strategy, Thatcher shrugs and lets him implement it, although she does not believe in it. Her millenarism convinces her that the ordinary people who work and are thrifty will be saved by the market-God. She believes that industry will solve the problem of pollution on its own, that new technologies will spring up and that God's chosen people will start their own businesses. She does not mention that the market is also the theater of bankruptcies, of speculation and of Darwinian struggles.

It remains to consider the themes that accompany language: accent, clothes and body language. Accent in Britain indicates not merely the class one comes from but the class toward which one is heading. Thatcher was unashamed in speaking with a would-be upper-class accent. She demonstrated that she was conquering society, which in her eyes was more important than being born into a great family. In the sphere of clothing, Thatcher took care to be well dressed—dresses and skirts, nothing bohemian. As she grew more powerful she appeared less in Marks and Spencers's outfits and more in designer suits or else in clothes bought from her favorite shop, Aquascutum. She favored blue—the color of the Conservative Party—but also black. People wrote in to comment on her dress, so she hired a woman to help her. Meanwhile the Labour Party was trying its hardest to stop Michael Foot wearing socks of different colors and to substitute dark suits for his rumpled sports jackets. Like her clothes, Thatcher's gestures revealed control over herself and, increasingly, the world. Her body language was designed to indicate this self-control. She did not wave her arms around and her hand movements were brief and precise. She leaned forward in her seat when discussion grew heated to strengthen her sense of conviction.

Thatcher used her womanhood in many different ways, some of which overlap with language. She could be harsh when debating with men, who did not dare to respond with rudeness since they were arguing with a woman. Kinnock, who came from matriarchal South Wales, was especially at a loss. During the Falklands War Thatcher was the mother who grieves for her dead sons. At EC meetings she was the housewife defending her family's budget—"We want our money back" was her refrain.

Some of the Conservative Party grandees considered Thatcher vulgar and hated the thought that she was representing Britain. Foreigners, accustomed to aristocrats like Lord Hume or union leaders like Ernie Bevin, found Thatcher hard to grasp, Europeans more than Americans. The supposedly aristocratic President Giscard d'Estaing, who, it is said, came from a middle-class family that had bought the "de," dismissed Thatcher as "the grocer's daughter."

In general Thatcher's discourse was different from that of previous Conservative leaders. It was the antithesis of MacMillan's long, elegant sentences. It was a response to the British crisis and hence it was bound to attract the attention of journalists and writers. They did not miss the occasions when Thatcher used her womanhood in arguments with male politicians. She got along well with Mitterrand, although he was a socialist, and with Charles Haughey, who was a nationalist and considered anti-British. Both of them, she declared correctly, liked women.

The Other Margaret

It was natural that Thatcher should clash with writers and intellectuals, since she clashed with so many other social groups. Oxford rebelled against her and would not grant her an honorary degree. The official reason was that she had damaged education up and down the country by her spending cuts. Since Oxford had never cared much about education up and down the country, this was not very convincing. Thatcher had not really liked Oxford and the two had little in common: irony and flippancy versus work and, even worse, talking about work. Harold MacMillan had relished the pageantry of Oxford; therefore Thatcher did not.

For writers and intellectuals the 1980s were the beginning of a period when their role was less flamboyant than it had been. In this context it is noteworthy that Thatcher and Drabble found a battlefield in the 1960s rather than in contemporary Britain. In the 1980s the German Greens completed their long march through the institutions and entered the Bundestag. But the SPD went into opposition and the long reign of Helmut Kohl began. In France Mitterrand undertook his historic task of legitimizing socialism while voiding it of any content. Italy was in a far worse plight because the age of Craxi had arrived: anti-communism grew cruder and corruption more expensive. Pasolini had been murdered in 1975 so the political class was freed of its sharpest critic. Nowhere was commitment flourishing: Sartre was dead and post-modernism was gaining ground. In Britain the Thatcher-Drabble clash is best seen as a defensive struggle waged against Thatcher's new and more aggressive brand of politics.

The politics of consensus, which had sparked Sillitoe's hostility, had given way to the politics of conviction, which aroused more vigorous debate. Thatcher found an ally in the popular press, whose language vulgarized hers: inflammatory titles, repetition and antithesis, magic devices. Papers like *The Sun* displayed an exasperated patriotism, heaping anathemas on French truck drivers who went on strike solely to ruin the plans of British holiday-makers. From the "up-yours, Delors" to the "Butcher of

Bagdad," the popular press delighted in setting out its notion of Thatcher's nation.

It supported Thatcher in her battles within the government. One example will be sufficient: "The Man betraying Thatcher's children."[8] The *Mail* attacked the Minister of Education, appointed by Thatcher but incapable of resisting the powerful lobbies: of the teachers' union, of civil servants and of fanatical progressives. Unions, the public sector and people who believed in a future that would be different from the past were natural targets for the *Mail*. Thatcher wanted an education system based on common sense, but her minister had allowed himself to be convinced by mere "gobbledegook." This episode shows the alliance between the "ordinary people" and Thatcher the populist against Thatcher, the Prime Minister and the Conservative Party élite. It is worth comparing the British popular press with *Bildzeitung*, as seen by Heinrich Böll.

If Thatcher could not lose such battles, things were different with her two greatest intellectual opponents: Ken Loach and Margaret Drabble. Loach has already been discussed and it remains only to repeat that, whereas Thatcher silenced the working-class, Loach allows it to speak.

Drabble was a very different kind of opponent. Of all Thatcher's critics her views were the most organic: they emerged out of her work and they had been developed before Thatcher came to power. Drabble's early novels, like *The Waterfall* and *The Millstone*, depicted and were narrated by young women, who came from working-class families in the North, who had escaped to Cambridge and from there found their way to London. They had no fear of men and some women readers considered that Drabble was doing harm in underestimating male power. Meanwhile Drabble, who wrote a book on Arnold Bennett, changed her range and began writing novels with a broader social skein. They were sometimes "écrivant" rather than the work of an "écrivain": Drabble set out to describe people's habits, what they wore and how they earned and spent their money. She was well-suited to explaining how British society worked and in the *Radiant Way* trilogy she would chronicle the Thatcher years. The two women had much in common: Drabble too revealed the presence of the grammar school in British society. She too bore the marks of a low-church Protestant upbringing, even if hers was less strict and less triumphalist than Thatcher's.

The Ice Age catches the crisis that seemed irresolvable in the late 1970s. Published in 1977, it anticipates *The Winter of Discontent*. Here is a not untypical passage:

> Nevertheless, over the country depression lay like fog, which was just about all that was missing to lower spirits even further.... All over the nation,

families, who had listened to the news looked at one another and said "Goodness me" or "Whatever next" or "I give up" or "Well fuck that...." All over the country, people blamed other people for all the things that were going wrong—the trade unions, the present government, the miners, the car-workers, the seamen, the Arabs, the Irish.... Nobody knew whose fault it really was.[9]

This catches well the so-called British disease: it was so deeply entrenched in history that it was difficult to unearth the economic issues or to isolate the actors. Yet by the 1970s the sickness had penetrated most of British society so the unions could be blamed as easily as the IRA. Drabble does offer some explanations: when they come down from Oxford, Anthony and his friends do not think of entering industry. Advertising and television are more enjoyable and have greater prestige. Drabble's dispute with Thatcher has, however, nothing to do with the presence or absence of an industrial culture. It is a dispute about the moral principles underlying politics.

One might approach their disagreement indirectly, first looking at one of Drabble's themes. Anthony, the main, male character in *The Ice Age*, is visiting a friend in prison: "Only the women talked, he noticed. As in a hospital, the visiting men—fathers, brothers, sons?—sat silently, grim, depressed. But the women had made a little home for themselves, even here, even in a waiting room. Some had brought their knitting, and they gossiped and exchanged the small coins of living, making something out of nothing, making a little company even out of this grim sojourn."[10] The two uses of the adjective "grim" reveal the gender difference: the men are at best stoical or resigned and at worst simply do not know how to cope. The women take the grimness of the prison and overcome it by imposing their own lives on it—by transforming a non-place into a home. Knitting is an activity associated with non-working women whose activity centers around the family rather than the market. The phrase "coins of living" implies these women have found an alternative to the market but that Drabble has no heroic or revolutionary vision of social life. Its key trait is just solidarity with others and feeling comfortable with oneself, which are attained via language. Just as the coins are small and the company is little, so language is no more than gossip, which implies invention and stolentelling but not of a high order. Indeed knitting and gossip are the most traditional, stereotypical activities of woman, which is another reason for the unhappiness of Drabble's women readers. Yet knitting and chatting allow these women to turn what a French scholar has called a "non-lieu" into a human habitat[11] and to outdo the male contingent.

This marks the presence of another value—modesty. In the context of a prison waiting room modesty is linked with meekness, which is a key value in the Sermon on the Mount—"Blessed are the meek for they shall possess the land." These women can achieve nothing by protest or defiance, but they soften the control of the prison authorities by daring to be themselves.

Drabble opposes this modest struggle against the inhuman to the cult of power that she saw behind Thatcher's "politics of conviction." This is an argument between two women and two exponents of low-Church Protestantism. The influence of this religion on Thatcher has already been noted: it encourages the individual to seek wealth as a modern form of salvation. The novel in which Drabble explains the full implications of her own religious sense is *The Needle's Eye* (1972).

Drabble's usual world of ambitious, prosperous professionals with their big houses in Hampstead, their public-sector jobs but private-sector incomes, their ceaseless dinner parties, their left-wing opinions expounded in detail and their carefully forgotten pasts in Northern industrial towns and grammar schools—this world is intact. We recognize without difficulty Drabble's natural Thatcherites who have risen in society by their talent and work, helped occasionally by rich marriages, but then Cecil Parkinson and Thatcher herself received such help. One of Drabble's characters, Simon, was pushed upward by his mother and filled with a "sad mistrust"[12] of wealth. His ally is Rose, who was marked for life by a puritanical maid and who gives away her fortune and lives in a slum.

Rose is happy there: stuffing putty into the cracks of her house "she persevered, she had faith, she built up brick by brick the holy city of her childhood."[13] She likes bringing up her children there because her neighbors "minded their own business and didn't try to upset one another."[14] Drabble draws a radical political conclusion: "Those that have may not reject those that have not: they may not in any way accuse of greed those that have less than themselves."[15]

Reversing in advance Thatcher's re-interpretation of the parable of the Good Samaritan, Drabble offers a new version of the parable of the Talents: the group just wanted to make money. Refusing Thatcher's exhortations to create wealth, Rose finds her own ideal text long before the prosperous Victorians in *Pilgrim's Progress*, which tells the difficult story of a self-denial that leads via poverty to salvation.

Finally, if Thatcher demonstrates that women can be as hard and as acquisitive as men, Drabble shows men—Simon here and Anthony in *The Ice Age*—looking after children, showing distrust for wealth or ambition and growing more like women. The feminization of the world—universal nurturing—is one of Drabble's major themes.

The radical strain in Drabble does not emerge often, for she also believes in common sense and is suspicious of extremes. Again this is associated primarily with women, as one tiny incident in *The Radiant Way* reveals. Alix and husband, Brian, are attending a party. Alix is tired, concerned about the baby-sitter and eager to leave. But Brian has just got involved in a discussion about left-wing politics in Britain. He is on the Labour left while his interlocutor favors the nascent SPD. Surely this is the usual case of a wife bored by political debate and concerned only with the trivialities of domestic life? But no. The male conversation is just words because Brian achieves nothing for the Labour left while the SPD enthusiast accepts a pleasant academic post in the United States. Once again Drabble undercuts male seriousness to praise the caring values of women. A small matter, but little things count. Male arrogance consists of ignoring little things but blowing up men's talk into earth-shattering issues.

Drabble's broadside against Thatcher is fired off on December 21, 1988, in the *Guardian,* the voice of the English moral conscience. Thatcher's position was weakened by Lawson's too generous budget, which was—probably incorrectly—held responsible for a wave of inflation. The poll tax issue was being discussed and entry to the EMS (European Monetary System) was being forced on the reluctant but weakened prime minister. Drabble's first attack is on Thatcher's language, which she considers much too harsh. Drabble picks up the verb "eliminate" and the noun "crusade," both used in connection with socialism. Instead she calls for the use of "convert" and "persuade," which are milder words and recognize the interlocutor's right to hold her own opinions. The general swing to the right is Drabble's next target: the market may work well for the distribution of hamburgers but it cannot be trusted with medical care. In this distrust of the market Drabble joins many but not all of the European left; she would not have Tony Blair on her side.

Thatcher regularly attacked the 1960s, a period of violence and of the break-down of authority, in which she sees the origins of the Brixton and Toxteth riots: "riots, football hooliganism and crime generally had been on the increase since the 1960s."[16] Drabble praises the 1960s as the period of collectives and of social reform, like the abolition of the death penalty. Drabble's article is a good example of a writer who criticizes a politician via her language. Unlike Leonardo Sciascia, Drabble does not pretend that her own language is qualitatively different from the language of politics. Rather a political aberration has arisen and must be combated.

Drabble was not alone in this struggle. A group of writers came together to combat Thatcher. They were in some ways an implausible group and they provided *Private Eye* with excellent material. They included John Mortimer, former barrister and successful TV writer, Harold Pinter, who was quite uncommitted in the 1950s but now wrote the short play about a people whose language is banned, *Mountain Language,* and Drabble's companion, Michael Holroyd, a biographer of Bloomsbury. The *Eye* depicts them as much too grand for the nitty-gritty of a political campaign.

Of these other writers Pinter is the best and his evolution the strangest. Although he denied any commitment, he has since acknowledged one: his ability to match linguistic nuances to subtle traits of class allowed him to explore the depths of English society. Then, at exactly the moment of Drabble's attacks on a weakening Thatcher, Pinter wrote *Mountain Language,* which has an obviously political theme, the willful destruction of a living language. Pinter denied that it was a play about the Kurds and, following our theme of the silence imposed on the working-class by Thatcher, we would see it as a disguised play about Britain. Pinter would probably not agree.[17] He has added the spice of anti-Americanism to his political cocktail. The Americans "are brutal, indifferent, arrogant and devoid of scruples." Via their faithful servants in the World Bank and the International Monetary Fund, they have ruined Haiti, Nicaragua and most of the Third World.[18]

To return to Drabble, her attack on Thatcher—or her self-defense—did not win over feminist critics, one of whom considers Drabble's women to be "a picture of predatory narcissism." The development of a female universe where men take on female characteristics like nurturing (Anthony in *The Ice Age*) and leave to women only negative traits like the despair of Allison in the same book supposedly allows Drabble to avoid the reality of women's lives.[19] We shall return to the "narcissism" of women in chapter 12. In the meantime let us praise both Margarets: Drabble for having the courage to take on Thatcher and the PM for having invented a language that could express her political vision.

Chapter Nine

The Selling of *Ulysses*

In this chapter we take up a story that we started in chapter one but have since neglected. One form of commitment is to the nation. It is predominantly, although not exclusively, a right-wing commitment and one example in France—one of several—is Charles Maurras and his Action Française. Another way of saying this is that Maurras identified with France, with one of several Frances. The word "identity" is much used today probably because the thing identity has become problematic. In particular Europe seems to lack identity. Low turn-out in European elections, a nameless, faceless Brussels bureaucracy and complicated EU regulations on fish, beer, street markets and other good things that would not appear to have need of EU interference, such are a few of the complaints made about Europe.

Do they prevent the creation of a European identity? Not in themselves, but they make it more difficult. European identity is blocked by a more general lack of substance. Then too one identifies with something and against something else. Russia is no longer able or willing to act as "the other." The United States could play the role if the euro grows strong enough to challenge the dollar. But as yet the financial markets do not trust the euro.

Good writing can do much to create an identity. The part played by Racine, Corneille and Molière in creating a French identity cannot be measured but it must be considerable. To write well is not enough. The writers must exhibit—or the reader must be able to discover—traits that are genuinely French but are presented in new and interesting ways. Here Europe is at a disadvantage because of its linguistic diversity. Whether for this or other reasons, Europe does not play a great role in contemporary writing.

Paradoxically it was more important when it had no political existence. I have tried to show that the beginning of the Europe of writers goes back to the pre-1914 era when Valery Larbaud published *L'Europe*. The trenches increased the fervor of the disgusted, peace-loving "Europeans" and, for approximately ten years until the Depression, several groups—of which we shall look at only one—set about creating works in which "Europe" was an active participant.

A number of introductory points may be made about this venture. Firstly, some of the main actors had not been involved in trench warfare: Joyce and Larbaud are just two names that come to mind. Secondly, there were Americans in and around the group of "Europeans": some like T. S. Eliot joined in; others like Hemingway went on with their own work; yet others, like William Carlos Williams, tried to re-work their identity as Americans. The general view of 1920s Paris as rootless and individualistic is not so much wrong as incomplete: "Europe" was a reaction against such rootlessness. Finally, the "Europeans" disliked polemics, virulent writing and even long, rational arguments to which they preferred creative works and suggestions rather than explanations. Therefore the political influence of the "Europeans" was slight. But they did serve as a model to good, young writers.

After the discussion of *Ulysses*, which takes up most of this chapter, we shall glance at one "European" and one meeting between Europe and America.

Making Europeans

After the war was over James Joyce made his way from Zurich—and before that Trieste—up to Paris. Why, why now and why Paris? The answer is that Joyce was now ready: he had gained a certain fame or notoriety through the publication of episodes of *Ulysses* in the *Little Review* and he was getting ready to publish the work as a whole. Paris was a much better base than Zurich or Trieste; the publishing houses were known, and new writing was much appreciated. Once he arrived in Paris, Joyce set about finding friends whom he could exploit. This was his way of surviving: to put it crudely, he scrounged off a circle of friends who provided him with money, helped him publish his difficult books and looked after his difficult family. In Paris the leading figure in the support group was Sylvia Beach, an ex-patriate American who ran a bookshop called Shakespeare and Co.

Beach also knew Larbaud, whom she had met via her friend Adrienne Monnier when he returned from Spain in 1919. Larbaud's Spanish sojourn is linked with his friendship with Joyce and deserves a word of explanation. In 1914 Larbaud had roughly the same reaction of moderate patriotism as Gide. Unable to join up because of health problems, he went to work as a volunteer in the hospital of his hometown, Vichy. But he grew more and more dissatisfied with the never-ending flood of wounded soldiers and he turned against the war. In 1916 he assembled the right documents and left for Spain, the largest of the countries that remained neutral.

Larbaud had virtually stopped writing in these two years but Gaston Gallimard succeeded in enlisting him for a project. The war prevented Gallimard from publishing, so he formed the plan of amassing books that could be published when the war was over. Many of these books were to be English novels because the *NRF* group was attracted to England as the country of the novel before the war—see Jacques Rivière's essay on the adventure novel. Gallimard obtained the rights to Conrad, Meredith and others and influenced a whole generation of French readers. As the leading expert (a word he would have hated) on England, it was natural that Larbaud be involved. Then too Larbaud looked on translation as an act of service, a form of humility and the subordination of self to another writer. Translation was also a form of freedom—the creation of a new self via a different language and another writer's texts. The two ran together but in this case there was the added spur of the war. Larbaud had fled the war and he did not shrink from calling himself a deserter. But his aim in 1916 was to render service to his Europe—the Europe of writers not of warriors—by taking on a work of translation. The choice of writer would be his own: Gallimard had acquired the rights to many English novelists. From this list Larbaud selected Samuel Butler. Why Butler? Because he was anti-Victorian. All through the years when he was friendly with Joyce, Larbaud went on translating and writing criticism on Butler. One may go as far as to say that Butler's book *The Authoress of the Odyssey* helped guide Larbaud to the Homeric parallels in *Ulysses*.

Larbaud met Joyce at the end of 1920.[1] He already knew both Monnier and Beach, who were important contacts for him—Monnier, who had her own bookshop, La Maison des amis des livres, publicized his books; Beach introduced him to the ex-patriate Americans. When he met Joyce, Larbaud had already read *Dubliners* and *Portrait of the Artist*. Inevitably he liked the figure of Stephen Dedalus, who incarnates a familiar Larbaud theme of the young artist trapped in a hostile environment. Stephen in Dublin joins Leopardi at Recanati, Butler at Langar,[2] Stendhal at Grenoble and of course Larbaud at Vichy. Then Beach gave him the numbers of the *Little Review* containing the installments of *Ulysses*. Larbaud was very enthusiastic, he offered to translate some fragments and publish them along with an article in the *NRF*. The plan was changed: in 1919 Larbaud had given a lecture on Butler at Monnier's bookshop. He would do the same for Joyce. To help Joyce finish his book, Larbaud lent Joyce and family his flat on the rue Cardinal Lemoine. In 1921 the two men spent much time together, sometimes accompanied by Robert McAlmon.

Larbaud gave his lecture on December 7, 1921, a few hours after the announcement in London that an agreement had been reached between the Irish rebel delegation, headed by Michael Collins, and the British government. The official date for the signing of the agreement is December 6, 1921, but since the negotiations did not end until 2.30 A.M., the agreement and the lecture took place on the same day. The question of *Ulysses's* relationship to Ireland could hardly have been posed more dramatically. The lecture was published in the *NRF* in April 1922 and Eliot translated parts of it into English and published them in *Criterion*. The fragments of *Ulysses*, read at the lecture, were translated into French by Jacques Benoist-Méchin, with help from Joyce, Larbaud and Léon-Paul Fargue, whose verbal flair greatly appealed to Joyce.

The setting for the lecture, the Maison des amis des livres; the speaker, Larbaud, considered the epitome of the international avant-garde in his many roles as friend of Gide, translator of Butler, novelist whose work formed part of the *NRF*; the author, an Irishman who had lived in several countries, whose work was difficult and who had the support of the expatriate Americans as well as the *NRF*—all these things combined to make *Ulysses* the banner of the young avant-garde, which looked to other capitals and which was represented also by the travel-writing of a Paul Morand.

This view of *Ulysses* was strengthened by a difference of opinion within the *NRF* and by a polemic without. The opinions were those of Larbaud, for the moment head of the "Joyce crowd," and of Jacques Rivière, the editor of the *NRF*.[3] Rivière had to fight on various fronts. Firstly he had to defend the review against an Action Française bid to take it over. Then he went on the offensive and had some success in imposing Proust as the great writer of the age. This had a political and an aesthetic aspect, and Rivière tried to blend the two. In his articles he depicted Proust as a master of psychological analysis who broke down human character into irrational fragments devoid of intention as of coherence. Such profound analysis was typical of French culture. Thus Rivière offered his readers avant-garde writing that was in a French tradition.

To Rivière Joyce was an unwelcome intruder. Joyce was not French and his inner monologue lacked precision. When Larbaud tried his hand at the new technique in two short novels, he did not attempt to convey the whole flux of thought but limited himself to certain key themes. This pleased Rivière, who wrote to Larbaud praising him but condemning

Joyce: with Larbaud "one always feels where one is going" whereas with Joyce one encounters "the arid wanderings of thought." The two novels were called *Amants heureux amants* and *Mon plus secret conseil.*

The Battle with Boyd

Ernest Boyd was a well-known journalist and literary critic. In 1920 he left Ireland and settled in New York, where he imitated H. L. Mencken's irony, did not hide his distaste for Prohibition and went on writing about Irish literature. He was the author of *Ireland's Literary Renaissance,* which went through several editions.

Boyd read Larbaud's April 1922 article and disliked it. He replied: "The doctrinaire zeal of a coterie seems to be bent on leaving the profoundly Irish genius of James Joyce in possession of a prematurely cosmopolitan reputation."[4]

Boyd did not believe in Europe. If Joyce was a good writer, then he must be Irish; conversely if Joyce was a creature who haunted the Left Bank, then he must be a bad writer. This view ran through *Ireland's Literary Renaissance,* which was published in a new edition in 1923. The book argued that there was an Irish identity, separate from English identity, and that it had produced this magnificent body of writing. Joyce was Boyd's latest and most dazzling recruit, so Boyd was horrified to see him presented to the public outside an Irish context.

The polemical solution was to claim that Larbaud knew nothing about Ireland. This was an exaggeration but it was not wholly incorrect. Larbaud knew less about Ireland than about England and he was not interested in Yeats. But Boyd's polemical solution was irrelevant because Larbaud saw no contradiction between being Irish and being European. On the contrary, Larbaud's ideal European writer was rooted in the culture of his country. In addition—but it must be an addition—he was rooted in the culture of other European countries and he was read by their élites as well as by his own.

As always in this kind of dispute there were other, hidden issues. Boyd dismisses the Homeric parallels, which fascinated Larbaud, because he perceived Joyce as a realist writer: *Dubliners* is for him "that superb collection of studies of middle-class Dublin life."[5] Larbaud belonged to the next generation in France and he had little use for the realist novel. Larbaud believed in the 1920s avant-garde, which was experimental and seemed to Boyd gimmicky. In a private letter to Larbaud he says as much: "At heart what separates us is your faith in certain literary innovators of whom I am skeptical."[6] This can be seen in the way supporters line up: Paul Morand castigates Boyd and Archibald MacLeish congratulates Larbaud.

So *Ulysses* was sold as the great work of the Europe of the 1920s. Another indication of the reality of this Europe is the selling of *La coscienza di Zeno*. Svevo supported Larbaud against Boyd, which is no more than fitting. Svevo was himself one of the "Europeans." When he published *La coscienza* in 1923 it was his first novel since *Senelità* (1898) and he was barely known in Italy outside Trieste. Initially this book did little to make him known. But Svevo had a newly powerful friend in James Joyce. Joyce told him to send the book to Larbaud, Eliot and Benjamin Crémieux, the *NRF's* leading Italianist. Larbaud liked the novel and he and Crémieux translated fragments of *La coscienza* and of *Senelità* for Adrienne Monnier's revue *Le Navire d'Argent*. They also persuaded Gallimard to publish a French translation of *La coscienza*. Some Italians resented this interference in their literature and dismissed Svevo as a "scoperta francese," but Eugenio Montale supported him. Reviewers compared Svevo with Joyce and Proust and he became Italy's representative in the European literary élite.[7]

A full discussion of the European identity would include a study of the review *Commerce,* where Marguerite Caetani was the owner and Larbaud and Fargue were both directors and that published some of Larbaud's essays on Italy as well as his translations; a longer discussion of the role of translation; and of a quest for tradition that included Eliot's re-discovery of the metaphysicals as well as Larbaud's essays on the French poets of the sixteenth century and even Ernst-Robert Curtius's *Die lateinische Literature des europaischen Mittelalters,* where the author, faced with the madness of Nazi nationalism, looks back to the unity of medieval Europe.

There is one translation that cannot be left unmentioned and that is the French version of *Ulysses*. This was supposed to be the model translation. Mooted at the 1921 launching of the English version, it was supposed to be published by Adrienne Monnier. Larbaud was the obvious translator but, with characteristic concern for his freedom, he backed out as early as March 1922. The logical substitute was Auguste Morel, translator of poetry and in particular of John Donne. Two years went by and in 1924 Morel began work. He had been promised Joyce's help but Joyce had started on what would, very much later, become *Finnegans Wake* and so he was not often available. Joyce's crowd began to change: Eugène and Maria Jolas were at the center because they published the fragments of *Finnegans Wake* in their review *Transition*. Samuel Beckett arrived from Ireland in 1928. Larbaud was not a member of this crowd and, by now, he had grasped Joyce's flair for exploiting people. Larbaud began seeing less of Joyce. A retired English civil servant, Stuart Gilbert, turned up in Paris and Joyce quickly enrolled him to correct Morel's version of the slang. Larbaud was to correct Gilbert's French and give an overall style to Morel's version. By now it was 1926 and Adrienne Monnier had been waiting four years to publish *Ulysses*. She had a furious quarrel with Larbaud, for whom this was one piece of work among several. He began his revision in the summer of 1927 and finished a year later in Italy where he had gone to escape from Monnier, who was no longer a friend but an implacable enemy.

When the book was launched in June 1929 there was a lunch at which none of the three translators was present. *Ulysses* remains, however, one of the great achievements of the "Europeans." It was also one of their last. The world was changing and other kinds of commitment—fascist and communist—would overtake Europe. They were tougher, more disciplined and more extreme. Anyway Europe could hardly offer unity when it was split into pro- and anti-fascist. In 1935 Larbaud had a stroke and could not write or speak. It is no coincidence that this is the year that Mussolini invaded Abyssinia or that next year the Popular Front came to power in France. "Europe" is linked with the little reviews that could not survive the depression and with the hopes of the post-war years. We must now look at another, very different "European," Charles du Bos.

A European Mystic

Du Bos and Larbaud had an amusing meeting in 1927 when Larbaud was writing the preface to a new translation of Shakespeare's sonnets and Du Bos was worried that Larbaud would devote too much space to the theme of pederasty. The two men had much in common but they were very different. They were both born rich but died poor after failing to look after their wealth. Larbaud's was new money and his family were provincial bourgeoisie; Du Bos's father was a member of the Jockey Club and he frequented the English aristocracy. Larbaud struggled with the French education system; Du Bos went to Balliol College. When he went to Germany, he met not only Ernst-Robert Curtius but the financial aristocracy of Berlin. Each created his own Europe but they were, despite certain overlaps, very different Europes. That did not matter because nearly all "Europeans" were tolerant.

Du Bos was a regular at the "décades de Pontigny," an abbey near Auxerre where a select group of writers met each year and discussed contemporary issues. The *NRF* was well represented because Gide was always present, often flanked by Rivière and François Mauriac. Larbaud, although frequently invited, never arrived. There were no young girls at

Pontigny and Larbaud's enthusiasm for long, serious, all-male debates was strictly limited. Du Bos, however, was a brilliant talker and in Gide's eyes "Charlie" was the leader of the Pontigny group.

Du Bos's critical method, if one may use such an unsuitable phrase, was quite different from Larbaud's. He looked in a work not for what was new about it nor even for its themes but for the "soul" that was behind it. The "âme" was not the everyday self; it was of no interest to biographers; it was the creative force: both aesthetic and religious. By contrast, the body does not interest Du Bos unless it is the dancer's body, which defies corporeal limits. He went to an Isadora Duncan performance and thought it was a liberation without a monologue.

Separate from what we call reality was the autonomous metaphysical structure that the work created. Although he did not return to the Church until 1927, all Du Bos's work has this spiritual dimension, for the spiritual is an extension of the aesthetic. "The kingdom of God is within us. Universal goodness is in us, it is us and it is not us."[8] Du Bos did not hesitate to take the final step and argue that if the soul existed, then God must exist too. Books and writers thus opened up a treasure house of experience for the ill-named critic. His task was not to distance himself from the writer but to join with him and recreate him. A Du Bos text could be placed alongside the works of the author he had studied.

Du Bos's Catholicism was the richest part of the treasure. It left intact his entire way of life, including his favorite writers from Keats onward. Du Bos was too individualistic to care much about the structure of the Church, he was not enough of a nationalist to support the Action Française and he was too much of a "European" to be interested in the virulence of a Léon Bloy. His Catholicism was that of the *NRF*, akin to the "fruitful humility" of Jacques Rivière.[9] It also cost him his friendship with Gide, who had seen too many of his friends become Catholics and denounce him for his homosexuality and for the appalling example he was giving to French youth. He and Du Bos continued their dialogue in their respective diaries.

Du Bos likes to begin an essay with one word from his author: with Pascal, one of his favorite authors, it is "explosive." He moves on to consider Pascal's short sentences, delighting in their spiritual energy. This energy is expressed directly and there is no need to bother with the artifices of rhetoric. Du Bos mentions Pascal's fear of silence, of the godless universe and therefore his willingness to gamble on God's existence.

So what has all this to do with Europe? These "âmes" are European and they are brothers or comrades of Du Bos. It is not just his life or his education. It is rather that he cannot envisage a Keats or a Thomas Mann outside the cultural framework of Europe. There is in Du Bos a touch of that belief in the West, which we called hubris in a previous chapter. But Du Bos is not excluding anyone: his essays on Germany may be read as a contribution to Franco-German reconciliation. Moreover Du Bos has a vision of Europe that is not the Europe of power politics.

"Europe" needs above all else a development of the critical spirit. Here Du Bos distinguishes between a genuine self-criticism and an apocalyptic pseudo-synthesis,[10] by which he means one of the several brands of "Untergang des Abendlandes." He then rebukes the Victorians for being insufficiently self-critical and for withholding some basic principles from criticism. His admiration goes to Butler, because nothing escapes his sharp gaze, and to Hardy, who has no new vision of the world but is all the better able to see the tragedy of things as they are. After Butler and Hardy have left behind a Europe without disguises or illusions, it is necessary to undertake a work of spiritual reconstruction.

This is probably the best way to read Du Bos's own work. His essay on Joyce argues that Joyce's work is the expression of "a revolt of the spirit which leads to the destruction of the world."[11] So the soul remains triumphant in *Ulysses* but is left stranded in a metaphysical nihilism. An example of reconstruction is given by Coventry Patmore, the Victorian poet of marriage. This requires a word of explanation since to mention Patmore in the same sentence as Joyce seems an aberration today.

But Patmore is an important figure to the "Europeans." Before 1914 Larbaud wrote a long piece on him for the *NRF* and Claudel translated some of his poems.[12] There are at least two reasons for Larbaud's interest. First, he wanted to dethrone Tennyson, the great poet of the Victorians, and replace him with a poet whose work was in the private sphere. Second, he was attracted by what he perceived as an upsurge of sexual love, which guided Patmore to a revelation of divine love. Claudel argued with him about this, maintaining that the sexual element must be purged before this love can guide man to God. Larbaud, who, like almost everyone at the *NRF*, was terrorized by Claudel, carefully avoided meeting him to discuss the matter. But the difference between what Claudel called "sacramental" and Larbaud "sexual" love was significant. Du Bos, writing some twenty-five years later, was closer to Claudel. But he also wished to see in Patmore a poet working for that spiritual revival that was overtaking Europe. The tragedy of Hardy and the metaphysical nihilism of Joyce were not the goals to be reached. Patmore, for whom truth was love, could take man more deeply into his own soul and hence closer to God.

The "essential European fact" was not, however, yet accomplished. Du Bos welcomes those who are still clearing the ground. He praises Lytton Strachey for his attacks on Victorianism. He applauds John Middleton Murray for his aesthetic intuition. Edmond Gosse, who had known Larbaud before 1914, gets a word of approval for setting his writers in a European rather than a British literary milieu.

When he turns to Germany, Du Bos asks the same questions. He dwells most on the poets, in particular Hugo von Hofmannsthal and Stefan George. Of George he writes that there is a tension in his work between the void of ordinary life and the force of the "âme." Du Bos also agrees in 1926 to make the welcoming speech in honor of Thomas Mann, who is on an official visit to France. The occasion does not allow Du Bos to discuss Mann's work in his own special language but it enables him to talk about the state of Europe. He is unashamedly aristocratic: "For as long as there is, in our two countries and more generally in Europe, a group of people endowed with a sense of authentic values and capable of keeping this sense alive in themselves, we do not have the right to despair."[13]

Du Bos was not troubled by the change in writing and politics that marked the 1930s. His study of Patmore was published in 1936 but he does not mention the Popular Front. Du Bos was now short of money and he had to accept a teaching post in the United States. His health was deteriorating and he died in August 1939. While the world changed around him Du Bos remained a "European" and a mystic. Joyce also ignored the changes: he considered the war an unnecessary distraction that took people's attention off the newly completed *Finnegans Wake*, perhaps the most European of all books. The Nazis would use the term "Europe," too: among the forces that invaded the USSR there was a Division Charlemagne. But Hitler's Europe demands a study of its own.

Europe Tries to Help Make America

As already argued, the American ex-patriates in Paris had some contact with the "Europeans" and reacted in different ways. It is tempting to assume that their reaction depended on their own reflections on their American identity, but no such blanket generalization can be made. Anyway their definition of themselves as Americans overlapped with their definition of themselves as individuals. We shall be on slightly firmer ground, if we limit ourselves to two writers.

William Carlos Williams was the anti–T. S. Eliot. Eliot opted for European tradition, whereas Williams flaunted his allegiance to Patterson, a small town in New Jersey. In 1923 Williams published *The Great American Novel* and Larbaud reviewed it. *The Great* is a series of satirical sketches about the American writer in search of something to write about. It weighs up Joyce and the surrealists and condemns them. Joyce's innovations constitute "a fragile fog . . . his art consists of words."[14] The book was published by Robert McAlmon, who still had access to the fortune of his ex-wife, Bryher.

If Joyce separates words from things, then Williams separates Europe from America. European culture has no value for him. In the second half of *The Great* Williams's writer seizes on scraps of American history and life and tries to make something of them but he cannot. The conclusion is that the task of the American writer is only starting and it will be hard.

In his review Larbaud is skeptical about the separation of Europe and America. He points out that, despite castigating Joyce, Williams uses the inner monologue. For Larbaud, America can be vast, Whitmanesque and free, while still having close ties to Europe. Indeed such an America had helped foster the pre-1914 "Europe."

When Williams came to Paris in 1924 Adrienne Monnier brought him to meet Larbaud at the rue Cardinal Lemoine. They had a long chat that found its way into *In the American Grain* (1925). This is a kind of anti-history where Williams knocks down the official great men of American history—Benjamin Franklin and Alexander Hamilton—and replaces them with heroes of his own like Aaron Burr and Daniel Boone. Such men were devoted to America, the unexplored wilderness. They hated the puritan, who is afraid of the vast, new continent, and they manifested the American virtues of generosity and courage. *In the American Grain* makes good reading seventy-five years after it was published.

Unfortunately the chapter that contains the conversation with Larbaud is a travesty of Larbaud's views. Williams turns him into the typical European intellectual, who loves books more than life, who is attracted to America but incapable of appreciating the rough grandeur that is its special and non-European trait.

Larbaud was right in thinking that Williams was exaggerating his dislike of Europe. *Patterson* shows many traces of avant-garde European writing. But this attempt to form an alliance between the "Europeans" and the Americans who thronged Paris was a failure. Williams needed Europe as "the other" and Larbaud, who wanted "America" as an ally, could not dissuade him.

In conclusion one might note that a strong American identity helps the development of a European identity by acting as the other against which Europe can take form. Boyd was an ideal other, an outspoken nationalist. An America as unsure of itself as Williams's cannot, however, dispense with a stereotypical Europe that is cultured but lifeless. Finally one remembers that to create an identity for a small group of writers is a very different task from the creation of a democratic, mass European identity.

Chapter Ten

Struggling on the Left

If we are right in arguing firstly that the post-war impulse toward a different and more socialist society ran its course by about 1960 and secondly that capitalism proved more flexible and more sophisticated than had been hoped or feared, then the 1960s would not be a promising decade for the left. Initially this was true. In Britain the Harold Wilson governments, 1964–1970, achieved little in democratizing the country, did a good deal of damage to the Labour Party by siding with the United States over Vietnam in return for support for the pound and began the quarrel with the unions that led eventually to the Winter of Discontent. The only liberating measures were private member bills that put an end to the death penalty and allowed homosexual relations between consenting adults. In France the 1960s belonged to Charles de Gaulle and then, unforeseen by most journalists and historians, came the student uprising of May 1968, accompanied by a workers' movement that the PCF succeeded only belatedly in bringing under its control. In Italy, where the government was weaker, the workers' and students' movements began earlier and lasted longer, even if they may retrospectively be seen to have peaked in the hot autumn of 1969. They were accompanied by left-wing terrorism and by a backlash of right-wing terrorism, probably aided by segments of the state and by the secret services of friendly countries. The PCI reacted to this complex situation with the Berlinguerian historic compromise.

Culturally the open, simple protest of neo-realism gave way to more sophisticated and individualistic forms of dissent. In Italy the cinema of Michelangelo Antonioni depicted the alienation of capitalist society from the viewpoint of the individual in films like *The Red Desert* (1964) or *Blow Up* (1966).

The 1960s was a great period for cinema and in France directors like Jean-Luc Godard satirized the tensions created by rapid, economic growth: Godard's *Weekend* mocked the motorcar, motorways and the fairly new habit of mass exodus from Paris at the weekend. Another film, *The Chinese*, depicts a group of Maoist militants achieving very little in Paris. François Truffaut sided with ill-treated children in films that ranged from *Les 400 coups* to *L'argent de poche*.

As already argued, Sartre's influence waned in the sixties. To revive left-wing enthusiasm he and others turned to the Third World. Sartre and Simone de Beauvoir went to Cuba to examine Castro's revolution. Sartre was in Havana when he wrote his essay on Nizan, designed to offer French youth a model of militancy. A hymn of praise for guerillas came from Régis Debray. *Révolution dans la révolution* was very successful in France. Debray followed Ernesto Ché Guevara to Bolivia and was arrested and jailed. In Italy Giangiacomo Feltrinelli would have liked to publish a big book by Fidel Castro explaining his revolution. But Castro, although willing enough to talk, would not talk about a fixed subject at a fixed time. This unwritten book had a different life: it caused Feltrinelli to spend much time in Latin America, radicalized his thought and contributed to his choice of clandestinity and to his early death.[1]

In Germany the students' attempt to make contact with the workers failed more completely than elsewhere. But the Greens kept going and growing more than in other countries and in 1983 they entered the Bundestag. The SPD (Social Democrats) came to power in 1966 as part of a grand coalition with the CDU (Christian Democrats) and then with the much smaller Freie Demokraten. Its policies based on the twin pillars of the Ostpolitik and the Rechtstaat, it remained in power until the "Wende" of 1982. Among German thinkers Jürgen Habermas continued to be influential. Although he broke with the New Left, his sense of the need for democratic controls in society made him a reference point for mainstream center-left thought. Achille Occhetto was fond of appealing to Habermas during the "svolta" (1989–1991). Germany also produced a great film director in Rainer Werner Fassbinder, whose string of films satirized the Bundesrepublik, from the victory over Hungary in the 1954 World Cup *(The Marriage of Maria Braun)* onward.

Meanwhile Ireland—in particular Northern Ireland—re-entered history by creating a free speech movement that set out to overcome the old politics of nationalism, religion and the Six Counties. Its leaders, among them Bernadette Devlin, wanted to introduce more modern, lay politics but the movement's first marches were interpreted by Protestants as a Catholic attack on the existence of the Six Counties. A rising level of violence among Protestants restored prestige and purpose to the IRA, initially mocked by a distortion of the acronym into "I ran away." Britain sent in troops and a Thirty Year War began, which was the latest episode in a Three Hundred Years War.

From this all too brief synopsis, one may see that the left was struggling. Its triumph lay in the student movements of the late 1960s: despite prosperity and relative privilege, there was still alienation and the possibility of protest. Conversely the number of people who wanted to live in a collectivist society was small. The New Left would have to discover new ways of gaining support.

Marcuse: Revolution or Co-option

In 1964 Herbert Marcuse published one of the most influential books of the decade: *One Dimensional Man*.[2] It has not stood the test of time and today one wonders at its importance. At the time it could be read in two different ways. Marcuse's thesis is that the working-class has been co-opted by advanced capitalism, which rules in Western Europe and North America with a philosophy of authoritarian permissiveness. Sexual activity, which is anathema to the party in *1984*, is encouraged but is linked to work: partners should come from the same office or factory; to consumption—creams and deodorant; and to technology—cars. There is no opposition because a combination of "warfare" (the Cold War) and "welfare" has destroyed the development of awareness of which Marx had written. Capitalism has subjugated both nature, turning it into parks where the trees as well as the visitors are subject to controls, and culture—Bach is played in supermarkets. Politics takes place within the limits set by capitalism: there are no longer any anti-capitalist parties. The Soviet Union offers no hope, although Marcuse considers the notion that a state bureaucracy is less caught up with capitalism and hence more easily overthrown than the owners who dominate Western politics. Nor does Marcuse see any hope in the Third World, where he thinks development might bring more rather than less violence than it has done in Europe.

On language Marcuse follows Orwell, although he does not anticipate the rise of a newspeak. But he thinks language will become evermore "operational," by which he means limited to making changes in how industry or government is run in order to make it more efficient, but never posing the question of why it is run that way. Some of his examples are taken from labor relations, which were indeed turning into class-free "human resources" around this time. Marcuse also reserves a chapter for LP (linguistic philosophy), which he accuses of leaving the world as it found it.

And he sees the growth of "magical" elements in the language of the powerful that make it harder to analyze what is being said or written.

Who is running this society? Marcuse does talk of a ruling class, but not often; he also talks about the machine process. He is halfway between the Marxist concept of a bourgeoisie and the Foucauldian notion that every man is his own jailor.

Philosophy and science have been subordinated to technology. Philosophy has lost its ethical sense, which drove Socrates to judge our society as well as to explain or measure it. It becomes especially difficult to maintain that ethical slant when the new society in the shape of the working-class and its anti-capitalist culture is no longer present to serve as an example.

There is no prospect of rebelling against this modern capitalism because the workers are happy. Consumerism has imposed a false consciousness on them and has hidden from them the alienation in which they live. Yet there are two, very different conclusions to be drawn from this book: the first is indeed that the dream of revolution is over and that humans are condemned to a permissive but alienated and indirectly authoritarian society. Or there is still some hope of piercing that false awareness, some hope that there are un-co-opted members of the working-class, such as immigrants or the long-term unemployed.

When *One Dimensional Man* was first published, the pessimistic interpretation dominated. In May '68, however, Marcuse was acclaimed as the prophet who had foreseen the emergence of that new social actor, the student. The politics of '68, which were theatrical and unstructured, were designed to awaken new forms of consciousness. Culture played a greater role and "l'Imagination au pouvoir" was a widely used slogan. Marcuse had changed his mind about several matters. The use of the language of the subordinate classes, like black American, which had been summarily dismissed as an admission of defeat, was now praised as an attack on the dominant culture. The *Essay on Liberation* was a more hopeful book than *One Dimensional Man*.

Evolution of the New Left

The student and worker movements of the New Left dismissed the communists and social democrats of the Old Left, to borrow an expression that was not much used outside the United States. The Old Left had been trapped in reformism and parliamentarianism; the New Left's aim was revolution. The belief ran deep that the workers were almost ready to rebel and needed only a few examples. This was entirely wrong and it imposed on the New Left militants difficult choices, once the big demonstrations were over. Intellectually there was a split between those who believed in political action and those who sought to create an alternative culture.

There are, of course, many historical reasons for the explosion of the New Left. One stresses the role of the university: in all four major European countries it had expanded very rapidly to meet the demands of a growing population. In Italy there had been one professor to every ten students in 1911; in 1967 there was one to fifty. The "new" student was unfamiliar with the university, s/he might be the first member of her/his family to reach university, s/he was defensive behind a superficially aggressive stance and s/he was not a worker. Despite the expansion, only 1.5 out of every 10 students had a father who was a worker or a peasant.[3] Not all such students were left-wing by any means—in Britain some were Thatcher's children—but those who were left-wing flaunted their opinions and were willing to be led into battles with the university authorities and with the police. Culturally the New Left was a mixture of many trends: there was a Marxism that was like a catechism, there was an admiration for doers like Mao and Ché, there was an interest in heretical Marxists like Marcuse or Althusser.

In Italy the New Left was stronger and the state weaker. The students managed to make contact with the workers. An excellent work of fiction on the worker movement that peaked in the hot autumn of 1969 is Nanni Balestrini's *Vogliamo tutto*. Balestrini was close to the leaders of the very radical Potere Operaio and he fled to France when a wave of them was arrested in 1979.[4] The first two of these three "novels" are in fact neither fiction nor novels. For our purposes we might say they bridge the gap between political and literary discourse and they were a part of the protest. Ballestrini creates a historically accurate proletariat: a Southerner come to Turin to work at Fiat allows him to use the "I" and traces his political evolution. But within this framework the character is free and there is no determinism, Marxist or otherwise. He seems to have inherited his father's dislike of work, but this is stated not stressed. The narrator does not, like a Sartrian character, invent himself a destiny. He accepts Fiat for what it is and then, since it is not a place he likes, he combats it. There are not the fireworks of existentialism. Put the other way around, the narrator does not feel that he is free so he surrounds himself with paragraphs and pages, neatly arranged to convey his sense of being imprisoned. This, Balestrini feels, is all that one can hope for. Total freedom from Fiat is unreal in this period. Balestrini does not use his own language, and the rhythm of his writing is more important than the content.

Balestrini starts the trilogy of novels, *La grande Rivolta*, of which *Vogliamo tutto* (1971) is the first, with a long, doggerel poem that is an appeal to the reader. As if to keep up the pressure on Orwell, Balestrini begins by affirming that "2+2 hardly ever makes 4." He goes on to state that literature is a pack of lies and that the society of spectacle has brought about a general disintegration. An army of commentators has created the belief that the movement of '68 eats babies and has no respect for the sacred parties born of the Resistance. The movement does not wash or work and it is capable of any kind of subversion. Fortunately, other, well-paid chroniclers have explained how the forces of order and of civilization gained the upper hand. Thus the 1980s have seen a yuppie renaissance, "this is the age of opportunistic cynicism and history is finishing. Here we are again with Kossiga, owners who flaunt their domination, amnesties for those poor people who paid bribes, there is a cultural void . . . for this reason we call on our well-loved readers, as we often did in the dark years during which it was almost a crime to talk of revolution. Listen to us once more with indulgence."[5]

Balestrini dismisses the post-Liberation left. Indeed his remark about the sacred parties born of the Resistance undermines that entire regime. The 1980s are the Craxi years. Although his poem is dated 1993, Cossiga's term ended in 1992 and Balestrini does not foresee the effort of reform that accompanies the onslaught on bribery. For him the second period in post-war Italian history has come to an end. The task of writing about it remains.

After the poem comes *Vogliamo tutto,* the story of the Southern boy who moves from seasonal work in agriculture to the Fiat conveyor belt. The narrative discourse is the most important aspect and Ballestrini chooses a "low" Italian, untouched by dialect but also devoid of elegance and rhetoric. Everything is seen through the eyes of the protagonist. But his language "has no body, no intensity and no weight . . . everything is missing . . . it is frozen and fragmented. It interrupts itself frequently, refusing to say more."[6]

This language de-ideologizes the notion of revolution itself. It is indifferent to the events it narrates, plain but not coarse, precise but not rich or varied. The aim of such a discourse is to rob the narrator's role in the Fiat strike of all grandeur without, however, stressing its absurdity.

The unit of Balestrini's prose is the paragraph that averages around ten lines. It is divided into sentences and its punctuation—here—is normal. One line is left white between two paragraphs, which makes the page look orderly. Visually the repetition of paragraphs that have roughly the same length imposes sameness on the book. This is a technical not an aesthetic impression. It is strengthened by the absence of inverted commas around the direct speech.

At the outset the narrator, who has come from such work as tomato picking, gets a job on the assembly line and takes no interest in politics. He unashamedly describes himself as a "qualunquista." Yet he has strong views on the factory—"the most absurd, nastiest thing in the world."[7] On May 1 he knows nothing about the labor movement and laughs at the crowds who chant the name of Mao-Tse-Tung without knowing who he is.

The narrator, however, is a natural protestor. He is not the kind of worker who found his way to the PCI in the previous generation of the 1950s. This worker was austere, enjoyed working and resented the alienation that the company imposed on him. The narrator condemns the profit-motive, work and factory. He picks up without help the way that Fiat uses numbers to give the worker a series of inauthentic identities: he has a corridor number, a work-place number, a changing-room number, a locker number, a number of pieces he must make during the day, and so on.[8] His life is controlled by these statistics. The narrator is no reformist: if his life is to change, then the entire capitalist system must change.

Balestrini belongs to the segment of the New Left that is most hostile to the PCI: "bureaucratic trade unionists who belong to the communist party, false Marxist Leninists, police and fascists have one thing in common: they are all afraid of the workers' capacity... to organize their struggle autonomously inside and outside the factory."[9]

As the book and the strike go on, the narrator's expertise grows. This is not really artificial because his basic feelings rather than thoughts remain: work is unpleasant so the workers can and must organize their struggle against it. "The workers' struggle evades attempts to control it. Each day a new struggle begins and the decisions about it are made by the workers."[10] Similarly the workers demand equal wage increases for everyone. This reduces the difference between a skilled and an unskilled worker and a backlash by skilled workers in the late 1970s and early 1980s brought defeat for all workers. But in the 1960s this was a logical demand for unskilled Southern workers to make.

Ballestrini ends his novel with two resounding statements. The first is that class antagonism is normal and inevitable: "We have nothing in common, we are two different worlds, we and they are enemies and that's all there is to it."[11] (This statement is reminiscent of Sillitoe.) The second is that this hostility inevitably produces violence and Ballestrini endorses this. "Let us say yes to the worker's violence."[12] *Vogliamo tutto* was first published in 1971 and it reflects the high hopes of the late sixties. The last chapter describes an uprising in Turin that spreads outward from the Fiat plant. The difference between the end of the novel and the 1993 poem tells us much about left-wing politics in the last thirty years.

The New Left made an immediate impact in several countries. In France it arguably led to de Gaulle's departure in 1969. He was followed by Georges Pompidou and then in 1974 by Valéry Giscard d'Estaing, both of whom had even less in common with the New Left, although Giscard was haunted by the fear of protest and revolt at least up to 1977. The movement took several courses: many members gave up and went home; others joined one of the factions or "tendances" of the existing left-wing parties—one group of militants followed a segment of Michel Rocard's Parti socialiste unifié (PSU) into the Socialist Party (PS); another group threw in its lot with Jean-Pierre Chevènement's Centre d'études de recherche et d'éducation socialiste (CERES). This was the most left-wing of the "tendances" in the PS. But the New Left militants were still agreeing to play by the rules of "bourgeois democracy." Conversely Mitterrand's victory in '81 showed that there was space on the left but it was not what the New Left considered left-wing.

In Britain the small New Left groups sometimes practiced "entrism" (Militant). They had their roots in student politics and the anti-Vietnam movement—(Tariq Ali), even if there was a Trotsky-ite element that was older. They were small, unimportant groups and their rise to significance was a sign of Labour's crisis. After the party's defeat in 1979 these groups helped form the hard core of a left that allied with the older Tribunite left and came close—but less close than they and their opponents claimed—to taking over the Labour Party in the run-up to the 1983 elections. That they failed with the party and the country is partly to be explained by political errors. But in a more fundamental way collectivist values did not suit the post-'68 electorate.

This was also true in Italy although it was less obvious. In the 1972 and 1976 elections, some of the New Left movements formed *partitini* and ran on their own. Although they were helped by the pure PR voting system, these converted movements won only a handful of votes. The electoral gains went to the PCI, now transformed, in all but name, into a "mild" left-wing party. As always, however, the name was important.

The New Left's form of government was via the "assemblea." This form of direct democracy, where at least in theory everyone had the same amount of power and all decisions were unanimous, was in practice extremely tiring, produced very few decisions and did not prevent the rise of would-be charismatic leaders. The Italian New Left inherited many of the faults and few of the virtues (if there were any) of the Third International: it was painfully slow, needlessly bureaucratic but fortunately it lacked a Stalin to make use of it. At times one felt it was less a political organization than one of the many forms of "stare insieme."

The next problem, which one cannot avoid facing, is whether the terrorist groups, which considered themselves left-wing, were an integral part of the post-'68 left. Commentators, eager to deny this, point out that many terrorists had little experience of New Left politics. A significant contingent of the Red Brigades, for example, came from the Trento sociology faculty but, although the faculty was left-wing, the future Red Brigades group, Renato Curcio, Mara Cagol and others had little contact with campus politics and saw themselves as a small élite. This explanation would not serve, however, to explain the second core group in the BR (Brigate rosse), the Reggio-Emilia contingent. Reggio was culturally dominated by the PCI and the future BR leader, Alberto Franceschini grew up in a communist family. He drew the conclusion that his mission was to complete the work left unfinished by the partisans and to bring about a revolution in Italy.[13] Nor was Franceschini unacquainted with New Left organizing in the factories: he tried it for a while in Milan before turning to exemplary violence and then to ordinary violence.

It seems to me that terrorism offers one, aberrant answer to the New Left's dilemma. It believed that the working-class was ready or almost ready to revolt. The workers were held back by the policies of the owners and by the double-dealing of the PCI. But these could be overcome by an energetic New Left. When the working-class still did not revolt, violence was the necessary catalyst. The terrorist continued to see himself as part of the struggle of the masses, whereas in reality s/he was ever more isolated. This is present in her language, which becomes a jargon, full of clichés from the Marxist catechism. The "masses" are a remote abstraction that are talked about but do not talk.

Franceschini continues to claim that his BR were part of a mass, revolutionary movement and that there were hundreds of thousands of young people intent on destroying the state. He admits the BR was wrong in believing that the collapse of the state was inevitable but he will not give up the mass movement.[14]

THE 1977 MOVEMENT, OR IRONY TAKES POWER

In most European countries the New Left peaked in the late 1960s and went down afterward, at least as a force in its own right. France belatedly produced a small terrorist group, Action directe, but Charles Pasqua broke it up easily when he became Minister of the Interior in 1986. (He had more trouble with the Middle Eastern terrorists.) Although isolated actions continued, the Stammheim suicides destroyed the ruling group of the Baader-Meinhof band. The IRA grew stronger but it disliked the Italian and German terrorists whom it considered too bourgeois and too Marxist. Individuals survived from 1968, like Daniel Cohn-Bendit, but not organizations or politics or languages.

Except in Italy, where there was a second great upsurge in 1977. But before examining that we must glance at the relationship between politics and culture in the New Left. Many of the individuals and groups discussed above were wary of culture as a distraction from politics. There was, however, a strong group that held the opposite view.[15]

It has been argued convincingly that the political side of the New Left was the last upsurge of messianic Marxism, whereas the cultural movement was far more modern. Typical of the new protagonists was the Roman group "Non," which rejected all notions of the leading role of the working-class now reduced, as Marcuse had foreseen, to an alienated consumerism, as well as of economic issues, which would in the future be resolved by automation.

The oil crisis that hit Italy in 1973 would reveal the optimism of such economic thinking. The "Non," however, demonstrated the split in the 1970s between the historic left, which was preparing to come to power with a project to fight inflation and a belief in the Berlinguerian notion of austerity, and the younger non-parliamentary groups who preferred game-playing and "joke-demonstrations."[16]

The aim of such irony was to provoke the listener, who was seen not as a possible ally to be won over but as an enemy whose worldview must be called into question. We are light years away from Togliatti's attempt to turn the PCI into a worthy inheritor of Italy's neo-Hegelian tradition. Moreover since they do not attach the same importance to the working-class, the young protestors left themselves open to the criticism of the guardians of PCI orthodoxy, like Giorgio Amendola, and of heretics like Pasolini, who attacked them as the children of neo-capitalism.

One of the dominant traits of this culture is its sense of being a counter-culture. It challenges what it considers official culture not only in the name of some vision of the future but on an everyday basis. It is a militant culture that arrives at its positions via a negative process that includes overthrowing the revealed truths of TV, safely under the control of the DC, of the school and of the factory. It has links with avant-garde culture: it is influenced by futurism, whose subversive tendencies it welcomes. But it is hostile to certain figures of the contemporary élite like Moravia, who possess an aristocratic air that reminds the New Left that theirs is a culture of the masses, although not a mass culture.

To challenge the official truths, the protestors take the struggle to the streets. They put on "happenings," which ignore the rules of traditional theater. As in Brecht, the object was to sketch out new relationships between actor and spectator. Julien Beck and the Living Theatre were the models. The future Nobel Prize winner Dario Fo was an ally.

The language of the counter-culture directed its irony at the language of modernization and especially of consumerism. The New Left rallies often gave the impression of a crowd of small-town or country kids lost in big cities and unused to everyday technology. In this sense they were conservatives, although they would not admit it. Often the New Left's language seemed to imitate the tongue of consumerism: simplified grammar and lists of objects. But the attempt was serious: to break up the movement from producer to consumer, as in the TV commercials, and to introduce a third and mocking voice.

Some movements tried to combine the political and the cultural. The groups that were purely political and made scant distinction between official and counter-culture did not last long. By the early 1970s they were reduced to small sects. Those like Autonomia or Lotta continua that aimed at a synthesis of politics and culture were more interesting: Lotta continua had a flair for picking up what was new in society; its work in prisons is but one example. The difficulty of resolving its own contradictions was, however, great and Lc dissolved at its Rimini congress of 1976 at least partly because of pressure from its women members.[17] Lc's militants often went straight into the 1977 Movimento. Lc was never well organized but its newspaper provided information on the New Left that the regular press ignored, while its letter page was an agony column for over-ideologized adolescents. Some branches of Autonomia, which by now had absorbed Potere Operaio, went over to violence, often a spontaneous violence considered inherent in the class struggle, according to spokesmen who took issue with the planned violence of the highly organized BR. They helped spawn another terrorist movement, Prima Linea, which tried to combine killing the enemies of the working-class with political organizing. Prima Linea quickly discovered that it was not an acceptable political interlocutor.

In 1977 the Italian Movement went through a second great upsurge. This has in our view been neglected outside Italy because, unlike '68, it was a purely Italian and not European movement.[18] It was also—except in the most superficial aspects—very different from '68. It emerged after the New Left's bad showing in the '76 elections, when it gained less than 2 percent of the vote. "It was the end of an era"—said one acute observer from Lc.[19] The Movement was also a reaction against the PCI strategy of the historic compromise. One feels, however, that the 1977 Movement was beaten before it took the field of battle. Its politics were officially revolutionary but in reality they were defeatist. Its culture was a prolonged exercise in self-irony. One of its supporters described it as "a vast, creative fauna that desecrated but was not violent." It was, he added, "a generation that was culturally shaped in front of the television screen, that grew up with the most beautiful ballads in the history of rock running around in its head."[20]

It had one interesting artist: Andrea Pazienza. His satirical cartoons depicting clashes between militants and the police were funny and bitter. A film based on his cartoons has just been issued in February 2002: *Paz* depicts a group of supposed militants in flight from politics and engaged in their own lives, which consist of hanging around together and scrounging money for drugs. This viewpoint displeased many ex–77-ites, who complained about the lack of politics. Women are depicted as stronger and more stable than men, whose need for a mother-figure is satirized. More important was the general lack of interest in the film, which appealed only to people who had experience of the Movimento. The non-exes stayed away.

The Movement had a short life-span, which ran between two victories. On February 17 it prevented the Communist trade union leader, Luciano Lama, from speaking at Rome University. This was politically coherent: Lama was identified with the PCI strategy of austerity, in particular of offering wage restraint in return for measures to fight unemployment. This was a reasonable bargain for workers who had jobs, but the Movement represented the young unemployed. The Movement also pointed out that Lama brought with him a loudspeaker and a podium, indicating that his would be a monologue not a dialogue and that, although a communist, he was a man of authority.

The Movement's own demonstrations were feasts. The largest came in September when, to protest against the death of Francesco lo Russo, a militant killed by the police, it took over the PCI's showcase city of Bologna. Bloodshed was avoided when the Communists flooded the city center with working-class militants instructed to talk to the demonstrators. These also heeded the peacekeeping efforts of their "servizio d'ordine," although tension was apparent in the assemblies. Representatives of Autonomia refused to call the BR "comrades in error" and insisted they were "comrades tout court." During the weekend of the occupation Bologna was divided in two: Piazza Maggiore belonged to the PCI and the townspeople, while Piazza Verdi was awarded or ceded to the Movimento.

The atmosphere of feast was heightened by two habits that resembled *potlatch*. One was the "proletarian expropriation," in which a militant who saw something s/he liked in a shop simply went in and took it in the name of the working-class. The second was "self-reduction," in which a member of the Movement went to a fashionable restaurant and ate heartily. When the bill came, s/he paid as much as a worker could have afforded, usually a fraction of the price. Such habits did not win the Movement any support among the Bologna shopkeepers, but they would have amused Croquignole and his creator, Charles-Louis Philippe.[21]

The element of "play" led the Movement to invent certain characters, usually gifted with fantasy and opposed to the dreary rationalism of modern capitalism. The first was the witch newly re-endowed with her magical powers. Young women with big hats and broomsticks marched in the demonstration chanting: "Tremate, tremate/le streghe sono tornate" ("Tremble, tremble/ the witches are back"). Metropolitan Indians, survivors of a race that was exterminated to permit the rise of the world's greatest capitalist power, came from nowhere and demanded chunks of Bologna for their reserves. Alice's name was used to symbolize the return of fantasy. The Bologna Movement's radio station was called Radio Alice. All these characters contain pre-capitalist elements.

Language follows the same pattern. Marx is satirized and his thought used in graffiti, such as "After Marx, April. After April, May," where the Italian word "mai" means "never." This is nonsense language but nonetheless meaningful. Other examples are "Più sacrifici, meno dentifrici" (More sacrifices, less toothpaste), which mocks the PCI's policy of austerity, and the transformation of the PCI slogan "E ora, è ora di cambiare, la classe operaia deve governare" into "E ora, è ora, miseria a chi lavora." The Movement presents itself as a new kind of interlocutor. Different from the political parties, whose complex discourse is designed to exclude and whose rationalism masks the quest for power, the Movement speaks with a voice that is more female than male, the voice of many women, a kind of mass Molly Bloom soliloquy.

This sort of political movement could not hope to last long or to exercise great influence. Its social base was too narrow; it was too prone to violence and too chaotic. It subsided quickly after its Bologna triumph and, while it left among young people a residual hostility to the PCI, which the next mayor of Bologna, Renzo Imbeni, tried hard to eliminate, it ceased to be a protagonist in its own right. The film director Francesca Archibugi made a film, *Verso Sera*, which looks back on the '77 Movement. Although more broadly based than *Paz*, *Verso Sera* too emphasizes the personal turmoil of many young militants.

Once more it was Nanni Balestrini who wrote the requiem of the politico-cultural New Left. *Gli invisibili* (1987) is a more complex work than *Vogliamo Tutto*. The structure of the two books is superficially similar but *Gli invisibili* has no punctuation, its vocabulary is richer and in particular it makes the body live for us. Body or rather bodies: the New Left bodies stripped, beaten and kicked by the police, occasionally happy after some dinner cooked in the most rudimentary manner in a prison cell, flashes of physical beauty like China's long hair falling over her face. These bodies tell the truth of the class struggle, as Sartre had foreseen. Order is present again through the paragraphs. They provide lists of things, seen or touched: these things are locked inside the narrator, whose name we never know. They are silent, except when he can speak of them, as when all the militants, female and male, come together to be tried: "to be able to speak of so many things, to be able at last to talk about everything."[22] Such ironically privileged moments are rare.

The short chapters are not in a chronological pattern nor is there one plot. The narrator lives in that gray area where he does not choose targets for violence but violence takes place as part of the social order. We see him at different moments: in school when he has just finished his "maturità" and has gone to live with China and three other comrades, for he says that "the movement was my family"[23]—a revealing remark; in prison during the repression when he, along with others, is savagely beaten; taking part in the occupation of a factory; preparing himself for defeat and a long spell in a special prison.

One of the most dramatic moments in the book is the debate within the small group of friends about the move to clandestinity and organized violence. The representative of this view is Scilla, who is depicted as being temperamentally violent and possessing little sense of politics. Scilla turns out to be a police spy, which is a somewhat facile interpretation of the Red Brigades. At the end of the book the narrator, who has broken with China and is locked away in his isolated prison, makes torches as a protest, but they can be seen by almost no one. He is truly invisible.

Of all Balestrini's books this must be one of the best. He has fused a piece of writing for writing, which describes the Movement as fully as possible, with the political goal of winning sympathy for an oft-calumniated political force. He consciously writes against the mass media. He writes of people emarginated by the press and TV and he shows how the prison system is used to prevent them from engaging in the social struggle.

The 1980s saw a de-politization of the New Left militants, their withdrawal into private life and an enormous increase in the drug trade. At least such is the legend, and the signs of drug trading in Bologna were indeed far more visible in the mid-1980s than they had been in the mid-1970s. Yet there is evidence that young people were unconvinced by the mass media and that, when confronted with publicity and consumerism, they reacted with skepticism.[24] In the 1970s the counter-culture hoped in vain to establish the beatnik as the figure to be admired and imitated. But the beatnik was defeated by the forces of tradition and by the left-wing terrorist. The post-modern, with its sense of fragmentation, was at hand. At the national and international level the left fared badly. In Italy the PCI lost its last great leader in 1984 when Enrico Berlinguer died in those dreadful days in Padua. Abroad Thatcher was the model and the watchwords were free enterprise, economic deregulation and the politics of conviction. The publication of J. F. Lyotard's *La condition postmoderne* coincided with the founding of the European Monetary System (EMS) by Schmidt and Giscard d'Estaing.[25]

Before moving into the 1990s we may attempt to sum up the impact of '68 on Italy and—very cursorily—on Europe. In both areas the direct political effect was short-lived. But the social consequences were far greater.[26] The Divorce Law of 1970, the Referendum of '74, the Abortion Law of '78 and the Referendum of '81 contradicted the collectivist thrust of New Left politics. They increased the individual's power to control her/his private life. Decisions, originally made by the Church, then by the State, pass to the individual or the couple. As if to demonstrate this, one of the spheres where the greatest change takes place is the role of women. So '68 did not contradict the powerful thrust in Western societies toward individualism and, where it did, it failed to convince.

From the 1980s on politics and writing tended to go their own separate ways in Italy. The students remained sufficiently dissatisfied to launch the Pantera protest (1991) and by taking over their university's fax machines, they realized their old dream of a nationwide network of alternative information. When the political crisis exploded in 1992, however, it did not lend itself to left-wing protest. Meanwhile writing had taken a new turn with the work of Pier-Vittorio Tondelli (1955–1991). In *Altri Libertini* (1980) he described groups of people, stressing gays, hippies and others who were marginal or excluded. By not passing judgment on them Tondelli turns them into subjects and lets them speak for themselves. Punks with dyed blue hair give their opinions on life as they wander from bar to bar. There is not the vicious strain that one finds in Martin Amis's novels and Tondelli's characters are also more provincial.

They are not the shock troops of a new Movement, for they have little interest in politics. They are opposed to the social order, however, if only because it does not much care for punks who dye their hair blue. They mix with the Johns Hopkins students and perhaps the CIA spies on them but they do not care, for they believe they are not worth the agency's time.[27] Balestrini had called more mainstream people than these the "invisible," while Foucault used the term "the marginals" and the 1977 Movimento thought of its members as "emarginati." As the Europe of the EMS and, after Maastricht, of Monetary Union prepared for its goals by long bouts of rigor, so the weaker social groups were pushed aside. The old who voted in great numbers managed to keep their share of a diminished Welfare State. Young people, unless their families could help, floundered amid unemployment, job-training schemes and government-backed "stages" that often led to nothing but other "stages." In France unemployment was the price that had to be paid for the strong franc and the

Franco-German alliance. Britain was forced out of the EMS in 1992, which increased hostility toward monetary union. Italy was forced out, which was lived as a national humiliation.

This is the unspoken background to Silvia Ballestra's *La guerra degli Antò*, a book that shows the influence of Tondelli. Her young characters are doubly alienated because they came from the Marche and the Abbruzzo to Bologna and have to face grasping landladies and prejudiced citizens. Their position as exploited Southerners pushes them to the left. Then too some of them inherit the political passions of the 1970s. During the Gulf War they pay attention only to Rai 3 and they are opposed to the myth of an easy American victory. The second Antò, convinced that he will be drafted and sent to the Middle East, decides to flee. The Bologna wing of the group has one Marxist militant, Fabio de Vasto, who takes a conventional view of the imperialist war and forges false documents for Antò.

The book's climax is reached when Fabio takes on the author in a political debate. Fabio is studying politics and condemns the author's ignorance in the name of Marx. She has read Céline and Derrida and the reader feels that her irony is truer than Fabio's certainties. She brings to a final end the long Italian tradition of alternative political movements, replacing it with a critical awareness of language. Her joust with Fabio could be read as the battle of the post-modern and the modern. To her attack she adds a feminist argument, that is deliberately simple and seems practical, about how the women in the Abruzzo and the Marche sacrifice themselves to the men.

The political energy in Tondelli and Ballestra has declined, although the linguistic skills have not. They share the sense of a cheapened modernity made up of TV programs like *Chi l'ha visto* and sundry kinds of space invaders. This is junk modernity and it is quite unlike the language used to depict it. We shall return to Ballestra in the next chapter, but one must note before finishing this one that, if in most of Europe the last years of the millennium showed little imagination in protest as in high politics, the social centers showed some awareness of the 1977 Movimento even as they adopted a minimalist language of protest.

In April 1998 the "squatters" left their social centers and headed for Turin, where one of their members had committed suicide in prison. Like their predecessors they practiced self-reduction on the trains and ate "the people's sandwiches," which were very much cheaper than the listed prices. The traditional ambivalence toward the United States emerged again: one slogan was "McDonald's must be burned," but one of the centers was called El Paso. The '98 demonstration had even less trust in its ability to change society than the 77 Movement. They were content to stamp on the walls words like "anger," which formed isolated, atomized graffiti. Equally short were the messages transmitted by their radio, which bore the incongruous, contradictory name of Radio Blackout. It is a long way from Radio Alice to this radio, which implies a lack of content and conjures up images of the Luftwaffe bombing London.

It is tempting to conclude that, unlike the works of Paul Klee, the social centers do not wish to make contact with humanity. Perhaps they detect no signs or messages welcoming them. But new writers and political movements may come forward to express the reality without the empty triumphalism of the end of the millennium and to tell the story of an unwanted social group. An attempt is being made in the cinema: in Britain of Ken Loach, in France at a simple level in *La Haine* and at a more complex level in Chabrol's *La Cérémonie*. Balestrini has switched his attention to soccer violence, which he depicts in *I Furiosi* (1994). He depicts it as a phenomenon in its own right that is barely connected with the match or support for the home team but constitutes a necessary outlet for violence, which then spreads throughout our society. The social centers are not an end in themselves. They help young marginals to survive until those welcoming signs and messages appear in the sky.

By February 2002 none had appeared, although the storm clouds of globalization loomed ever darker. The meeting of the G8 at Genoa provided an occasion for the anti-global movements to demonstrate against the political leaders of the advanced countries. It was tempting and sure enough the protest was international, the police brutal and the media generous in their coverage. The Black Bloc, about whom little was known but who are thought to be anarchists, became the leading object of interest. Clad in black overalls, they were expert street fighters. A book entitled *Bloc Book* was published about them by the underground—Stampa alternativa. It turned out to be a kind of "do it yourself" or "how to set up your own anarchist group." The Black Bloc must become subjects and deploy a language of their own before they can become worthy successors of Andrea Pazienza and Lotta continua.

Chapter Eleven

The Empire Strikes Back

Until now we have virtually avoided the entity of culture, whether as a word or as a thing. Or at least we have refrained from discussing it openly or at length. Presuppositions about culture underlie all our attempts to define and distinguish various kinds of language. Here we shall try to bring culture into the open. This chapter deals with the meeting of European and non-European peoples to whom Europeans ascribe a different culture (or none at all).

Discussion of culture can be dangerous since a culture, at least in Europe, is usually defined against another culture, which is then dismissed as inferior. Multi-culturalism is new and foreign in Europe, although it is spreading in big cities and has inspired films such as *Sammy and Rosie Get Laid*, the script of which was written by Hanif Kureishi. But European culture has dominated its neighbors for so long that its spokespeople forget how much they owe, for example, to Arab culture. Instead they tend to dismiss "Moslem fundamentalism" as the core of an Arab culture that is unfailingly hostile and backward. In fact fundamentalism, at least in the Moslem communities in Europe, is often the consequence of a failed attempt at integration, itself the result of a European refusal to accept Moslems.

Such tendencies can only be banished by a fair-minded discussion of culture, even if being fair is more difficult than it seems. We shall begin by defining culture; then we look at the phenomenon of colonialism, which shaped Europe's attitude toward the world outside; finally we shall deal with non-European writers writing about Europe.

We cannot avoid September 11, although we are still too close to it to make definitive judgments on it. Moreover, the prime impact of the assault on the World Trade Center towers has been, obviously, on the United

States. The Europeans have been reacting to the American reaction as much as to the assault itself. President Bush has made declarations of war. Directed against whom? President Bush says against terrorism, but one cannot go to war against terrorism. One goes to war against terrorists, who have bases and money and whose organizations can only flourish with the support of sovereign states.

The destruction of the World Trade Center towers revealed one important cultural difference between the United States and Europe and another between "Western" and "Moslem" terrorists. The United States sees itself as the sole remaining superpower and believes it has the right or even the duty to maintain a world order, by force if necessary. The Europeans, after fifty years of American protection-hegemony, are reluctant to take the initiative or to use force or to spend more money on defense. The difference in terrorists is that the Red Brigades were prepared to risk death but not to go to a certain death. The hijackers of September 11, like the Palestinians who blow themselves up on the crowded streets of Jerusalem, are willing to go to their deaths.

Before lapsing into vague generalizations about the European concern for life, let us define culture.

What is Culture?

One might begin with the definition of culture offered by Edward Said: culture is "all those forms of description, communication and representation which possess a relative autonomy from the political, social and economic realities." Culture also contains "a refining or elevating element." It is attached to a state or nation, in short to "us" and not to "them."[1] This definition seems generally correct, although there have been periods, like the Paris of the 1920s, when the national gave way, in certain, small and well-defined circles, to an international or a European culture. This opened up the "us" to include "some"—a carefully chosen "some"—of the "them."

Mostly Said denies that this "opening up" takes place. He is not concerned with the distinction between Europe and one of its member states but rather with the clash of West and East. In *Orientalism* (1978) he demonstrates that there has been precious little serious study of the East by the West. Rather what is called "orientalism" is a discourse constructed from Western sources that is designed to conceal or to justify the use of Western power to conquer the East and to gain control of its natural resources. There is much to quibble about with this judgment: it implies, for example, a rapacious but rational behavior by the West that is rare indeed and was certainly not present in the last rush to divide up Africa in the late nineteenth century. But the notion that the West is guided by an unflagging drive for power, that hides behind a carefully crafted series of intellectual discourses, has been expounded by Foucault. Said also demonstrates how the mythical figure of T. E. Lawrence, champion of Arab freedom, was both manipulated by the British authorities and living out his own thoroughly Western dream of deserts, the Bedouin and homosexuality.

The nineteenth century was a great period for orientalism. An initial impulse came from Napoleon's invasion of Egypt and the crowning achievement was the construction of the Suez Canal, which was built by Ferdinand de Lesseps, whose father had gone to Egypt with Napoleon. The Canal was the symbol of imperialism, which explains why Nasser's recovery of it in 1956 was greeted with such joy by the Arabs and was such a humiliation to Britain and France. It marked that moment that Sartre describes when the colonized ceases to see everything through the eyes of the colonizer and imposes her/his own view on the colony.

The orientalist's view is static, minimizing the possibility of change. His discourse is designed to fit into a Western frame of knowledge and to strengthen Western supremacy. Even France's Louis Massillon, who envisaged a meeting of what was best in the two cultures, weakened mainstream Islam by his interest in Arab mysticism. Said denies having affirmed that only a black could write about blacks or only a Moslem about Islam. But he certainly stresses the need to live within a culture in order to know it and Western man's difficulty in penetrating and living within any culture but his own is well established. Said's judgment on Europeans is harsh: almost every European is "a racist, an imperialist and almost totally ethnocentric."[2]

Said's work is more important than ever because the Cold War is over. As long as it dragged on, ideological criteria continued to function. Even if, as I believe, the Soviet threat was never as great as the prophets of anti-communism would have us believe, the sound and fury of the Cold War drowned out other clashes, such as ethnic disputes. Now they have, thanks to Samuel Huntington and others like him, returned to the front row. The ongoing Gulf War with the periodic bombing of Iraq is only one example.

The word "culture" is used in a very different manner by the French poet Hughes Labrusse.[3] Culture is an apparatus that envelops writers as well as readers. It is a weapon with which the ruling élite, by careful allocation of resources, is able to block kinds of research that might threaten it. Labrusse lists the defects of the present network: there is too much culture, it is too much like an industry, it is nowadays a matter of marketing—as one markets the Disneylands. This kind of culture will grow stronger as recorded, predictable language, on which it thrives, grows more common. Art is quite separate from culture, but in the massive spread of culture by states who see in it a diversion—cinemas and fashion parades (along with soccer) are the opium of the masses—art suffers. Culture, however, goes on, heedless of its own superfluity. As an integral part of the political and social systems, culture will become global. It possesses powerful allies in international business and politicians desperate for reelection. By contrast artistic creation is fragile and heretical.

Culture in Labrusse's sense of the word is the negation of life values. It is reminiscent of Baudrillard but without the self-mockery. Labrusse is surely correct to maintain that the culture industry is growing and that, as it exists in most European countries, it takes the products of artistic creation and uses or abuses them as it sees fit. Examples would be public subsidies for young (rock?) musicians or the rapid swings of the art market. We ask how Europe perceives other continents. That Europe will, its worldview established, drape it in the costumes and trinkets of the culture industry, is certain. But in our view there is something that Said calls culture, which exists in its own right, prior to the creation of Disneylands, the Millennium Dome and even the fringe theater of the Edinburgh Festival.

Time is an important issue. It moves in its usual linear way: from novels that are set in the grand period of Empire like Joseph Conrad's *Lord Jim* and E. M. Forster's *Passage to India* via the break-up of colonialism in the Algerian and Vietnam Wars and the writing of Albert Camus, to the present, when movement goes in the opposite direction and immigrants from the former colonies come to Europe to work and to write. Yet along with the linear time there is a kind of eternal present. For the adolescent reading Conrad, *Lord Jim* was published yesterday; the Algerian War lives on in France.[4] Meanwhile the North African immigrants seem to Le Pen's supporters like a new battalion of the FLN (Front de libération nationale).

The only major criticisms we wish to make of Said's work are firstly that his notion of imperialism is too monolithic: we have already argued that Ireland was not a colony in the sense that Ghana or Nigeria was. The second, overlapping thesis is that awareness of imperialism, whether in the shape of guilt or especially of criticism-rebellion, was more difficult for Western writers than the author of *Culture and Imperialism* might think it should have been. Moreover the problem of the "other" culture appears often as "unsaid," words that the writer of the dominant culture does not know how to say.

A Man from Poland
and the British Empire

Conrad found in the English language a security that comes of much effort. Similarly he is aware of the well-ordered lives of the people who speak it. He, Joseph Conrad, whose real name was long and very Polish, might have no home to go back to other than the acquired linguistic home of English, but the Britishers could all go home, indeed this was the occasion when "they rendered account" (or were judged, as Satta would have said). In *Lord Jim*, Conrad makes great play with going home: he invents, imagines Jim's house: "the red front of the rectory gleamed with a warm tint in the midst of grass-plots, flower-beds and fir-trees."[5] Conrad is original in his use of irony, which he introduces into almost every paragraph, juxtaposing one sentence against another, here contrasting the age and tradition of the rectory with the light-hearted way Jim decides that his life's vocation is to go to sea.

Light-hearted is not, however, the word to describe what happens to Jim. The sea tests a man: the sea is beautiful but—this is a key point in Conrad's descriptive writing—it changes rapidly. Sooner or later there is a storm to test young Englishmen. When Jim fails the test, he cannot go home but neither can he leave the Empire. Australia would seem one possibility; Argentina or the West Coast of the United States would be two more. None of these enters Jim's mind: there is nothing outside the Empire. (Australia was of course part of the Empire, but as a white settler colony it was very different from Malaya.)

Within the Empire reigns a strict hierarchy with the English at the top, other Europeans, who have an order of precedence of their own with the French and the Germans high up and the Portuguese at the bottom, just above the Australians. Then come the indigenous peoples who in one case possess legitimate leaders and a political order—Doramin and his wife—but are mostly subject to the law of hunger. Among these people the prestige of the white man is great but with it comes the responsibility of which Kipling writes so eloquently. Jim, having failed to assure the boatload of devoted Moslems an untroubled journey toward Mecca, seeks out the country of Patustan. He imposes justice on it and thus regains, in the eyes of the handful of people who have kept in touch with him, and yet more important in his own eyes, the trust that was offered to the Englishman. Unlike Kipling, Conrad does not dwell on the class differences within the British colony; his Europeans are mostly traders and form a bloc with a few outcasts like the Portugese, Cornelius.

Jim was "one of us,"⁶ and one possible reading of the novel is that he wished to fit into the Englishman's exalted niche and would accept no other. This would explain the book's ending. In Brown Jim saw a white who had taken precisely the opposite path from his own. Brown's gratuitous cruelty would prove that the world was inhuman; Jim's unselfish determination to do good would demonstrate that the world was livable. Brown alludes to "their common blood,"⁷ and the narrator berates him for it. But is there not something true about the comparison? Both men were romantics seeking to live exceptional lives. Empire provided countries devoid of laws, policemen and management consultants where they could measure themselves against a wild nature and against each other. Both were selfish, Brown more obviously, but Jim too in his refusal to live for the girl rather than seek out a sacred death at the hands of his friend's father.

Jim is presented as an Englishman. He is not especially clever but he works hard, he is devoted to his family back in England. Perhaps there is an element of selfishness in his refusal to go home: his family might have preferred seeing a non-hero to talking about their brave Jim.

But Jim inspires trust in men like Marlow. Marlow is the narrator and we rely on his memory so the events of the novel are less certain than in the realist novel. Moreover Marlow takes information where he finds it, so his is a multiple narration: much of the ending is recounted to Marlow by Captain Brown.

Brown is, of course, very hostile to Jim. Throughout the novel there is an aversion running alongside Marlow's sympathy. This is the critique of European culture that takes Britain and Empire as its main targets. Yet the reader's sympathy goes out to Jim if only because reader and character seem to have little choice. This is a novel about Western culture of which Conrad was knowingly a part. Jim's romantic idealism is different from but akin to Kim's energy in *Jungle Book*. Europe needed colonization. The language of the great colonial novels belonged to the literary avant-garde; there is far too much doubt in the way *Lord Jim* is told to make it an "écrivant" piece of writing.

Using a different vocabulary, one might accuse Jim of hubris. He takes it for granted that the "natives" will obey and follow him. Another way of expressing Jim's worldview is to see it as a public school ethic. Not that Jim attended one of the leading public schools but their values were felt in society as a whole. They were designed to support the colony against the factory within the British economy and to set in the colonies an example that could not be followed by the indigenous people. Theirs were romantic values: Conrad could not but remember his parents' fate and he was critical of this romanticism. But he could see that Empire rested on the white man's burden–prestige.

Orwell and the Good Colonizer

Conrad sailed in and out of Eastern ports, whereas Orwell knew the life of the British who stayed a long time. They were not, like the *pieds noirs*, a settler colony that had no "home" to go to but neither were they traders. Orwell's parents were Indian civil servants, underpaid, undervalued and suffering from the heat and the humidity. By now the British Empire was changing. Orwell sees 1914 as the watershed. Until then the wealth of the English upper-classes was taken for granted; not so afterward. Orwell saw, as Conrad had done, that Empire rested on the prestige of white skin. But he saw this prestige decline as Ghandi told Indians to wear shirts they had made themselves and to use salt they had cut themselves.

Orwell served in the Burmese police force after leaving Eton and he wrote a short piece called *Shooting an Elephant* about the burdens of working in a colony. A rogue elephant is terrorizing a village, which asks the police to send men to shoot it. By the time that the narrator and his colleague arrive, the elephant is calm and tranquil. Yet, although the animal offers no danger to anyone, the two white men have to shoot it. Why? To show they are not afraid of it. Because they have said they will shoot it. Because the entire village is waiting for the spectacle. Because the two men are policemen. Because they are white. Naturally all these reasons overlap and at the core is the principle of white authority. Thus the colony undermines the ethical principles and the rational decisions on which Western society is supposedly based.

Orwell left the Burmese police force: his military training stood him in good stead in the Spanish Civil War. But the main result of his colonial experience was the novel *Burmese Days* (1935). Here Orwell distinguishes between what Albert Memmi calls good and bad colonizers: the bad colonizer, like Ellis, welcomes the Burmese with kicks, spends every evening drinking in the "no-natives-allowed" club, and yearns for a non-existent Britain where there are no Burmese but where there are, miraculously, servants. The bad colonizer has scant knowledge either of Burma or Britain and he is suspicious of whites who speak the indigenous language or who know much about "native" life.

Flory is such a character in *Burmese Days*. He feels a fascination for Burmese customs and he dislikes the English club. He exemplifies ironically Edward Said's remark about the "refined" element in culture because, while he is refined in a real sense, he is considered treacherous or mad by the gin-drinkers of the club. Flory explores the forest, getting away from the logging companies and discovering villages where no Englishman has set foot. Flory's ambition is to marry a white woman who shares his interest in Burma and to go on living in Burma and working for an English company with a European salary.

One does not need to be a Marxist to see the contradictions in this view. The woman with whom Flory falls in love hates Burma and is concerned only with her social position inside the English community. The Burmese do not welcome Flory, convinced that such an unusual Englishman must be even worse than the usual kind.

There are several Burmese characters in the novel, one of them well drawn. The minor figures are Dr. Veraswami, who is fawningly pro-British, and Ma Hla May, whose sole ambition is to be a white man's mistress. U Po Kyn is more interesting because he understands that the discourse and the practices of colonialism are quite separate. He would agree with Edward Said that most Europeans are xenophobic and racist. Starting from this realistic view, U Po Kyn prospers under colonialism.

Outside U Po Kyn's shrewd remarks there is no attempt to see the colony from a Burmese point of view. This is in itself a sharp critique of the idealized vision of a European country helping a poorer country. But, while most Europeans paid lip service to this vision, it was not taken seriously by many. Orwell's un-said elements include Flory's fear of the judgments passed on him at the club and his complementary fear that the Burmese will reject him. His silences are eloquent. Pierre Macheray accounts well for such silences or absences.[8] Ideology—in this case imperialism—holds the written work together but when ideology turns against itself, as it does when confronted with the flagrant injustice it fosters, then language collapses and the structures of the work along with it.

This is what happens when the revolt—if that is the correct word—takes place and whites find guns pointed at them instead of at the Burmese. Language is important because a new vocabulary would be needed if a more tolerant society came into being. It was, however, no nearer when Orwell published *Burmese Days* than it was when Conrad wrote *Lord Jim*. But there is a difference between the two novels that cannot be explained by the different character traits of their authors, even if this kind of explanation were acceptable. In Conrad the Empire is the universe, which helps explain why Jim's crime is so much greater than it seems. In Orwell the colony is just that: one small, abused country among many. So the Burmese do not treat the whites with the genuine admiration they receive in *Lord Jim*. No European would admit to kicking a "native" in Conrad's novel. The world has grown harder in the some thirty-five years between the publications of the two books—more hostile, more racist, and more clearly headed toward war. Orwell was conscious of this and, although he shared Kipling's defense of the lower social orders among the colonizers and treats the aristocrat Verrall with contempt, there is not the sense of the Empire projecting its own values and then defending them by its examples, as was the case in Lord Jim. Burmese Days has a Manichean structure that is common in the language of politics; there are arguments about how best to defend oneself and much unnecessary talk about rape. Europe was preparing to do battle to save its colonies.

The great colonial powers naturally produced the colonial novels, but from Italy's belated attempt to build an empire in Africa came one good, original book: Ennio Flaiano's *Tempo di uccidere*.[9] After the war Flaiano teamed up with Leo Longanesi to form a satirical right, the closest Italy came to having a right like Roger Nimier's. Flaiano also wrote film scripts and he worked on several Fellini films.

In this book Flaiano asserts himself as a writer at the outset: "I wish to put to an end any doubt about his importance in this story."[10] Then for the next 200 pages we hear nothing more about the fair-haired, young worker. One cannot help feeling doubt about his role in the story and about the narrator. After those 200 pages the fair-haired worker is mentioned as the possible reason for a massacre conducted by Mussolini's troops. This is not certain, however, so we are left wondering whether the narrator has been making fun of us.

The colonial setting is not to be questioned. Africa is omnipresent and menacing; it is the antithesis of Italy. Like Jim the narrator wants to come home but the geography of the book makes it impossible for him to flee. He cannot help returning to the place where he buried Mariam. The menace of Africa is represented by the immobile crocodiles patiently waiting and watching in the river; they haunt the dreams of Ethiopians, much less Italians. The contrast with Italy is indicated by a watch that the narrator gives to Mariam. She is delighted but the present is worthless in an Africa where the simplest forms of technology are unknown and time is measured in centuries.

By contrast the colonizer's home country shrinks to an ill-defined object of desire. The narrator wants to get to Naples but it is not clear why. The other Italian cities barely receive a mention. Colonial Europe is present in the book: the Suez Canal is mentioned in the early pages, while a huge advertisement for whisky dominates Port Said and the closing pages. In this way Mussolini's invasion of Ethiopia is placed not in the context of the break with the League of Nations but in the long history of attacks by Europeans on neighboring peoples.

The European characters are not named but are given their military titles. They are thus stripped of their personal identity and they receive non-names—major, captain, et cetera—which associate them exclusively with the war. The Abyssinians possess first names, which are used by any and every European. It is uncertain whether Mariam was really the first name of so many Ethiopian women or whether the colonizer ignored them and imposed on them a first name chosen by him. This would be a milder version of the Auschwitz method.

Such motifs set Flaiano's novel in the mainstream of colonial writing: names, especially last names, link the individual and the state, whether to exact from her/him acts of duty or to provide her/him with money and welfare. So the absence of names marks Ethiopia as a non-state. The military titles remind us that colonies are perpetually on the brink of rebellion. Flaiano sees Abyssinia not as a state in its own right nor as an Italian conquest but as a dark, amorphous entity on which the Europeans have made little impact. The main male Ethiopian character, Johannes, spends his time not preaching a new messiah but watching over the dead.

The presence of and the contact with Italy is via the written word. Indeed it is the written word. It consists of a sheaf of letters that the narrator has received from an unnamed "Lei." Of her we know little except that she bears a certain resemblance to a minor, inevitably unnamed film actress. This extra layer of illusion makes her even more remote. She and the narrator were married a year before he was sent to Ethiopia. The longer he stays in Africa, the more that year disintegrates. Her letters lose their power: they are used as cigarette paper; they become unreadable because they have been soaked in the river. They are destroyed because they were written to a different, healthy man. In turn the narrator ceases to write back to "Lei." The written word no longer enables a character to isolate a part of her/his life, which he lives as he did in Italy. The colony has its own form of the written word, which is the death sentence an officer reads to a soldier who is about to be executed.

By contrast, the Abyssinians rely on other forms of communication. The visual and the oral are combined when the narrator draws pictures of animals and has Mariam tell him their names in her language. No European appears to speak this language, while the Italian taught to the boy Elias is full of indecent expressions. He, the prophet of Mussolini's Abyssinia, makes an effort to learn Italian so that he can become a smuggler and black-marketeer. The Abyssinians's inability to use the written word increases their respect for it: they carry around with them "documents" containing flippant or obscene messages written on them by soldiers. Johannes chooses to speak his own tongue but reveals his alienation by speaking to himself in Italian.

The question posed by the fair-headed worker and debated throughout the correspondence with "Lei" is whether it is possible for a European colonizer to write a novel about colonized Africans. The narrator expresses his doubts directly: in Africa "distances are deceptive because of the light which makes the most remote or trivial object stand out."[11] By contrast people fade into the immense African night: "His face grew smaller and soon the white spot of his clothes merged into the shadow." The narrator casts himself as reader and decides that he can read nothing in the eyes of Ethiopian women except the boredom of decadence.

Fear, guilt, unfamiliarity and sheer ignorance do not suffice to explain the problem of writing. Certainly this is no *Bildungsroman*, in which the narrator acquires wisdom and improves morally. Instead he goes downhill until he manages to escape at the end. This is another case where in our view Edward Said is asking for too much: he argues that the writer give up the ideology of imperialism and side with the indigenous movement that is combating it.[12] This could, however, lead to the boy-girl-tractor version of socialist realism or else to the 1960s cult of Third World guerrilla leaders—the various Castros, Chés and Ho-chi-Minhs.

During the Algerian War a group of French intellectuals, led by Francis Jeanson, who contributed to Sartre's *Les temps modernes,* but including a Catholic group associated with *Esprit,* offered their services to the FLN. The FLN leadership was suspicious and the French group was small and very well versed in the colonial issue. This was not an exception to the rule that even the good colonizer cannot see the colony as the indigenous population sees it because these people are mostly intellectuals from metropolitan France.

One might arrive at a preliminary conclusion: a piece of writing may well criticize the literary or political brands of language. It will also make statements about events that it perceives as unwelcome. But it will encounter greater difficulty in criticizing its culture with which its links are more organic. It takes a situation of real crisis before a language will turn against itself. Said seems to underestimate the resources of a colonial society when he implies that one can see through it easily. The invasion of Abyssinia was popular at first.

To return to *Tempo di uccidere,* the essential problem is not whether the narrator can reconstruct the colony as an Ethiopian rebel would have seen it. He cannot and, if he could, the problem of colonialism would be less intractable. It is like asking a male inter-war writer to write about women in a way that satisfies the contemporary militant feminist. What one can ask is that the male inter-war writer be aware of the alienation undergone by inter-war males and females alike.

In *Tempo di uccidere* the key question is whether Flaiano's language acts as a critique of the way language is used in the colony. Johannes, who stays in the sacked village to watch over the dead, speaks his own language in what the European thinks of as an "unpleasant, guttural" voice.[13] In his defiance of the narrator and of European methods, he prepares his own food and cures the narrator's wound with an ointment he prepares himself. Yet there is no such thing as a pure language or culture. Johannes has served in the Italian army, so he speaks Italian and receives a tiny pension from Rome.

The narrator remains at the center of a web of relationships that are structured like the author-reader dialogue. The Ethiopian courtesans read Milan fashion magazines, which is a simple sign of their alienation. The doctor reads out-of-date Italian newspapers and the narrator joins in. This marks their isolation from Italy. Then the narrator tells the doctor the story of an engineer who comes to Africa and catches leprosy. The doctor, a good if unsubtle listener-reader, grasps the oral tale's unsaid and offers the narrator a book on leprosy. The book, written by a European and hence unreliable, reinforces the narrator's fears and leads to his attempt to shoot the doctor. This reveals the danger that the reader runs, even if the doctor escapes. The little book contains an account of the isolation of a leper. It raises the narrator's fear to fresh heights.

The major is not a reader but somehow he has learned part of the tale. He is more a character in the story: the narrator had foreseen that the major would have a part to play. He is, to use Memmi's categories again, the classic "bad" colonizer "who hated this land, hated its inhabitants, hated everything."[14] The narrator robs him and tries to kill him but uncertainty persists into the last chapter. This takes the form of a review of the narrator's story conducted by a sub-lieutenant, who has until now been depicted as an enthusiastic reader.

The chapter is entitled "Punti oscuri" (Obscure Points) and the exact interpretation of the issues raised by the sub-lieutenant is less important than the discussion of them. The two are not able to arrive at complete clarity, although they do establish that the major is dead. But no one is looking for the narrator, although he is responsible for two deaths. The lack of an investigation of Mariam's death shows the injustice of imperialism: the murderer leaves the colony free.

More important is the ambiguous position of the novel, *Tempo di uccidere,* which does not succeed in telling the full story of the conquest of Abyssinia, as seen by an Italian. Near the end the Bible is introduced. Perhaps that text has more authority? But the unexplained elements in Flaiano's novel indicate the non-society in which it is set and the unsaid in its language.

Meanwhile France was producing colonial novels, one of which was written with the studied ambiguity of Henry de Montherlant. Often assumed to be a right-winger, Montherlant in fact adopted various and contradictory positions, engaged in a cult of virility, wrote books denouncing women, liked sports and was, like Pasolini, a dedicated hunter of young boys.

La rose de sable was written between 1930 and 1932 but Montherlant refrained from publishing it because he feared it would be read as an anti-colonial book. The love story sections were published in 1954 but once more Montherlant would not publish the book in its entirety during the year of Dien Bien Fu. It was finally published in 1967, some five years before Montherlant committed suicide.

The hero, Auligny, is an officer in the French army in Morocco. He seems to have the usual prejudices of his caste. He describes a group of Jewish businessmen: "they had teeth like lama which stuck out of their mouths and they shook like dogs with desire to be included in the conversation."[15] Auligny has a similar opinion of Spaniards, Maltese and all the other peoples who intruded on this French possession. For Arabs he has a special contempt and he is reluctant to believe his friend, Guiscart, who tells him that Arab servants steal no more than French. Two forces drive Auligny to criticize the role of the French army in Morocco. The first is that same aristocratic sense of how one should behave toward, for example, aged and defeated Arabs. He is displeased with his fellow officers who do not hide their distaste. He begins to question his own behavior.

The second factor is the love affair he conducts with a young Arab girl on whom he confers the name Ram. That her "real" name is something else reinforces Auligny's effort. The student of Montherlant's life is tempted to believe that Ram is a transposed boy. It matters little, however, since at their first meeting s/he makes him feel the distance that separates the indigenous population from the French army. She obeys or disobeys him without showing any feelings toward him. This sends Auligny off on a long quest in which he examines the role of the French army in Morocco and his own role in the army.

Very popular in the inter-war period were Paul Morand's short stories. They depicted an ultra-modern world of jazz, travel among the various European and non-European capitals and many different races. Morand was drawn to this modernity, but he feared it, too. Race provided an identity amid the swirling, speeding mass. Put the other way around, one cannot escape one's racial background. A black American singer, called Congo (modeled on Josephine Baker?) conquers Paris but she has to return to her home in the Deep South when her grandmother dies. The Mississippi is flooded but Congo cannot wait. She plunges in her big car and the water closes over her head. This is an eminently suitable end for a black singer, triumphant but uprooted in Paris. It will come as no surprise that Morand threw in his lot with Vichy or that de Gaulle vetoed his candidacy for the Academy. This kind of fixed identity awarded to African or Asian people is dangerous. It makes no difference whether the identity is favorable or not.[16]

The speed and confusion of cosmopolitan modernity is very different from the colony of Algeria. Here one approaches a kind of colonialism that, from the outset in the 1830 conquest, was very different and that was yet more different when the troubles peaked in the Battle of Algiers in 1957. First, Algeria was a settler colony, like Southern Rhodesia, which caused Britain such trouble. Bugeaud, whose methods were not gentle, led the French forces and brought the country under control. Algeria was not a strong state but rather an outlying province of the Ottoman Empire. Nor was it a fervent Muslim community: Islam broke through in Algeria in the 1930s as one early form of anti-French nationalism.

There are two conflicting views about Algeria's first century as a French colony. The first is that the *pieds-noirs* or European community looked upon this chunk of the Mediterranean coast as home and expected to live there forever with an Arab community whom they could dominate with help from France. The second is that, despite Bugeaud, the Arabs were never really defeated and that fighting continued after 1830: the Emir Abdelkader battled on after the Dey surrendered. In the mountains of Kabylia fighting went on for decades after 1830 (as well as in the year 2001!). After the French defeat in the war of 1870 there was a strong Arab reaction against the number of immigrants who were choosing to remain French and were settling in Algeria. In 1911 there were demonstrations in Tlemcen against the drafting of young Arabs into the army.

The Dreyfus Case had produced noisy demonstrations among the Europeans, most of whom had Spanish or Maltese blood. Anti-Semitism was a way of proclaiming they were French. Drumont, author of the dreadful *La France juive,* was elected to parliament from Algeria. So the massive celebrations for the hundredth anniversary in 1930 had undertones of conflict. Messali Hadj, the first Arab nationalist although then a communist, chose 1930 as an opportune moment to visit the USSR. The agricultural recession of the inter-war period forced small, often Arab farmers off their land, while the larger farmers hung on and bought up land cheaply. Arabs came flooding into the cities and Camus noticed the increase in his own neighborhood of Belcourt.

The decade of the 1930s had complex effects on Algeria. It strengthened the left, both the European and Moslem components. Cheik El Okbi's trial, which Camus covered as a journalist, was a way to get rid of a nationalist leader. It went wrong and El Okbi was vindicated. At the same time, the right was strong enough to defeat the left and French-Algeria would fall easily to Vichy. The reforms, such as an extended franchise, offered by the Popular Front had gone nowhere and the newspaper *Alger Républicain,* created to support the Popular Front and staffed by the underestimated Pascal Pia and the young Camus, was a beacon of honesty but lacked money. After the war it became the newspaper of the PCA, Camus had a circle of left-wing friends whom he had met at the University of Algiers or via his membership in the PCA (Parti communiste algérien). But Camus and all his friends envisaged an assimilation of the Arabs. There was to be no separate state but the Arab population of Algeria was to have the same rights as the French population of France.

This was entirely unacceptable both to the French electorate, which had no desire to share its welfare funds, and to Arab opinion, which grew more convinced that independence was the only road. In the 1930s not many Arabs had reached that level of awareness and one could make the claim that the reforms offered by the Popular Front represented the last hope of a peaceful settlement. But that seems to us an exaggeration of the Popular Front's power.

The hopes aroused by the Free French vanished when they departed in 1945 and when the "normal" administration of French civil servants and of officials elected by the *pieds-noirs* regained power. Arabs rioted across Algeria and they killed a certain number of Europeans at Sétif. The French security forces used planes to machine-gun the insurgents and killed a much larger number of them. Camus returned to Algeria for the first time in three years. In his articles on Sétif, Camus condemned the violence on both sides but ignored the discrepancy in firepower between the insurgents and the security forces. From this point on there was scant hope of a peaceful settlement. In November 1954 the Algerian War began, as General Jacques Massu had forecast.

The struggle was especially harsh and drew in many different actors. On one side was the French colonial army, humiliated by its Indochina defeat, which it blamed on French civilians and especially on the government, which became the second actor. A third actor was de Gaulle, eager to use this crisis to return to power. Next came the *pieds-noirs* determined to hold "their" Algeria. On the other side stood the FLN willing to use whatever methods were necessary to defeat the French, who were using torture. Then came the Arab population over which the other protagonists were fighting, and finally the remnants of Sartre's party, this time allied with *L'Esprit*.

Among the books, written on this war and that have in common the attempt to substitute the discourse of words for the discourse of violence, as Seamus Heaney might have put it, the best is by Mouloud Feraoun. Feraoun was a friend of Camus', a model of assimilation and a protagonist of the discourse of dialogue. Yet Feraoun sums up the psychology of colonialism: "They were good, we were bad. They were civilized and we were barbarians... we finished up by convincing them that they were sincere with us, that they were good and superior. Now they'll have to change their tune."[17] Feraoun had no love for the FLN and yet he admitted they had changed people's thinking through the use of violence—"the clandestine struggle wins people over as soon as it begins fighting the oppressor." Feraoun realized that his assimilation had been a sham and that he must look into himself for a new self. This new self will be Algerian and it was only possible because the FLN had constructed a new Algerian identity by its use of terror. Feraoun is prescient in his view of the FLN: they are brutal and any government they create is likely to be dictatorial. But he sees the value of FLN violence: "Terrorism has forced many of us to abandon our lethargy and our reluctance to think."[18] In Algiers terrorism took the form of random bombings. But the French government countered by putting Algiers under the control of General Massu and his parachute troops. The "Battle of Algiers" went on for most of 1957 and Massu won it. But on his own admission he used torture. He justifies it by citing the number of lives saved, but it was a sad blow to French culture.[19]

Feraoun was killed by right-wing Europeans. His views on terrorism are not widely shared (neither, fortunately, are Massu's) in an era that has seen violence at work in Belfast and Bosnia. Yet he faces the unpleasant fact that sometimes terrorism is the only way to counter-balance the better armed, more professionally trained forces of the colonizer.

This was the case in Algeria. In 1956 a peace-making maneuver attempted by the socialist Prime Minister, Guy Mollet, and backed by Jean-Jaques Servan-Schreiber's *L'Express*, which in turn had enlisted Camus and Mauriac as well as Jean Daniel and Alexandre Astruc, met with clear failure. It was an exemplary piece of commitment by the writers, and Camus went further: in January '56 he went to Algiers to make a speech in which he called on Arab and Frenchman to break the cycle of terrorism and repression. The whole occasion may have been manipulated by the FLN. Anyway Camus proved that committed writing could not on its own achieve a great deal. The end of commitment was foreshadowed in the same numbers of *L'Express*, which contained Alain Robbe-Grillet's book reviews. Dismissing the Sartre-Camus view of the close relationship between art and the working-class, Robbe-Grillet wrote: "There must surely be parallels between the crisis of writing and the crisis of our society but it is highly unlikely that the solutions to these two crises will be at all the same."[20]

Guy Mollet's visit to Algeria in February 1956 made Camus's seem like a summer picnic. Crowds of angry *pieds-noirs* followed him around, fearful of a socialist sell-out. They succeeded in convincing Mollet to widen the war. Next year came the Battle of Algiers and, although Massu won it, the French army could not defeat the FLN. Fears of a sell-out by Paris politicians haunted the army and the *pieds-noirs*. In 1958 Algiers threatened Paris with a coup and took over Corsica to show it meant business. De Gaulle's relationship to the coup was and remains a subject of debate, but he used Algiers' hopes and Paris's fears to bring about his own May 13, 1958, coup.

Whatever de Gaulle thought of the Algerian War when he returned to power—and mostly he was guarded in his language, throwing an occasional "I have understood you" or a "French Algeria," into his early speeches—he gradually became convinced that France could not and should not remain in Algeria. De Gaulle envisaged a quite different international role for France. A modernized army equipped with its own nuclear weapons should be ready to take its place in the East-West conflict. Slowly but inexorably de Gaulle moved toward independence. Lined up against him were his own supporters, who had brought him back to power to win the war and to keep Algeria French; the élite of the army, determined to avoid a second Dien Bien Fu; and the *pieds-noirs,* who were fighting to defend their homes. On the same side as de Gaulle, although hardly supporters of his rule, were the PCF and the growing number of French people who were sick of the war and whose sons were being drafted into the army.

In 1960 Camus died, killed in an automobile accident, leaving an aura of uncertainty over what he would have thought or done. In my opinion he would have supported the *pieds-noirs,* although by peaceful methods. Camus also left behind an unfinished novel, *Le Premier Homme,* which shows a young boy growing up in Algiers, his life linked to place with a great intensity. Such fervor may have been the result of the colonial setting. A short time after Camus's death the *pieds-noirs* rose up in the Revolt of the Barricades, which de Gaulle put down. It was followed by the Revolt of the Generals (see chapter 1). De Gaulle began the Evian talks with the FLN and the despairing forces of the far-right formed the OAS (Organisation de l'armée secrète) to assassinate him. They came close at Petit-Clamart, where they raked the presidential car with bullets. Miraculously de Gaulle was untouched.

The Evian talks went ahead. The French delegation, led by Louis Joxe, agreed to Algerian independence. De Gaulle wanted to make Franco-Algerian relations a model for ex-colonial powers. Devoid of exploitation, the goal of the oil trade was to bring about improvement of relations between First and Third Worlds as well as to furnish the new state of Algeria with the money it needed to "take off" and to provide France with a secure supply of energy. The effects of the end of colonialism were great but less positive than de Gaulle had hoped. In Algeria the FLN became an eternal party of government and of corruption. In France the war had the effect of forcing political change. De Gaulle had returned to power, the constitution was changed to introduce direct election of the president and a newish political class was created. The state became perhaps more important than ever. A million *pieds-noirs* returned to France but the high growth rate—around 5 percent to 6 percent—enabled them to find jobs. Not that they felt gratitude; forty years later people too young to remember the exodus talk about the beauty of *their* Algeria with tears in their eyes. Some but not all of them feel an intense dislike of Arabs and give their vote to Jean-Marie Le Pen.

The value of Algeria as an example of colonialism is not that it was typical but that it shows the extremes to which Europeans would go to defend their colonies. Algeria was officially an integral part of France and to many settlers it was more precious than France. Then, when Algeria became independent, the ex-settlers were aggrieved, while other segments of French society were happy to form an alliance with the authoritarian FLN. France did not, despite de Gaulle, come well out of de-colonization. In the smaller West African colonies like Senegal and Mali, France remained a dominant influence after independence, making and breaking leaders. Similarly Britain allowed Ian Smith, the leader of the white minority in Southern Rhodesia, to declare independence. Britain also helped Smith to circumvent the sanctions imposed by the international community. De-colonization, which initially seemed such a humiliation to some right-wing Europeans, did little to alter the arrogance with which Europe viewed the Third World.

French-Algeria produced a literature with themes and motifs of its own, although its language marked it as French. Lack of space compels us to consider only Camus and only some aspects of his work. Firstly, Camus thought of himself as French-Algerian, which included being French but was not limited to it. The Algerian part meant belonging to a new nation where men were tougher and more independent than the Parisians. After life on the Left Bank soured on Camus, when he lost—in French eyes—the battle of *L'Homme révolté* to Sartre, and during the years when journalists plagued him with questions on the Algerian War, Camus would have preferred to be somewhere other than Paris. He would also have liked to remain silent with that Rilkean silence that is charged with meaning.

Camus used to tell his friends in Algiers how much he would have liked to stay with them. But by now he was not only French-Algerian but a member of the French élite and a great writer. Proof came in the shape of the 1957 Nobel Prize, which was spoiled for him by the same, old questions. He was trapped by his admission that the FLN had much justice on its side. As a French writer, Camus took his place in a distinguished tradition. He had been taught in Algiers by Jean Grenier, who was published by the *NRF*, and he learned journalism from the unorthodox Pascal Pia, who later sent the manuscript of *The Stranger* to André Malraux. Camus had joined the PCA, encouraged by Jean Grenier, who did not, however join but instead had published *L'essai sur l'esprit de l'ortodoxie*. Grenier's doubts about dogmatism suited the *NRF*, which also needed Camus some years later as the representative of a new generation. Jean Paulhan, however, thought Camus's work was simplistic.

Camus seemed to, but in reality did not, omit the subject of the Arab in *The Stranger*. We have elsewhere argued that Meursault has an affinity for Arabs, which is part of his being a French-Algerian inspired with a mild dislike for metropolitan France. This affinity turns into rivalry and leads to the fight on the beach, which is set in a typically Algerian landscape.[21] Similarly the stories of *L'Exil et le royaume* depict the good colonizer, the *pied-noir* like Daru in *L'Hote*, who is drawn to Arabs and wants to live with them as equals but is forced by the colonial system into the role of disciplining Arabs.[22] Daru is a schoolteacher and on his blackboard the rivers of France are drawn. They illustrate the ideal of assimilation. But when Daru returns at the end, having sent the Arab, however reluctantly, off to prison, there is a new piece of writing on the board to mark the presence of a new, FLN-run state: "You have delivered up our brother. You will pay for it."[23] Daru feels alone in Algeria: the country he has loved has brought him a crushing disappointment. The prospect of a state where Europeans and Arabs live together has been revealed as an illusion. Although the second-person familiar form, the "tu" form, is twice used to refer to Daru, he is conspicuously excluded from the fraternal group, indicated by the "our" or "notre." *L'Exil* takes us up to the start of the Algerian War.

But the most moving of the stories is also the one most removed, superficially, from political discourse. Daru operates in a setting he cannot control but that he—and the reader—can understand. At the outset of *Le Renégat* this narrator-renegade tells us his tongue has been cut out and a second language is taking possession of him. Although he can no longer speak it, the first language was one of order, a language that had evolved out of his first set of experiences, when he was trying to become a priest and a missioner in order to obtain power. He harks back to confession, where one recounts one's sins. As a young missionary, he looks forward to doing battle with the inhabitants of Taghasa. He is not immune from the hubris that pervades our culture—"I would subjugate these savages like a powerful sun."[24] Certainly he possesses that lust for power that leads Europeans to conquer their neighbors. So what is the narrator-renegade trying to tell us?

If these people seem the antithesis of Europeans—a closed society based on religion, hierarchies and violence—we have in fact much in common with them. Camus satirizes their lust for power and for torture. The missionary gives way to them because their world is so familiar to him. By an initiation ceremony he becomes the servant of the fetiche as he has been the servant of the Christian God. This second text, far from contradicting the first, becomes a co-text. When the French army comes and he could free himself, he at once opts for the tribe, their white city and their cruelty.

This text leads by its concision to many interpretations. But, following our general theme in this chapter, *Le Renégat* is both the hell of the FLN and of the French army. Each deserves the other. It is a world of fanaticisms, devoid of measure, play or acting. The term "renegade" applies to Camus, who has left his tribe and exchanged his moral discourse for the discourse of the mother, but it refers also to the French forces and the FLN, whose use of torture has robbed them of any legitimacy. The writing in *Le Renégat* is strong and there is much play with the color white, as there was in *L'Etranger*.

There are various kinds of post-colonial writing, which we would distinguish sharply from writing by the post-independence generation of the colonized. Their work is an integral part of the new country. Their task is to act as watchdogs over the new language of politics and to inject all the freedom possible into the language of literature. They are suspicious of the new, indigenous political class. To study them it helps to know something about the traditional life of the country.

The first group is more varied and less serious, for history has left it behind. When that happens one must laugh or weep. Anthony Burgess always laughed when he was writing this kind of a book. *Time for a Tiger* is about a thoughtless Englishman, living in Conrad's territory but quite unsuited to being Conrad's character. He is more content with Burgess, who has him drink lots of the local beer, called Tiger. The colony is becoming independent, but the Englishman has made no plans: then something turns up and he wins a large sum of money in the national lottery. As far as we know he lives happily or at least carelessly in the post-independence, ex-colony that continues to produce Tiger.

Right to an Answer is about a product of colonization who turns up in England. This is obviously a variant on the Tiger-drinking kind of novel. Burgess depicts the antics of a young man who escapes from the colony and goes to university in England. He is a wonderful cook and wins over the English provinces to beef curry and chicken tika. He has, however, a desperate need for English women, which brings him to disaster. *Right to an Answer* has a serious strain: the difficulty the home country has in absorbing inhabitants of its ex-colonies.

More serious still are Graham Greene's novels that might be considered post-colonial, such as *Comedians*, *The Quiet American* or *The Hon-*

orary Consul. The last of the three has as hero a man who is half-English and half-Argentinian and who decides to live in a smallish city near the Paraguay border. Pfarr is recognizably Greenian in his outer loneliness and his rather unhappy womanizing. But he also has a vein of spirituality that leads him to throw in his lot with a group of rebels from Paraguay who half-believe in liberation theology. He is a half-critic of the Argentinian socio-political system, but he is mostly an Englishman whose solitude marks the end of an Empire (Argentina was an honorary colony) in which he did not believe.

IMMIGRANTS TELL TALES OF EMPIRE

In the 1950s and 1960s Western companies did all they could to summon labor from the ex-colonies. During the boom—which ran very roughly from 1955 to '65—London transport set up recruitment-offices in the larger Caribbean islands. British buses were to be driven and British tickets checked by people from the former colonies. Many immigrants came from the ex-colonies because they knew the language of the home country as well as some of the habits and because they had the correct documents.

This process, which one might call "bringing the Empire home," ran into difficulties when unemployment increased in the late 1960s. Enoch Powell saw the Thames full of blood, and treatment of Turks in Germany grew harsher. People began to complain that immigrants abused the welfare system because they had several wives and several children by each. Today immigrants are accused of having larger families, of letting their teenagers run drugs, of anything and everything. They continue to get unskilled jobs even if they have qualifications and to encounter great difficulty in obtaining lodgings. In Italy the term used to describe them is "extra-comunitari," which means that they come from countries outside the EU but implies general exclusion. One of them has written that their bodies are considered productive forces that have no needs.[25]

Meanwhile the immigrant community, particularly in its second generation, which is neither French nor Algerian or which is Pakistani and British, produces its own writers who live through the contradictions of their upbringing. Hanif Kureishi, author of *The Buddha of Suburbia* (1990) and the less good but more revealing *Black Album* (1995), is second generation and has a sharp eye for anomalies.

He orchestrates the second book around the clash between a Western culture, which is in steep decline, and a banal, authoritarian version of Islam. Indeed the climax of the book is what attitude this group of

Moslems should adopt toward the sentence meted out to Salman Rushdie for his *Satanic Verses*.

Shahid is a student in London whose mind has been opened by Alice Walker, Toni Morrison and Richard Wright. Far greater has been the influence of Deedee, Shahid's English teacher, who brings together the usual traits of sexual emancipation: feminism, left-wing politics, promiscuity and drugs, all of them described lavishly. This may be seen as a debased version of the Gidian theme of freedom and Riaz, the head of the orthodox Moslem band, is not altogether wrong in seeing a link between such an individualistic morality reserved for Westerners, while authoritarian rule is considered normal for the East.

The Strapper, a drug-dealer, sums it up: he and Shahid have much in common because "You a Paki, me a delinquent."[26] Yet the various attitudes adopted by Pakistanis toward Britain are at least as important as the blanket British prejudice against Moslems. Shahid opts for Deedee and a London where people dress to be looked at. Riaz writes a sheaf of poems that Shahid is supposed to type for him. Shahid makes alterations, which may be seen as a challenge to Riaz's control of the English language. In so doing Shahid opens the way to many kinds of English.

Kureishi's earlier novel, *The Buddha of Suburbia,* is a richer work. It too has as hero a young Moslem who is exploring himself and London. His Indian family is not poor and his father takes advantage of his neighbors' spiritual vacuum to introduce them to Oriental philosophy. His real talent lies, however, in his charm: "charm, rather than courtesy or honesty, or even decency, was the primal social grace."[27] His son wants to live "always this intensely: mysticism, alcohol, sexual promise, clever people and drugs."[28] The Indian community has no illusions about Britain: its decline is apparent to them.

The second generation sets out to explore. Jamila emulates Simone de Beauvoir and makes love to the hero, but she agrees to an arranged marriage rather than let her father kill himself in a hunger strike. She will not, however, allow her husband to touch her and she becomes a model of feminism. The hero, Karim, fails all his school examinations but he also succeeds in abandoning the suburbs and moving to London. Karim wants to be an actor but the only part he is offered is Mowgli from Kipling's *Jungle Book*. He has to correspond to the English view of the subcontinent—boot polish to make him look brown, nude except for a loincloth, a thicker Indian accent. This horrifies Karim, who finally accepts in return for being treated a little better than the other actors—the choice of individualism over collectivism has been made. Karim's friend Charlie becomes a nihilistic pop singer. Jamila thinks the Kipling production is neo-fascist.

Then Karim manages to get a part in a much better play where he is to imitate Jamila's chosen husband, Changez. Karim advances in London society as the kind of nice innocent boy whom Gide used to like.[29] But "English" London society is depicted as cruel and hard, while the Moslems suffer both from the prejudice against them and from the tensions imposed by their own religion. Jamila fares best: a tough, committed Indian woman, who ends up in two relationships, one lesbian, the other heterosexual. Karim learns the paradox of acting: to become someone else you have to be yourself. Changez does not even realize he is being used for Karim's role. Karim is a success and the play goes to New York. Here it is not a success but Karim returns to England and gets a part in a TV soap as a rebellious son in a Moslem family.

This is almost as much a stereotype as the Kipling role, although it will bring lots of money. The book ends when Karim takes his entire family out to dinner to celebrate his TV role. History, which has been discreet throughout the book, now makes an appearance to inform us that Thatcher is coming to power.

Kureishi does not believe, however, that the lives or the fortune of social groups are shaped by a few big historical events. Rather members of the Indian population have individual goals that fit or do not fit with the aims of the general population. These goals have less to do with raw political power—although this remains important—than with sexual and emotional success. There is a sense that the characters and their community are young and that they will change. Indeed this sense goes as far as believing that the new Pakistani and Indian contingent will make or break England (not to mention the England cricket team).

The writers of the Empire Strikes Back take as a starting point the stance of the good colonizer. But they take the next step or it is taken for them. We see the former colonial power through their eyes and their gaze is rapid, brutally honest and acquisitive. It does not question capitalism although it has ideas about redistribution. It identifies with the most modern side of the ex-colonial power: the London of Sammy and Rosie. It has no use for wars, regional loyalties or heavy industry. It expects discrimination but believes it can overcome it. It is fighting on several fronts since the fathers of this generation are men of strict, traditional morality who came to England to make money but not to change their values. These men thought the Empire would live on, the next generation knows it is dead and believes it will itself be able to build something in its place. This is the new culture of post-colonialism.

Silvia Ballestra offers a variation on this development. Instead of having a non-European as a narrator, she keeps her habitual narrator, a student of French post-modernism and reader of Jacques Derrida, but inserts an African into this most European of settings. The best example is *La fidanzata di Henrix da Piccolo* in *Gli Orsi*. (1994). At the outset an old man is trying to get down from the train while his wife hectors him. She has to step aside before he manages to descend. There is no great exaltation of freedom in the story but it is permeated by the notion that people should make their own decisions, while taking account of other people. The narrator boards the train to discover five black men sitting like kings. Ballestra now assumes that they are all together but soon four of them get off. Once again the narrator wonders if there is some hidden explanation for this but concludes she would be wrong in looking for one: she would have seen nothing unusual had the five "kings" been white. She does, however, view the whole event through *Heart of Darkness*. She is creating a text by building on and contradicting an earlier text. This does not mean the Africans are pawns in a European chess match or minor characters in a novel written by and about Europeans.

Next a gang of youngsters gets on the train and once more the issue of discipline is raised as Henrix eats his chewing-gum instead of sharing it. The African, however, sees things the other way around: he is under thirty and already has five children. His presence in the story is to present to the European on his home-ground a set of very different values: he stirs the narrator to admit there is something good about having children young. Or rather about holding different values?

One comes to the introduction of a black character into an otherwise all white setting. Alone the black is easily massacred; or else different from the whites, he may incarnate some kind of goodness. In Harold Pinter's *The Room* (see chapter 3) the entry of the black, Riley, who is blind, triggers a crisis in Rose. When he calls her Sal and asks her to go home, he takes away her present identity and plunges her into a past. The bond between them, which she will not admit, is revealed when he is killed by Rose's truck-driver companion and she goes blind in his stead. Pinter shows that the white prejudice against blacks is based on an unrecognized communion or else that the black represents some power that the white does not possess.

The late and very good French dramatist Bernard-Marie Koltès used black characters in a similar but more developed way. In *Quai-Ouest* there is a family of Latin American or rather of Quéchuan Indians struggling to survive in a Western slum. One is or in any case looks Asian—Faq. Another is black—Abad (A bad or Ahab?). He has been mistreated by his father, who took away his name. Abad does not speak, except to his brother Charles, who wants to leave the family. At the end of the play Abad kills Charles. Koltès tells us that Abad is the positive element.[30] In *Combat de nègre e de chiens* the action is set in Africa and Horn, the old

Africa hand, tells us that what he admires about Africans is that they place no value on life or death. This is surprising since the African, Alboury, has come for the corpse of another African who has been killed on the construction site. But the fascination of Africa runs through the play: Léonie, who has come to marry Horn, breaks up with him and slashes her face with the ritual cuts she has seen on Africans. Koltès denies that his play is neo-colonial but admits the French characters look different in an African context.[31]

Koltès is the model of a writer who sees that the Europeans are entering a new phase of their history. Shortage of labor, low birth rate and increasing life expectancy will outweigh illegal, leaking boats with their cargo of immigrants. The EU is attempting via its Barcelona agreement to fix its Southern borders and with the help of NATO peace-keeping forces to do the same in the East. It talks more than in the past about integrating the immigrant communities that have settled in the EU. To live with other peoples will require an effort of imagination. It will mean discarding the arrogance of colonialism that survived de-colonization. It is not enough, as Pasolini wrote, to tolerate. One must welcome people of other religions or cultures. In particular Islam.

Chapter Twelve

The Long, Unfinished March toward Women's Rights

Tahar Ben Jelloun is a Moroccan who writes in French, who has acquired a large French public and has won the Prix Goncourt. The very successful *Les yeux baissés* (Le Seuil, 1991) may be read for two reasons: as a post-independence novel about a young girl who moves between her village, situated in distant South Morocco, and France, where her father finds work; and as a novel written by a male novelist about a female growing up. Both themes are fleshed out. To consider the second here, the heroine becomes a woman in her own right, torn between France, which is associated with the school, the dictionary, electricity and freedom,[1] and her village, where silence, the invisible, water and light are the essence of life.[2] The heroine has lovers and is also able to dispense with men. Regardless of her victories and defeats this woman dominates the book, as the female characters discussed earlier cannot do. They existed in their relationship to men: Julia in the second half of *1984* who allows Winston to run their affair and to lead them to O'Brien; Estelle in *Huis clos* who cannot survive without male admiration.

Between these two very different kinds of women—or rather women characters—lies May '68 and the wave of feminism. Martin Amis has affirmed that Gloria Steinem convinced him of the justice of feminism. It would be wrong, however, to see here the beginnings of women's protest. For that we must look back to the pre-1914 years, to the period of Dreyfus when so many skirmishes were fought, which turned into the battles of the twentieth century. Here we encounter the suffragettes who dared to disturb the great events of Britain in order to draw attention to the relatively bad situation in which women lived in the center of the Empire. A militant threw herself under the king's horse at Ascot.

The women's movement already had the difficult dilemma of deciding whether it was akin to a class-based protest organization, which should seek alliances with the new working-class movements. In Germany the SPD (German Socialist Party) could boast of leaders like Clara Zetkin and Rosa Luxemburg, who became a martyr of the left when she was executed after the Spartacus Rebellion. The right to vote was a major goal of these early militants and they won it in 1919 in Germany and in 1928 in Britain. In France, despite the outstanding achievements of such women as Louise Michel, a leader of the 1870 Commune who was deported to New Caledonia and became an expert on the flora and fauna of the island, women did not get the vote until 1944, in Italy 1945. Togliatti favored votes for women although he knew they would mostly support the DC in 1948.

This brings us back to the relationship between the women's movement and radical politics. The leaders are usually on the left because they see sexual or gender oppression as linked with class-based or colonial oppression. An example would be Jamila in *The Buddha of Suburbia*. The followers, concerned with their own situation and not consistently with anyone else's, are influenced by the forces that reign in their world, in this case by the Catholic Church. If this led them to vote DC in 1948 Italy, then today they are guided, across Europe, toward the center-left parties. The gulf between leader and follower has been narrowed. But the issue of whether or not to allow men into the organization has remained.

The second phase of the women's movement took place in the aftermath of the Second World War. It has long been accepted by historians that the war had a democratizing effect: young men were drafted and lived in entirely different circumstances from pre-1939.[3] Children were evacuated out of London to the countryside and women were sent into the factories. They had little choice in the matter: the labor market needed people. But with men posted abroad, women had to take care of their own lives as they had rarely done—at least theoretically—until then.

Germany took its own fascist road, summed up in the slogan "Kinder, Kirche, Kuche." German women were to be protected from factories, males of inferior races and almost everything that existed outside of church and family. The fascist concern for the strength of the race meant that women were perceived more and more as instruments of procreation. Mussolini gave special awards to numerous families and seemed not to worry how the children would fare as they grew older. These policies became more difficult to defend as the war swung against Hitler and Mussolini, but traces of this attitude survived into the post-war and were taken up by the CDU-CSU.

Idealists who hoped that women would fare better in a united Europe were doomed to disappointment. The only woman's issue prominent in the early discussions of the EC was equal pay, supported by France, which had it anyway and wanted to raise wage-costs in other countries to its level. Social affairs lagged behind trade and growth in the EC, where the notion that high growth could solve all problems was dominant until the late 1960s.

The Women's Movement

Feminism has survived better than most other forms of protest that emerged in the aftermath of May '68. There seem to be two reasons for this. The first is that women belong to all social classes, including the highest. This means they bring culture and self-confidence to the political struggle. The second is that many things they are fighting for would indeed benefit them as a gender but would also result in a shift of power toward individual women. This fits with our interpretation of May '68.

It was no easy task to get the movement off the ground. A French feminist, a radical of the FMA (Féminin/Masculin/Avenir,) states with satisfaction that her meeting had drawn more than thirty people for the first time in the two years that have gone by since May '68.[4] The meeting was opened by Simone de Beauvoir, who had launched the women's movement with *Le Deuxième Sexe,* but who was criticized by younger women for her alleged subservience, both intellectual and personal, to Sartre.

It is surprising that de Beavoir should see her work on women as a particular example of what Sartre called inauthenticity. But then she also underestimated the hurdles she had to surmount to avoid the conventional life that her family had mapped out for her. Moreover her book encountered opposition: Camus said, for example, that she had ridiculed French males.

Now de Beauvoir gave a talk on the need for women to excel; only thus can they impress men and get the chance to be perceived as equals. Here again de Beauvoir offers her audience men as a model and work as the means to attain their goals. She does not spend time on lesser themes: women must dare to dare, such is her messsage.[5]

The impact of Simone de Beauvoir was great. Clearly she had been forgiven in return for lecturing on the obstacles women encounter rather than on their weaknesses. The debates about whether feminism is part of the class struggle and whether men can be allowed to attend meetings ended with victories for the hardliners. The question of men is all the harder because many women the 1960s and 1970s entered feminist groups via the New Left, where they were very disappointed with the sexism of their male comrades. Even Régis Debray talked about peasant women cooking for the guerrillas in the mountains.

Meanwhile the struggle of women in the workplace continued. The obstacles they faced included the generally higher unemployment rate of the post-'73 economy, the avoidance of equality by downscaling jobs women often held (this demanded the re-writing of job descriptions, which provided well-paid work for mostly male consultants) and the reluctance of husbands to help out at home, which increased the double-burden on women. In turn this led women to accept part-time or temporary jobs, which offered less chance of promotion and fewer welfare benefits. Finally there were significant areas of industry—the technical sphere—that were considered unsuitable for women. The private sector was less welcoming—or more unwelcoming—than the public sector, which had repercussions on women's attitudes and their voting habits.

The theme that could unite most women was control over their bodies. There was a popular saying that no Third World country was as colonized as a woman's body. De-colonization meant contraception, divorce and abortion and more recently fertility treatment. Hitherto control had been exercised by the state or the church. This was a case where the historical difference between Catholic and Protestant made itself felt. Protestant countries adapted more easily. Ireland, that bastion of Catholicism, managed to pass a divorce law but abortion is still a forbidden topic. Italy's special role as housing the headquarters of the Catholic Church made these issues particularly difficult.

France had a divorce law that had been passed in the early years of the Third Republic, while an abortion law was passed under President Giscard d'Estaing. In Italy a divorce law was passed in 1970 and then the bid to repeal it came in 1974. At the time it seemed to many like a right-left struggle. The DC secretary, Amintore Fanfani, hoped to use the repeal to re-launch his flagging party. Enrico Berlinguer feared that the repeal campaign would provide a platform for anti-communism and for the old 1948 accusations that communists devour babies and break up the family.

To the surprise of DC and PCI alike, the "no repeal" position was backed by 59 percent to 41 percent. But this was not a vote for the PCI or even for the left. Pasolini was right to see it as a vote for modernity, against ideologies of all kinds and in favor of the individual and, in Pasolini's eyes, of hedonistic consumerism. It was a complex matter because Berlinguer had modernized the PCI and part of its increased vote came from the contrast between its honesty and efficiency and DC corruption. But the size of the victory in the referendum showed that different forces were at work.

Other pieces of legislation like the May '75 law on family rights put an end to the father's automatic right to be head of the family and to the wife's duty to take her husband's last name.[6] On May 22, 1978, the PCI-backed Andreotti government passed a law allowing abortion. This encountered less opposition than was feared and the new pope's attempt to reverse it by referendum was heavily defeated in 1981.

John Paul II did not give up the struggle (he rarely does) and not only does the Church teach that abortion is a grave sin but it never misses a chance to say so. Catholic politicians are warned that they must oppose abortion; compromising or accepting majority opinion constitutes a sin. Similarly the Church has, in recent years, fought hard against third-party donors and in favor of awarding fertility treatment to established couples only. The Church argues that it is defending not merely the family but the foundation of society itself, whereas its opponents will create a fatherless, motherless non-society.[7]

The battle of ideas goes much further and much deeper. Whereas Anglo-Saxon women fight hardest to obtain equality, Italians and French seek to assert difference. The world is shaped to suit men: the values of ambition, self-assertion and gaining power are male. It is not in the interest of women—or humankind—to create equality or emancipation, defined as right of entry into the male world as it is now constituted. Rather women must fight for space in which to exercise nurturing, caring and tenderness. Clearly the notion of difference is a more radical goal to set oneself. It leaves less space for men and more conflict with them. The female child requires a period of isolation from men if she is to develop a womaness that they cannot know.[8] Then young women need to discover "sexed" thought. Philosophy seems to get rid of the specific and to neutralize the world. But man remains and the philosophical universe falls into place around him. Therefore women must assert themselves as a gender and develop their own way of thinking. In so doing they will destroy the spurious universality of what is in fact a male-dominated universe. The values of courage and endurance will be revealed as male values and women will develop different values.[9]

In particular difference requires a different mother-daughter relationship. It is firstly a closer relationship (a theme that has, in the author's opinion, gained acceptance by many males). Secondly Freud's view, popularized as female envy for the penis, which drives girls toward their fathers and into conflict with their mothers, must give way to the primacy of a harmonious relationship with the mother. This will require a re-organization of the family to rid it of male domination. The barrier to the close mother-daughter bond is the daughter's disappointment with the mother's lack of authority and submission to the father. It is not envy of the father in himself. On this point the women's movement takes issue with Freud.

One drawback of this otherwise sensible body of thought is the risk of taking not just power but responsibility from the father. In Italy matriarchy abounds, even if it varies from region to region. The privileged relationship was, historically, between the mother and the eldest male child(ren). In this sphere the mother's role should be cut back. Juggling these different spheres is no easy matter, especially since the family has been forced by high unemployment to allow all children to remain at home longer.

Politically—here we are talking of an ideal politics; politics, as it really is, will be discussed in the next section—has its starting point in the "relationship of entrustment" among women. Trust is rarer among women, so the women's bookshop in Milan maintains because there is a dearth of women's institutions, whereas men have clubs, sports teams and the like.[10] A comparative study would surely rank Italy lower in male groups and clubs than Britain. The same is true of trust: there is a Machiavellianism in everyday life in Italy that works against trust. Gender-based studies should always be checked against national—and class-based studies. Support for the women's bookshop's views comes from an unlikely source. Their argument on trust and the lack thereof is offered by Margaret Thatcher, who notes that opposition to her being awarded a winnable seat in parliament came not from the men in the local conservative parties but from the women.[11]

The "relationship of entrustment" is a lived, personal bond between women, often between an older successful woman and another who is less experienced. It is quite a different bond from representation, which hides the gender struggle behind a false universality. Nor is entrustment to be attained by reformist, quantitative methods such as increasing the number of women in parliament or in other institutions. Such pseudo-solutions ignore existing and everyday male oppression, thus they further them and become instruments of them. Delegation and mediation are also instruments of repression.

Naturally women's organizations should not be monolithic, but the ideal that emerged from the lively if obscure women's debate on whether the PCI should be dissolved or not (1989–1991), was of a party of men and women united to combat the present economic order, while, simultaneously, the women united against the men to fight sexism. Carrying on these two battles at the same time would be a difficult operation. But then there is a pessimistic strain in female (or is it Italian?) activists, summed up in a reflection on silence: women are stalked by silence; they try to combat it by re-discovering neglected women painters or writers, but this absence of language is a deprivation, "a profound and secret sign of our wretched state."[12] If one wished to be optimistic one could argue that the bonds that exist among women, because they combine feelings—liking and affection running all the way to lesbianism—with political alliance, are stronger than among men.

The Political Language of Women

There are far more women—so it seems—in public life than ever before. A woman has been not just prime minister of Britain, but the most formidable P.M. of the post-war years. Martine Aubry is number 2 in the French Socialists and a good bet to become the first woman president of France. In Germany Angela Merkel won the race to succeed Helmut Kohl as opposition leader but was easily defeated by the Bavarian Prime Minister, Edmund Stoibe, in the struggle to become "Kanzlerkandidat." Ireland has just had a competent president in Mary Robinson. Italy lags behind: the colorful Emma Bonino was thrown out of the European Commission to make room for Romano Prodi. She had run for president of Italy but stood no chance against Carlo Azeglio Ciampi. Italy's president is chosen by an electoral college and when Bonino ran for the European parliament, she fared rather better. Once more Italy was in advance of its political class. Bonino was identified with Marco Pannella, with the Partito Radicale and with dangerous issues like divorce and abortion. This immediately cut her off from the Catholic vote. Berlusconi has no powerful women in his new government and his level of sophistication in dealing with women's issues is roughly equal to his sophistication in discussing non-Western cultures.

There is nothing inevitable about women's advancement: during Tony Blair's first term there were 118 women in parliament; in his second term there are 101. Blair did make his secretary a peer and sent her off to the Lords to answer unpleasant questions about why there were fewer women.

Just as male politicians use their gender to convey strength or moral rectitude, so women must use theirs. JFK was handsome and virile, while Mitterrand, in his 1988 version but not in his '74 or '81 campaigns, was Tonton François, the elderly, reassuring relative who would keep the hotheaded Chirac under control. As already noted, Thatcher was a mother to the young soldiers who were fighting in the Falklands. Elsewhere she adopted the discourse of the housewife in order to appear ordinary. She talked frequently about boiling eggs and peeling potatoes (chapter 8). Handsome women do not seem able to profit from their appearance as much as their male counterparts: Giovanna Melandri may be the rare exception.

We have affirmed (chapter 5) that women are given either posts linked with the traditional role of women or else difficult posts, where they are unlikely to be successful. In the latter post they need to find a language as quickly as possible. Edith Cresson is the best example of a woman politician in search of a language. She was appointed prime minister by Mitterrand in 1991. She replaced Michel Rocard, who had been popular and was widely considered competent. Moreover the historical moment was difficult. In the first years of German Reunification other EC-EU countries found that German demand was high, so their exports went up. Then Kohl's decision to finance the turn-around of the former DDR by borrowing rather than by increasing taxes raised interest rates across Europe and had a strong, deflationary effect. French unemployment was stubbornly high and growth was lower than it might have been.

Cresson had no power over these two ills and she tried to divert attention from them by colorful and populist language. Since the Socialist élite had been to the *grandes écoles* and mostly used a technocratic language (while denying that they were technocrats), this was a grave mistake. In a short time Cresson had alienated Britain by declaring that most British males were homosexuals who never looked at her on the street. She followed up with an attack on the Japanese, who were like "ants." She went on to declare that "Japan is an adversary who does not respect the rules and whose overwhelming desire is to conquer the world."[13]

There can be little doubt that Cresson, who was middle-class and to whom such populism did not come naturally, had made a bad choice of language. But the British forgot that they were famous for their calm humor and they were very rude in reply. Moreover rumors swept Paris that Cresson owed her exalted position to the intimate relationship she had had with Mitterrand. Here we see the difficulties women face. Would anyone bother to gossip about the past love affairs of a man?

Cresson remained in power for one year. She could make no impact on unemployment and neither could her successor, Pierre Bérégovoy. He lost the '93 elections badly and committed suicide. Cresson was a forerunner in the Parti socialiste: after her came Martine Aubry, who is Jacques Delors' daughter, although to see her as that and no more is to overestimate the role of a father and underestimate the capacity of a daughter; and Elisabeth Guigou, who became Jospin's Minister of Justice, a post not usually given to women and not impossible; and others.

Meanwhile in Britain Tony Blair gave an impossible post to Mo Mowlam: she became secretary of state for Northern Ireland. Someone must surely have reminded her of the old saying that Ireland was a graveyard for English politicians. In fact Mowlam was directly responsible for the signing of the Good Friday Agreement and her language was a key factor.

She made no pretence of knowing any Irish history or, if she did know any, she did not talk about it. So she was not weighed down under the Battle of the Boyne, the Wolf Tone rebellion, the death of Michael Collins or even the Easter Rebellion. Mowlam went as far as claiming that the Good Friday Agreement was not supposed to be an answer to the Easter rebellion, but one has doubts about this. In general, however, Mowlam substituted for the sacred "stolentelling" of Catholics and Protestants alike a worldview based on the values of women. In the Maze prison she talked about early releases, kids hooked on hard drugs and in need of guidance and how to go about getting a job.

Mowlam's subsequent misfortunes are described in chapter 5, but on taking leave of her we would like to reiterate that she—perhaps more than anyone—has shown what women can achieve in politics. The Labour Party has the dubious distinction of having in its ranks a woman who is especially badly treated by men. Claire Short does not suffer in silence and she often goes on the attack. But she has been subject to insults and gibes of a kind rarely heard in the "Mother of Parliaments."

Women are not a monolithic bloc; they vote for various parties. They tend to vote less for parties of the far-left and the far-right: in France this means the PCF and the FN (Front National). The reasons lie in their distrust of extremism, which might threaten the stable social structures that children and families need. The tendency to vote center-left stems from a desire to protect public intervention in its social forms of maternity and paternity leave, day care centers and the like. This center-left vote has replaced the center-right voting of the 1950s, which has declined along with churchgoing.

Women have learned from their experience: in '68 about one third of Italian university students were women and many of them were active in the New Left. But few reached positions of importance and many discovered that men who were left-wing on most issues were no less sexist than right-wingers. Régis Debray was far from untypical. The PCI was slow to understand feminism, although once he grasped its importance Enrico Berlinguer was energetic in supporting it. But for a long time the PCI viewed feminism as an American import that appealed to women who did not work.[14]

Women Who Write

There have always been women writers, even if there have been far more men and if the women have not been feminists. The Bronte sisters did more to encourage female writers than anyone else could have done.

Cathy's "Oh but I am Heathcliff" speech is a cry of passion outside of or rather beyond any political motif.[15] Still the last thirty years of this century have seen a more committed literature that debates the male-female dialogue and conflict. The word "commitment" conveys the belief in a literature that can help young women who are making a start in society. But since there are no more party secretaries like Togliatti to establish an orthodoxy of organic intellectuals, or hatchetmen, like Alicata, to enforce the secretaries' decisions there are more debates and fewer certainties inside the women's movement. We may use the term "commitment" as long as we remember this is a milder, more flexible brand than the commitment discussed in chapter two.

An example of a woman writing specifically about women is Pat Barker's *Union Street*.[16] Barker poses the problem of women working in a small, cake-making factory. They are clearly working-class, some of them sub-proletarian, but while Barker stresses their poverty, she does not dwell much on the notion of class. It is replaced by the notion of gender: the manager is male and there are sundry husbands and fathers who lay claim to authority at home. It is because they are women that these workers are exposed to exploitation. A verbal sign is the way that, in a variant on the theme of names, the manager refers to them all as girls, regardless of their age. Then, as well as their exploitation at work, they must face the full range of sexual problems: unwanted pregnancies, husbands who disregard contraception, brutality and so on. When one adds the hardships of old age and the extra difficulties it brings to the poor and to women, this is a bleak life. Yet a certain solidarity is present alongside frequent quarrels: "violence between women was unthinkable," writes Barker,[17] and this is no small achievement.

To take this problem further we have chosen to look at Crista Wolf and in particular at her novel *Kassandra*.[18] Crista Wolf was born in the Oder-Neisse provinces, which are the part of Germany that lies to the East and that were ceded to Poland at the end of the Second World War. This was the first uprooting for Wolf; the second would come in 1989 with Reunification. Growing up under the Nazis left its mark on Wolf, who describes it in *Kindheitsmuster* (1976). She was struck by the ordinariness in which Nazism was cloaked: a relative bought a shop from a Jew who had to sell and hence set a price lower than he would otherwise have done. The relative was pleased by his bargain and did not inquire into the reasons for it. Wolf's father had been at Verdun and deeply disliked all wars. This made the family generically anti-Nazi, but they did not ask questions. Wolf has an odd "Angsttraum": a Jewish boy is being beaten up but she does not join in and hit him, which awakens guilt in her.

On this trip to the "lost provinces," the narrator is accompanied by her daughter and her brother. One of her goals is to teach Lenka, who has never heard of Eichmann, something about the German past. But Lenka, who has grown up in the comfortable DDR, cannot really understand what her mother is saying. When they made the choice between East and West Germany, it was those members of Wolf's family most aware of the Nazi past who chose the DDR (Deutsche Demokratische Republik), but ideologies have changed and withered. The narrator's brother represents the scientific worldview that has become dominant in Europe. When asked what he believes he replies that "it is possible to construct a machine that has a predictable efficiency."[19] As for the narrator she believes "in the importance of communicating what one thinks is truth."[20]

As often with Crista Wolf, one has the impression of hearing a voice out of the German past. The narrator's thought has been molded by an idealism that does not seek contact with science, which it considers inferior. Instead it holds that moral values suffice unto themselves. This is old-fashioned in its view of language because it ignores both deconstructionism and the various brands of newspeak.

A Woman and a Prophet

Wolf's situation when this book was published was solid (in so far as anything was ever solid in the Communist bloc). She had been successful with her first novel *Der geteilte Himmel* (1963), which is a fairly simple work about young love caught between East and West. From then on her books were acclaimed. She enjoyed the privileges of the literary establishment, travel and country houses. Not the least of these privileges was the belief that one was leading an opposition to the DDR's ruling Communist Party. This opposition was based on moral values; it was anti-capitalist and it had far less popular support than it believed or professed to believe.

Feminism swept over Wolf and it is the dominating force in *Kassandra* and in her latest work, *Medea*. From where did it come? It might be part of the growing Western presence in the DDR: an unintended byproduct of Brandt's "Ostpolitik." Certainly it fits with the anti-war stance that DDR intellectuals adopted when Brezhnev invaded Afghanistan and threatened Europe with the SS20s. We could also turn the question around and ask what was the effect of feminism: it gave new life and energy to Wolf's writing. What the discovery of Marx had been to her in the 1950s, feminism was now. One might broaden the argument and claim that it was the last upsurge of a dying system that had few ideas and still fewer emotions.

Wolf takes an empowering myth and stands it on its head. The myth is none other than the *Iliad*, which has offered models of bravery, beauty and occasional compassion to many societies. The hero is Achilles, who is a model of male virtues, although in the Greek version he is dressed as a woman at the outset because his mother does not want him to go to Troy. Wolf's aim is to present Achilles as the model male but to emphasize his cruelty and his love of shedding blood. There is a gruesome account of how he strangles Kassandra's younger brother, Troilus.

The new version of the myth is accompanied by a modern segment, which recounts Wolf's plane journey to Greece and some of her experiences there. The theme of women is introduced in a minor key when Wolf notes there are two stewards and two stewardesses "who carry out the instructions of their male colleagues" and a group of Syrians where the women "obey unconditionally the signals from their men folk."[21] The cultural pessimism, which is inherited from the German past, makes itself felt when Wolf comments on the availability of bottled water: "the eternal, wearisome gurgling of our civilization, leading nowhere."[22] There is a similar note in her criticism of Greece, which is trying to modernize too quickly.

But Wolf reiterates her belief in "the Logos, the word as fetish—perhaps the deepest superstition in the West."[23] Clearly she sees herself as an "écrivain" and politics will have to take account of the supreme value of language. Yet Wolf also believes literature understands the cruelty of Western culture and so helps to structure the double code, killing and thou shalt not kill. Gide used to call the first "la part du diable" and it makes of the writer a necessary bringer of scandal and of her/his work an act of destruction.

Here again Wolf situates herself within this Western tradition and not as the bearer of some new brand of Marxism or of capitalism. Her worldview looks back to Kant and Schiller and forward to the stand she will take in 1989.

Most relevant to the tale of Kassandra is the shift in ancient Greece from rule by women to rule by men. Women's achievements were greatest in Crete, which is sacred territory to modern feminists, although a dispute rages about whether this was a slave-based economy. But by Homer's age men had won out so Kassandra interests Wolf as an illustration of the fate women would undergo for the next 3,000 years: to be turned into objects.

Running through the meditation on Greece is the contemporary theme of war where Wolf professes to believe in unilateral disarmament. More interesting is her admission of the impact the Kassandra motif makes on her, an experience comparable to the discovery of Marx or to Goethe's discovery of "Die Mutter" in *Faust II*, but the last word is Kassandra's. She affirms that the whites are coming, that they will always come and that they will be re-born brown or black but still be white. It is not stated here but the whites are all male and the spells of women are useless against them.

Kassandra the Prophet

The Kassandra we meet in the opening pages has suffered, has lived through the Trojan defeat and her prophecies have encountered disbelief spiced with hostility. She has evolved, having passed through two different phases. She is still uncertain, especially about the transmission of her truth to future generations, but her understanding of herself and others is much greater than it was.

Kassandra's first phase is marked by ambition and success at the price of prophesying banal orthodoxy. As a child she was close to her father Priam who was a kindly monarch but lacked any sense of statecraft. Her mother, Hecuba, felt that Kassandra did not need her. (So much for the harmonious mother-daughter relationship!) Her early experiences with men brought a strong negative reaction: she could not stand Apollo, whose priestess she was and who imposed disbelief as a punishment for her rejection of him. She tolerated the chief priest Panthous and she liked/loved Aeneas because he made no demands on her. Kassandra is driven by ambition: she ousts her sister from the race for priestess. With hindsight she recognizes that "my privileges intruded between me and the most necessary insights."[24]

Kassandra noticed, however, the inevitable drift toward war. Firstly the increasing power of Eumelos, the bureaucrat, who intervenes in language to create a newspeak, in which a "war" becomes a "sudden attack." Eumelos is a modern figure, the forerunner of Albrecht Speer or Robert McNamara. The chief priest Panthous, who is Greek, is followed and harassed. Paris boasts of his conquest, although Helen is seen by no one, which is another proof that her beauty was invented by males.

Achilles' laughter at Troilus has homosexual overtones and is designed to reveal the truth about male heroism. It brings about the great change in Kassandra, who turns against the war and who in the ruling council calls for a serious negotiation with the Greeks. The logic of war works, however, in the opposite direction: Troilus must be avenged. The city of Troy changes in war: it does not become more democratic; rather it becomes more police-ridden, like the England that Orwell had foreseen at war with Germany. Kassandra has periods of silence because she has learned that group silence is the start of protest.

All the violence of the war has its origins in gender clashes. Kassandra's sister, Polyxena, dreams that her father is violating her. The effect of the war on Kassandra is to destroy her belief in the gods. The women have learned to fear not the Greeks but "the men on both sides who seemed to have joined forces against our women."[25] Penthesilea, the Amazon queen, offers one solution, but it would destroy the "difference" between the genders. Penthesilea aims at equal treatment and gets it: she is killed by Achilles.

At her funeral her followers lose their reason and dance wildly: "Let the wilderness engulf us again. Let the undivided, the unmanifested, the primal cause, devour us. Dance Kassandra."[26] The women kill the Greek priest and carry Kassandra off to their caves. But she will not give way to the irrational nor will she acquiesce in the plan, drawn up by the Council to kill Achilles by using Polyxema as a decoy. She is now finding her own path.

That path leads, however, to imprisonment. She fights deprivation, the other prisoners and she weakens the prison walls. The plot to kill Achilles has worked but she continues to say no. Anchises, Aeneas's father, sends her one of his sculptures of animals, which are tokens of solidarity and of living close to nature. Kassandra lives in the women's caves, outside of the war. She is dragged back when her father sells her in marriage to a king who brings soldiers. From the viewpoint of Kassandra and Wolf, he is the ideal husband. In one night he impregnates her and the next day he is killed in battle. The reader might think he is rather the model of the irresponsible father. Kassandra warns against bringing the horse into Troy and encounters her usual disbelief.

For a while she had been part of a community of women, enjoying the "stolentelling" in the evenings and the absence of power struggles. (In this context stolentelling is seizing men's stories and telling different versions of them.) Now Agamemnon's captive, she is alone again. She refuses to accompany Aeneas, knowing that his destiny is to found Rome and become a hero. She despises Agamemnon and she foresees and welcomes his death. He is murdered by his wife, Klytemnestra, who takes her revenge for Agamemnon's sacrifice of their daughter, Iphigenia. (In Goethe's version of this myth Iphigenia incarnates moral goodness. His play could be read as a co-text to Wolf's.) Alone, Kassandra's words are "uncolored by hope or dread:"[27] they do not console but they do bring knowledge. She has always appreciated images more than words, she says in a comment that surprises us. But she means that images, like Anchises's wooden animals, bring people together in peace whereas her language is caught up with war and death. Words die before images but are truer.

The Kassandra who is waiting to be killed by Klytemnestra is aware of the price she has to pay to be a writer. She thinks conflicts and persecution are an integral part of her vocation as a stolenteller. And who is to be her reader? She calls for a slave-girl with a good memory: her aim is to gain women-readers and to de-legitimize the *Iliad*. Her book has no single ending and it defies simple interpretation. Kassandra is an enigmatic figure and her fate as a writer is undecided.

The same is true of her creator. In 1990 Wolf published *Reden im Herbst* in which she opposes immediate reunification as a sell-out to powerful West German interest groups. She "doubts whether in the long run the capitalist system will be able to solve the problems that are facing all humanity."[28] She appeals to people not to leave the DDR but rather to seek out what was distinctive and worth preserving about the regime. But the vast majority of East Germans saw nothing worth preserving in the DDR and supported Helmut Kohl's policy of immediate reunification. West German critics were sarcastic about literature-as-opposition in the DDR. Wolf, they declared, was not ready for freedom; she knew only the show of opposition, which in fact strengthened the Communist regime by making it seem tolerant.

Wolf made her own case worse by publishing *Was bleibt* (1990). It describes how she was kept under government surveillance. The moment was ill chosen: Wolf had clearly not suffered much and other people had suffered much more. Moreover Wolf's name turned up on the Stasi's list of informers. This was a fairly trivial matter: Wolf had informed for the Secret Police from 1959 until 1962 and there is no evidence that people had suffered greatly as a result of the reports she had sent in. This was also the period when Wolf's belief in the regime was at its peak.

Every time a West German critic savaged Crista Wolf, a French or Italian critic came forward to defend her (and attack the German). In our context her adherence to feminism may be seen as a form of commitment that is all the more intense because the official worldview of the DDR was growing weaker. This gives to certain passages of *Kassandra* a force that is rare in Western or Eastern European writing. It remains paradoxical that the women's movement should be revitalized by a dying communism.

But then the women's movement has survived and is flourishing because of its ability to take different forms, many of them compatible with modern capitalism. To observers like Foucault and Lyotard, the risk was that women's movement would lose the radical traits that enabled it to reach out to other groups like gays. It would defend female sexuality as equal to male but it would no longer defend the various "banned" forms of sexuality. This may be correct, but surely the essential trait of the women's movement is that decisions about women are made by women. The role of men is to respect them.

> PMC. Throughout this chapter I have argued in favor not of one brand of feminism rather than another but of having women make their own decisions. It is appropriate to end the chapter with the words of a woman, who has much experience and knowledge of the women's movement.
> Q PMC: What are the major problems that women face today?
> A FM: The Italian movement has to rethink its view of representation. By attaching so little importance to having women in parliament, by rejecting quotas, it has helped to make women invisible.
> PMC: Instead of?
> FM: Woman as citizen. We must avoid the situation where women's rights are treated as one isolated sector of politics. Women are half of the human race and any major—or even minor—decision affects them. When a local authority decides to give its entire budget for sport to encouraging soccer; that affects women negatively because only boys play soccer. There is much more to equality than equal pay.
> PMC: What are the achievements of the women's movement in the 1970s and what were its mistakes?
> FM: The mistakes are what I have just been talking about. The achievements are the Divorce Law and all the accompanying legislation. The restrictions on women's freedom—the husband was automatically the head of the family—were scrapped.
> PMC: Is peace still a major women's cause?
> FM: Yes, "the women in black" are influential. There is a group of Israeli and Palestinian women who meet . . .
> PMC: I had no idea . . .
> FM: No, no one pays attention to action by women. There is another group in the ex-Yugoslavia. The women in black appeal to young women and they are important for us because they're coming back to feminism.
> PMC: Are the young in favor of a return to politics?
> FM: Yes, although the general feeling among women is so negative. Did you know what the abstention rate was among women in the last general election? Around 40 percent.
> PMC: That's amazingly high for Italy. Let me ask you a couple of different questions to finish. Are there men in the various women's movements?
> FM: Not in Italy. In other countries there are and there are also male groups that meet to discuss masculinity in the light of feminist theory
> PMC: Who are the cultural figures you admire?
> FM: Well I like Crista Wolf too, especially *Kassandra*. Then there was Simone de Beauvoir. I'd like just to mention someone very different—bell hooks. She is a black American feminist who poses the problem of being black and being a woman.
> PMC: Thank you very much.

Our role as students of politics and literature is to note the success of the women's movement in an otherwise dull period. We should then move on to a host of new problems, to post-modernism, the excluded, the language of contemporary politics *et à bien d'autres encore.*

Conclusion

In the approximately four months this manuscript or would-be book has spent lying on the tables of friends, being re-worked by me and re-read by my patient, tolerant publisher, Amanda Johnson, much has happened to the characters and themes in my piece of stolentelling. Politically, the Provisional IRA has agreed to set dates for giving up its weapons. At least one of Sinn Féin's ministers, Martin McGuiness, is considered by his civil servants to be doing an excellent job. The "Irish Question" is still with us but relations between Catholics and Protestants are at the very least better than they were in 1998 when the Good Friday Agreement was signed. One should not expect too much. A reluctant acceptance that they must live together has replaced or disguised the outright hatred between the two tribes. The case of the Catholic children, subjected to abuse as they make their way to school through a Protestant area of Belfast, shows how reluctant that acceptance is.

The political and economic situation in Western Europe gives one scant reason to reverse the pessimistic judgments of the last three chapters. The euro is widely used but it remains weak against the dollar. The mighty German economy is like an old, weary locomotive that is barely strong enough to pull behind it its four million unemployed. The French presidential elections are not likely to remove the unsaids of France's European policy. The price the Europeans have paid for monetary union is high.

European-U.S. relations are going through a troubled phase and Joschka Fischer feels the need to inform the world that the Western Europeans are not "satellites."[1] But unless the Europeans are willing to spend more money on their own defense, the United States will continue to dominate. In Afghanistan Bush demonstrated that he did not need the Europeans militarily. The EU is finding the work of a regional power difficult enough—the problems of ex-Yugoslavia are far from resolved—it has neither the energy nor the imagination to play the difficult role of a superpower. A strong America, we have suggested, makes for a healthier Europe; an overwhelming military power makes for a weak, dependent Europe.

Politics is still preoccupied with September 11 and the fear of terrorism is running high. In turn that gives fresh meaning to Edward Said's view of the way the West behaves toward the East: the dumping of the Al Qaeda prisoners in Cuba, the treatment meted out to the Taliban who remained in Afghanistan and the comments of Donald Rumsfeld provide ample evidence that Said is right. The destruction of the World Trade Center towers and the deaths of nearly 3,000 people (at Omagh, Northern Ireland, 29 people died) left President Bush little room for maneuver. And yet, after his Afghan triumph, he has more freedom. Talk of the "axis of evil" or of invading Iraq is unnecessary. A privileged observer in my comfortable university, I should brood on my chapter 11 and remember that de-colonization did not put an end to Western European arrogance or to the problems faced by developing nations. Our goal is to talk not about but to Islam.

The example of what not to say was set by Silvio Berlusconi. Speaking in Berlin, a sacred city to Westerners because of the airlift, he asserted calmly that the West should approach Bin Laden "with an awareness of its superior culture, for the two cultures cannot be put on the same plane." Expanding on his theme Berlusconi explained that Western culture "guarantees a respect for human rights, political and religious, which certainly does not exist in Moslem countries."[2] Having resolved that problem, Berlusconi left himself free to ignore the issue of conflict of interest. The internet is advancing more slowly than we imagined two years ago. Nor has it brought the liberty some hoped for. Whereas the internet used to be regarded as "an exciting new frontier where a lawless freedom prevails," it turns out that governments in China, Singapore and South Korea engage in heavy censorship, and that the Europeans have been quieter and more subtle but almost as intrusive.[3]

Television remains the most important mass medium and it offers "entertainment," which means shorter or more aimless political discussions, so-called talk shows dominated by the professional TV presenter, more frequent zapping by the younger watchers, an absence of history and an abundance of packaging to turn every and any subject into a variety show. Even wars and massacres can make thrilling programs; in the case of Bosnia guilt for the EU's tardiness in taking action added spice to the tale. Silence as harbinger of real discourse is not practiced on TV. An occasional advertisement juxtaposing real and virtual reality is the best thing to be seen. Unsurprisingly, the advertisements are often better than the programs among which *Quelli che . . . Il calcio,* a bland mixture of pornography and soccer-chatter, devoid of sex and soccer, is surely the worst.

Meanwhile the e-weapons keep up their guerrilla war against the autonomy of our thought. They marshal other people's words and anonymous words to persuade us to forget our own words or simply to spend time and money on the internet. This will go on, albeit more slowly than we thought two years ago.

So what of social and cultural developments? The current of May '68, while it never posed much of a challenge to capitalism, became a spur to social change (chapter 10). It also gave voice to segments of the population, especially to the young, who had hitherto been silent. But the process that began in '68 has now run its course. One would like to believe that politics will find a new language to fit some of the new actors and issues but we found scant trace of it.

Intellectuals no longer commit themselves or enter politics directly and full-time but they are often willing and eager to allow their research to be used. They do not imagine that they can have a privileged relationship with the now shrunken working-class: there is no contemporary equivalent of Il-ne-faut-pas-désespérer-Billancourt (chapter 3). Identity, the sense of belonging to a country or a Europe that has its own values that one shares, is, in my opinion, going through a difficult period. Europe is remote and bureaucratic; the bargaining state is perceived as too weak.

Meanwhile Ken Loach has made another splendid film, *The Navigators*, about a team of workers whose job is to keep the railway line in good condition. Here again Loach's actors convey the techniques, the fatigue and the male bonding of heavy manual labor. Here again women are, so we think, confined in roles of looking after small children and refusing or offering sex. The film is set in the period just after the privatization of the British railways and it depicts the clash between the two different ways of running them.

There is no need, then, to worry about culture with a small "c." One might give an example of a thinker who has tried to deal with contemporary issues. Pierre Bourdieu, who died during these four months, set out his view of language in 1982. *Ce que parler veut dire* rejects the structuralist tenet that language can be examined from within. Terms like "sign," "signifier" and "signified" have no meaning unless they are placed in their social context. Structuralism flourished when commitment began to fade. The model was no longer the communist militant but rather the semiologist-anthropologist who would use the instruments given to him by Ferdinand de Saussure and Claude Lévi-Strauss, first to break down the object and then to offer a rational purified version of it. The outside world is not so much ignored as assumed to be fairly stable.

Bourdieu disagrees with this, arguing that our age has produced global clashes than run through our national societies. In 1995 he joined in a protest against Prime Minister Alain Juppé, who deflated the economy so that France could enter the European monetary union. Bourdieu had a range of targets that included one of particular interest—the fatalism of neo-liberalism. He conducted this polemic in a series of short, fairly cheap books, entitled "Raisons d'Agir" and designed for a wider public.

He produced long, massive volumes for an academic public, from *Les Héritiers* (1964, with Jean-Claude Passeron) onward. His vision of society is class-based, but not guided solely by the economic infrastructure. Instead the various social groups fight over symbolic power. "Symbolic" is a term that Bourdieu uses to define political and cultural struggles that result in a victory for one social group that acquires a form of capital that is recognized by the losers. It enables the class that possesses it to dominate, while the defeated class is dominated.

Bourdieu has been attacked for his view of domination. The editor of *L'Esprit*, Olivier Mangin, argues that Bourdieu leaves no place for the resistance of the non-dominating classes and hence no place for politics. Mongin follows up with an attack on Bourdieu's view of intellectuals who are alone able to see through the consent of the dominated.[4] One of their tasks is to correct the language of the mass media, which is littered with clichés like "the global village." This fits with our argument—in chapter 4—of writers acting as watchdogs over the language of politics.

Writers should, of course, be read for themselves, for the freedom they demonstrate in their use of language. In Western Europe we have fine writers, novelists like Martin Amis, Ian MacEwan and Jean Echenoz, to name only a few. It is appropriate to single out V. S. Naipaul not because he has just received the Nobel Prize but because his is a view that comes from the outside (see chapter 11). Born in Trinidad in 1932 into a Hindu family, he has written many travel books and he sets London in a global context as one interesting city among many others.

The first book by Naipaul that we wish to mention is, however, *Miguel Street* (1961). This is a group of short stories set in the slums of Port of Spain. The characters' lives are limited by their social disadvantages, of which they are conscious. Speaking good English is much valued, although they mostly speak an ungrammatical patois: "My mother say she ain't have four cents" (p. 47). Speaking well is associated with the whites. But the power structure is complex because during the Second World War the Americans arrive and are different from the English community. There are many eccentrics on Miguel St. but on closer inspection their odd actions are ways of coping with alienation. Cricket is a source of prestige so the narrator's uncle, who does not play cricket, beats his wife with a cricket bat. She understands that this is a sort of honor for her so she keeps the bat oiled and ready. Naipaul's writing contains a populism that creates a community on Miguel St. but the characters are really all trying, each in her/his own way, to live with their lack of power.

Half a Life (2001) is the story of a young Indian who comes to London before going on to Portugese Africa. His life in India has been shaped by caste, in London race and class are important and in Africa it is hardest if one is African and better if one is a quarter or a half Portuguese. Naipaul is aware of a sincerity or an intensity in African life—"there was something in the African heart that was shut away from the rest of us and beyond politics" (p. 186). But Naipaul lives in the world where one is exposed to power and struggles to survive. The conflicts around what Bourdieu would have called symbolic capital are Naipaul's real subject. He does not concentrate on Willy, his young Indian hero. At the outset Willy's father dominates, then the people Willy meets in London and toward the end come the intricacies of the Portuguese colony. Naipaul organizes these half-told stories with the skill of an "écrivain" whose psychological and sociological insights are a pre-text to play with language.

We are conscious of all that we have neglected: post-modernism and the language of contemporary politics are only two of the topics left out for lack of space.

We shall end this book with a plea for language whether it be political like Joschka Fischer's speech on the EU or a well-written website open to all who are surfing the internet (web sites are not all equally bad). Most liberating is the stolentelling of Joyce and Céline. (Imitating Joyce one might use the expression "lace-telling" to introduce the discourse of *Féerie.*) *Finnegans Wake* may be impossible to read from cover to cover but a fifteen-minute dip into the tale of Shem and Shaun frees one from the language of bureaucracy or of Umberto Bossi and hence from bureaucracy and Bossi themselves. One can no longer discover a destiny via commitment, but "bits and pieces" of freedom must be seized whenever the chance is offered or constraint permits.

Bologna, February 2002
Patrick McCarthy

Endnotes

Introduction

1. Ruth Padel, "The Death of the Reader," *Prospect,* January 2002, pp. 62–64.
2. Tony Judt, *A Grand Illusion* (New York: Hill and Wang, 1996), p. 70.
3. James Joyce, *Finnegans Wake* (London: Penguin 1961, first published 1939), p. 424.

Chapter One

1. Pietro Ingrao, *Le cose impossibili* (Rome: Riuniti, 1990), p. 8.
2. Roland Barthes, *Degré zéro de l'écriture* (Paris: Le Seuil 1953), Chapter 1.
3. Claus Gatterer, *Schöne Welt, böse Leute* (Vienna: Verlag Fritz Molden, 1969).
4. Cardinal Martini, *Pastoral Letter,* 1991.
5. Rainier Maria Rilke, *Die Sonette an Orpheus* (Leipzig: Insel-Verlag undated, written 1921–1922), p. 5.
6. Paolo Flores d'Arcais, "Dio esiste?" in *Micromega* 2/2000, pp. 17–40.
7. *Féerie* is best read as a summa of the sounds of the night, which shuns everyday words as much as possible.
8. Roya Ghafele Bashi, *Verbale und Non verbale Kommunikation im Landervergleich Österreich Frankreich.* Diplomarbeit Universität Wien, 1999.
9. Jean Paulhan says that "modern art strives obstinately for some unspoken reconciliation between the real world and man." By "real world" he means not the technological world that man measures and exploits (Note: Jean Paulhan, *Les incertitudes du language* [Paris: Gallimard 1970] but given on French radio 1952), p. 135.
10. Charles du Bos, "Paul Valéry," *Approximations* (Paris: Editions des Syrtes 2000, first published 1922), p. 311.
11. *Economist,* May 1, 1989, p. 13 and foll.
12. For a study of how de Gaulle re-worked his manuscript see Jean-Luc Barré, "Les repentirs du Général, Inédits," *Revue des deux mondes,* March 2000, pp. 129–141.
13. *Le Figaro,* July 18, 2000. The article formed part of the ongoing battle in France over reform of spelling.

14. The film is based on Norman Mailer's book *The Fight* (New York: Penguin 1975), but the language is Ali's.
15. Muhammed Ali quoted in David Remnick, *King of the World* (New York: Random House 1999), p. 287.
16. See Christopher Hitchens, "Hooked on Ebonics," *Vanity Fair,* March 1997, p. 96.
17. *La Repubblica,* May 27, 1999.
18. See for example *L'ordre du discours* (Paris: Gallimard 1971), p. 25: "the lyrical dream of a discours which is born again in its every detail absolutely new and innocent."
19. *Le Figaro,* September 13, 2000.
20. Phoebe Hogan, *Basquiat* (London: Quartet Books 1998) and *Basquiat,* a film directed by Julian Schnabel, 1997.
21. Norman Fairclough, *New Labour, New Language* (London: Routledge 2000), pp. 21–50.
22. For an interesting evaluation of Bobbio and language see Alistair Davidson, "Noberto Bobbio, liberal Socialism and the problem of Language" in *Citizenship Studies,* vol. 2, no. 2 (1998), pp. 223–265.
23. Jonathon Knight, "Lost for Words" in *New Scientist,* August 12, 2000, pp. 16–17.
24. Amos Oz, *Israel, Palestine and Peace* (London: Vintage 1994), p. 54.
25. *Sonette an Orpheus,* p.15.
26. Stefano Pivato, *Il nome e la storia* (Bologna: Il Mulino 1999), p. 23.
27. Cardinal Giacomo Biffi, *Contro Maestro Ciliegia* (Milan: Jaca Book 1977).
28. Harold Pinter, *Mountain Language, TLS,* October 7, 1988.
29. *Le Figaro,* July 17, 2000.
30. Hannah Arendt, *Politics and Lies,* translated into Italian as *Politica e Menzogna* (Milan: Sugar Co. 1985), p. 239.
31. Roland Barthes, *Essais critiques* (Paris: Le Seuil 1964), pp. 147–154.
32. *Degré zéro de l'écriture* (Paris: Le Seuil 1953). Some of the articles, however, were completed as early as 1947.
33. *Essais critiques,* p. 9.

Chapter Two

1. Michel Winock, *Le siècle des intellectuels* (Paris: Le Seuil 1998), pp. 11–64.
2. Albert Thibaudet, *La république des professeurs* (Paris: Grasset 1927), pp. 229–258.
3. Sarah Vajda, *Maurice Barrès* (Paris: Flammarion 2000), p. 154.
4. Antonio Gramsci, *Quaderni del carcere,* edited by V. Gerratano (Turin: Einaudi 1975). See also Antonio Gramsci, *Selections from Cultural Writings,* edited and introduced by David Forgacs and Geoffrey Nowell-Smith (Cambridge: Harvard University Press, 1985).
5. Billancourt, just west of Paris, used to be the home of the great Renault works, which was a bastion of the PCF.

6. See Lucien Goldmann, *Pour une sociologie du roman* (Paris: Gallimard 1964).
7. Roberto Roversi, "I giovani di Vidiciatico" in *Pasolini e il Setaccio*, edited by Mario Ricci (Bologna: Cappelli 1977), p. 181.
8. See Alberto Asor Rosa, *Scrittori e popolo* (Rome: Savelli 1965), Chapter 1.
9. P. McCarthy, *Camus* (London: Hamish Hamilton 1982), p. 197.
10. *Les Temps modernes* no. 1 (October 1945), pp. 1–7.
11. Edward Said, a very original thinker in this field, would not agree with Gide and probably not with me. See chapter 11.
12. Auguste Anglès, *André Gide et le premier groupe de la NRF* (Paris: Gallimard 1978), Volume 3, pp. 504–511.
13. Valery Larbaud, "Les poèmes de Lèon-Paul Fargue" in *Mercure de France*, juin 1963, but first written 1912, p. 256.
14. See Valery Larbaud, *A.O. Barnabooth- Europe* Oeuvres complètes, Pléiade edition (Paris: Gallimard 1958), pp. 63–79.
15. Walt Whitman *Oeuvres choisis* (Paris: Gallimard 1918).
16. Paul Claudel to André Gide, September 9, 1914, *Correspondance* (Paris: Gallimard 1949) p. 222.
17. See Robert Brasillach, *Notre avant-guerre* (Paris: Plon 1941).
18. Robert Belot, *Lucien Rebatet* (Paris: Le Seuil 1994), pp. 405–415.
19. Pierre Drieu la Rochelle, *Gilles* (Paris: Gallimard 1942, 1939 edition with passages then taken out by the censor now included), p. 679.
20. Denoel was shot at the Liberation. *Les Décombres* was republished in 1976, with some cuts and a warning to the reader not to be shocked, by Editions Jean-Jacques Pauvert as the first volume of *Les Mémoires d'un fasciste*. The material used here is taken from *Les Mémoires d'un fasciste II, 1941–1947*, published at the same time, 1972. *Les Deux Etendards* was published by Gallimard 1952.
21. See *Les Abeilles de Delphes* (Paris: Editions des Syrtes 1999), pp. 136–169.
22. *Les abeilles de Delphes*, p. 331.
23. Jean Paulhan, *Les incertitudes du langage* (Paris: Gallimard 1970, but given as a series of radio broadcasts in the early 1950s), p. 94. See also: Paulhan's *Lettre aux Directeurs de la Résistance* (Paris: éditions Ramsay 1987).
24. Paolo Turi, *L'ultimo segretario: Vita e carriera di Alessandro Natta* (Rome: Cedam, 1996), p. 45.
25. Interview with Renzo Renzi.
26. For a good analysis of Silone's spying see Giulio Ferroni, "Uscite e segrete di Ignazio Silone" in *La Rivista dei Libri*, February 2001, pp. 27–31.
27. *Selections from cultural writings*, p. 100.
28. J.-P. Sartre, "Préface" to Paul Nizan, *Aden Arabie* (Paris: Maspéro 1960, first published 1931), p. 8.
29. See our "Sartre, Nizan and the dilemmas of political commitment" in *Sartre after Sartre Yale French Studies*, no. 68, pp. 191–205.
30. *Fallen Oaks*, 1971.
31. On intellectuals in the 1930s see Mark Gilbert's D. Phil. thesis "Foreign policy and propaganda in the progressive press 1936–1945," Swansea University 1990.

32. Hans-Peter Schwarz, *Das Gesicht des Jahrhunderts* (Munich: Goldmann 2001), p. 297.
33. On Ryan see J. Bowyer-Bell, *The Secret Army, the IRA*, Third Edition (London: Frank Cass 2000), p. 133.
34. W. B. Yeats, "Coole Park and Ballylee," *Collected Poems*, p. 239.
35. Interview with Renzo Renzi.
36. Bologna won the Italian championship in 1936, 1937, 1939 and 1941.
37. Gianni Scalia, "Due o tre cose su Pasolini" in *Pasolini e il Setaccio* edited by Mario Ricci (Bologna: Cappelli 1977), p. 186.
38. Mario Ricci, "Pasolini a Bologna," *La Società*, no. 33 March 1980, p. 61.
39. PPP, "Per una morale pura in Ungaretti" in *Pasolini e Il Setaccio*, pp. 52–54. All references are to this anthology rather than to *Il Setaccio*, which is virtually unobtainable.
40. On *Architrave* see Nazario Sauro Onofri, *I giornali bolognesi nel ventennio fascista* (Bologna: Editrice moderna 1972).
41. Agostino Bignardi, *Crediamo Architrave*, February 1941, p. 8.
42. Galvano della Volpe, "Vecchio e nuovo umanesimo," *Architrave*, December 1941, p. 3.
43. Agosto Bignardi, "Appunti su Ungaretti," *Architrave*, January 1941, p. 11.
44. Nino Betocchi, "Del Premio Bergamo," *Architrave*, December 1940, p. 14.
45. Roberto Mazzetti, "Atto di nascita," *Architrave*, December 1940, p. 1.
46. Dioniso Romano, "Cultura e rivoluzione," *Architrave*, April 1941, p. 49.
47. Renzo Renzi, *Il Fascismo involontario* (Bologna: Cappelli 1975), p. 150.
48. Carlo Betocchi, "Acqueforti di Bartolini" *Architrave*, May 1942, p. 5.
49. PPP, "Umori di Bartolini," *Pasolini et il Setaccio*, pp. 168–170.
50. *Architrave*, January 1942, p. 2.
51. PPP, "Cultura italiana e cultura europea a Weimar," *Pasolini e il Settacio*, pp. 68–71. Pasolini republished this piece in *Il Setaccio*.
52. PPP, p. 51.
53. PPP, "Ragionamento per il dolore civile," *Pas*, pp. 56–58.
54. PPP, "Per una morale pura in Ungaretti," *Pas*, pp. 52–54.
55. PPP, "Dino" e "Biografia ad Ebe," *Pas*, pp. 73–77.
56. PPP, "Fuoco Lento," *Pas*, pp. 59–62.
57. PPP to Luciano Serra (July-August 1963) *Lettere agli amici* (Guanda 1976), p. 33.
58. Michel Contat, "On n'en a pas fini avec Sartre" *Le Monde*, April 21, 2000.
59. Tony Judt, *Marxism and the French left* (Oxford: Clarendon Press 1986), pp. 169–238.
60. Simone de Beauvoir, *Mémoires d'une jeune fille rangée* (Paris: Gallimard 1958), p. 337–355.
61. Jean-Paul Sartre, *La nausée* (Paris: Gallimard Collection Folio 1983, first published 1938), p. 117.
62. *L'age de raison*, p. 146.
63. p. 151.
64. p. 152.

65. Simone de Beauvoir, *Le deuxième sexe* (Paris: Gallimard 1949), p. 16.
66. Mavis Gallant, "A Couple and their Family," *TLS*, September 14, 1990, p. 963.
67. *L'age de raison*, pp. 215 and foll.
68. J.-P. Sartre, *Les communistes et la paix* in *Les Temps modernes*, July 1952, p. 48.
69. Republished in *Situations l* (Paris: Gallimard 1947), pp. 100–121.
70. Bernard Crick, *George Orwell, A Life* (Boston: Little, Brown and Co., 1980), pp. 15–46.
71. Quoted by Crick, p. 84.
72. Beatrix Campbell, "Wigan Pier and Beyond," in *New Statesman*, December 16, 1983, p. 23.
73. This conflict is still being fought out. See Ken Loach's treatment of Spain in *Land and Liberty* in chapter 3.
74. *The Collected Essays, Journalism and Letters of George Orwell* (London: Penguin Books 1970), volume 1, p. 301–325.
75. Crick, p. 308.
76. *Collected Essays*, volume 3, pp. 25–26.
77. George Orwell, *1984* (New York: Signet 1981), p. 59.
78. Crick, p. 397.
79. p. 120. All references to the play are to the Suhrkamp Verlag's pocket edition published in 1962 in Frankfurt.
80. John Fuegi, *Brecht and Company: Sex, Politics and the Making of the Modern Drama* (New York: Grove Press, 1994).
81. p. 8. Allusions are to the 1962 edition by Suhrkamp Verlag, Frankfurt.
82. pp. 91–92.
83. *Brecht on Theater*, edited by John Willet (New York: Hill and Wong, 1964), p. 14.
84. *Brecht on Theater*, p. 15.
85. The quotation has been left in German because it has the simple beauty of the Volkslied. A literal translation would be: "Because I have carried you so far and because my feet hurt, because the milk was so expensive, you became dear to me," p. 50. All references are to the Suhrkamp edition of the play (Frankfurt 1962).
86. *The Caucasian Chalk Circle*, p. 110.
87. Albert Camus might have agreed: this is another theme of the period.
88. *The Caucasian Chalk Circle*, p. 116.
89. Roland Barthes, *Essais critiques* (Paris: Le Seuil 1964), p. 144.
90. Franco Fortini, *Verifica dei Poteri* (Milan: Mondadori 1965), p. 200.
91. Franco Fortini, "Il Metellismo" *Dieci Inverni* (Bari: De Donato 1973. This essay was written in 1955), pp. 121–126.
92. Roland Barthes, "La critica brechtiana" in *Ragionamenti*, no. 7 (October-November 1956), pp. 163–165.
93. *The Caucasian Chalk Circle*, p. 96.
94. p. 101.
95. p. 53. Goldstein's book in *1984*.

Chapter Three

1. Bruno Vercier, "Préface" to *La Mère et L'enfant* (Paris: Gallimard, 1983, first published 1900), p. 9.
2. Interviews carried out in Ygrande 1985 and 2000.
3. Philippe Muller, *Vive l'Ecole républicaine* (Paris: EJL 1999).
4. For the story of the French education system see Eugen Weber, *Peasants into Frenchmen* (Stanford: Stanford University Press 1976) and for the role of the state see Ernest Gellner's *Nations and Nationalism* (Oxford: Blackwells, 1983).
5. Charles-Louis Philippe, *Oeuvres complètes* (Moulins: éditions ipomée, 1986) volume 2, pp. 159 and 199. All references to Phillippe's work are to this edition, unless otherwise stated.
6. *OC*, vol. 3 p. 126.
7. The best piece of criticism on Philippe is David Roe's essay in vol. 1 of the *OC*. For Philippe and the *NRF* see Auguste Anglès, *Andrè Gide et le premier groupe de La Nouvelle Revue Française*, vol. 1, pp. 221–243.
8. *OC*, vol. 2, p. 230.
9. Letter from Francis Jourdain to Valery Larbaud, undated (Summer 1911), Larbaud Archives, Municipal Library, Vichy.
10. *OC*, vol. 3, p. 143.
11. *OC*, vol. 3, p. 143.
12. *OC*, vol. 3, p. 119.
13. *OC*, vol. 3, p. 247.
14. Antonio Gramsci, *Cultural Writings*, edited and introduced by David Forgacs and Geoffrey Nowell-Smith (Cambridge: Harvard University Press, 1985), pp. 99–102.
15. Franco Solinas, *Squarciò* (Milan: Feltrinelli, 1993, first published 1956).
16. Franco Fortini, *Dieci inverni* (Bari: De Donato 1973 first published Milan: Feltrinelli, 1957), pp. 121–126.
17. Expression used by Auguste Anglès.
18. *Saturday Night and Sunday Morning*, p. 115.
19. *Saturday Night and Sunday Morning*, p. 109.
20. For a biography of Macmillan see Alistair Horne, *Macmillan* (London: Macmillan, 1989).
21. John Osborne, "Introduction," *The Entertainer*, p. 1.
22. John Osborne, *The Entertainer* (London: Faber and Faber, 1957), p. 54.
23. John Osborne, *Look Back in Anger* (London: Faber and Faber, 1960, first performed 1956, Royal Court Theater), p. 90.
24. *Look Back in Anger*, p. 81.
25. Alan Sillitoe, *Life without Armour* (London: Harper Collins, 1995), p. 232.
26. John Braine, *Room at the Top* (London: Methuen, 1989, first published 1957), p. 81.
27. Kingsley Amis, *Lucky Jim* (London. Penguin, 1961, first published 1954), p. 14.

28. *Saturday Night and Sunday Morning*, p. 114.
29. *Saturday Night and Sunday Morning*, p. 114.
30. *Saturday Night and Sunday Morning*, p. 111.
31. Alan Sillitoe, *The Loneliness of the Long Distance Runner* (London: Grafton Books, 1985, first published 1959), p. 20.
32. *The Loneliness of the Long Distance Runner*, p. 9.
33. *Life without Armour*, p. 235.
34. *The Loneliness of the Long Distance Runner*, p. 47.
35. *The Loneliness of the Long Distance Runner*, p. 12.
36. *The Loneliness of the Long Distance Runner*, p. 11.
37. Derek Birley, *A Social History of English Cricket* (London: Aurum Press, 1999), pp. 59–76.
38. *The Loneliness of the Long Distance Runner*, p. 13.
39. *The Loneliness of the Long Distance Runner*, p. 13.
40. Harold Pinter, *The Room* (London: Faber and Faber, 1991, first performed 1960), p. 10.
41. *Loach on Loach*, edited by Graham Fuller (London: Faber and Faber, 1998), p. 11.
42. *Loach on Loach*, p. 64.
43. Ken Loach specifically rejected this interpretation in a lecture given at Johns Hopkins University, Bologna, May 1, 1992. He said it was a coincidence that the two episodes of the mother and the girl were juxtaposed.
44. Loach, JHU May 1, 1992.
45. *Loach on Loach*, p. 12.
46. Ken Loach quoted in *La Repubblica*, May 12, 2000.

Chapter Four

1. Umberto Eco, "Il linguaggio politico" in Gian-Luigi Beccaria, ed., *I linguaggi settoriali in Italia* (Milan: Bompiani, 1987), pp. 91–105.
2. Alcide De Gasperi, "Le ragioni ideali della Democrazia cristiana" in *Discorsi Politici* (Rome: Cinque Lune, 1956), pp. 29–35.
3. *Discorsi politici*, p. 97.
4. "Intervento di Aldo Moro" in Giuseppe Rossini, ed., *I cattolici nei tempi nuovi della Cristianità* (Rome: Cinque Lune, 1956), pp. 189–199.
5. Palmiro Togliatti, "L'anti-fascismo di Antonio Gramsci" in *Momenti della storia d'Italia* (Rome: Riuniti, 1963), p. 183.
6. Giorgio Amendola, "Coerenza e severità" in *Politica ed Economia* (July-August, 1976), p. 8.
7. Enrico Berlinguer, *Austerità, occasione per trasformare l'Italia* (Rome: Riuniti, 1977), p. 13.
8. Aldo Moro, "la terza fase" in *Storia della Democrazia cristiana*, ed. Francesco Malgesi, (Rome: Cinque Lune, 1989), pp. 551–555.
9. Leonardo Sciascia, *Nero su nero* (Turin: Einaudi, 1979), p. 216.

10. Palermo: *Sellerio*, 1978.
11. p. 31.
12. Leonado Sciascia, *La Sicilia come metafora* (Milan: Mondadori, 1979), p. 87.
13. Heinrich Böll, *The Lost Honor of Katharina Blum*, English translation by Leila Vennewitz (New York: McGraw-Hill, 1975), pp. 7–9.
14. Jack Zipes, "Political dimensions of the lost honor of Katharina Blum" in *New German Critique* (Fall 1977), no.12, p. 83.

Chapter Five

1. W. B. Yeats, "The Rose Tree," *Collected Poems* (London: Macmillan, 1958), p. 206. All references to Yeats's poetry are to this volume.
2. Terence Brown, *Ireland: A Social and Cultural History* (London: Fontana, 1985), pp. 1–195.
3. Declan Kiberd, *Inventing Ireland, the Literature of a Modern Nation* (London: Vintage Books, 1996, first published by Cape, 1995), p. 143.
4. Brian Freel, *Translations* (London: Faber and Faber, 1981), p. 21.
5. *La Repubblica,* February 4, 2000.
6. Michel Longley, Wounds, in *Poets of Northern Ireland*, édition bilingue publiée sous la direction de Colin Meir avec la collaboration de Jacqueline Genet (Caen: Amiot- Lenganey, 1991), p. 122.
7. *The Field Day Anthology of Irish Literature,* Volume 3, p. 328. I wish to thank Seamus Taggart for drawing my attention to this passage.
8. Seamus Heaney, "Whatever you say say nothing," *North* (London: Faber and Faber, 1975), p. 51.
9. Marjorie Mowlam, *The Stepping Stones to Peace,* Johns Hopkins University Bologna Center, Occasional Papers, 1998.
10. Ruth Torrens, "Political language and the peace process" in PMC edited *The Changing Political Language of Northern Ireland,* Johns Hopkins University Bologna Center, Occasional Papers, 1999, p. 61.
11. For the colonial theme in Irish literature see Declan Kiberd, *Inventing Ireland* (New York: Vintage, 1996, first published in London: Cape, 1995).
12. Seamus Heaney, "The Ministry of Fear," *North*, p. 57.
13. Derek Mahon, "A disused shed of Co. Wexford," *Poets of Northern Ireland*, p. 122.
14. John Hewitt, "The Glens" in *Poets of Northern Ireland*, p. 18.
15. W. B. Yeats, "The Man and the Echo," *Collected Poems*, p. 393. "Did that play of mine send out/certain men the English shot?"
16. Seamus Heaney, "At a potato digging," *Poets of northern Ireland*, p. 62.
17. S. H., "The Bog Queen," *North*, p. 25.
18. S. H., "Kinship," *North*, p. 33.
19. W. B. Yeats, "Three Songs to the One Burden," *Collected Poems*, p. 371.
20. Declan Kiberd, *Inventing Ireland*, p. 594.

21. S. H., "Whatever you say say nothing" *North*, p. 52.
22. Antony Easthope, "How good is Heaney?" *Prospect*, March 1998, p. 74. The accusation, made in Ireland by Desmond Fennell, is that Heaney creates no new myths, takes no risks and in his "Northern" poems is content to look on. The implicit comparison, made explicitly by Fennell, is that Heaney is too prudent, cannot be compared with Yeats and is a minor poet.
23. S. H., "The Toome Road," *Poets*, p. 76.
24. S. H., "From the land of the unspoken," *Poets*, p. 84.
25. S. H., "The Ministry of Fear," *North*, p. 57.

Chapter Six

1. On Lampedusa's life see David Gilmour, *The Last Leopard* (London: Quartet Books, 1988).
2. Carlo Feltrinelli, *Senior Service* (Milan: Feltrinelli, 1999), p. 166.
3. Giuseppe Tomasi di Lampedusa, *Il Gattopardo* (Milan: Feltrinelli, 1958), p. 40.
4. p. 252.
5. p. 286.
6. *The Last Leopard*, p. 168.
7. Mario Alicata, "Il principe di Lampedusa e il Risorgimento italiano" in *Intellettuale e l'azione politica* (Rome: Riuniti, 1976), pp. 276–289. First published *Il Contemporaneo*, April 1959.
8. Salvatore Satta, *De Profundis* (Milan: Adelphi, 1980), p. 16.
9. p. 79.
10. p. 115.
11. p. 79.
12. Salvatore Satta, *Il mistero del processo*, (Rome: Adelphi, 1994), p. 25.
13. *Il Giorno del giudizio*, p. 24.
14. For an unfavorable review of *The Book*, which contradicts many of the points made here, see Geofroy Grigson, "In the crab pots," in *The New York Review of Books*, November 5, 1981, pp. 43–44.
15. G. B. Edwards, *The Book of Ebenezer le Page* (New York: Knopf, 1981), p. 143. Hereafter cited in text as E.
16. Note: Quoted by John Fowles in "Introduction" to *The Book*, p. xii.

Chapter Seven

1. See Nicholas Hewitt, *The Life of Céline* (Oxford: Blackwells, 1999), pp. 198–255.
2. Primo Levi, *Se questo è un uomo* (Turin: Einaudi, 1969, first published 1947), p. 1.

3. Primo Levi, *La Tregua* (Milan: Einaudi, 1958), p. 191.
4. Gunther Grass, quoted by Ernestine Schlant, *The Language of Silence* (New York: Routledge, 2001), p. 204.
5. Primo Levi, *Il Sistema periodico* (Turin: Einaudi, 1975), p. 155.
6. *Il Sistema periodico*, p. 158.
7. *Se questo*, p. 75.
8. Levi places the lines from Coleridge at the head of *i sommersi e i salvati*.
9. *Il Sistema periodico*, p. 57.
10. L.-F. Céline, "Féerie pour une autre fois," *Oeuvres Complètes* (Paris: Gallimard Pléiade edition 1993), p. 5. Hereafter cited in text as "Féerie."
11. p. 13.
12. Albert Camus, "Le mythe de Sisyphe," *Oeuvres complètes* t2 Essais (Paris: Gallimard Pléiade 1965), p. 198.
13. *Féerie*, p. 20.

Chapter Eight

1. "Speech to the Chelsea constituency association" *Collected speeches of Margaret Thatcher* edited by Robin Harris (London: Harper Collins 1997), p. 27
2. *Collected speeches of Margaret Thatcher*, p. 12
3. "Speech to the General Assembly of the Church of Scotland," *The Collected Speeches of Margaret Thatcher*, pp. 308–314. Jonathon Raban, *God, man and Mrs. Thatcher* (London: Cape 1989)
4. "Bruges Speech," *The collected speeches of Margaret Thatcher* (London: Harper Collins 1997) pp. 315–325
5. Neil Kinnock, "Speech to a group of Welsh Labour Party members," May 27, 1987. Text furnished by Neil Kinnock's office.
6. See "La conférence de presse du président de la république," *Le Monde*, September 8, 1990.
7. *Collected Speeches of Margaret Thatcher*, p. 113 and 115.
8. Daily Mail, April 2, 1990.
9. *The Ice Age*, p. 59.
10. *The Ice Age* (London: Weidenfeld and Nicholson 1977), p. 120.
11. Marc Augé, *Dialogo di Fine Millennio* (Turin: L'Harmattan 1997), p. 46 and foll.
12. *The Needle's Eye*, p. 8.
13. *The Needle's Eye*, p. 50.
14. *The Needle's Eye*, p. 140.
15. *The Needle's Eye*, p. 192.
16. *The Downing Street Years*, p. 144.
17. Harold Pinter, "Mountain Language" in *TLS* October 7, 1988. See also Guido Almansi, "Il Pintor Furioso" in La Repubblica, November 20, 1988.
18. See his "America ti odio" in Il Manifesto February 11, 1997, where Pinter plays skillfully with the phrase "the American people."

19. Elizabeth Fox-Genovese, "The ambiguities of Female Identity: A reading of the novels of Margaret Drabble" *Partisan Review* 2/1979 pp. 234–248.

Chapter Nine

1. Sylvia Beach says on Christmas Eve, *Shakespeare and Company* p. 67; Larbaud's biographer moves the date back to November—G. Jean-Aubry, note to Larbaud's *Oeuvres complètes* volume 3 (Paris: Gallimard 1950–1955), p. 459.
2. Larbaud's biographical study of Butler was published in April 1920.
3. PMC, "Le dialogue de Jacques Rivière et de Valery Larbaud," *Bulletin des amis de Rivière* 1977/2 pp. 7–19.
4. New York Tribune, May 28, 1922.
5. *Ireland's Literary Renaissance* (New York: John Lane Co. 1966, first published by Knopf in 1922 and by Grant Richards in 1923), pp. 411–412.
6. Ernest Boyd to Valery Larbaud, March 20, 1925. Valery Larbaud Library, Vichy.
7. Valery Larbaud, *Lettres à Adrienne Monnier* (Paris: IMEC 1991).
8. Charles du Bos, *Approximations* (Paris: Editions des Syrtes 2000), p. 350.
9. *Approximations*, p. 477.
10. p. 301.
11. *Approximations*, p. 1057. This is actually a quote from E.R. Curtius but it meets with Du Bos' approval.
12. Larbaud's article was first published in *NRF* volume 6, pp. 273–297 and pp. 398–419. It was republished with Claudel's translations in book form (Paris: NRF, 1912). It appeared again in Larbaud's *Oeuvres complètes* vol. 3, pp. 58–106.
13. *Approximations*, p. 667.
14. William Carlos Williams, *The Great American Novel* (Paris: Three Mountains Press 1923), p. 19.

Chapter Ten

1. See Carlo Feltrinelli on his father: *Senior Service* (Milan: Feltrinelli, 1999).
2. First published 1964 (London: Routledge, 1991).
3. Mino Monicelli, *L'Ultrasinistra in Italia* (Bari: Laterza, 1978), p. 10.
4. Franco Berardi, *La nefasta utopia di Potere operaio* (Rome: Derive-Approdi, 1998), pp. 155–163.
5. N. Balestrini, *Vogliamo tutto*, p. V.
6. Angelo Guglielmi, *Antologia critica* in Nanni Balestrini, *La grande rivolta–Vogliamo tutto, Gli invisibili, l'Editore* (Milan: RCS Libri, 1999), p. 339.

7. *Vogliamo tutto*, p. 30.
8. On Fiat at this period see Marco Revelli, *Lavorare in Fiat* (Milan: Garzanti, 1989).
9. *Vogliamo tutto*, p. 58.
10. p. 63.
11. p. 79.
12. p. 79.
13. Alberto Franceschini, *Mara, Renato ed io* (Milan: Mondadori, 1988), pp. 3–11.
14. *Mara, Renato ed io*, pp. 64–85.
15. For this discussion I rely heavily on Pablo Echaurren and Claudia Salaris, *Controcultura in Italia 1967–1977* (Turin: Bollato Boringhieri, 1999). See also my review of the book in *Polis* 2/1999, pp. 330–334.
16. *Controcultura*, p. 32.
17. Nanni Balestrini's success in reconciling these divergent pressures at the level of the individual writer is the key to his achievements.
18. An exception is Robert Lumley's *States of Emergency: Cultures of Revolt in Italy* (London: Verso, 1990).
19. "This was the end of an era," Luigi Bobbio, *Lotta continua* (Rome: Savelli, 1979), p. 171.
20. Pier Vittorio Tondelli, *Un weekend postmoderno* (Milan: Bompiano, 1990), p. 205.
21. Chapter 3.
22. *Gli invisibli*, p. 95.
23. p. 166.
24. See Agostino Massa, *Giovani e comunicazione elettorale* (Turin: L'Harmattan, 1999).
25. See J. F. Lyotard, *La Condition postmoderne*.
26. Percy Allum, "Italian society transformed," in P. McCarthy edited *Italy Since 1945* (Oxford: Oxford University Press, 2000), pp. 26–30.
27. *Altri Libertini*, p. 90.

Chapter Eleven

1. Edward Said, *Culture and Imperialism* (New York: Knopf 1993), p. xii.
2. *Orientalism*, p. 204.
3. See his essay "L'art sous le règne de la culture" read in manuscript form.
4. There is a very common French expression—"La France n'a pas fait son deuil pour L'Algérie" (France has not mourned for Algeria)—the present perfect tense is always used to imply that France should be mourning now.
5. Joseph Conrad, *Lord Jim* (London: Penguin Books 1989, first published 1900), p. 47.
6. p. 74.
7. p. 329.

8. Pierre Macheray, *Pour une théorie de la production littéraire* (Paris: Maspéro, 1966).
9. Milan: Mondadori 1993, first published 1947.
10. p. 7.
11. p. 20.
12. Edward Said, "Introduction" to *Culture and Imperialism*.
13. *Tempo di uccidere*, p. 59.
14. p. 107.
15. *La Rose de sable Romans 2* Pleiade edition (Paris: Gallimard 1982), p. 16.
16. Paul Morand, *Nouvelles complètes* (Paris: Pleiade edition 1992), pp. 514–529.
17. Mouloud Feraoun, *Journal 1955–1962* (Paris: Le Seuil, 1962), p. 27.
18. Mouloud Feraoun, *Journal 1955–1962*, p. 76.
19. Jacques Massu, *La vraie bataille d'Alger* (Paris: Plon, 1972), pp. 164–179.
20. *L'Express,* December 20,1955.
21. Patrick McCarthy, *Camus' "The Stranger"* (Cambridge: Cambridge University Press, 1988).
22. See "Camus, Orwell, Greene: The Impossible Fascination of the Colonized," in Adèle King edited *Camus' "The Stranger" fifty years on* (Hampshire: Macmillan 1992), pp. 20–30.
23. *OC* Pleiade édition, p. 1623.
24. p. 1581.
25. Hamid Bichri, *I soldi della miseria* (Bologna: Extra Edizioni, 1995), p. 38.
26. *The Black Album*, p. 145.
27. *The Buddha of Suburbia*, p. 7.
28. p. 15.
29. p. 192.
30. Bernard-Marie Koltès, *Quai-Ouest* (Paris: editions de minuit, 1985).
31. Bernard-Marie Koltès, *Combat de nègre et de chiens* (Paris : éditions de minuit, 1989).

Chapter Twelve

1. *Les yeux baissés*, p. 109.
2. p. 148 and foll.
3. Paul Addison, *The Road to 1945* (London: Pimlico, 1994).
4. Anne Tristan and Annie de Pisan, "From de Beauvoir to the Woman's movement" in *French Feminist Thought* edited by Toril Moi (Oxford: Basil Blackwell 1987), p. 35.
5. Simone de Beauvoir, "Women and creativity" in *French Feminist Thought*, pp. 17–32.
6. Luisa Passerini, "Gender Relations" in *Italian Cultural Studies,* edited by David Forgacs and Robert Lumley (Oxford: Oxford University Press, 1996), pp. 144–159.

7. Patrick McCarthy, "The Church," in *Italy since 1945* (Oxford: OUP, 2000). p. 146.
8. "Introduction. Coming from the South," in Paola Bono and Sandra Kemp edited *Italian Feminist Thought* (Oxford: Blackwells, 1991), pp. 1–25.
9. Adriana Cavarero, *Italian Feminist Thought*, p. 181.
10. *Italian Feminist Thought*, p. 123.
11. Margaret Thatcher, *The Path to Power*, p. 94.
12. "Il Centro culturale Virginia Woolf di Roma" in *Italian Feminist Thought*, p. 151.
13. *The Economist*, May 18, 1991, p. 26.
14. Stephen Gundle, *Between Moscow and Hollywood* (Durham: Duke University Press, 2001), pp. 150–160.
15. Emily Bronte, *Wuthering Heights* (London: Penguin, 1995, first published in 1847), p. 92.
16. Virago Press, 1972.
17. p. 84.
18. Darmstadt: Luchterhand Verlag 1983, translated by Jan Van Heurck and published in London by Virago Press, 1984.
19. Crista Wolf, *Kindheitsmuster* (Berlin: Aufbau-Verlag 1976) *A model childhood* (London: Virago, 1983), p. 378.
20. Ibid.
21. *Kassandra*, p.151. References are to the Jan Van Heurck translation
22. p. 153.
23. p. 162.
24. p. 53.
25. p. 104.
26. p. 122.
27. p. 41.
28. Crista Wolf, *Reden im Herbst* (Berlin: Aufbau Verlag 1990), p. 88.

Conclusion

1. Joschke Fischer, "Wir sind keine Satelliten," *Die Welt*, February 12, 2002.
2. Quoted in *Il Giornale*, September 25, 2001.
3. *The Economist*, August 11, 2001.
4. Olivier Mangin, "Les impasses de la politique," in *Magazine littéraire*, no. 69 (November 1998), pp. 65–67.

Suggestions for Further Reading

Some books in French, German and Italian have been included in order to help convince the supposedly reluctant Anglo-Saxon reader that s/he cannot understand a country without knowing its language. Obviously this list is arbitrary and many fine books are left out. Books that are easily available are listed only by author and title. The same is true for the list of films. I wish to thank Scott Vine for helping me with this task.

Chapter One

George Steiner, *After Babel*
———. *Language and silence* (Oxford: OUP, 1998)
Roland Barthes, *Writing Degree Zero, Critical Essays*
Michel Foucault, *A Discourse on Language*
George Orwell, *1984* (chapter on Newspeak)
Harold Pinter, "Mountain Language" (*TLS* October 7, 1988.)

Chapter Two

Antonio Gramsci, *Cultural Writings*, edited and introduced by David Forgacs and Geoffrey Nowell-Smith (Cambridge: Harvard University Press 1985)
Michel Winock, *Le siècle des intellectuels* (Paris: Le Seuil, 1998)
Eugen Weber, *The Action française* (Stanford: Stanford University Press, 1962)
J-P. Sartre, *No Exit, The Flies, Dirty Hands, Nausea, The Age of Reason*
André Malraux, *The Human Condition, Man's Hope*
L-F. Céline, *Bagatelles pour un massacre* (Paris: Denoel, 1937)
George Orwell, *The Road to Wigan Pier* (London: Golancz, 1937)
Bernard Crick, *George Orwell: A Life* (Boston: Little, Brown and Co, 1980)
Paul Addison, *The Road to 1945* (London: Pimlico, 1994)
Graham Greene, *The Power and the Glory*
Albrecht Speer, *Inside the Third Reich* (NY: Macmillan, 1976)
Berthold Brecht, *Leben des Galilei*

Films: Leni Riefenstahl, *Die Götter des Stadions;* Jean Renoir, *Les règles du jeu;* Marcel Carné, *Hotel du Nord* and *Les enfants du paradis;* Georges Clouzot, *Le corbeau;* Luchino Visconti, *Ossessione, La terra trema, Rocco e i suoi fratelli;* Federico Fellini, *La Strada.*

Chapter Three

Charles-Louis Philippe, *Bubu de Montparnasse* (English translation, preface by T.S. Eliot. Paris: Crosby Continental Press, 1932)
Alain-Fournier, *Le grand Meaulnes*
André Gide, *Paludes*
Auguste Anglès, *Histoire de la Nouvelle Revue Française 1908–1914,* 3 volumes. (Paris: Gallimard, 1978)
Eugen Weber, *Peasants into Frenchmen* (Stanford: Stanford University Press, 1976)
Albert Thibaudet, *La république des professeurs* (Paris: Grasset, 1927)
Alan Sillitoe, *Life without Armour*
Gunther Grass, *The Tin Drum,* translated into English by Ralph Mannheim, (London: Minerva, 1997)

Chapter Four

Leonardo Sciascia, *The Day of the Owl* (Manchester: Carcanet)
———. *Todo Modo*
———. *Nero su nero*
———. *La Sicilia come metafora* (Milan: Mondadori, 1979)
———. *Una storia semplice* (Milan: Adelphi, 1999)
Heinrich Böll, *Biliard um halb zehn*

Chapter Five

Conor Cruise O'Brien, *Maria Cross*
———. *States of Ireland*
———. *Ancestral Voices*
Terence Brown, *Ireland: A Social and Cultural History* (London: Fontana, 1985)
Patrick Kavanagh, *The Great Hunger*
W. B. Yeats, *Collected Poems* (London: Macmillan, 1958)
J. M. Synge, *Playboy of the Western World*
Seamus Heaney, *Station Island* (London: Faber and Faber, 1984)

Chapter Six

Evelyn Waugh, *Vile Bodies* (London: Penguin)

———. *A Handful of Dust*
———. *Brideshead Revisited*
———. War trilogy: *Men at Arms; Officers and Gentlemen; Unconditional Surrender.*

Chapter Seven

Jorge Semprun, *L'écriture ou la vie* (Paris:Gallimard 1994)
Primo Levi, *La Tregua.*
L-F. Céline, *Journey to the End of the Night,* translated by Ralph Mannheim (New York: New Directions, 1987)
———. *Mort à crédit*
———. *D'un chateau l'autre*

Chapter Eight

Margaret Thatcher, *The Path to Power* (London: Harper-Collins, 1995)
———. *The Downing Street Years* (London: Harper-Collins, 1993)
———. *Collected Speeches* (London: Harper-Collins, 1997)
Margaret Drabble, *The Needle's Eye*
———. *The Radiant Way* (3 volumes)
Jonathon Raban, *God, Man and Mrs. Thatcher* (London: Cape, 1989)

Chapter Nine

James Joyce, *Dubliners*
———. *Portrait of the Artist as a Young Man*
———. *Ulysses* (London: Bodley Head, 1963)
———. *Finnegans Wake* (London: Penguin, 1992)
Richard Ellmann, *James Joyce* (Oxford: OUP, 1983)
Ernest Hemingway, *The Movable Feast*
Sylvia Beach, *Shakespeare and Co.*
Valery Larbaud, *A.O. Barnabooth, ses poèmes et son journal*
Amants heureux amants (Paris: Pléiade, 1961)

Chapter Ten

Herbert Marcuse, *An Essay on Liberation*
Jurgen Habermas, *Towards a Rational Society*
Mino Monicelli, *L'ultra sinistra in Italia*
Nanni Balestrini, *Vogliamo tutto; Gli invisibili; L'Editore*
Barbara Ehrenreich, *Long March, Short Spring.*
Patrick Seale and Maureen McConville, *Red Flag, Black Flag*

Henri Mendras, *Europe and the Europeans*
Alberto Franceschini *Mara, Renato e io*
S. Aust, *The Baader-Meinhof Group*
Films: Rainer Fassbinder, *The Marriage of Maria Braun, The Bitter Tears of Petra Von Kant;* Werner Herzog, *Aguire or the Wrath of God;* François Truffaut, *Shoot the Piano-player, The 400 Blows;* Jean-Luc Godard, *La Chinoise, Le week-end;* Federico Fellini, *La Dolce Vita, Eight and a Half, Julietta and the Spirits;* Michelangelo Antonioni, *Eclipse, The Red Desert, Blow-up;* Luchino Visconti, *The Leopard, The Stranger*

Chapter Eleven

Edward Said, *Orientalism* (NY: Penguin, 1991)
———. *Culture and Imperialism* (NY: Knopf, 1993)
Albert Memmi, *The Colonizer and the Colonized*
Albert Camus, *Le Premier Homme* (Paris: Gallimard, 1994)
E.M. Forster, *Passage to India*
Joseph Conrad, *Heart of Darkness*
Graham Greene, *Heart of the Matter*
V. S. Naipaul, *Miguel St.* (London: Penguin, 1971)
———. *The Mystic Masseur* (London: Penguin, 1964)
———. *Half a Life* (Picador, 2001)
Films: Gilles Pontecorvo, *The Battle of Algiers*

Chapter Twelve

Simone de Beauvoir, *The Second Sex*
———. *Memoirs of a Dutiful Daughter*
Luce Irigaray, *I, You, We—Towards a Culture of Difference*
———. *J'aime à toi*
Vicky Randall, *Women and Politics*
Crista Wolf, *Medea*
———. *Selected Essays* (London: Virago Press, 1992)

Index

A.C. Milan 110
Abyssinia 222–224
Action Française (AF) 29, 31, 33–34, 53, 183, 186, 190
Adams, Gerry 118
Adenauer, Konrad 14, 110
Afghanistan 257–258
Alain-Fournier (Henri-Alban Fournier) 76, 78, 83; *La Miracle de la Fermière*, 78
Algeria ix, 10, 59, 127, 226–231; Algerian War xiv, 10, 51, 216, 223, 227, 229–230; Algiers 68
Ali, Muhammed ix, 7, 17; and *When We Were Kings* (1997) 7
Ali, Tariq 202
Alicata, Mario 142, 248
Alto-Adige 2, 15, 133
Amendola, Giorgio 108, 204
Amis, Kingsley 91–92, 119; *Lucky Jim*, 91–92; *The Old Devils*, 119
Amis, Martin 209, 239, 260
anti-politique (anti-politics) x, 73, 75, 78, 104
anti-Semitism 27–28, 53, 226
Antonioni, Michelangelo 102, 195; *Blow Up*, 195; *The Red Desert*, 195
Archibugi, Francesca 207; *Verso Sera*, 207
Architrave 44–48
Arendt, Hannah 22
Artaud, Antonin 9, 68, 70
Aubry, Martine 245–246
Audoux, Marguerite 76–77, 83; *Marie-Claire*, 76–77
Auschwitz xiii, 2–3, 19, 35, 105, 157, 159, 222
Autonomia 205–206

Baker, Josephine 225
Balestrini, Nanni xiii, 199–201, 207, 209, 211; *I Furiosi*, 211; *La grande Revolta*, 199; *Gli invisibili*, 207; *Vogliamo tutto*, 199–201
Ballestra, Silvia 210, 235–236; *La Guerra degli Antò*, 210; *Gli Orsi*, 236
Balzac, Honore de' 75, 80, 106, 127, 162
Barker, Pat 92, 248; *Union Street*, 248
Barrès, Maurice 27, 31; *Un homme libre*, 27; *Le jardin de Bérénice*, 27; *Sous l'oeil des barbares*, 27
Barthes, Roland 2, 9, 23, 58, 70–71, 96; écrivain vs. écrivant, 23, 37, 66
Basquiat, Jean-Michel 12, 15; *Zydeco* 12
Bassani, Giorgio 136; *The Garden of the Finzi-Contini*, 136
Baudelaire, Charles 6, 138, 140, 163; *Le Cygne*, 163; *Voyage à Cythère*, 138
Baudrillard, Jean 216
BBC (British Broadcasting Corporation) 164
Beach, Sylvia 184–185; and Shakespeare and Co. 184
Beckett, Samuel 20, 42, 131, 188
Ben Jelloun, Tahar 239; *Les yeux baissés*, 239
Berlinguer, Enrico xiv, 1, 3, 108–109, 150, 208, 242, 247
Berlusconi, Silvio 13–14, 16, 110, 245, 258
Bernanos, Georges 33
Bevan, Aneurin 87
Beveridge, William 85
Bevin, Ernest 85, 176
Bin Laden, Osama xiii, 258
Black Bloc, the 211
Blair, Tony x, 14, 22, 104, 106, 110, 124, 175, 181, 245–246
Bo, Carlo 29
Bobbio, Norberto 14
Böll, Heinrich xii, 111, 113–116; *Die verlorene Ehre der Katarina Bloom*, 111, 113–116

Bologna 43–46, 85, 206–208, 210
Bosnia 228, 258
Bossi, Umberto 16, 110, 261
Boulanger, General 27
Bourdieu, Pierre 22, 259–261; *Ce que parler veut dire*, 259; *Les Héritiers*, 260
Boutang, Pierre 35
Boyd, Ernest 187–188, 193; *Ireland's Literary Renaissance*, 187
BR (Brigate rosse) *See also* Red Brigades
Braine, John 85–86, 88–90; *Room at the Top*, 86, 90–91
Brasillach, Robert 34, 35
Brecht, Bertolt 41, 43, 64, 66–72, 98, 140, 204; and commitment 66–72; *Arturo Ui*, 67; *Der Kaukasische Kreidekreis (The Caucasian Chalk Circle)*, 43, 66–69, 72; *Leben des Galilei*, 41, 64, 67; *Mother Courage*, 68; *Three Penny Opera*, 66
Brigate rosse (RB) *See also* Red Brigades
Burgess, Anthony 232; *Right to an Answer*, 232; *Time for a Tiger*, 232
Bush, George W. xiii, 214, 257–258
Butler, Samuel 185–186, 191; *The Authoress of the Odyssey*, 185

Calvino, Italo 26
Camus, Albert ix, 30, 35, 51, 56–57, 59, 68, 95, 127, 163, 166, 216, 226–227, 229–232, 241; *L'Etranger (The Stranger)*, 12, 23, 56, 95, 231–232; *L'Exil et le royaume*, 231; *L'Homme révolté*, 56, 230; *L'Hote*, 231; *Le mythe de Sisyphe*, 166; *Le Premier Homme*, 229; *Le Renégat*, 231–232
Carnetin group 76, 83
Carta, Maria 1, 25
Castro, Fidel 103, 196, 223
Catholic Church, the 16, 26, 33, 43, 55, 67, 107, 119–120, 128, 190, 209, 240, 242–243
CDU-CSU 240
Céline, Louis-Ferdinand ix, 4–5, 7, 22, 30, 35, 57–58, 63, 135, 143, 157–158, 162, 164–170, 210, 261; *Les beaux draps*, 35; *D'un chateau l'autre*, 35, 170; *Féerie pour une Autre Fois*, x, 1, 30,143, 157–158, 162–165, 167–169, 261; *Féerie pour une Autre fois II*, 158, 169–170; *Mort à crédit* 4, 167; *Voyage au bout de la nuit* 4, 158, 165, 167–169

CERES (Centre d'etudes de recherche et d'education socialiste) 202
Chabrol, Claude 22, 163, 211; *La Cérémonie* 22, 211
Chaplin, Charlie 110; *Modern Times*, 110
Ché Guevara, Ernesto 196, 199, 223
Chevènement, Jean-Pierre 202
Chirac, Jacques 245
Churchill, Winston 9, 85, 89
CIA (Central Intelligence Agency) 22, 113, 209
Ciampi, Carlo Azeglio 245
Claudel, Paul 13, 32–33, 168, 191
Clay, Cassius Marcellus see Ali, Muhammed
Clean Hands investigation, the 13, 109
Cold War, the 56–58, 61, 93, 215
Collins, Michael 42, 118, 186, 247
Collodi, Carlo 17 Works: *Pinocchio* 17
colonialism 213
Combat 30
commitment: and Antonio Gramsci 36–37; and Gide 31–33; and Sartre 50–57; and socialism 25–26; in England 40–41; in Germany 41–42
committed writing x
conceptual art 13
Conrad, Joseph 20, 185, 216–220, 232, 236; *Heart of Darkness*, 236; *Lord Jim*, 216–218, 220–221
Conservative Party 85
Cooke, Henry 122
Corneille, Pierre 183
Craxi, Bettino 109, 177, 200
Cresson, Edith 124, 246
Crick, Bernard 58, 60, 63–65
Criterion 186
Croce, Benedetto 26, 36, 145
cultural hegemony 52
culture 213; definitions 214–216

D'Annunzio, Gabriele 29, 36
Dante Alighieri 107, 111, 161
DC (Christian Democrats–Democrazia cristiana) 21, 29, 106–112, 204, 240, 242
de Beauvoir, Simone 30, 50–51, 55, 196, 234, 241, 254; *le deuxième sexe*, 55, 241
de Gasperi, Alcide, Prime Minister 107
de Gaulle, Charles ix, xiv, 5, 20–21, 29, 39–40, 88, 106, 157, 166, 195, 201, 225,

227, 229–230; and authority 10; *Mémoires de Guerre* 5
de Lubak, Henri 33
de Valera, Eamon 42, 118–120
Déat, Marcel 29
Debray, Régis 196, 242, 247; *Révolution dans la révolution,* 196
deconstructionism 249
Delors, Jacques 246
Dench, Judi 92
Depression, the x, 10, 28, 59, 87–88, 90, 184
Derrida, Jacques 210, 235
Di Pietro, Antonio 14
dissent: in graphic arts 13; in literature 12–13; in technology 13–14
Doriot, Jacques 29
Dossetti, Giuseppe 107
Drabble, Margaret 153, 177–182; *The Ice Age,* 178–180, 182; *The Millstone,* 178; *The Needle's Eye,* 180; *The Radiant Way,* 178, 181; *The Waterfall,* 178; *The Winter of Discontent,* 178–179
Dreyfus case xi, 26–28, 30–31, 77, 118, 226
Drumont, Edouard 226; *La France juive,* 226
Du Bos, Charles 4, 189–192
Duncan, Isadora 4, 190

EC (European Community) 51, 87–88, 125, 176, 241, 246
Echenoz, Jean 260
Edwards, G. B. 150–153; *The Book of Ebenezer le Page,* 150, 154
El Okbi, Cheik 226
Eliot, T. S. 61, 85, 184, 186, 188, 192
EMS (European Monetary System) 181, 209–210
EU (European Union) xi, 52, 105, 111, 183, 233–237, 246, 257, 261
existentialism 50, 51, 55, 169, 199

Falklands War, the 176
Fanon, Frantz 126
Fargue, Léon-Paul 83
Fascism 3, 29, 34, 37, 44–47, 143
Fassbinder, Rainer Werner 196; *The Marriage of Maria Braun,* 196
Fèin, Sinn 123, 125
Fellini, Federico 137, 221; *La Dolce Vita,* 137

Feltrinelli, Giangiacomo xi, 26, 70, 103, 136, 196
feminism x, 239, 241, 247, 249, 253–254
Feraoun, Mouloud 227–228
Fianna Fàil 119, 125
Fine Gael 119
Fischer, Joschka 257, 261
Flaiano, Ennio 221, 223–224; *Tempo di uccidere,* 221, 223–224
Flaubert, Gustave 30, 140
FLN (Front de libération nationale) 51, 216, 223, 227–232
FMA (Féminin/Masculin/Avenir) 241
FN (Front National) 247
Forster, E. M. 20, 216; *Passage to India,* 216
Fortini, Franco 84–85; *Ragionamenti,* 85
Foucault, Michel 9, 14, 20, 22, 44, 51, 80, 103, 107, 209, 215, 253; and power 9; and the unsaid 20, 22
Fowles, John 155
France 10, 15, 20
Freel, Brian 119; *Translations,* 119
French Communists 20
French Resistance, the 157
French Revolution, the 78
Freud, Sigmund 243–244
Friuli 49
fundamentalism 213
futurism 204

Gaitskill, Hugh 87
Gallimard, Gaston 35, 185, 188
Gentile, Giovanni 36
Gide, Andre 28, 31–33, 63, 73, 80, 167, 169, 185–186, 189–190, 235, 250; *Corydon,* 32; *L'Immoraliste,* 31, 32; *Journal,* 33; *Nourritures terrestres,* 31; *La porte étroite,* 31; *Paludes,* xiv; *Retour de l'URSS,* 32
GUF (Giovani Universitari Fascisti) 43–48
GIL (Gioventù italiana del Littorio) 44, 48
Giscard d' Estaing, Valery 10, 176, 201–202, 209, 242
globalization 14–15, 52, 211
Godard, Jean-Luc 196; *The Chinese,* 196; *Weekend,* 196
Goethe, Johann Wolfgang von 250, 252; *Faust II,* 250
Good Friday Agreement, the 117, 123–125, 129, 246–247, 257

graffiti 11–12; in Paris 11
Gramsci, Antonio xii, 1, 26–27, 36–37, 44, 52, 73, 75, 79, 83–85, 138, 144; *Quaderni del Carcere,* xii
Grass, Gunther 159
Greene, Graham 41, 97, 132, 232; *Comedians,* 232; *The Honorary Consul,* 233; *The Ministry of Fear,* 132; *The Quiet American,* 232
Grenier, Jean 230–231; *L'essai sur l'esprit de l'ortodoxie,* 230–231
Guardian, the 181
Guigou, Elisabeth 246
Guillaumin, Emile 76–77; *Baptiste et sa Femme,* 77; *La Vie d'un simple,* 76
Guilloux, Louis 83
Gulf War, the xi, 210, 215

Habermas, Jürgen 196
Hancock, Tony 96–97
Hardy, Thomas 79, 191
Heaney, Seamus xii, 117, 123, 128, 130–133, 227; *Kinship,* 132; *North,* 131, 132; *Strange Fruit,* 131; *Whatever you say, say nothing,* 132
Hemingway, Ernest 26, 142, 184
Hewitt, John 129; *The Glens,* 129
Hitler, Adolf 10, 20, 28, 34, 41–42, 66, 95, 158, 171, 192, 240
Ho-chi-Minh 223
Hooks, Bell 254
Hugo, Victor 106
Huntington, Samuel 215
Huysmans, J-K. 126; *A Rebours,* 126

Iliad 250, 253
Imbeni, Renzo 207
inauthenticity 241
Ingrao, Pietro 2, 108, 110, 142
internet 5, 7, 8, 258–259
IRA (Irish Republican Army) 18–19, 117–121, 123–124, 130–132, 173, 179, 196, 203, 257
Iraq 215, 258
Ireland x, 18; and 2001 Referendum, xi, 105
Irigaray, Luce 153
Islam xiii, 226, 233, 237, 258
Italian Unification 6, 16–17

Jarrow marches, the x, 10, 40

Jeanson, Francis 57, 223
Johns Hopkins 209
Jourdain, Francis 78
Joyce, James xi, xiii, xiv, 20, 42, 58, 127, 130, 131, 136, 163, 184–189 191–193, 261; in Paris 184–187; *Dubliners,* 127, 185, 187; *Finnegans Wake,* xiv, 42, 127–128, 130, 188, 192, 261; *Portrait of the Artist as a Young Man,* 185; *Ulysses,* xii, xiv, 1, 8, 127–128, 163, 183–186, 188–189, 191
Judt, Tony xi, 50, 52

Kavanagh, Patrick 130
Kennedy clan, the 123
Keynes, John Maynard 85–86, 88
Kinnock, Neil 7, 174, 176
Kipling, Rudyard 217, 220, 234–235; *Jungle Book,* 218, 234
Klee, Paul 4, 13, 211
Koestler, Arthur 39, 40, 65
Kohl, Helmut 110, 177, 245–246, 253
Koltès, Bernard-Marie 236–237; *Combat de nègre e de chiens,* 236; *Quai-Ouest,* 236
Kureishi, Hanif 213, 233–234; *Black Album,* 233; *The Buddha of Suburbia,* 233–234, 240; *Sammy and Rosie Get Laid,* 213

La Maison des amis des livres 185–186, 188
la Rochelle, Drieu 34; *Gilles,* 34
Labour Party, the xiv, 58, 60, 85, 87, 98, 172, 175–176, 195, 202, 247
Lagerdeutsch 160
Lama, Luciano 206
Lampedusa, Giuseppe Tomasi di 136, 138–144, 148; *Il Gattopardo (The Leopard),* 136, 138, 140–141, 143, 150, 153–154
Lang, Fritz 41
language: and authority, 9–10; bureaucracy 19; and death 19; and freedom 1; and naming 15–18; and nationalism 14–15; and silence 2; and the state 6; and violence 18; as protest 17; of discontent 10; of literature 1; see political language, spoken language, literary language; see silence
Larbaud, Valery xi, 32, 83, 184–191, 193; *Amants heureux amants,* 187; *L'Europe* 32, 184; *Mon plus secret conseil,* 187

Le Pen, Jean-Marie 30, 216, 230
League of Nations, the 221
Lega Nord 16
Levi, Primo xiii, 4, 19, 157–163, 170; *Se questo è un uomo*, 161, 163 ; *Il sistema periodico*, 159, 161; *I sommersi e I salvati*, 159
literary language 116
Little Review, the 184–185
Loach, Ken: x, 75, 87, 98–100, 102–104, 178, 211, 259; *Bread and Roses*, 104; *Carla's Song*, 103; *Kes*, 98–90; *Ladybird, Ladybird*, 103–104; *Land and Freedom*, 104; *My Name is Joe*, 104; *The Navigators*, 259; *Poor Cow*, 98; *Raining Stones*, 102; *Riff-Raff* 75, 99–100, 102–103; *Which Side Are You On?*, 100
Longhi, Roberto 43
Longley, Michael 121, 129
Lotta continua 205, 211
Lyotard, J. F. 209, 253; *La condition postmoderne*, 209

Maastricht Treaty xi, 110, 209
MacEwan, Ian 260
Macherey, Pierre 220
MacMillan, Harold 85, 87–89, 93–94, 96, 98, 172, 177
Mafia 111–112
Mahon, Derek 129
Mallarmé, Stéphane 3, 27, 41, 52
Malraux, Andre 25, 39–40, 59, 71, 104, 231; *Les chenes qu'on abbat*, 40; *La condition humaine*, 25; *L'Espoir*, 25, 39;
Mann, Thomas 41, 144, 190, 192; *Zauberberg (The Magic Mountain)*, 144
Mao-Tse-Tung 16, 39, 199, 201
Marcuse, Herbert 41, 85, 173, 197–199, 204; *One Dimensional Man*, 197–198
Maritain, Jacques 29; *Humanisme intégral*, 29
Marx, Karl 16, 23, 69, 85, 94, 197, 207, 249–250
Marxism xiii, 36, 38, 50–52, 71, 199, 204, 250
Massu, Jacques 227–228
Mauriac, François 34, 53, 55, 167, 189, 228; *Bloc-Notes*, 34
Maurras, Charles 31, 33–35, 183
May 1968 195, 198, 239, 241, 259
McAlmon, Robert 186, 193

McGuiness, Martin 257
Memmi, Albert 219, 224
Michel, Louise 240
Michelangelo Buonarotti 107
Mitterrand, François 10, 21, 110, 124, 174, 177, 202, 245–246
Molière, Jean-Baptiste 6, 183
Mollet, Guy 228
Monnet, Jean 52
Monnier, Adrienne 184–186, 188–189, 193
Montherlant, Henry de 224–225; *La rose de sable*, 225
Morand, Paul 188, 225
Morandi, Giorgio 45
Moravia, Alberto 204
Morel, Auguste 188–189
Moretti, Nanni 104; *Aprile* 104
Moro, Aldo xii, 107–111, 113
Mossad 113
Mowlam, Mo 124–125, 246
Mussolini, Benito 2, 16, 34–36, 42–45, 47–49, 63, 105, 111, 143, 189, 221–222, 240

Naipaul, V. S. 260–261; *Half a Life*, 261; *Miguel Street*, 260
names: and power 16; and social identity 16–18
NATO 174, 237
New Left, the 197–199, 201–205, 207–209, 241, 247
newspeak 61, 63, 65, 197, 249
Ní Houlihan, Cathleen 130–131
1977 Movimento 109
Nizan, Paul 29, 37–38, 50–51, 53, 55, 73, 83, 196; *Aden Arabie*, 38; *Le cheval de Troie*, 38; *Les chiens de garde*, 38; *La condition humaine*, 29, 39; *La Conspiration*, 38
NRF (Nouvelle Revue Francaise) 28–29, 31–34, 53, 80, 82, 126, 185–186, 189–191, 230–231

OAS (Organisation de l'armée secrète) 229
Occhetto, Achille 110
orientalism 214–215
Orwell, George x, 8–9, 16, 22–23, 33, 40, 53, 57–65, 72, 104, 115, 135, 139, 167, 175, 197, 200, 219–220, 251; and commitment 57; and *Tribune; 1984*, 23, 28, 43, 58–64, 72, 115, 197, 239; *Animal*

Farm, 60–61, 64–65; *Burmese Days*, 59, 219–221; *Coming Up for Air*, 60; *Down and Out in London and Paris*, 40, 58–59; *Homage to Catalonia*, 59; *Inside the Whale*, 60; *The Lion and the unicorn*, 60; *The Road to Wigan Pier*, 40, 58–59, 175; *Shooting an Elephant*, 219; *Such, Such Were the Joys*, 57–58
Osborne, John 86–87, 89, 96, 98; *The Entertainer*, 87–89; *Look Back in Anger*, 86, 89–90, 92
Osti, Maurizio 13
Owens, Jessie 41

Pantera movement 13, 209
Papon, Maurice 21
Parnell, Charles Stuart 28, 117, 130
Pascal, Blaise 190
Pasolini, Pier Paolo 5, 12, 26, 29, 32, 42–43, 56, 62, 70, 72, 84–85, 109, 111–112, 136, 141, 162, 177, 204, 224, 237, 242; and commitment 43–50; *Cultura italiana*, 47; *Officina*, 85; *Poesie a Casarsa*, 44; *Ragazzi di vita*, 84–85; *A Violent Life*, 84–85, 136
Pasternak, Boris xi; *Dr. Zhivago*, xi, 26, 136
Patmore, Coventry 153, 191–192; *The Angel in the House*, 153
Paulhan, Jean ix, 35, 158, 231
Pazienza, Andrea 206–207, 211
PCA (Parti communiste algérien) 56, 227, 231
PCF (Parti communiste français) 38–39, 52, 56, 195, 229, 247
PCI (Italian Communist Party) xi, xiv, 3, 10, 21, 26–27, 36, 43, 70, 84–85, 106–110, 112, 136, 142, 150, 195, 201–208, 242–244, 247
Pearse, Padraig 117–118, 120, 123–124, 128, 131
Péguy, Charles 26, 30, 33; *Cahiers de la quinzaine*, 26
Philippe, Charles-Louis 75–86, 89–90, 94, 97, 100, 206; *Bubu de Montparnasse*, 79–80, 85–86; *Croquignole*, 78–82, 90, 94; *Le Grand Meaulnes*, 76, 83; *La Mère et l'enfant*, 76–78, 83; *Le Père Perdrix*, 76, 78–80
Pia, Pascal 30, 226, 230
Pinocchio (Collodi) 17

Pinter, Harold 97, 181, 236; *Mountain Language* 19, 182; *The Room*, 97–98, 236
political language 1, 116; and France 20–21; and the unsaid 20–22, 110–111; and Ireland 117–125; and Margaret Thatcher 172–178; and Italy 21–22; and literary language 1–2, 4, 22–23; spoken 5–6; as storytelling 105–118; written 5
Pompidou, Georges 201
Popular Front, the 226–227
Potere Operaio 199, 205
POUM (Partido obero de unificaciòn marxista) 59
Powell, Enoch 233
Pratolini, Vasco 84; *Metello*, 84, 142
Prima Linea 19, 205
Prodi, Romano 14, 245
Profumo affair 88
Proust, Marcel 28, 136, 186, 188
PS 110, 202
PSI 110
PSU (Parti socialiste unifié) 202

Raban, Jonathon 173
Radio Alice 207, 211
Radio Blackout 211
Rebatet, Lucien 30, 34–35; *Les Décombres*, 34–35; *Les deux étendards*, 30, 35
Red Brigades, the 8, 18–19, 109, 113, 203, 205–206, 208, 214
Resistance, the 20–21, 29, 35, 52–53, 157, 167; Italian 200
Revolt of the Barricades, the 229
Revolt of the Generals, the 229
Rilke, Rainier Maria 16, 23, 49, 155; *Sonette an Orpheus* 3
Risorgimento, the 107
Rivière, Jacques 29, 185–186, 189–190
Robbe-Grillet, Alain 228
Robinson, Mary 245
Rocard, Michel 23, 171, 202, 246; *L'inflation au coeur de la crise*, 171
Rodano, Franco 85
Rote Armee Fraktion 19
Rushdie, Salman xii, 234; *Satanic Verses*, 234
Rutelli, Francesco, 104
Ryan, Frank 42

Said, Edward 214–216, 219–220, 223, 258; *Culture and Imperialism*, 216; *Orientalism*, 214
Sands, Bobby 19
Sardinia 1, 84
Sartre, Jean-Paul ix, x, xiv, 28, 30, 38–39, 43, 50–57, 62–63, 69, 71, 73, 78, 103, 135, 139, 163, 166, 168–169, 177, 196, 207, 215, 223, 227–228, 230, 241; and Camus 56–57; and *Le Temps modernes*, 30, 56; and Paul Nizan 37–39, 53; *L'Age de raison*, 54, 56; *Les Communistes et la paix*, 56; *La critique de la raison dialectique*, 51; *L' etre et le néant*, 51; *Huis clos*, 54, 239; *Les Mouches*, 53–54, 62; *Le Mur*, 53; *La Nausée*, 38, 52, 53, 56; *Les mains sales*, 54, 62; *Portait d'un anti-sémite*, 168; *Situations I*, 53; *Situations II*, 30
Satie, Erik 13; *Morceaux en forme de poire* 13
Satta, Salvatore 1, 143–144, 148–150, 217; *De Profundis*, 143, 147; *Il Giorno (The Day of Judgment)*, 135, 144, 149, 150, 153, 155; Il *Mistero del processo*, 144; *La Veranda*, 144
Schiller 250
Schmidt, Helmut 110, 209
Schröder, Gerhard 5–6, 104
Sciascia, Leonardo xii, xv, 109, 111–113, 181; *L'affaire Moro*, xii, 111–113, 116; *Il Contesto*, 112; *Il giorno della civetta*, 111; *Todo Modo*, 111
Second World War ix, xi, 21, 53–54, 59, 85–86, 89–90, 143, 152, 158, 169, 240, 248, 260
September 11th xiii, xv, 213–214, 258
Serra, Luciano 47; *Un esame di conscienza*, 47
Il Setaccio 44, 46, 48
silence: and communication 4; and God 3; and Irish society 122–123; and privacy 5; and technology 5; and violence 18; as action 3; as resistance 3; as reward 4; imposed 2–3; *see also* language
Sillitoe, Alan 75, 85–88, 90, 92–97, 100, 177, 201; *Loneliness of the Long Distance Runner*, 85, 88, 94–95; *Saturday Night and Sunday Morning*, 85–87, 94–95
Silone, Ignazio 36, 39, 65; *Pane e Vino*, 36

Sinn Féin 257
Solinas, Franco 84; *Squarcio*, 84
Southern Rhodesia 226, 230
SPD (German Socialist Party) 240
Stalin, Joseph xii, 20, 36–38, 41, 64, 66–67, 115, 202
Stasi, the 253
Steffin, Grete 66–67
Steinbeck, John; *The Grapes of Wrath* 2
Stendhal 63, 106, 136, 185
stolentelling ix, xiii, xiv, 247, 252, 257, 261
Strachey, John 41; *The Coming Struggle for Power*, 41
Sud-Tirol 2, 15, 133
Suez Canal, the 215, 221
summa, the 127, 165
Svevo, Italo 188; *La coscienza di Zeno*, 188; *Senelità*, 188
Synge, John 119, 127; *Playboy of the Western World*, 127

Tennyson, Alfred, Lord 110, 191
terrorism xiii, xv, 214, 258
Thatcher, Margaret 7, 87, 99, 100–101, 104, 110, 116, 127, 136, 171–182, 199, 208, 235, 244–245
Third Republic 27, 76–79, 86
Third Way, the 14, 22
Togliatti, Palmiro 25–26, 37, 84, 107–108, 136, 142, 204, 240, 248
Tondelli, Pier-Vittorio 209–210; *Altri Libertini*, 209
trasformismo 137, 140
Tribune 58, 60
Trimble, David 117
Trollope, Anthony 26, 88, 162–163; *Phineas Finn*, 26, 162
Trotsky, Leon xii, 37, 64, 202
Truffaut, François 196; *L'argent de poche*, 196; *Les 400 coups*, 196

United States 76, 87–88, 104, 126, 174, 183, 195, 210, 213–214

Vatican 107
Vichy 34, 35, 225–226; and Vichy government, the 29, 54
Vietnam War 7, 195, 216
Visconti, Luchino 84, 102, 137, 142; *Death in Venice*, 142; *The Leopard* 137, 142;

Ludwig, 142; *Ossessione,* 142; *Rocco and his Brothers,* 142; *La terra trema,* 84
Vittorini, Elio 25, 136, 142
Von Runstedt. Karl 35

Wales 133
Waugh, Evelyn 41, 92, 97, 136, 143
Weber, Max 145
Weigel, Helene 67
Welfare State, the 152, 154
White, Carole 98
Wilde, Oscar 32, 126
William of the Orange 121
Williams, William Carlos 184, 192–193; *In the American Grain,* 193; *The Great American Novel,* 192–193; *Patterson,* 193
Wilson, Harold 195
Wittgenstein, Ludwig 3
Wolf, Crista x, xiii, 248–250, 252–254; *Der geteilte Himmel;* 249; *Kassandra,* 248–254; *Kindheitsmuster,* 248; *Medea,* 249; *Reden im Herbst;* 253, *Was bleibt,* 253
World Cup, the 14

Yeats, William Butler x, 42, 117, 119–120, 130–132, 187
Yugoslavia (ex) xiii, 15, 133, 254, 257

Zola, Emile 30, 75, 80; *J'accuse,* 30

OHIO UNIVERSITY LIBRARY

Please return this book as soon as you have finished with it. In order to avoid a fine it must be returned by the latest date stamped below. All books are subject to recall after two weeks or immediately if needed for reserve.

CF